2012
青岛统计年鉴

QINGDAO STATISTICAL YEARBOOK

(总 第33期 VOL.33)

青岛市统计局
国家统计局青岛调查队 编
QINGDAO MUNICIPAL STATISTICS BUREAU
NBS SURVEY OFFICE IN QINGDAO

中国统计出版社
China Statistics Press

(京)新登字041号

图书在版编目(CIP)数据

青岛统计年鉴: 2012 /青岛市统计局编.--北京:中国统计出版社 ,2012.7

ISBN 978-7-5037-6590-2/C.2671

Ⅰ. ①青… Ⅱ. ①青… Ⅲ. ①统计资料－青岛市－2012－年鉴 Ⅳ. ①C832.523-54

中国版本图书馆CIP数据核字(2012)第158050号

青岛统计年鉴-2012

作　　者/ 青岛市统计局 国家统计局青岛调查队
责任编辑/ 陈越月 张 进
封面设计/ 青岛天之韵广告文化传播有限公司
出版发行/ 中国统计出版社
通信地址/ 北京市西城区月坛南街57号　邮编/ 100826
办公地址/ 北京市丰台区西三环南路甲6号
电　　话/ (010)63376907
网　　址/ http://csp.stats.gov.cn
印　　刷/ 青岛星球印刷有限公司
经　　销/ 新华书店
开　　本/ 890x1240毫米 1/16
字　　数/ 1152千字
印　　张/ 26.375
印　　数/ 1-1000册
版　　别/ 2012 年 7 月第 1 版
版　　次/ 2012年7月第 1 次印刷
书　　号/ ISBN 978-7-5037-6590-2/C.2671
定　　价/ 280.00元

全市生产总值构成（%）
Composition Of Gross Domestic Product（%）

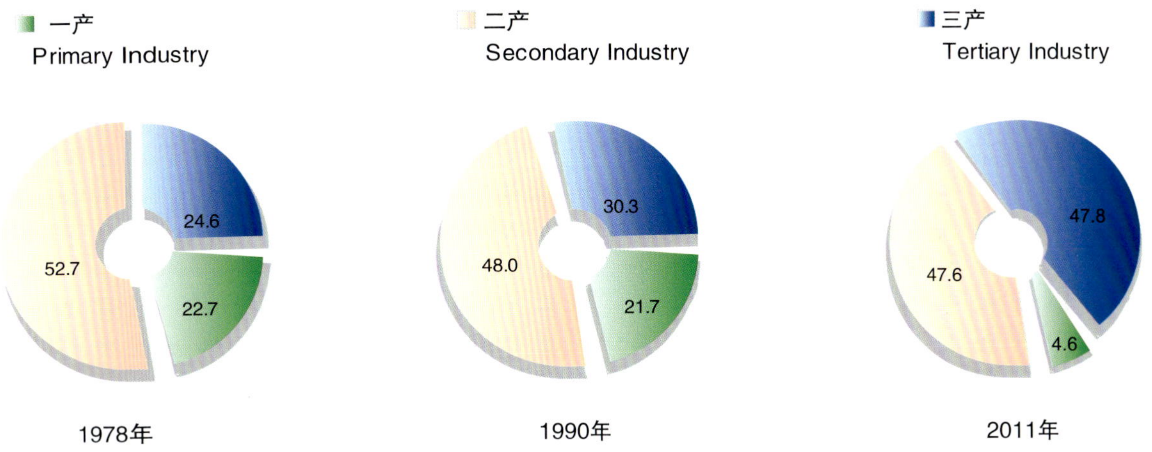

全市生产总值（亿元）
Gross Domestic Product (100 million yuan)

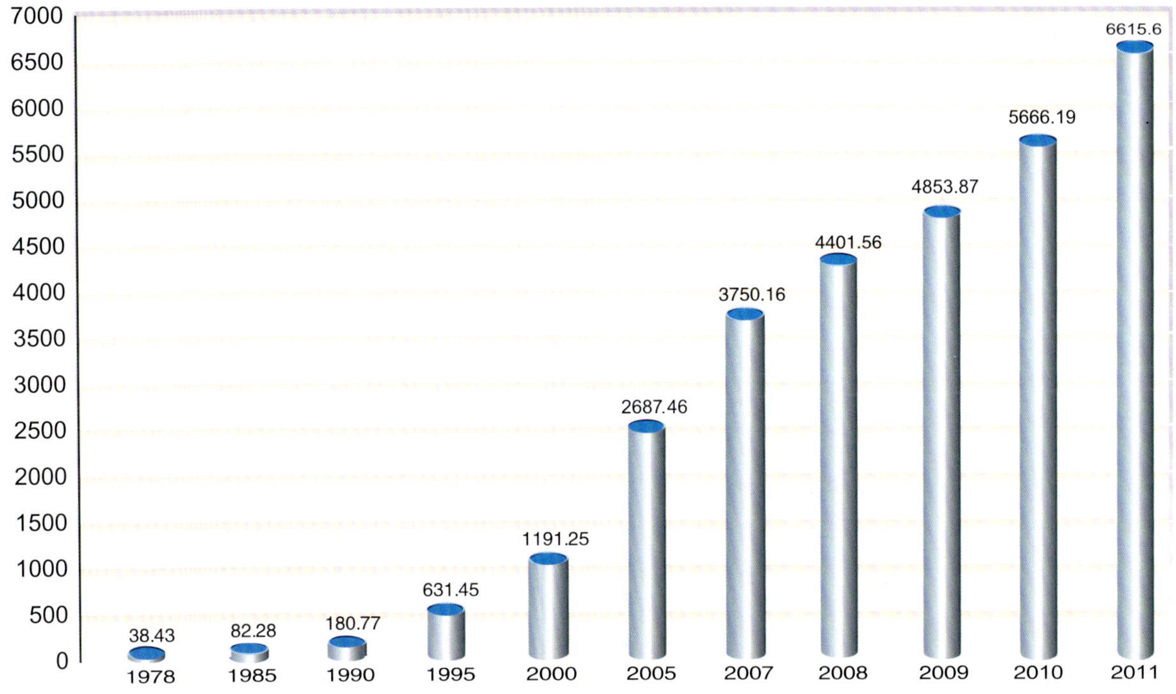

农林牧渔业总产值（亿元）

Gross Output Value Of Agriculture (100 million yuan)

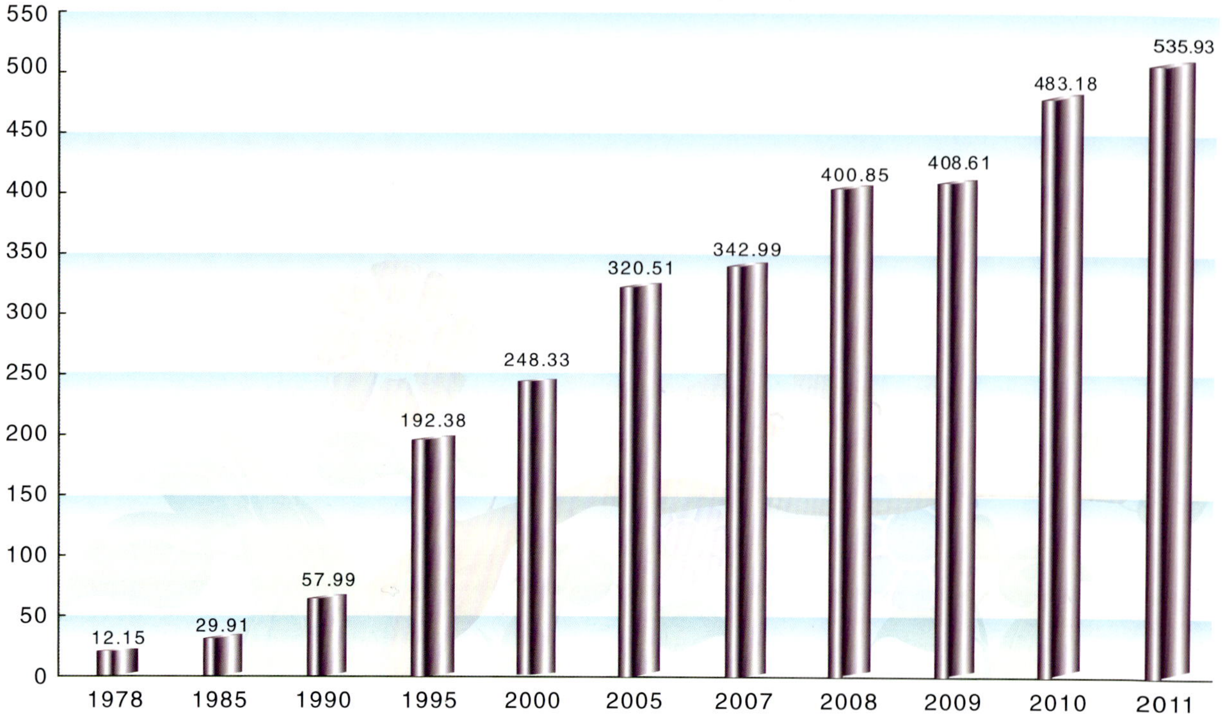

主要农产品产量（万吨）

Output Of Farm Products (10000 tons)

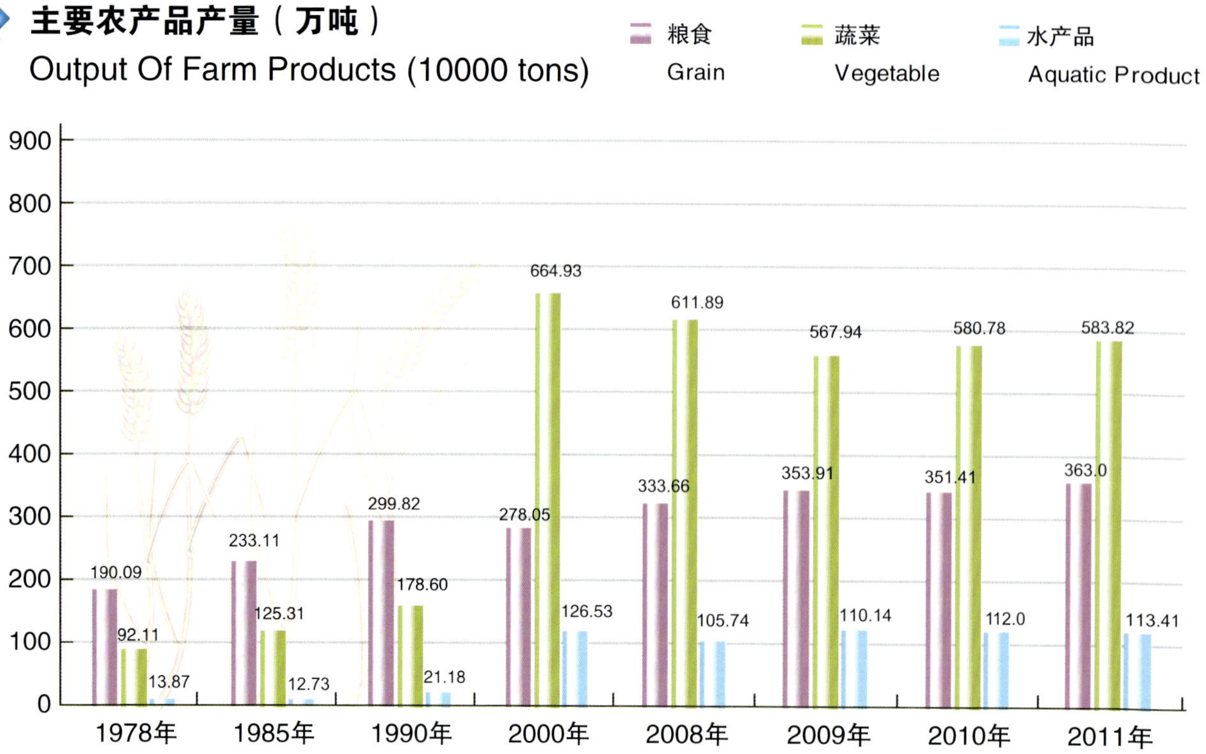

工业总产值（亿元）
Gross Industrial Output Value (100 million yuan)

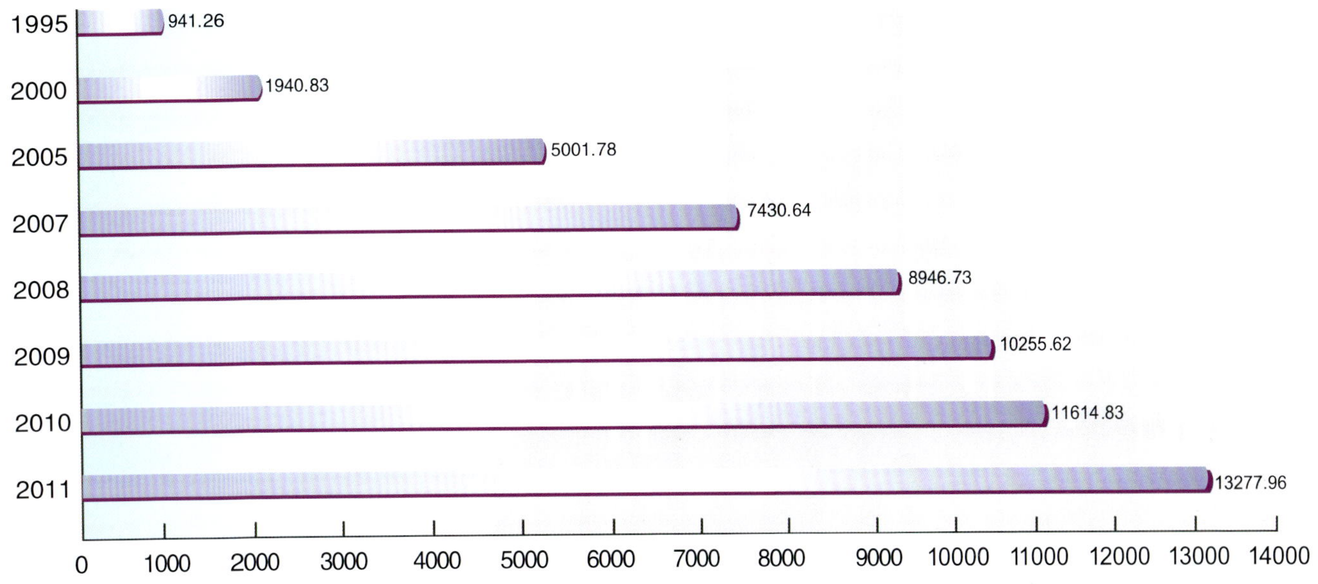

规模以上工业实现利税总额（亿元）
Total Profits And Taxes Of Industry Above Designated Size (100 million yuan)

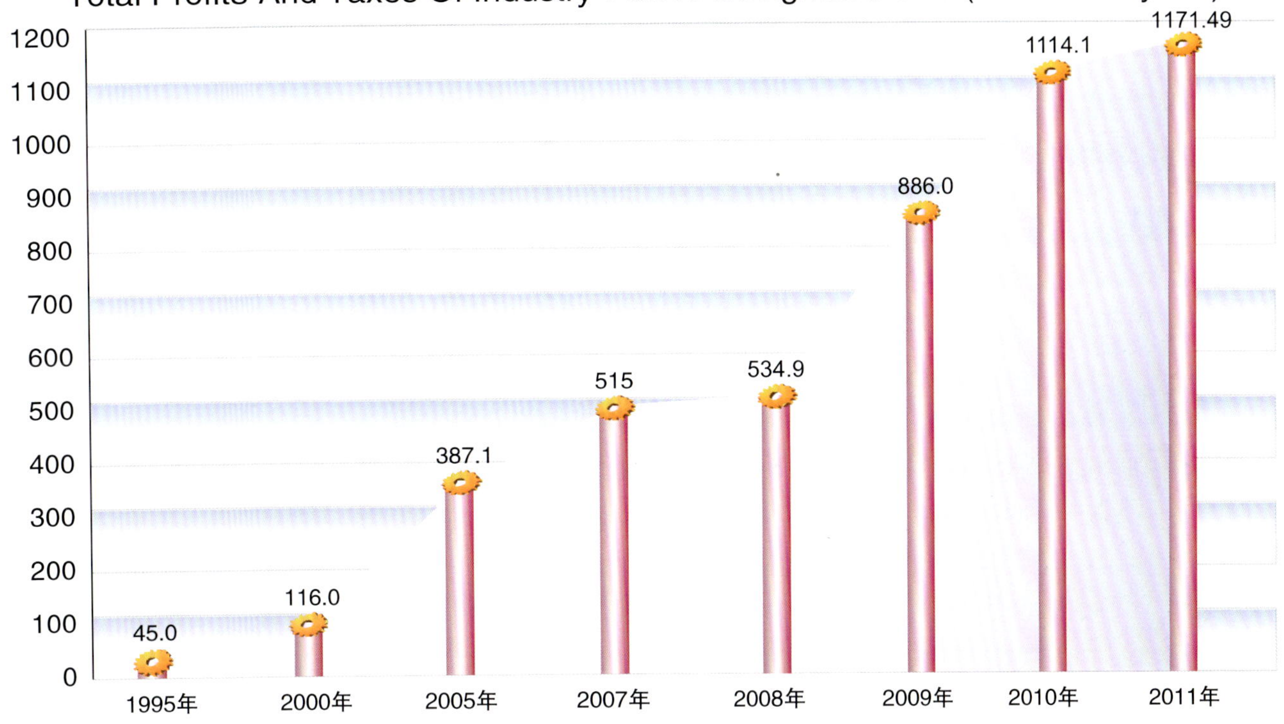

规模以上固定资产投资（亿元）
Investment In Fixed Assets Above Designated Size (100 million yuan)

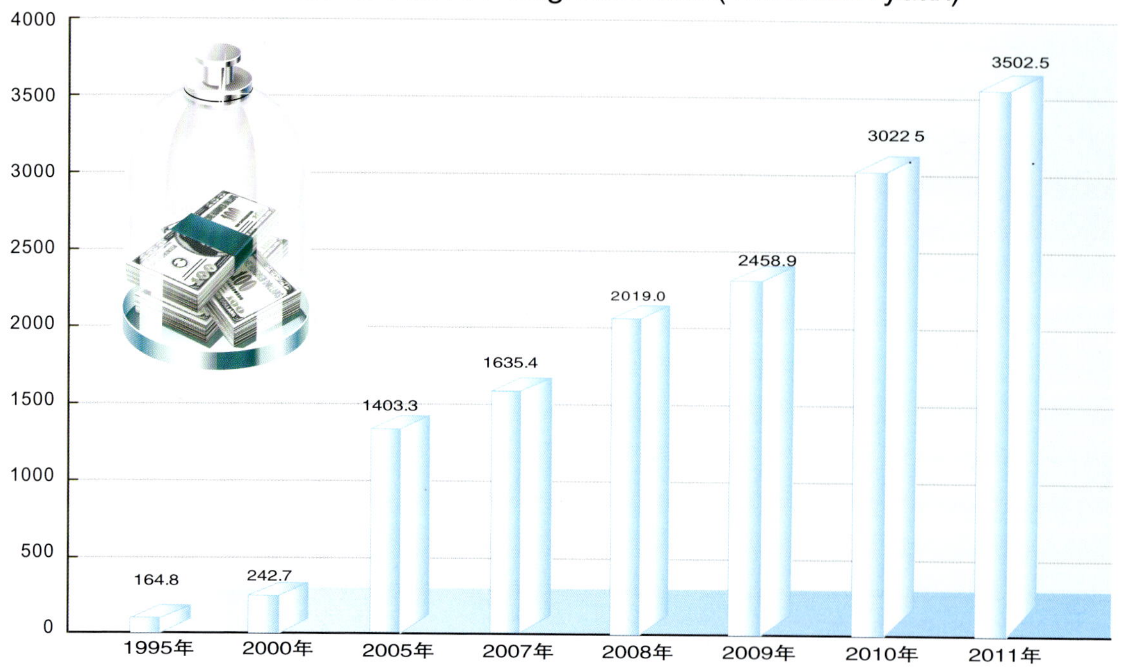

房屋竣工面积、住宅竣工面积（万平方米）
Floor Space Of Buildings Completed，Floor Space Of Residential Buildings Completed(10000 sq.m)

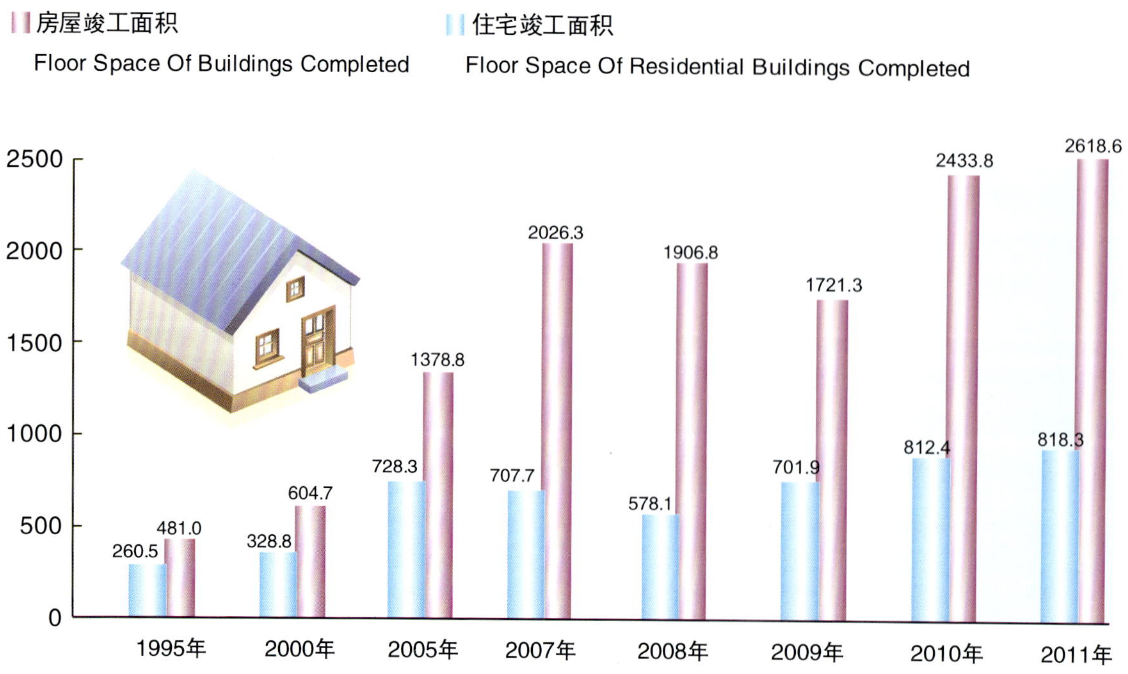

消费构成（%）(2011年)
2011 Composition Of Consumption (%)

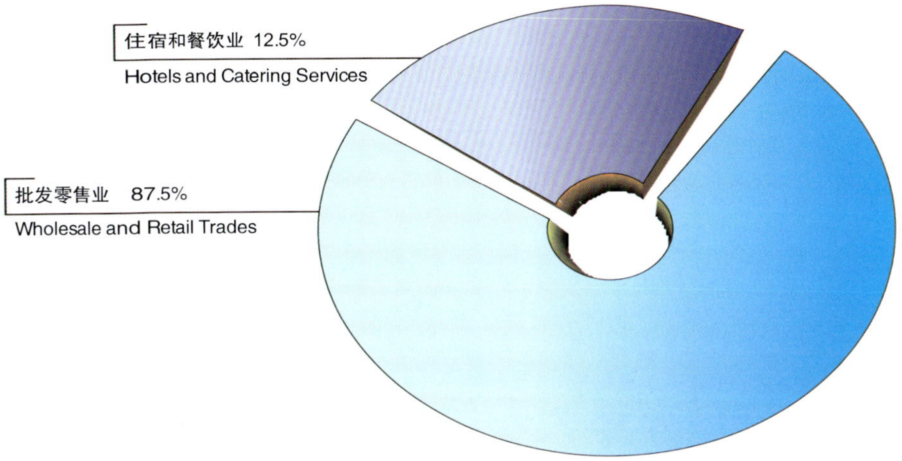

社会消费品零售总额（亿元）
Total Retail Sales Of Consumer Goods(100 million yuan)

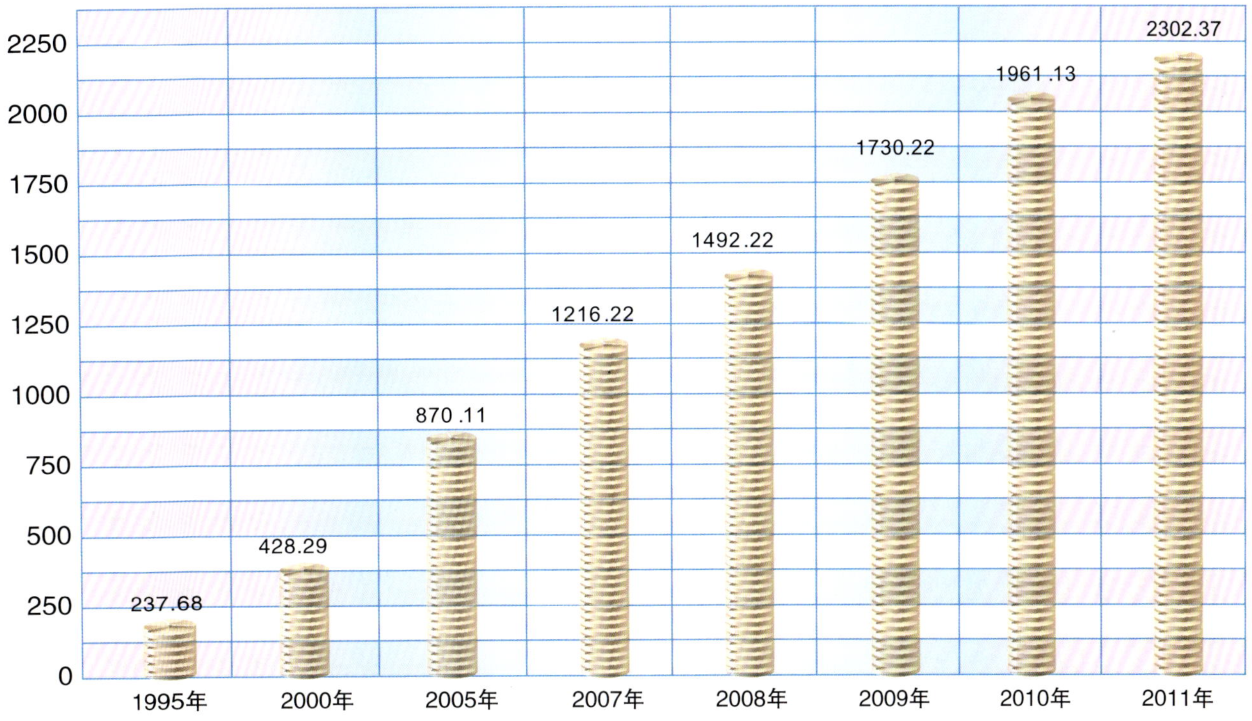

社会从业人数(万人)
Social Employment(100 million persons)

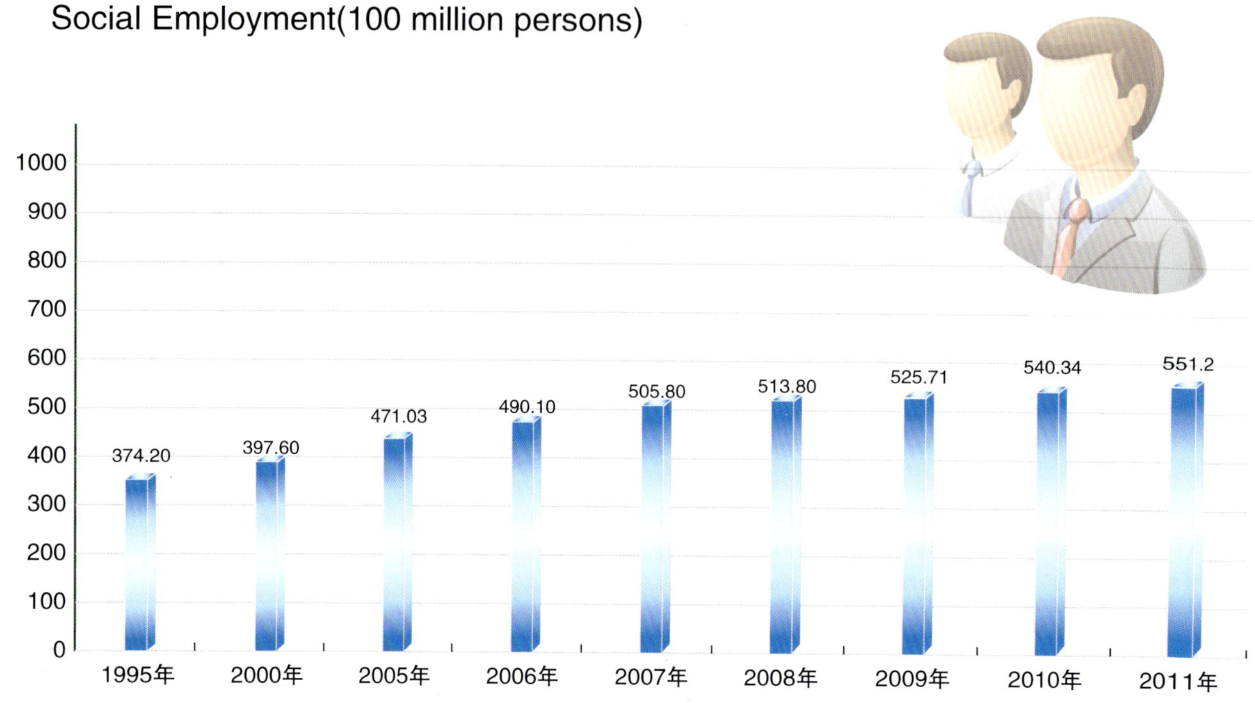

在岗职工平均工资(元)
Average Wage Of Employed Staff And Workers(yuan)

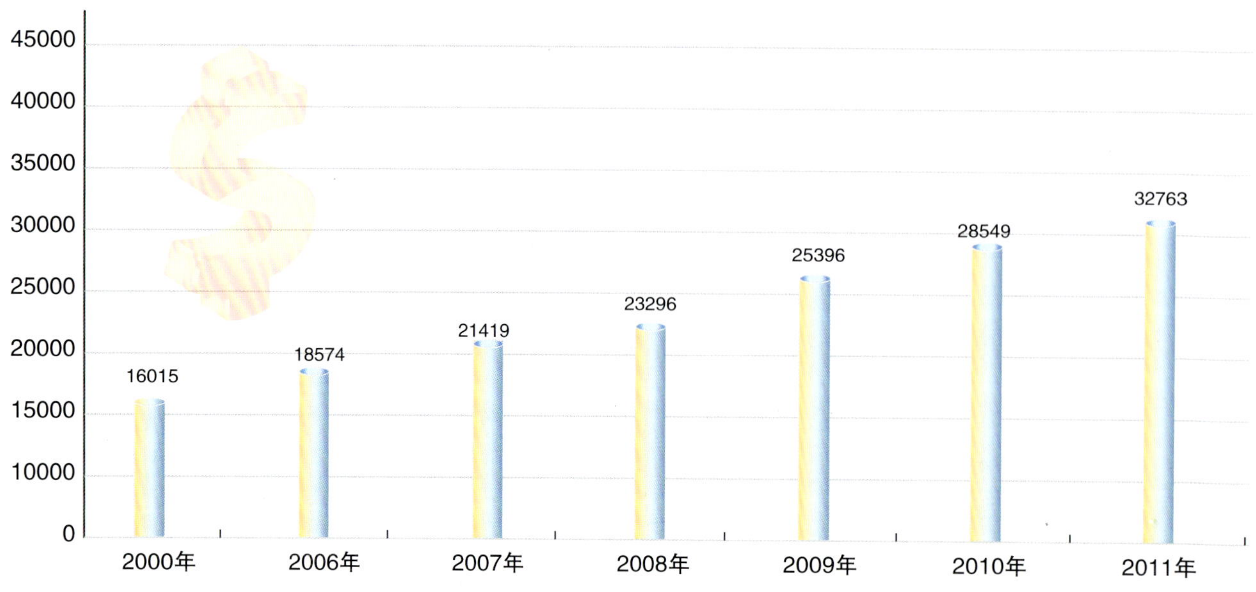

城乡居民收入（元）
Income Of Urban And Rural Households (yuan)

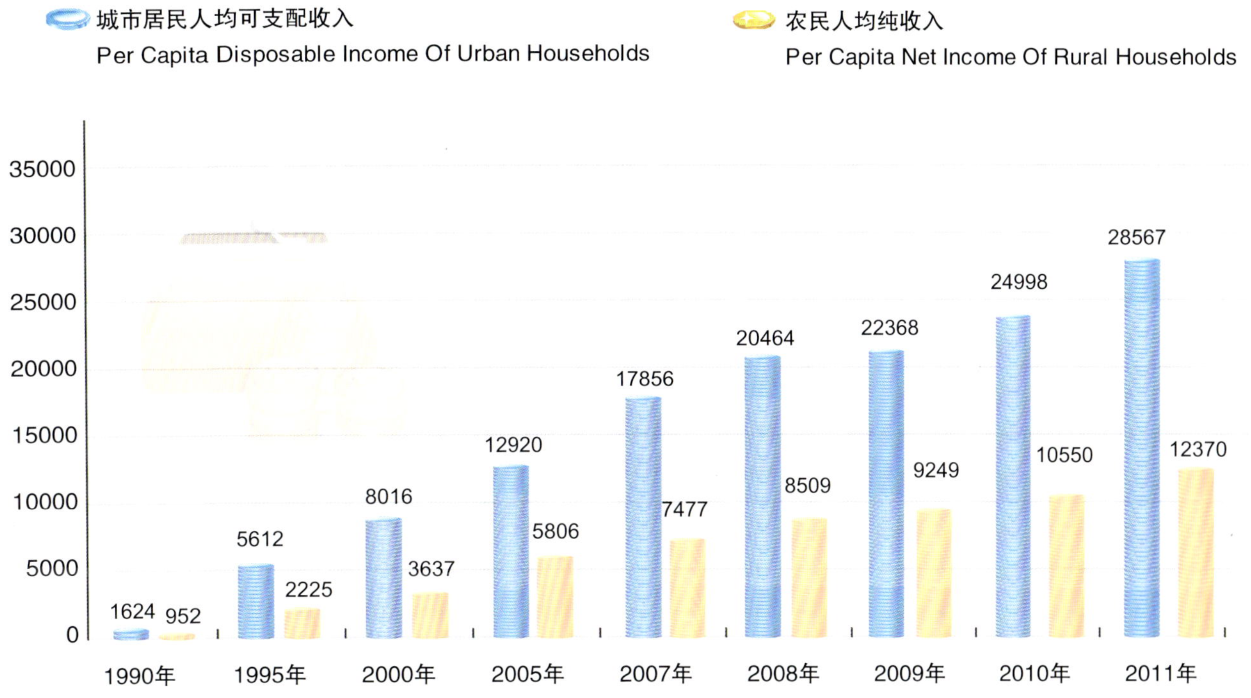

城乡居民人民币储蓄存款余额（亿元）
Savings Deposit Of Urban And Rural Households (RMB)(100 million yuan)

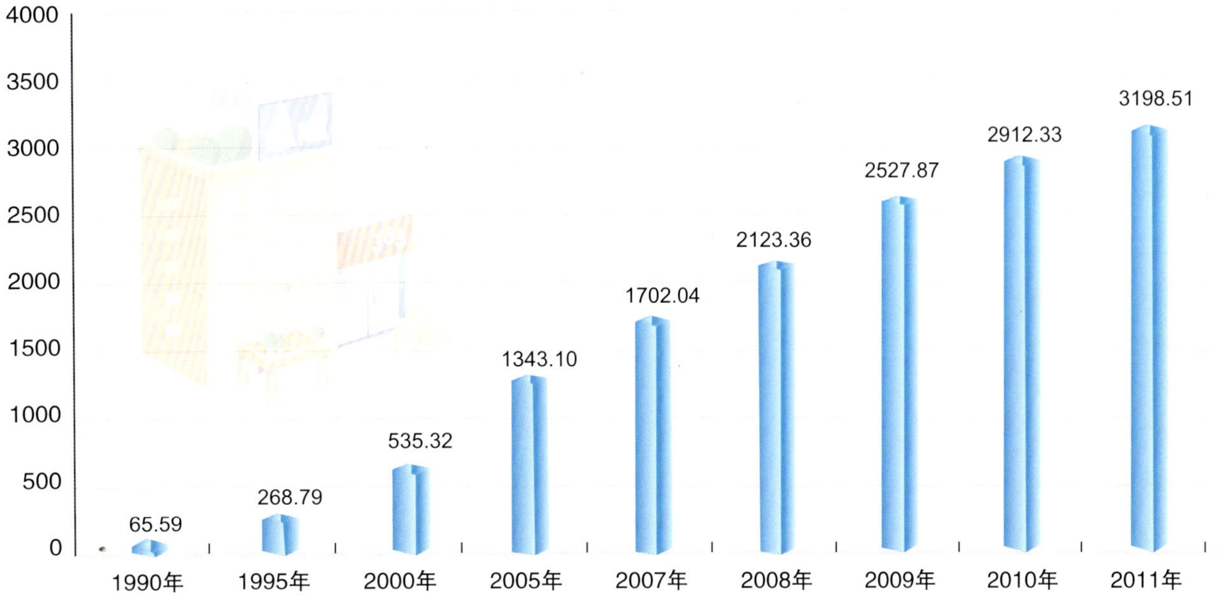

居民消费价格指数(上年=100)
Consumer Price Indices(preceding year=100)

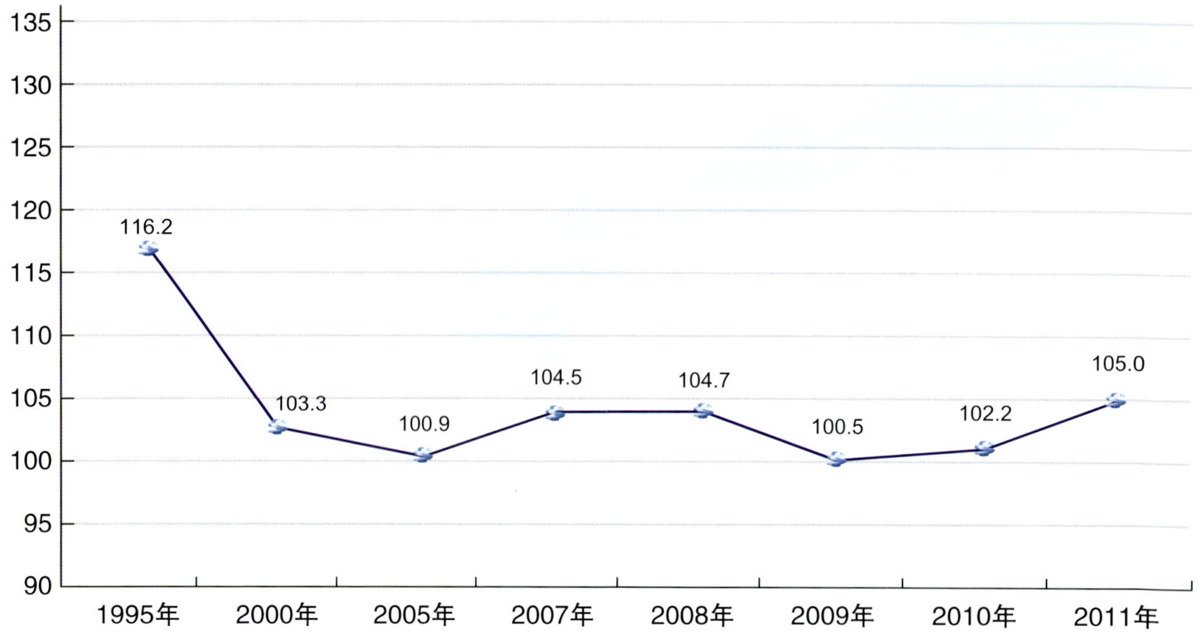

商品零售价格指数(上年=100)
Retail Price Indices(preceding year=100)

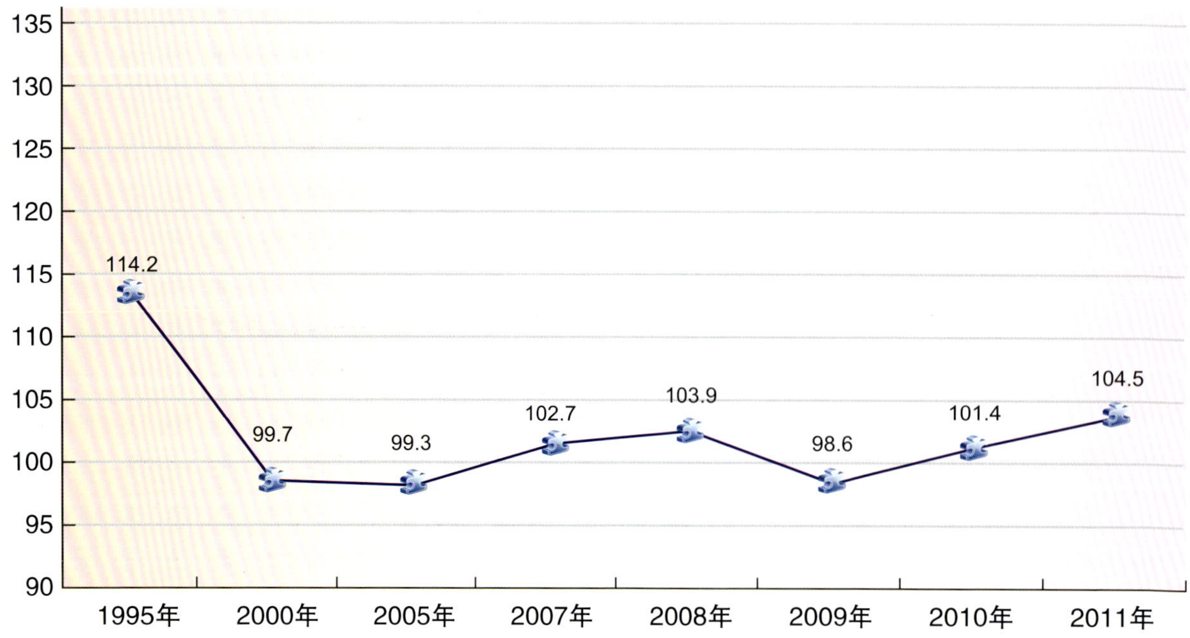

城市建成区面积、铺装道路面积
Developed Area Of the City And Area Of Roads

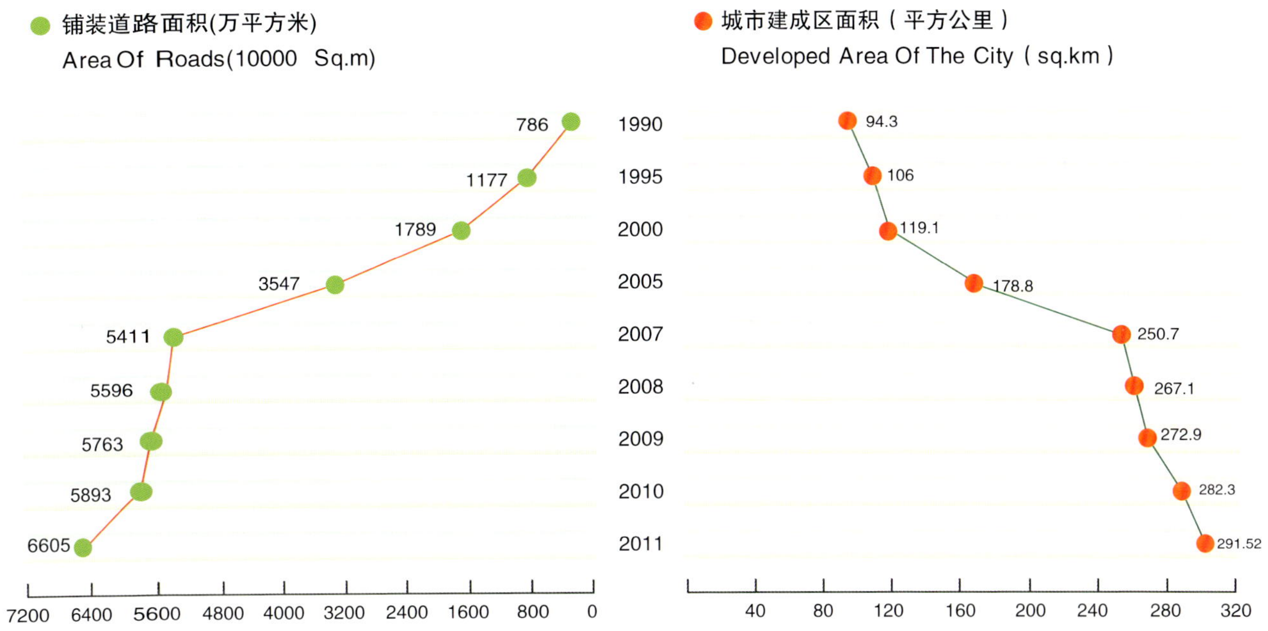

建成区绿化覆盖率（%）
Green Coverage Rate Of Developed Area(%)

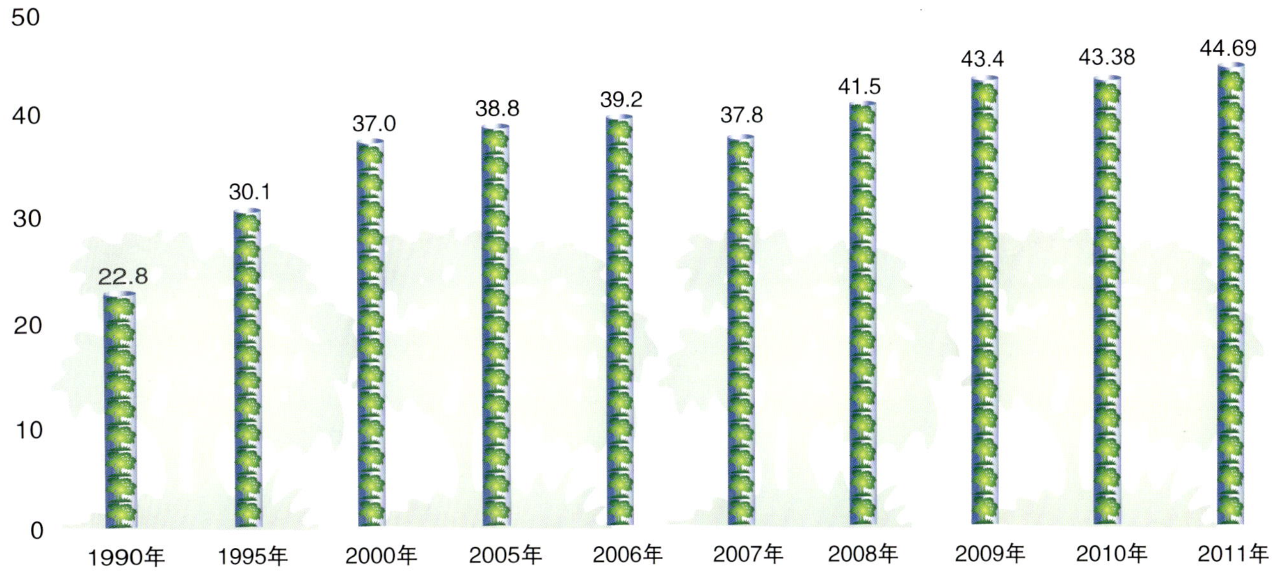

Editor's Note

Ⅰ. *Qingdao Statistical Yearbook 2012* is a very important reference book, which reflects various aspects of Qingdao's social and economic development and contains High-density information.

Ⅱ.The yearbook contains the following four parts: achievement graphs, statistic gazette, statistics and appendixes.

Statistics contains all kinds of data on Qingdao's social and economic development in 2011,and data in significant year or data since the beginning of reform and opening up, including: General Survey; Population; Employment and Wages; Investment in Fixed Assets; Foreign Trade; Consumption of Energy; Government Finance,Financial Intermediation and Insurance; Price; People's Living Conditions; City Construction and Environment Protection; Agriculture; Industry; Construction;Transport,Postal and Telecommunication Services; Wholesale and Retail Trades; Hotels,Catering Services and Tourism; Education,Science and Culture; Sports,Public Health and Civil Affairs, Judicial Affairs; Enterprises Survey.

In brief introduction at the beginning of each chapter, main coverage, data sources and statistical coverage are concerned. Meanwhile explanatory notes on major statistical indicators have been attached for readers to use the data correctly.

Ⅲ. All of the data in the book are in accordance with new administrative division.

Some of the data have been adjusted on the basis of statistics of economic census. In any case the data of this book shall be deemed as the authentic ones.

Ⅳ. Marks in this book:

"(blank)" indicates that the figure is not large enough to be measured with the smallest unit in the table, the data is not available, or the data is not available;

"#" indicates the major items of the total.

Ⅴ. Previous editions of *Qingdao Statistical Yearbook* have won wide acclaim among the readers. In order to excel, we welcome all candid comments and criticism from our readers.

Editorial Board

July, 2012

目　　录
CONTENTS

一、综　合
Chapter 1. GENERAL SURVEY

二、人　口

Chapter 2. POPULATION

三、从业人员及职工工资

Chapter 3. EMPLOYMENT AND WAGES

四、固定资产投资

Chapter 4. INVESTMENT IN FIXED ASSETS

五、对外经济贸易

Chapter 5. FOREIGN TRADE

六、能源消耗
Chapter 6. CONSUMPTION OF ENERGY

七、财政、金融和保险业
Chapter 7. GOVERNMENT FINANCE, FINANCIAL INTERMEDIATION AND INSURANCE

八、物　　价

Chapter 8. PRICE

九、人民生活

Chapter 9. PEOPLE'S LIVING CONDITIONS

十、城市建设、环境保护

Chapter 10. CITY CONSTRUCTION AND ENVIRONMENT PROTECTION

十一、农　业

Chapter 11. AGRICULTURE

十二、工　业

Chapter 12. INDUSTRY

十三、建 筑 业

Chapter 13. CONSTRUCTION

十四、运输、邮电

Chapter 14. TRANSPORT, POSTAL AND TELECOMMUNICATION SERVICES

十五、批发和零售业

Chapter 15. WHOLESALE AND RETAIL TRADES

十六、住宿、餐饮业和旅游

Chapter 16. HOTELS, CATERING SERVICES AND TOURISM

十七、教育、科技和文化

Chapter 17. EDUCATION, SCIENCE & TECHNOLOGY AND CULTURE

十八、体育、卫生和民政、司法

Chapter 18. SPORTS, PUBLIC HEALTH AND CIVIL AFFAIRS, JUDICIAL AFFAIRS

十九、企业调查

Chapter 19. ENTERPRISES SURVEY

附 录
APPENDIX

2011 年
青岛市国民经济和社会发展
统　计　公　报

青岛市统计局

国家统计局青岛调查队

(2012 年 3 月 27 日)

2011 年，面对复杂的国内外环境，在市委、市政府的正确领导下，以科学发展为主题，以加快转变经济发展方式为主线，全面落实中央一系列宏观调控政策，全市经济实现了平稳较快发展，社会事业全面进步，民生状况进一步改善。

一、综　合

初步核算，全市实现生产总值(GDP)6615.60 亿元，比上年增长 11.7%。其中，第一产业增加值 306.38 亿元，增长 5.0%，第二产业增加值 3150.72 亿元，增长 11.6%，第三产业增加值 3158.50 亿元，增长 12.4%。三次产业的比例关系由上年的 4.9：48.7：46.4 调整为 4.6：47.6：47.8。

图1 2006—2011年GDP

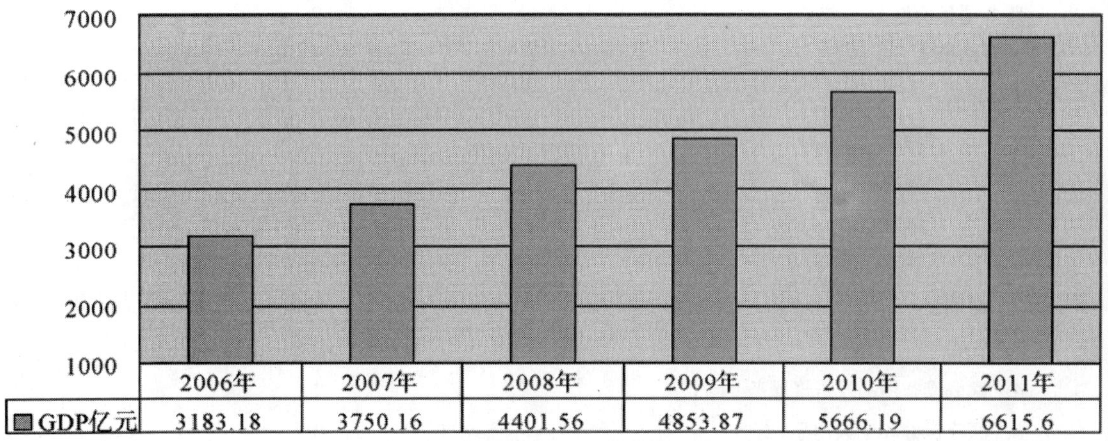

全年财政总收入实现 2407.76 亿元，增长 20.3%；地方财政一般预算收入 566.00 亿元，增长 25.1%；地方财政一般预算支出 658.68 亿元，增长 23.7%。全年国税系统组织税收收入(含海关代征)1222.71 亿元，增长 22.9%；其中，国内税收 521.44 亿元，增长 11.3%。地税税收收入 362.24 亿元，增长 27.9%。反映企业家对宏观经济环境信心的企业家信心指数年末为 114.3，反映企业综合生产经营状况和经济效益的企业景气指数为 127.7，企业家信心指数和企业景气指数分别处于相对景气和较景气区间。

图2 2006—2011年地方财政一般预算收入

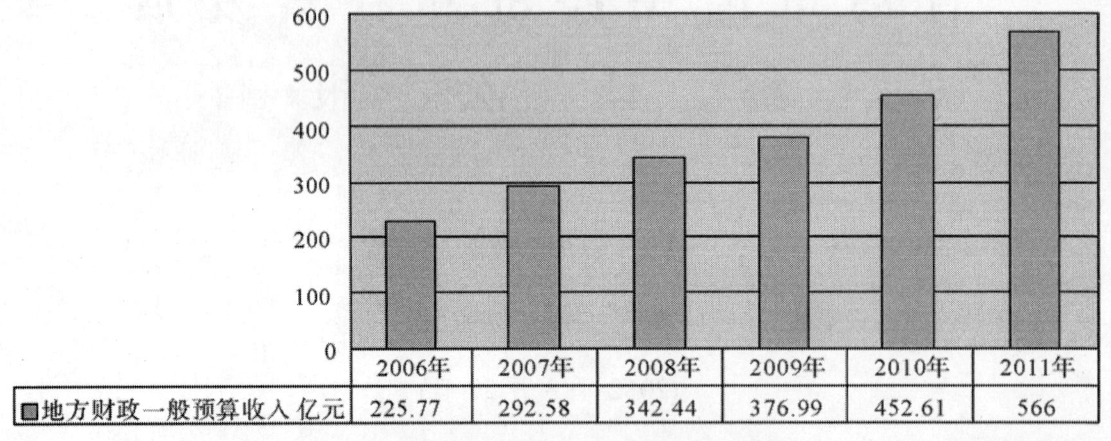

全年居民消费价格上涨5%(其中，12月份同比上涨4.8%),八大类商品价格不同程度上涨，食品上涨11.1%、烟酒上涨1.5%、衣着上涨8.2%、家庭设备用品及维修服务上涨1.0%、医疗保健和个人用品上涨1.7%、交通和通信上涨0.6%、娱乐教育文化用品及服务上涨0.7%、居住上涨3.5%。食品中，粮食、猪肉分别上涨7.2%、40.5%、鲜菜下降2.1%。12月份市区新建住宅价格同比上涨0.5%，环比下降0.3%；二手住宅同比下降1.2%，环比下降0.7%。全年工业生产者出厂价格上涨4.9%；工业生产者购进价格上涨9.4%。

表1：2011年居民消费价格比上年涨跌幅度

指标名称	比上年涨跌（%）
居民消费价格	5.0
非食品价格	2.8
服务项目价格	3.1
消费品价格	5.8
1. 食品	11.1
#粮食	7.2
猪肉	40.5
鲜蛋	11.1
鲜菜	-2.1
2. 烟酒	1.5
3. 衣着	8.2
4. 家庭设备用品及维修服务	1.0
5. 医疗保健和个人用品	1.7
6. 交通和通信	0.6
7. 娱乐教育文化用品及服务	0.7
8. 居住	3.5

全年实现海洋产业增加值669.25亿元，占GDP比重为10.12%，较上年提高0.28个百分点。

二、农 业

全市粮食播种面积 54.56 万公顷，增长 1.9%，粮食总产量达到 363.0 万吨，增长 3.3%。2011 年末全市实有耕地面积 41.98 万公顷，下降 0.2%。

表 2：2011 年主要农产品产量及增速

产品名称	产量(单位)	比上年增长(%)
粮食总产量	363.0 万吨	3.3
其中:小麦	165.34 万吨	0.4
玉米	190.64 万吨	6.2
花生	44.37 万吨	0.5
蔬菜	583.82 万吨	0.5
水果	80.52 万吨	0.3

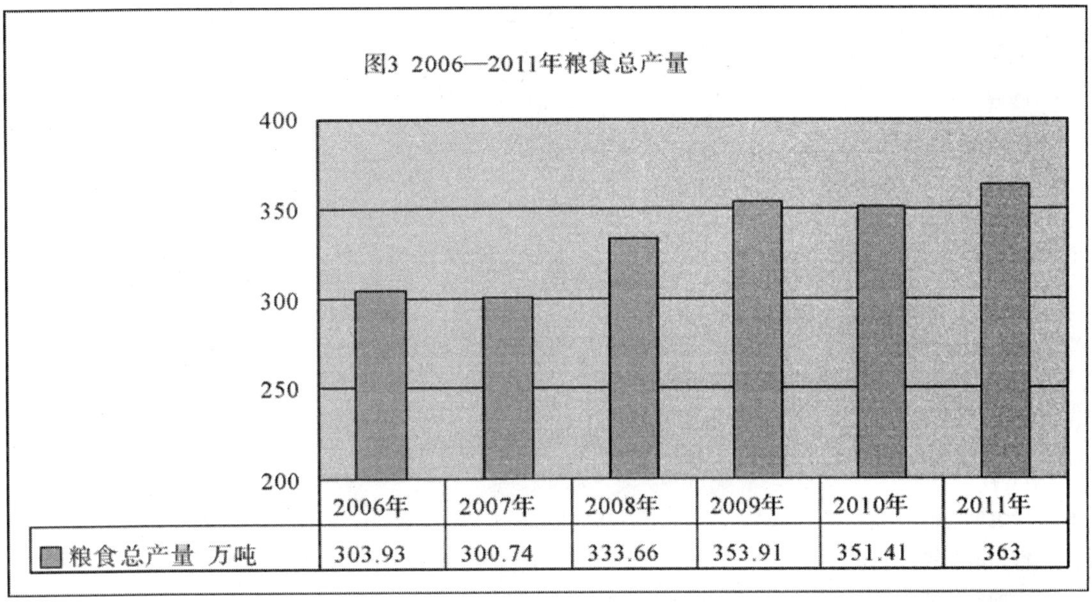

2011 年主要畜产品产量及增速

产品名称	产量(单位)	比上年增长(%)
肉类总产量	59.55 万吨	6.0
其中：猪肉	26.65 万吨	9.5
牛肉	0.98 万吨	1.7
羊肉	0.20 万吨	1.3
禽肉	31.47 万吨	3.4
牛、羊奶	37.17 万吨	2.8
禽蛋	19.14 万吨	1.0

全年完成造林面积 0.92 万公顷，增长 10.8%；森林覆盖率 37.77%，提高 0.87 个百分点。全年完成幼林抚育面积 1.2 万公顷，下降 8%。

水产品总产量 113.41 万吨，增长 1.3%，其中，捕捞产量 26.7 万吨，增长 1.1%；养殖产量 86.71 万吨，增长 1.3%。海、淡水养殖面积 5.49 万公顷，下降 2.5%。

2011 年末，全市拥有农业机械总动力 784.06 万千瓦，增长 2.7%。农用拖拉机 20.2 万台，增长 0.9%。农村用电量 43.16 亿千瓦时，地膜覆盖面积 16.45 万公顷。农田有效灌溉面积 33.17 万公顷，增长 0.8%，其中，节水灌溉面积 16.62 万公顷，增长 2.2%。

三、工业与建筑业

2011 年规模以上工业企业(年主营业务收入 2000 万元及以上的工业法人企业)4561 家。完成增加值增长 13.5%；其中，国有企业增长 13.2%，集体企业增长 4.7%，股份制企业增长 13.7%，外商及港澳台投资企业增长 11.8%，其他经济增长 27.9%。分轻重工业看，轻工业增长 15.1%，重工业增长 12.3%，轻重工业的比例为 40.5∶59.5。

全年规模以上工业企业共完成高新技术产业产值 4640.08 亿元，增长 11.2%，占规模以上工业总产值的 39.0%，比重较年初提高 1.0 个百分点；装备制造业完成产值 4375.42 亿元，占规模以上工业比重 34.6%；规模以上工业中战略性新兴产业产值 2192 亿元，增长 11.6%。

2011 年规模以上工业主要产品产量及增速

产品名称	产量(单位)	比上年增长(%)
纱	1.94 万吨	20.8
布	4.39 亿米	162.7
化学纤维	3.86 万吨	0.5
卷烟	522.56 亿支	1.9
啤酒	154.65 万千升	9.2
发电量	173.69 亿千瓦时	−4.7
钢材	332.20 万吨	6.1
原油加工量	1273.66 万吨	−6.5
烧碱	13.20 万吨	−4.8
纯碱	72.07 万吨	3.9
化学农药原药	1.73 万吨	31.9
橡胶轮胎外胎	4441.59 万条	15.3
水泥	530.80 万吨	19.0
汽车	48.88 万辆	−13.5
彩色电视机	1154.20 万台	3.9
家用电冰箱	718.54 万台	−9.7
房间空气调节器	411.56 万台	0.2

规模以上工业实现利税总额 1146.1 亿元，增长 11.6%；利润 627.9 亿元，增长 15.4%。主营业务收入 12273.8 亿元，增长 18.4%。资本保值增值率 124.1%，产品销售率 98.5%。

图4 2006—2011年规模以上工业

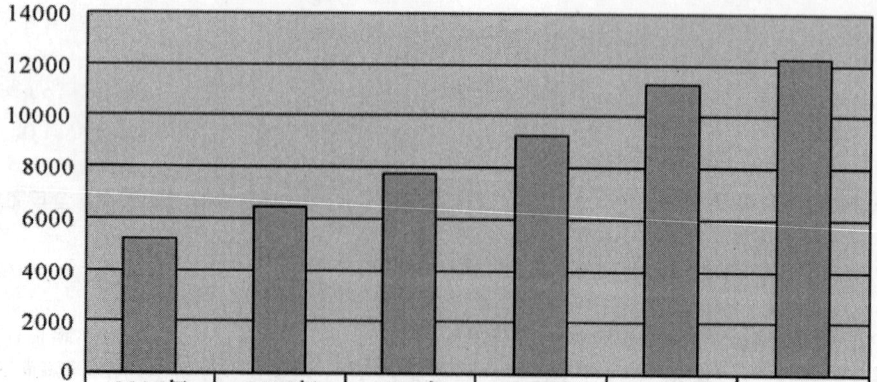

	2006年	2007年	2008年	2009年	2010年	2011年
主营业务收入 亿元	5190.77	6462.55	7813.77	9217.59	11264.04	12273.8

全年建筑业实现增加值 356.16 亿元，增长 13.5%。实现利税总额 56 亿元，增长 11%；其中，国有及国有控股企业实现利税 12 亿元，增长 10%。

四、固定资产投资

全市固定资产投资(包括城镇、农村 500 万元以上投资项目)3502.5 亿元，比上年增长 23.4%。其中，第一产业投资 42.2 亿元，增长 106.8%；第二产业投资 1472.6 亿元，增长 24.5%；第三产业投资 1987.7 亿元，增长 21.6%。

图5 2006—2011年固定资产投资额

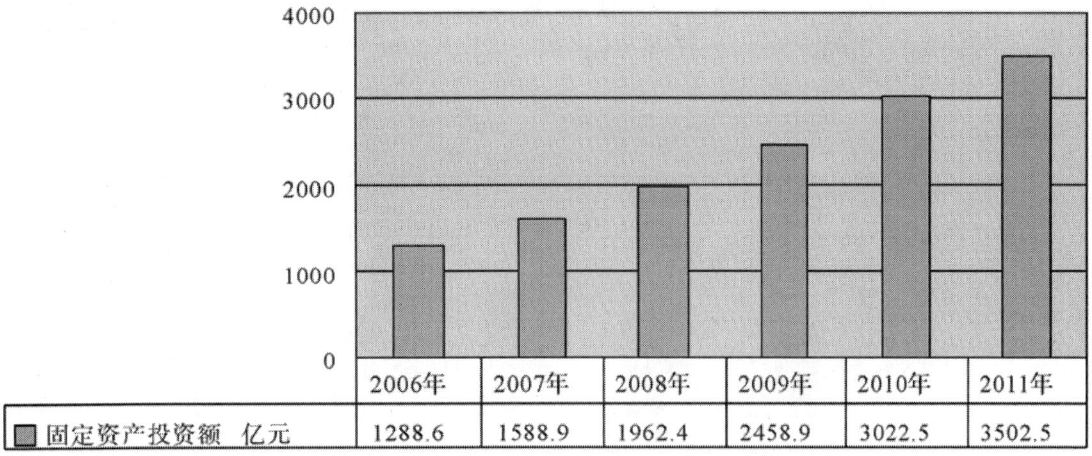

全年固定资产投资施工项目 4508 个，新开工项目 2681 个，竣工项目 2984 个；在建项目计划总投资规模 9706.5 亿元，增长 22.4%。全年新增固定资产 1992.3 亿元，项目建成投产率 66.2%，固定资产交付使用率 56.9%。

全年房地产开发完成投资 782.7 亿元，增长 29.9%。商品房竣工 905.9 万平方米，下降 11.2%；全市销售房屋面积 1028 万平方米，下降 24.5%。经济适用房施工面积 208.31 万平方米，竣工面积 43.64 万平方米。

五、国内贸易

全年实现社会消费品零售额 2232.88 亿元，增长 17.4%。分地域看，城市市场实现零售额 1851.31 亿元，增长 17.8%；农村市场实现零售额 381.57 亿元，增长 15.2%。分行业看，批发和零售业实现零售额 1954.48 亿元，增长 17.5%；住宿和餐饮业实现零售额 278.4 亿元，增长 16.7%。

图6 2006—2011年社会消费品零售总额

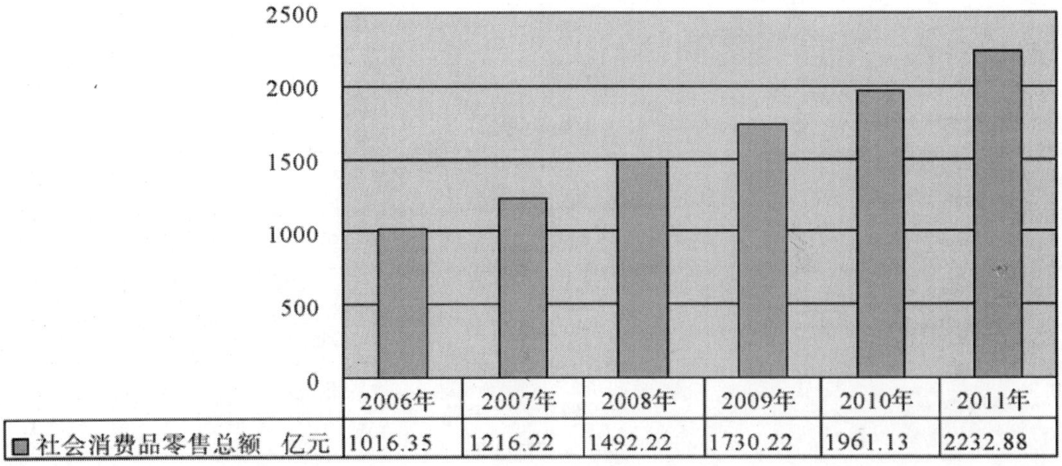

全年限额以上单位实现汽车类零售额 303.56 亿元，增长 29.1%；石油及其制品类零售额 102.93 亿元，增长 21.8%；粮油、食品、饮料、烟酒类零售额 104.25 亿元，增长 20.0%；日用品类零售额 25.67 亿元，增长 25.3%；体育及娱乐用品类零售额 7.25 亿元，增长 12.7%；化妆品类零售额 16.26 亿元，增长 33.0%；金银珠宝类零售额 21.64 亿元，增长 48.1%。

六、对外经济

青岛地区(含中央、省公司)实现外贸进出口总额 721.52 亿美元，增长 26.5%。其中，出口额 406.13 亿美元，增长 19.7%，进口额 315.39 亿美元，增长 36.3%。青岛市(不含中央、省公司)实现外贸进出口总额 712.63 亿美元，增长 27.2%。其中，出口额 400.56 亿美元，进口额 312.07 亿美元，分别增长 20.5%和 36.9%。外商投资企业出口额 193.31 亿美元，占全市出口额的比重为 48.3%。

图7 2006—2011年外贸进出口额（含中央、省公司）

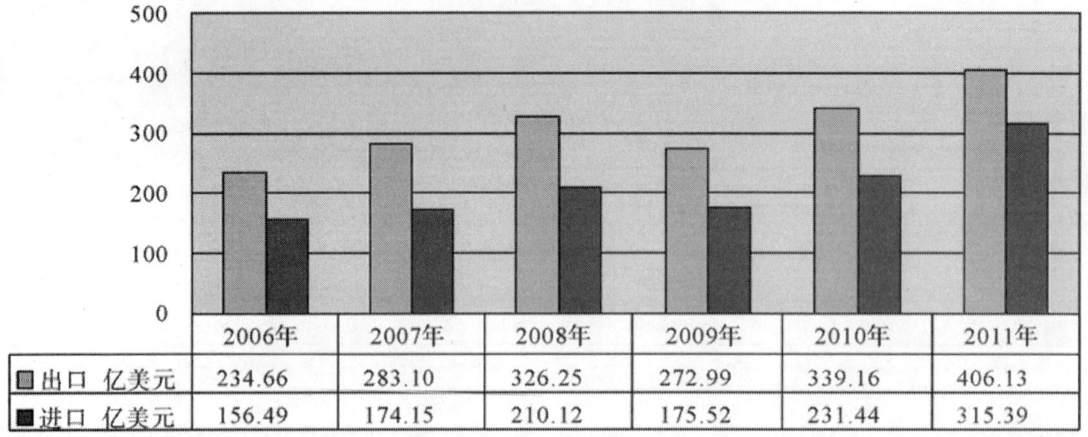

据青岛海关统计，青岛口岸对外贸易进出口总额 1510 亿美元，增长 26.7%，其中，出口额 730 亿美元，进口额 780 亿美元，分别增长 21.9%和 31.7%。

实际使用外资 36.34 亿美元，增长 27.8%。

全年完成对外承包工程和对外劳务合作新签合同金额 6.8 亿美元，增长 1.5%；营业额 13.5 亿美元，增长 25%；共派出各类劳务人员 7003 人次，增长 9.5%。

全市引进内资 818.5 亿元，增长 30.3%。

七、交通运输、邮电和旅游业

全年港口吞吐量(不含地方港务局)37971 万吨，增长 6.46%；外贸吞吐量 26726 万吨，增长 3.99%；集装箱吞吐量 1302 万标准箱，增长 8.41%。

表 5：2011 年各种运输方式完成的运输量及增速

运输方式	运输量(单位)	比上年增长(%)
客运周转量	184.57 亿人公里	6.2
铁路	51.65 亿人公里	9.7
公路	131.82 亿人公里	5.6
水运	1.1 亿人公里	-39.4
货运周转量	3819.45 亿吨公里	6.2
铁路	173.19 亿吨公里	13.2
公路	408.86 亿吨公里	10.6
水运	3237.4 亿吨公里	5.3

年末拥有国内航线 107 条，国际航线 9 条，港澳地区航线 3 条，全年航空旅客吞吐量达到 1171.6 万人次，增长 5.5%；航空行货邮吞吐量 16.65 万吨，增长 1.7%。

全年完成邮电业务总量 197.83 亿元，增长 11.9%。其中，邮政业务总量 5.68 亿元，增长 15.1%；电信业务总量 192.15 亿元，增长 11.8%。信函 9280 万件，增长 19.2%。2011 年互联网用户累计达 185.69 万户，下降 1.4%，使用时长达 1695.55 亿分钟，增长 15.1%。年末固定电话用户达到 251.33 万户；全市移动电话发展到 1094.88 万户，其中，年内新增 138.38 万户。

全年全市旅游总收入 681.39 亿元，增长 17.5%。其中国内旅游收入 637.34 亿元，增长 18.0%；国际旅游收入 6.89 亿美元，增长 14.7%。全年共接待国内外游客 5071.75 万人次，增长 12.6%；其中国内游客 4956.11 万人次，增长 12.7%；海外游客 115.64 万人次，增长 7.0%。年末 A 级旅游景区达到 60 处，星级饭店 153 家。

八、金融业

年末金融机构本外币存款余额 8901.27 亿元，比年初增加 1002.59 亿元；人民币存款余额 8638.50 亿元，比年初增加 985.80 亿元，其中，储蓄存款 3198.51 亿元，比年初增加 291.57 亿元。本外币贷款余额 7495.25 亿元，比年初增加 1145.40 亿元；人民币贷款余额 6947.75 亿元，比年初增加 1076.87 亿元。

全年全市承保金额 38082.96 亿元，增长 1.9%，实现保费收入 145.73 亿元，增长 8.5%。其中：财产保费收入 57.15 亿元，增长 13.2%；人身险保费收入 88.58 亿元，增长 5.7%。赔款支出金额 46.38 亿元，增长 23.4%；其中财产险赔付金额 29.1 亿元，人身险赔付金额 17.28 亿元。

九、科学技术和教育

初步统计，2011 年全市共取得重要科技成果 345 项。获得国家级科技奖励 14 项，其中，技术发明奖 2 项，科技进步奖 12 项；获得省级科技奖励 97 项，其中，自然科学奖 4 项，技术发明奖 4 项，科技进步奖 88 项，国际科技合作奖 1 项。

全年共成交技术合同项目 2352 项，成交额 20.75 亿元。全年专利申请量 19816 件，授权专利 9149 件。

2011 年末，全市共有各类大专院校(含民办高校)24 所，其中普通高校 22 所，在校学生 29.1 万人，增长 4.12%。中等学校 380 所，其中，普通中学 290 所，在校学生 37.3 万人，下降 1.79%；中等专业学校和技工学校 90 所，在校学生 13.5 万人，下降 12.9%。接受中等职业教育的学生占高中阶段在校生的 53%。共有小学 889 所，在校学生 48 万人，增长 3.6%。学龄儿童入学率 100%，初中入学率达 99%以上。

十、文化、卫生和体育

全市共有各类文化机构 470 处。其中，影剧院 40 处，文化馆(站)183 处，博物馆 9 处，公共图书馆 13 处，艺术表演团体 10 个，广播电台 1 座、12 套节目，电视台 1 座、15 套节目，全市有线电视用户达到 268.2 万户，数字电视用户达到 243.88 万户。全市出版各类杂志 2766 万册，出版报纸 107615 万份。全市共有档案馆 14 处。

年末全市共有卫生机构(含诊所)2549 处，其中，医院、卫生院 278 处，疾病预防控制中心 13 处，妇幼保健机构 13 处，门诊部(所)、卫生保健所、医务室 1861 处。年末各类卫生技术人员 4.8 万人，其中，医生 1.9 万人。全市拥有医疗床位 4 万张，其中，医院、卫生院床位 3.6 万张。

全市运动员在各项比赛中共获得金牌 352 枚，银牌 209 枚，铜牌 268 枚。共打破全国纪录 2 项。全市共有体育专业队 1 个，队员 125 人。重点体校 2 所，学员 1108 人，业余体校 12 所，学员 1516 人。群众体育运动蓬勃开展。

十一、城市建设

建成区面积 291.52 平方公里，增长 3.3%。城市平均每天供水量 96.22 万吨，下降 2.9%。城市全年实际用水量 3.11 亿吨，增长 0.8%，其中生产用水和生活用水分别为 1.38 亿吨和 1.73 亿吨。

城市使用液化气、煤制气、天然气的总户数达到 98.21 万户，全年供应液化气总量 8 万吨；供应煤制气总量 9137 万立方米；供应天然气总量 48308 万立方米，增长 35.4%。城市气化率达到 100%。

全社会用电量 313.44 亿千瓦时，增长 7.0%。其中，工业用电 203.42 亿千瓦时，城乡居民生活用电 50.13 亿千瓦时，分别增长 8.4%和 1.3%。全年新增供热面积 1010 万平方米，年末供热面积达到 8235 万平方米，增长 14.0%。

年末市区公共汽、电车线路 227 条，增长 10.7%。共有营运的公交汽、电车 5419 辆，增长 16.2%。年末全市共有出租汽车 9683 辆，增长 0.5%。

年末城市道路总长度 3544 公里，扩建、翻建道路 194 条，城市下水道总长度 5187 公里。

据抽样调查，年末城市人均现住房建筑面积 27.67 平方米，农民人均拥有住房面积 32.6 平方米。

十二、能源、环境和安全生产

节能减排主要指标完成国家和省下达的任务。监控的市重点用能工业企业 12 项产品单耗指标中，下降的占 83.3%，主要产品生产实现节能 22.5 万吨标准煤。风力发电建设力度继续加大，风电装机容量累计 13 万千瓦，增长 6.9 倍；风力发电 7800 万千瓦时，增长 2.6 倍。

全年空气质量按功能区达标率为 100%；市区空气质量优良天数达到 334 天，优良率 91.5%，比上年提高 0.8 个百分点。市区区域环境噪声平均值 53.7 分贝，市区交通干线噪声平均值 68.1 分贝。市区共植树 275.74 万株，增长 159.6%。建成区绿化覆盖率达到 43.81%。市区园林绿地面积达 18012.79 公顷，增长 8.4%；新增公共绿地面积 151.21 公顷，人均拥有公共绿地面积 14.58 平方米。全市现有公园、动物园 74 个。

各类生产安全事故 2585 起，死亡人数 427 人，分别下降 14.9%和 4.5%。亿元 GDP 生产安全事故死亡 0.065 人，下降 17.7%。道路交通事故万车死亡 2.3 人，下降 5%。未发生重特大事故。

十三、人口、人民生活和社会保障

年末全市户籍总人口为 766.36 万人，增长 0.36%，其中，市区 277.09 万人，增长 0.58%；五市(县级)489.27 万人，增长 0.23%。全年新出生人口 65793 人，出生率为 8.60‰；死亡人口 55537 人，死亡率为 7.26‰；人口自然增长率为 1.34‰。

城市居民人均可支配收入 28567 元，增长 14.3%；人均消费性支出 19297 元，增长 10.1%；城市居民家庭食品消费支出占家庭消费性支出的 37.5%。全市在岗职工平均工资 32763 元，增长 14.8%。

农民人均纯收入 12370 元，增长 17.3%；人均生活消费支出 7661 元，增长 15.0%；农村居民家庭食品消费支出占家庭消费总支出的 36.6%。

图8 2006—2011年城乡居民收入

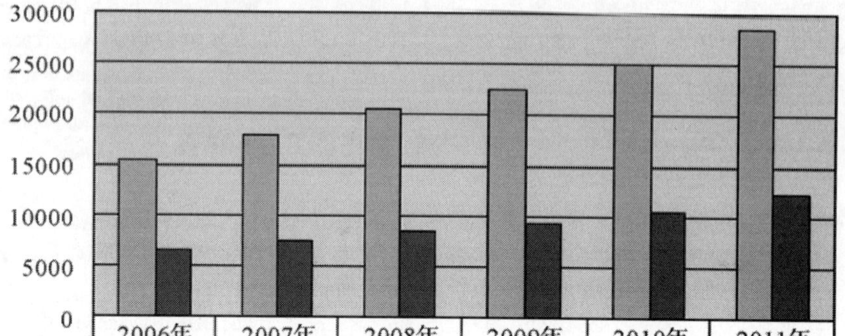

	2006年	2007年	2008年	2009年	2010年	2011年
城市居民人均可支配收入 元	15328	17856	20464	22368	24998	28567
农民人均纯收入 元	6546	7477	8509	9249	10550	12370

表 6：2006-2011 年城乡居民家庭食品消费支出占家庭消费性支出比重

指　　标	单 位	2006	2007	2008	2009	2010	2011
城市居民家庭	%	36.4	37	37.4	38.5	37.4	37.5
农村居民家庭	%	36.6	37.2	37.7	36.4	35.5	36.6

2011 年末全市单位从业人员 275.9 万人，增长 2.4%。年末全市城镇登记失业率为 2.95%，上升 0.03 个百分点。

年末全市基本养老保险参保缴费人数为 207.68 万人，参加失业保险人数为 155.58 万人，全年累计领取失业保险金的人数为 6.11 万人。2011 年全市新型农村合作医疗参合率达到 100%。

2011 年全市各类社会福利院床位达 27383 张，收养 18930 人。

注：

1、公报中统计数据均为初步统计数。

2、公报中全市生产总值、各产业增加值绝对数按现价计算，增长速度按可比价计算。

3、从 2011 年 1 月起提高工业、固定资产投资统计起点标准，其中纳入规模以上工业统计范围的工业企业起点标准从年主营业务收入 500 万元提高到 2000 万元；固定资产投资项目统计的起点标准，从计划总投资额 50 万元提高到 500 万元。

4、战略性新兴产业根据国家规划，现阶段主要包括节能环保、新一代信息技术、生物、高端装备制造、新能源、新材料、新能源汽车等七个产业领域。我市目前战略性新兴产业统计监测所涉及的行业主要包括节能环保、生物、高端装备制造、新能源、新材料、新一代信息技术等 6 个产业。

5、市话交换机总容量包括小灵通容量。

6、在岗职工平均工资是指各单位在岗职工在一定时期内平均每人所得的工资额，包括国有经济、集体经济、联营经济、股份制经济、外商和港、澳、台投资经济、私营经济单位等。

7、企业家信心指数也称“宏观经济景气指数”，是根据企业家对企业外部市场经济环境与宏观政策的认识、看法、判断与预期(通常为对“乐观”、“一般”、“不乐观”的选择)而编制的指数，用以综合反映企业家对宏观经济环境的感受与信心。其表现形式为纯正数，以 100 作为景气指数的临界值，其数值范围在 0−200 之间。

8、企业景气指数是根据企业家对本企业综合生产经营情况的判断与预期(通常为对“好”、“一般”、“不佳”的选择)而编制的景气指数，用以综合反映企业的生产经营状况。其表现形式为纯正数，以 100 作为景气指数的临界值，其数值范围在 0−200 之间。

STATISTICS COMMUNIQUÉ QINGDAO'S ECONOMIC AND SOCIAL DEVELOPMENT DURING 2011

Qingdao Statistics Bureau

NBS Qingdao Survey Office

(March 27, 2012)

In 2011, Qingdao saw steady rapid economic growth under the wise and effective leadership of local government. Taking the Scientific Concept for Development as their guideline for governance, local officials made great efforts to accelerate transformation of the economic development model and implement the central government's macroeconomic regulations and control policies. The city also witnessed overall progress in social programs and further improvement in personal incomes.

I. General

Preliminary statistics showed a gross domestic product (GDP) of RMB 661.56 billion, up 11.7% over the previous year. Of the total, primary industries contributed RMB 30.638 billion in added value, up 5.0%, secondary industries contributed RMB 315.072 billion, up 11.6%, and tertiary industries contributed RMB 315.850 billion, up 12.4%. The percentage of primary, secondary and tertiary industries changed to 4.6, 47.6 and 47.8 from 4.9, 48.7 and 46.4 in the previous year respectively.

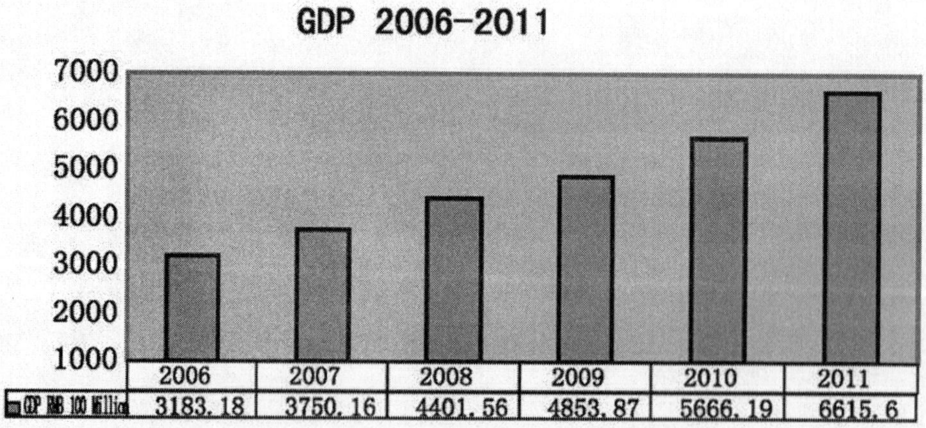

Qingdao realized RMB 240.776 billion in the local government's general revenue, up 20.3%, RMB 56.60 billion in the general budget revenue, up 25.1% and RMB 65.868 billion in the general budget expenditure, up 23.7%. The national tax revenue (including those collected by customs) rose by 22.9% to RMB 122.271 billion. Internal revenue increased 11.3% to RMB 52.144 billion and local tax revenue increased 27.9% to RMB 36.224 billion. The Entrepreneur's Confidence Index reflecting entrepreneurs' confidence and expectations for the macro economy was 114.3 while the Business Climate Index reflecting companies' overall production and operation status as well as earnings was 127.7. The Entrepreneur's Confidence Index and the Business Climate Index falls in the intervals of Relative Prosperity and More Prosperity respectively.

Local government's general budget revenue 2006-2011

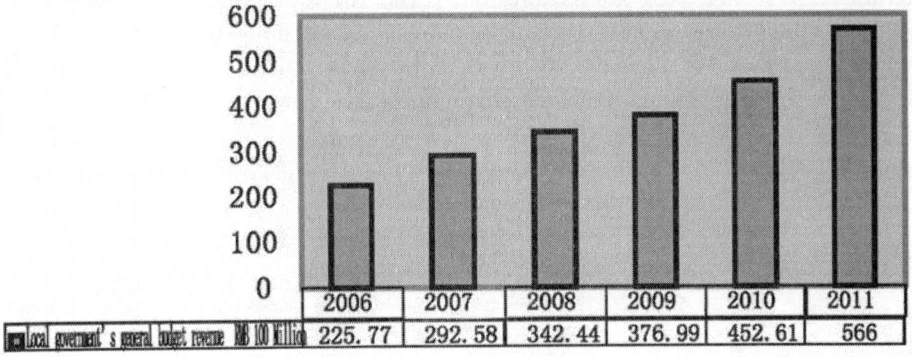

The total consumer price index increased 5% (in December, the index increased 4.8% year-on-year). Prices of products in eight categories rose to different levels; food prices rose 11.1%, tobacco and wine increased 1.5%, clothes surged 8.2%, household appliances and repair services increased 1.0%, medical care and personal articles climbed 1.7%, transportation and communication edged up 0.6%, entertainment, educational and cultural products and services went up 0.7% and housing rose 3.5%. In food, grain and pork prices rose 7.2% and 40.5% respectively, while fresh vegetables price declined by 2.1%. In December, urban newly-built residential housing prices increased 0.5% year-on-year, but declined 0.3% month-on-month. Second-hand residential housing prices decreased 1.2% year-on-year or 0.7% month-on-month. The factory price index for main industrial products rose 4.9%. The purchase price index surged 9.4%.

Table 1: Movements of Customer Price Index in 2011 over the previous year

Description	+/-% over the previous year
Customer Price Index	5.0
Non-food	2.8
Services	3.1
Consumption goods	5.8
1. Food	11.1
Grain	7.2
Pork	40.5
Eggs	11.1
Fresh vegetables	-2.1
2. Tobacco and wine	1.5
3. Clothes	8.2
4. Household appliances and repair services	1.0
5. Medical care and personal articles	1.7
6. Transportation and communications	0.6
7. Entertainment, educational and cultural products and services	0.7
8. Housing	3.5

The ocean industry realized a total added value of RMB 66.925 billion, accounting for 10.12% of GDP, up 0.28% over the previous year.

II. Agriculture

The sown area for crops totaled 545, 600 hectares, up 1.9%. The total grain output reached 3, 630,000 tons, up 3.3%. By the end of 2011, Qingdao had 419,800 hectares of cultivated land, down 0.2%.

Table 2: Output of major farm products and growth rate in 2011

Description	Output (ton)	+/-% over the previous year
Grains	3,630,000	3.3
Of which: Wheat	1,653,400	0.4
Corn	1,906,400	6.2
Peanuts	443,700	0.5
Vegetables	5,838,200	0.5
Fruits	805,200	0.3

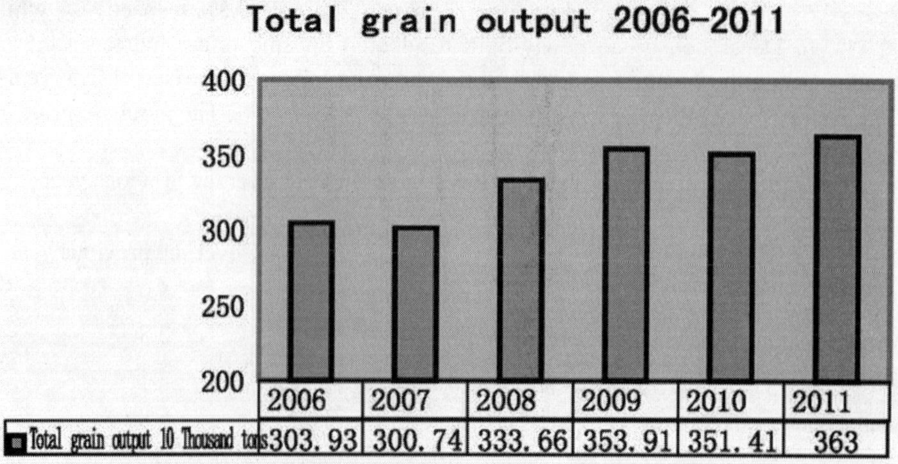

Table 3: Output of major livestock products and growth rate in 2011

Description	Output (ton)	+/-% over the previous year
Meets	595,500	6.0
Of which: Pork	266.500	9.5
Beef	9,800	1.7
Mutton	2,000	1.3
Poultry meet	314,700	3.4
Cow and goat's milk	371,700	2.8
Fowl eggs	191,400	1.0

9,200 hectares of trees were planted in the year, up 10.8%. Forest coverage reached 37.77%, up 0.87 percent. 12,000 hectares of young growth were cultivated, down 8%.

The total output of aquatic products reached 1, 134, 100 tons, up 1.3%. Of the total, 267,000 tons were from fishing, up 1.1% and 867,100 tons were from farmed fish, an increase of 1.3%. The combined seawater and freshwater farming area was 54,900 hectares, down 2.5%.

By the end of 2011, power from farming machines totaled 7,840,600 KW, up 2.7%. Farming tractors totaled 202,000 units, up 0.9%. Rural power consumption totaled 4.316 billion KWh. Total greenhouse area was 164,500 hectares. Effective irrigation area was 331,700 hectares, up 0.8%, including 166,200 hectares of water-saving irrigation area, up 2.2%.

III. Industry and Construction

In 2011, the Industrial Enterprises above Designated Size (Industrial Corporate Enterprises with an annual operating income of RMB 20,000,000 or more) numbered 4,561. Their industrial added value grew 13.5%; the state-owned enterprises grew 13.2%; collective enterprises increased 4.7%; shareholder enterprises rose 13.7%; enterprises invested by foreign companies and by compatriots from Hong Kong, Macao and Taiwan, increased 11.8%; and other types of businesses rose 27.9%. By industry, light industry increased 15.1% while heavy industry rose 12.3%. The ratio of light to heavy industry was 40.5:59.5.

The Industrial Enterprises above Designated Size finished a total output of RMB 464.008 billion in Hi-tech Industries, up 11.2% year-on-year, or 39.0% of the total industrial output value finished by Industrial Enterprises above Designated Size, an increase of 1.0 percentage from the beginning of the year; equipment manufacturing industries finished RMB 437.542 billion, or 34.6% of the total; strategic emerging industries increased 11.6% to RMB 219.2 billion.

Table 4: Output of Major Industrial Products by Industrial Enterprises Above Designated Size and increase/decrease in 2011

Description	Output	+/-% over the previous year
Yarn	19,400 tons	20.8
Cloth	439,000,000 meters	162.7
Chemical fiber	38,600 tons	0.5
Cigarettes	52.256 billion pieces	1.9
Beer	1,546,500 kilolitres	9.2
Power output	17.369 billion KWh	-4.7
Steels	3,322,000 tons	6.1
Crude oil processed	12,736,600 tons	-6.5
Caustic soda	132,000 tons	-4.8
Soda ash	720,700 tons	3.9
Chemical pesticide	17,300 tons	31.9
Tire casings	44,415,900 pieces	15.3
Cement	5,308,000 tons	19.0
Motor vehicles	488,800 units	-13.5
Color TV sets	11,542,000 sets	3.9
Household refrigerators	7,185,400 sets	-9.7
Room air conditioners	4,115,600 sets	0.2

Industrial enterprises above the designated size realized the total pre-tax profits of RMB 114.61 billion, up 11.6%, with after-tax profits of RMB 62.79 billion, up 15.4%. Operating incomes totaled RMB 1,227.38 billion, up 18.4%. The capital maintenance and appreciation ratio was 124.1 %. The sales ratio was 98.5%.

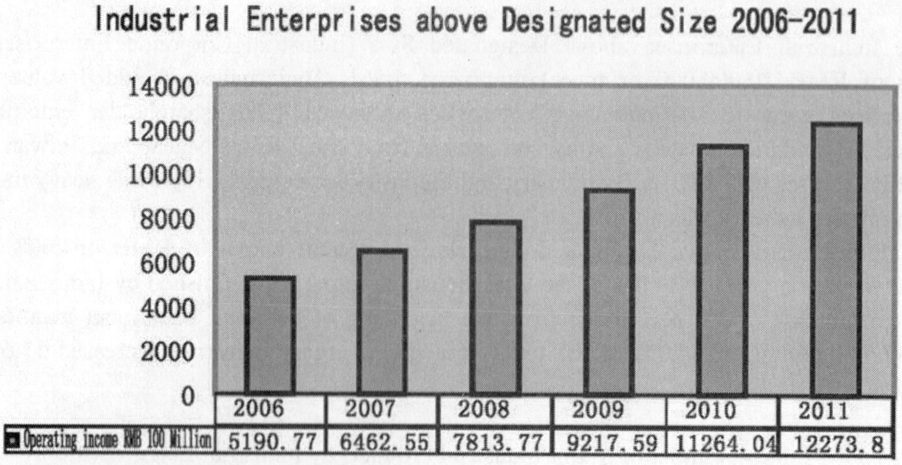

The construction industries generated RMB 35.616 billion in added value, up 13.5% and RMB 5.6 billion in pre-tax profit, up 11%, in which RMB 1.2 billion was finished by the state-owned and controlled enterprises, up 10 %.

IV. Fixed Assets Investment

The fixed asset investment (including the projects with investment over RMB 5,000,000 in townships and rural areas) totaled RMB 350.25 billion, up 23.4%. Of that figure, RMB 4.22 billion was made in primary industries, up 106.8%, RMB 147.26 billion in secondary industries, up 24.5% and RMB 198.77 billion in tertiary industries, up 21.6%.

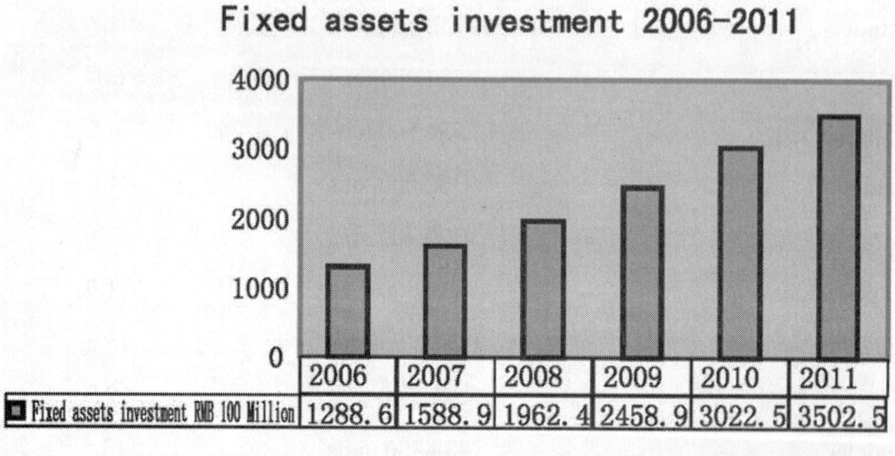

The fixed assets investment construction projects numbered 4,508. New start-up projects numbered 2,681 and completed projects numbered 2,984. The amount of investment in projects in progress was RMB 970.65 billion, up 22.4%. Another RMB 199.23 billion was invested in fixed assets for the whole year. The project completion ratio was 66.2% and the fixed asset delivery ratio was 56.9%.

Finished investment in real estate development for the whole year reached RMB 78.27 billion, up 29.9%. Completed commercial housing totaled 9,059,000 square meters, down 11.2%; sold housing floor area was 10,280,000 square meters, down 24.5%. The construction area of affordable housing totaled 2,083,100 square meters, of which, 436,400 square meters were completed.

V. Domestic Trade

In 2011, total retail sales of consumer goods increased by 17.4% to RMB 223.288 billion. Geographically, RMB 185.131 billion was generated by the urban market, up 17.8% and RMB 38.157 billion by the rural market, up 15.2%.

By industry, wholesale and retail industries realized sales of RMB 195.448 billion, up 17.5%, while the lodging and catering industries generated RMB 27.84 billion, up 16.7%.

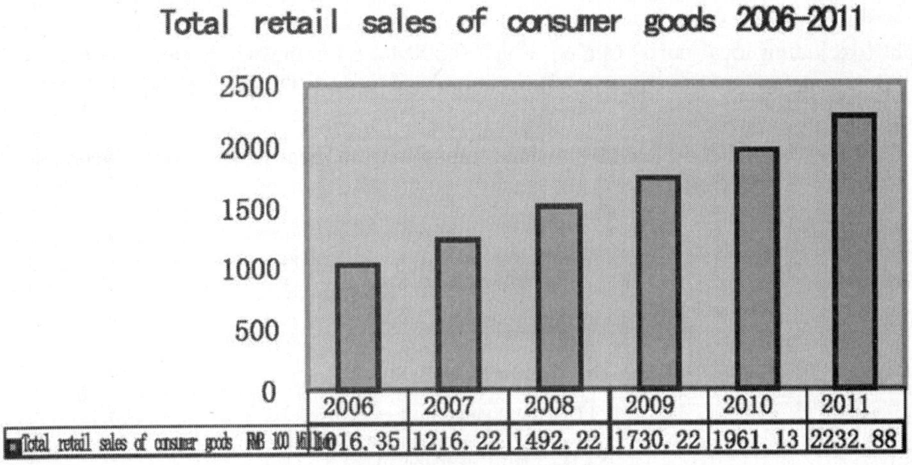

In 2011, the retail sales of motor vehicles above the limited value reached RMB 30.356 billion, up 29.1%; that of petroleum and petroleum products totaled RMB 10.293 billion, up 21.8%; that of grain and oil, food, beverages, cigarettes and alcohols amounted to RMB 10.425 billion, up 20.0%; that of daily necessities added up to RMB 2.567 billion, up 25.3%; that of sports and entertainment products amounted to RMB 0.725 billion, up 12.7%; that of cosmetics totaled RMB 1.626 billion, up 33.0%; and that of gold, silver and jewelry was RMB 2.164 billion, up 48.1%.

VI. Foreign Trade

Qingdao's import and export volume (including that of companies directly controlled by provincial and central governments) was USD 72.152 billion, up 26.5%, with exports amounting to USD 40.613 billion, up 19.7% and imports amounting to USD 31.539 billion, up 36.3%. Excluding companies directly controlled by provincial and central governments trade volume was USD 71.263 billion, up 27.2%, with exports amounting to USD 40.056 billion, up 20.5% and imports amounting to USD 31.207 billion, up 36.9%. Foreign investment enterprise finished an export amount of USD 19.331 billion, accounting for 48.3% of Qingdao's total exports.

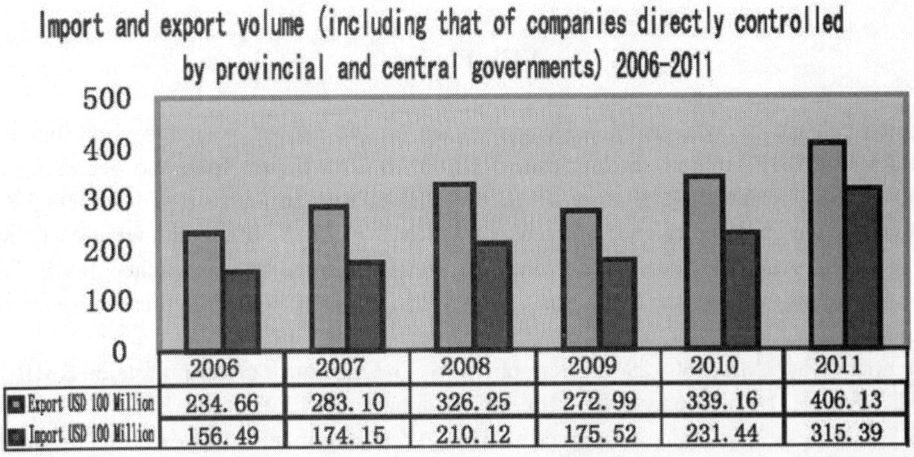

According to Qingdao Customs' statistics, imports and exports registered at Qingdao ports totaled USD 151 billion, up 26.7%. Of the total, USD 73 billion were exports, up 21.9% and USD 78 billion were imports, up 31.7%.

In 2011, direct foreign investment reached USD 3.634 billion, up 27.8%.

Total contracted value of overseas contractor projects and services was USD 680 million, up 1.5%. Turnover amounted to USD 1.35 billion, up 25%; the number of personnel sent overseas reached 7,003, up 9.5%.

Qingdao attracted a total domestic investment of RMB 81.85 billion, up 30.3%.

VII. Transportation, Post, Telecommunications and Tourism

Port throughput (excluding local ports) totaled 379,710,000 tons for the whole year, up 6.46%, with 267,260,000 tons handled for foreign trade, up 3.99%. Container throughput reached 13,020,000 TEUs, up 8.41%.

Table 5: Volume completed by various transportation means and increase/decrease

Transportation means	Volume	+/-% over the previous year
Passenger volume	18.457 billion person-km	6.2
Railways	5.165 billion person-km	9.7
Highways	13.182 billion person-km	5.6
Waterways	0.11 billion person-km	-39.4
Cargo volumes	381.945 billion ton-km	6.2
Railways	17.319 billion ton-km	13.2
Highways	40.886 billion ton-km	10.6
Waterways	323.74 billion ton-km	5.3

By the end of the year, there were 107 domestic airlines, 9 international airlines and 3 airlines to/from Hong Kong and Macao. The airport passenger throughput for the whole year reached 11,716,000 person-times, up 5.5% and air cargo and mail throughput was 166,500 tons, up 1.7%.

Postal and telecommunication service business transactions in 2011 totaled RMB 19.783 billion, up 11.9%. Of the total, RMB 568,000,000 was from the postal service, up 15.1%, and RMB 19.215 billion from the telecommunication service, up 11.8%. The total number of letters handled was 92,800,000, up 19.2%. Internet users numbered 1,856,900 in 2011, down 1.4% and time online reached 169.555 billion minutes, up 15.1%. At the end of the year, fixed-line telephone users numbered 2,513,300. Mobile phone users numbered 10,948,800, of which 1,383,800 were new users.

Tourism income for the year totaled RMB 68.139 billion, up 17.5%. Of the total, RMB 63.734 billion was from domestic tourism, up 18.0% and USD 689 million from international tourism, up 14.7%. Tourists to Qingdao during the year totaled 50,717,500 person-times, up 12.6%. Of the total, 49,561,100 were domestic tourists, up 12.7% and 1,156,400 overseas tourists, up 7.0%. By the end of the year, there were 60 A-rated tourist attractions and 153 star hotels.

VIII. Finance

At year-end, the balance of local and foreign currencies on the deposit accounts with financial institutions in Qingdao stood at RMB 890.127 billion, an increase of RMB 100.259 billion from the beginning of this year. The balance of deposits in local currency (RMB) was RMB 863.850 billion, an increase of RMB 98.580 billion from the beginning of the year. Of the total, the balance of savings was RMB 319.851 billion, an increase of RMB 29.157 billion from the beginning of the year. The loan balance in local and foreign currencies reached RMB 749.525 billion, an increase of RMB 114.540 billion from the beginning of this year. The loan balance in local currency (RMB) was RMB 694.775 billion, an increase of RMB 107.687 billion from the beginning of the year.

The insured amount was RMB 3,808.296 billion, up 1.9%. The insurance premium totaled RMB 14.573 billion, up 8.5%. Of the total, RMB 5.715 billion was for property insurance, up 13.2%; and RMB 8.858 billion for personal insurance, down 5.7%. Expenses for claims amounted to RMB 4.638 billion, up 23.4%. Of this figure, RMB 2.91 billion was for property claims and RMB 1.728 billion for personal claims.

IX. Science, Technology and Education

Preliminary statistics show that Qingdao achieved 345 key scientific and research results in 2011 and received fourteen (14) national scientific and technological prizes. Of the total, two (2) were for technological invention and twelve (12) were for scientific and technological progress; it also received 97 provincial-level scientific and technological prizes. Of them, four (4) were for natural science, four (4) were for technological inventions, eighty-eight (88) were for scientific and technological progress and one (1) was for international scientific and technological co-operation.

In 2011 there were a total of 2,352 technology transfer contracts completed with a value of RMB 2.075 billion; 19,816 patents were pending and 9,149 more were granted with patent certificates.

By the end of 2011, there were 24 higher education schools (including private schools) including 22 ordinary colleges and universities. There were 291,000 students enrolled, up 4.12%. Secondary schools numbered 380. Of them, 290 were ordinary middle schools, enrolling 373,000 students, down 1.79%; technical secondary schools and vocational schools numbered 90, enrolling 135,000, down 12.9%. The number of students in vocational secondary schools accounted for 53% of the number of senior middle school students. There were 889 primary schools enrolling 480,000 pupils, up 3.6% and 100% of pre-school aged children were schooled. The schooling of youngsters for junior middle school was over 99%.

X. Culture, Public Health Services and Sports

There were a total of 470 cultural institutions in Qingdao, including 40 cinemas and theatres, 183 cultural centers (stations), 9 museums, 13 public libraries, 10 performing arts troupes, one radio and broadcasting station with 12 programs and one TV station with 15 programs. Cable TV users numbered 2,682,000. Digitalization TV users numbered 2,438,800. 27,660,000 magazines and 1,076,150,000 issues of newspapers were published. There were 14 archives in Qingdao.

At the end of the year, there were 2,549 public health institutions (including clinics). Of the total, there were 278 hospitals, 13 epidemic prevention institutions, 13 children and women's health care centers and 1,861 clinical and medical health locations. There were 48,000 medical professionals, including 19,000 doctors. Medical beds numbered 40,000, with 36,000 beds in hospitals and clinics.

Qingdao athletes won 352 gold medals, 209 silver medals and 268 bronze medals in various games, creating 2 new national records. There were 1 professional sport teams totaling 125 members. Key sports schools numbered 2, enrolling 1,108 students. Part-time sports schools numbered 12, enrolling 1,516 students. Mass sports and fitness exercise programs were very popular and enjoyed all over Qingdao.

XI. Urban Construction

Built-up area reached 291.52 square kilometers, up 3.3%. Urban water supply averaged 962,200 tons per day, down 2.9%. The actual water consumption for the year totaled 311 million tons, up 0.8%, including 138 million tons for production use and 173 million tons for residential use.

Liquefied petroleum fuel, coal gas and natural gas users numbered 982,100. The total supply for liquefied petroleum fuel for the year was 80,000 tons, for coal gas was 9,137 cubic meters, and for natural gas was 483,080,000 cubic meters, up 35.4%. . The urban gas coverage was 100%.

Total electricity consumption was 31.344 billion KWh, up 7.0%, including 20.342 billion KWh for industrial use, up 8.4% and 5.013 billion KWh for residential use, up 1.3%. Total heating space increased by 10,100,000 square meters to 82,350,000 square meters by the end of the year, up 14.0%,

At the end of the year, there were 227 public bus and trolley lines operating in urban areas, up 10.7%. 5,419 public buses and trolleys were in operation, up 16.2%. Taxicabs numbered 9,683, up 0.5%.

Distance covered by roads in urban areas totaled 3,544 km, and 194 roads were expanded and rebuilt. The total length of underground sewers was 5,187 km.

A survey showed that the per capita average floor space in urban areas was 27.67 square meters at the end of the year, and the per capita average floor space for rural residents was 32.6 square meters.

XII. Energy, Environment and Work Safety

The targets set by the national and provincial authorities for energy-saving and emission reduction have been attained. Of the 12 indexes for energy consumption per unit of products by key manufacturers being monitored, 83.3% declined. 225,000 tons of standard coal was saved in the manufacture of major products. More investments have been made in the construction for wind power generation. The installed capacity of wind power totaled 130,000 KW, increasing 6.9 folds, and wind power output reached 78,000,000 KWh, an increase of 2.6 times the total of last year.

The air quality of functional regions all reached the desired standards. Acceptable air quality percentages in urban areas reached 334 days, accounting for 91.5% of the whole year, an increase of 0.8 percentage points over the previous year. Environmental noise pollution in urban areas averaged 53.7 dB. Noise pollution at traffic trunk lines in urban areas averaged 68.1 dB. A total of 2,757,400 trees were planted in the urban area, up 159.6%. "Green area" coverage reached 43.81%. The "green area" of parks and gardens totaled 18,012.79 hectares, up 8.4%. The increase in public "green area" was 151.21 hectares. Per capita "green area" was 14.58 square meters. There are 74 parks and zoos in the City of Qingdao.

There were 2,585 accidents happened at work, down 14.9%, with 427 people died, down 4.5%. The death toll from work accidents for every RMB 100 million of GDP was 0.065 persons, a decline of 17.7%. The road traffic death toll per 10 thousand vehicles was 2.3 persons, a decrease of 5%. No extraordinarily large accidents happened.

XIII. Population, Living Conditions and Social Security

At the end of the year, the total population was 7,663,600 (with permanent residence), up 0.36%. Of the total, 2,770,900 represent the population of the City of Qingdao, up 0.58%; 4,892,700 represent the population of the Greater Qingdao regions, up 0.23%. New births in 2011 totaled 65,793, a birth rate of 8.60‰. The number of deceased persons totaled 55,537, a percentage rate of 7.26‰. The population natural growth rate was 1.34‰.

The per capita average disposal income was RMB 28,567, up 14.3%. The per capita consumption expense was RMB 19,297, up 10.1%. The Engel Coefficient for urban areas was 37.5%. The wages of employees in Qingdao averaged RMB 32,763, an increase of 14.8%.

The average net income among farmers was RMB 12,370, up 17.3%; per capita consumption expense was RMB 7,661, up 15%. The Engel Coefficient for rural areas was 36.6%.

Income of urban and rural residents 2006-2011

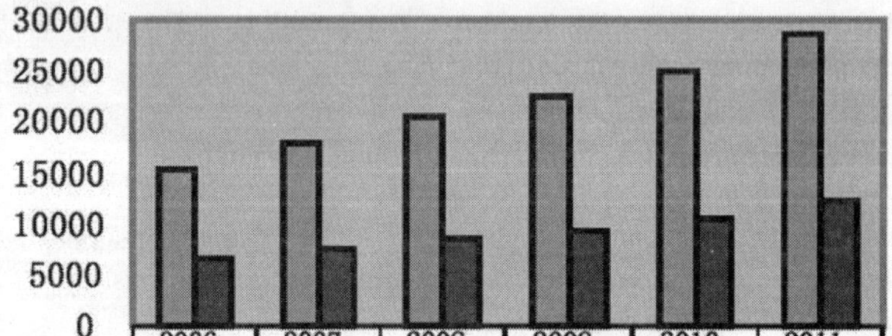

	2006	2007	2008	2009	2010	2011
Per capita average disposal income of urban residents RMB	15328	17856	20464	22368	24998	28567
Average net income of urban residents RMB	6546	7477	8509	9249	10550	12370

Table 6: The Engel Coefficient in urban and rural areas from 2006 to 2011

Index	Unit	2006	2007	2008	2009	2010	2011
Urban households	%	36.4	37	37.4	38.5	37.4	37.5
Rural households	%	36.6	37.2	37.7	36.4	35.5	36.6

At the end of 2011, the number of people employed in Qingdao was 2,759,000, up 2.4%. At year-end, the registered urban unemployment rate was 2.95%, up 0.03 percentage points.

The number of people covered under the basic pension program was 2,076,800, people who participated in the unemployment insurance program numbered 1,555,800, and people who received payment from the unemployment insurance program numbered 61,100. In 2011, the coverage of the new rural cooperative medical care program in Qingdao reached 100%.

Nursing homes registered 27,383 beds with 18,930 residents.

Note:

1. Figures reported herein are preliminary statistics.

2. The total production value and the absolute added value of the industries in Qingdao were calculated at current prices and growth rates were calculated at comparable prices.

3. From January 2011 on, the statistics starting point for industry and fixed asset investment was increased. The start point for those in the group of industrial enterprises above the Designated Size was increased from RMB 5,000,000 to RMB 20,000,00 in terms of annual operating income. The start point for fixed asset investment projects was increased from RMB 500,000 to RMB 5,000,000 in terms of total planned investment amount.

4. According to the national planning, the strategic emerging industries refer to the seven industries or sectors including energy conservation and environmental protection, the new generation of information technology, biology, high-end equipment manufacturing, new energy, new materials and new energy vehicles. At present, the strategic emerging industries being monitored for statistics in Qingdao cover 6 sectors, namely, energy conservation and environmental protection, biology, high-end equipment manufacturing, new energy, new materials and the new generation of information technology.

5. The total exchanger capacity for local calls included Xiaolingtong or Smart Phones.

6. Employees' average wage means the average wage paid at a certain time to employees by employers of such ownership types as the state-owned, collectively-owned, joint operation, shareholding, privately-owned and investment by foreign business people and by compatriots from Hong Kong, Macao and Taiwan.

7. The Entrepreneur's Confidence Index, also called Macroeconomic Prosperity Index, is generally identified as "Optimistic", "Average" or "Unoptimistic" according to entrepreneurs' understanding, view, judgment and expectation of the market economic environment outside the companies and macroeconomic policies, to comprehensively reflect entrepreneurs' perception of and confidence in the macro economy environment. It is expressed in pure positive numbers, with 100 as the critical value for prosperity index, ranging from 0 to 200.

8. Business Climate Index is generally identified as "Good", "Average" or "No Good" according to entrepreneurs' judgment and expectation of their company's overall production and operation status, to comprehensively reflect the conditions of their company's production and operation. It is expressed in pure positive numbers, with 100 as the critical value for prosperity index, ranging from 0 to 200.

综 合 1

GENERAL SUREY

简要说明

一、本篇资料的主要内容

本篇资料是对我市行政区划、气象情况、分行业法人单位数、各部门机构数和国民经济、社会发展的综合反映，主要包括行政区划、气象情况、分行业法人单位数、各部门机构数、国民经济主要比例关系、国民经济和社会发展主要指标占全国全省比重、国民经济和社会发展主要指标及其增长速度等资料。

二、本篇资料的来源

1、"行政区划"主要包括2011年底各区(市)街道办事处(乡镇)、社区居委会(村民委员会)区划资料，数据来源于市民政局。

2、"气象情况"包括分区市、市区分月气象资料，数据来源于市气象局。

3、"全市生产总值"来源于国民经济核算统计报表，由市统计局国民经济核算处整理提供。

4、国民经济和社会发展综合部分来源于本年鉴各篇章中的资料，由市统计局国民经济综合统计处加工整理。

Brief Introduction

I. Main Content

Data in this chapter cover the main indicators on divisions of administrative areas, meteorology, corporate units, number of grass-roots units and national economy and social development, including divisions of administrative areas, meteorology, number of corporate units, number of grass-roots units, average daily social and economic activities, ratio, and percentage of main indicators of Qingdao to the whole nation and the whole province and growth rate of main indicators.

II. Source of Data

(1) Data on divisions of administrative areas are mainly including the information on sub-district offices (villages and towns) and community neighborhood committees (villagers residents' committees) at the end of 2011.The data are provided by Qingdao Municipal Bureau of Civil Affairs.

(2) Data on meteorology are provided by Qingdao Municipal Meteorological Bureau.

(3) Data on gross national product are prepared according to the data of national accounts and compiled by the Division of National Accounts of Qingdao Municipal Bureau of Statistics.

(4) Data on general survey of economy and society are based on those of different chapters and compiled by the Division of Comprehensive Statistics of Qingdao Municipal Bureau of Statistics.

1 -1 行政区划(2011 年底)
ADMINISTRATIVE DIVISION(END OF 2011)

单位:个(unit)

市、区名称	Region	街道办事处 Subdistrict Offices 小计 Sub-total	社区居委会 Community Residents' Committees	镇 Town 小计 Sub-total	村民委员会 Villagers' Committees
全　市	**Whole Municipality**	**101**	**1 178**	**77**	**5 449**
市　区	Urban Area	74	954		1
市南区	Shinan District	14	65		
市北区	Shibei District	16	80		
四方区	Sifang District	15	93		
李沧区	Licang District	11	125		
崂山区	Laoshan District	4	146		
黄岛区	Huangdao District	6	204		
城阳区	Chengyang District	8	241		1
即墨市	Jimo	5	35	18	1 028
胶州市	Jiaozhou	7	51	11	811
胶南市	Jiaonan	6	55	11	965
平度市	Pingdu	4	58	26	1 783
莱西市	Laixi	5	25	11	861

1 -2 气象情况(2011 年)
METEOROLOGY(2011)

市、区名称	Region	平均气温(摄氏度) Average Temperature (℃)	极端气温 Extreme Temperature(℃) 最高(摄氏度) Maximum(℃)	最低(摄氏度) Minimum(℃)	降水量(毫米/年) Precipitation (millimeter/year)	日照时数(小时/年) Sunshine Hours (hour/year)	平均气压(百帕) Average Atmospheric Pressure(100 pa)
市 区	Urban Area	12.8	31.9	-10.4	717.2	2 022	1 009.0
崂山区	Laoshan District	13.4	33.3	-11.3	701.8	2 241	1 013.0
即墨市	Jimo	13.0	34.9	-12.8	610.5	2 275	1 014.5
胶州市	Jiaozhou	12.5	34.5	-13.2	780.2	2 089	1 008.9
胶南市	Jiaonan	12.7	33.1	-13.0	682.7	2 256	1 016.7
平度市	Pingdu	12.6	34.8	-13.8	832.4	2 382	1 011.8
莱西市	Laixi	11.7	35.0	-16.2	743.2	2 443	1 008.5

1 -3 市区分月气象情况(2011 年)
MONTHLY METEOROLOGY OF URBAN AREA(2011)

月 份	Month	平均气温(摄氏度) Average Temperature (℃)	降水量(毫 米) Precipitation (millimeter)	日照时数(小 时) Sunshine Hours (hour)
一月	Jan.	-2.9	0.1	188
二月	Feb.	1.6	25.8	147
三月	Mar.	6.0	4.5	249
四月	Apr.	11.4	8.4	230
五月	May	17.5	36.2	188
六月	June	20.0	57.9	131
七月	July	23.8	256.0	148
八月	Aug.	25.0	148.5	143
九月	Sept.	21.2	98.7	178
十月	Oct.	16.3	13.7	170
十一月	Nov.	11.3	46.6	116
十二月	Dec.	1.8	20.8	134
全年	Annual Total	12.8	717.2	2 022

1－4 各部门机构数(2011 年底)

GRASS-ROOTS UNITS IN VARIOUS SECTORS(END OF 2011)

项　目	Item	单位	Unit	机构数 Grass-roots Units
农村基层单位	**Rural Grass-roots Units**			
镇政府	Town Governments	个	unit	77
乡村户数	Number of Rural Households	万户	10 000 households	154.91
工业企业单位	**Industrial Enterprises**	**个**	**unit**	**81 998**
规模以上工业	Above Designated Size	个	unit	4 727
#国有企业	State-owned Enterprises	个	unit	147
集体企业	Collective-owned Enterprises	个	unit	31
外商及港澳台商投资企业	Enterprises with Funds from Hong Kong, Macao, Taiwan and Foreign Countries	个	unit	1 618
规模以下工业	Under Designated Size	个	unit	77 271
#个体	of which: Individual	个	unit	52 651
交通运输业	**Transportation**			
铁路	Railway	个	unit	
公路	Highway	个	unit	48
水运	Waterway	个	unit	16
邮电业	**Postal and Telecommunication Services**			
邮电局所	Post Offices	处	unit	739
建筑业企业	**Construction Enterprises**	**个**	**unit**	**584**
国有企业	State-owned Enterprises	个	unit	31
集体企业	Collective-owned Enterprises	个	unit	24
其他	Others	个	unit	529
批发和零售业、住宿和餐饮业	**Wholesale & Retail Trades, Hotels and Catering Services**			
限额以上批发业	Wholesale Trade above Designated Size	个	unit	809
限额以上零售业	Retail Trade above Designated Size	个	unit	521
限额以上住宿业	Hotel above Designated Size	个	unit	157
限额以上餐饮业	Catering Service above Designated Size	个	unit	208

1 -4 续表
continued

项　目	Item	单位	Unit	机构数 Grass-roots Units
教育事业	**Education**			
普通高等学校	Regular Institutions of Higher Education	所	unit	22
中等专业学校	Specialized Secondary Schools	所	unit	7
普通中学	Regular Secondary Schools	所	unit	290
普通小学	Regular Primary Schools	所	unit	889
幼儿园	Kindergartens	所	unit	2 476
科研机构	**Science and Technology Institutions**	**个**	**unit**	**47**
中央属	Central Level	个	unit	10
省属	Provincial Level	个	unit	11
市属	Municipal Level	个	unit	24
县级市属	County Level	个	unit	2
文化及相关产业	**Culture and Related Industry**			
文化事业机构	Cultural Institutions	个	unit	259
公共图书馆	Public Libraries	个	unit	13
影剧院	Cinemas	个	unit	40
广播、电视台	**Radio and Television Broadcasting Stations**			
广播电台	Radio Stations	个	unit	1
电视台	Television Stations	个	unit	1
卫生事业	**Public Health**	**个**	**unit**	**2 549**
#医院	Hospitals	个	unit	280
民政行政单位	**Civil Affairs Departments**			
#社会福利事业机构	Institutions of Social Welfare	个	unit	263

1 -5 按行业分法人单位数
NUMBER OF CORPORATE UNITS BY SECTOR

单位:个(unit)

行　业	Sector	2011	2010
总　计	**Total**	**145 788**	**130 509**
农、林、牧、渔业	Agriculture Forestry Animal Husbandry and Fishery	2 094	1 616
采矿业	Mining	393	387
制造业	Manufacturing	39 670	36 771
电力、燃气及水的生产和供应业	Production and Supply of Electricity Gas and Water	273	244
建筑业	Construction	7 543	6 648
交通运输、仓储和邮政业	Transport Storage and Post	4 851	4 306
信息传输、计算机服务和软件业	Information Transmission Computer Services and Software	3 326	3 069
批发和零售业	Wholesale and Retail Trades	46 819	39 925
住宿和餐饮业	Hotels and Catering Services	2 214	2 116
金融业	Financial Intermediation	350	282
房地产业	Real Estate	4 099	3 692
租赁和商务服务业	Leasing and Business Services	12 079	10 258
科学研究、技术服务和地质勘查业	Scientific Research Technical Services and Geologic Prospecting	2 669	2 318
水利、环境和公共设施管理业	Management of Water Conservancy Environment and Public Facilities	781	724
居民服务和其他服务业	Services to Households and Other Services	3 518	3 162
教　育	Education	2 591	2 532
卫生、社会保障和社会福利业	Health Social Security and Social Welfare	1 302	1 274
文化、体育和娱乐业	Culture Sports and Entertainment	966	910
公共管理和社会组织	Public Management and Social Organizations	10 250	10 275
国际组织	International Organization		

注:本表数据来源于基本单位统计年报。

Note: Data in this form are based on the annual report of basic units.

1-6 国民经济主要平均指标
AVERAGE INDICATORS ON NATIONAL ECONOMY

指　　标	Indicator	单　位	Unit	1990	1995
人口密度	Density of Population	人/平方公里	person/sq. km	626	643
每户年平均人口	Average Household Size	人	person	3.57	3.29
在岗职工年平均工资	Annual Average Wage of Employed Staff and Workers	元	yuan	2 400	6 164
城市居民人均年可支配收入	Annual Per Capita Disposable Income of Urban Households	元	yuan	1 624	5 612
农民人均年纯收入	Annual Per Capita Net Income of Rural Households	元	yuan	952	2 225
每一播亩平均粮食产量	Output of Grain Per Mu of Sowing Area	千克	kg	351	409
每亩蔬菜平均产量	Average Output of Vegetables Per Mu	千克	kg	3 017	3 274
每亩茶叶平均产量	Average Output of Tea Per Mu	千克	kg	35.0	8.0
每亩花生平均产量	Average Output of Peanut Per Mu	千克	kg	244	311
每亩棉花平均产量	Average Output of Cotton Per Mu	千克	kg	55	39
每台拖拉机负担耕地面积	Cultivated Area Ploughed by Per Tractor	亩/台	mu/unit	135	129
每亩耕地施用化肥量(折纯)	Chemical Fertilizer Consumption Per Mu(convert to pure amount)	千克	kg	27	43
每人平均消费品零售额	Per Capita Retail Sales of Consumer Goods	元	yuan	995	3 487
城市每天平均生活用水量	Daily Residential Consumption of Water	万吨	10 000 tons	11.70	22.60
城市每人平均公园绿地面积	Per Capita Public Green Areas	平方米	sq. m	3.70	5.40
每万人拥有医疗床位	Number of Hospital Beds per 10000 Population	张	bed	35.3	36.9
每万人拥有医生数	Number of Doctors per 10000 Population	人	person	20.6	20.2
每万人中高等学校学生数	Students Enrollment of Institutions of Higher Education per 10 000 Population	人	person	23	36
每万人中中等学校学生数	Students Enrollment of Secondary Schools per 10 000 Population	人	person	527	658
每万人中小学学生数	Students Enrollment of Primary Schools per 10000 Population	人	person	948	870

注:1990 年、1995 年在岗职工年平均工资统计范围为城镇单位全部职工。

Note: Annual average wage of employed staff and workers in 1990 and 1995 refers to average wage of units in urban area.

2000	2005	2006	2007	2008	2009	2010	2011
664	695	703	711	715	676	677	679
3.14	3.12	3.13	3.14	3.13	3.12	3.1	3.09
10 072	20 022	23 457	27 083	30 233	33 258	37 805	43 077
8 016	12 920	15 328	17 856	20 464	22 368	24 998	28 567
3 637	5 806	6 546	7 477	8 509	9 249	10 550	12 370
411	421	407	422	436	446	437	444
2 735	2 985	3 078	3 166	3 511	3 562	3 606	3 759
8.1	16.5	18.0	21.0	28.0	28.0	30.0	30.4
298	327	309	312	315	312	303	313
83	74	76	75	78	79	78	87
56	39	36	36	36	35	32	31.2
45	52	52	55	50	48	47	46.6
6 077	11 822	13 640	16 137	19 640	22 699	25 694	30 043
33.33	34.35	29.27	31.25	30.96	33.56	34.31	27.53
8.50	11.82	11.80	13.30	14.53	14.50	14.58	14.58
34.5	41.3	38.3	39.7	42.5	43.0	47.2	52.2
21.0	20.3	20.6	19.8	21.4	21.9	23.2	23.9
65	324	347	349	354	361	373	380
704	768	740	737	765	740	701	659
757	648	646	640	627	610	606	626

1-7 主要年份社会经济主要指标
MAJOR YEAR'S INDICATORS ON SOCIETY AND ECONOMY

指 标	Indicator	单 位	Unit	1990	1995
人口	**Population**				
总人口(年末)	Population at Year-end	万人	10 000 persons	666.65	684.63
男性人口	Male	万人	10 000 persons	339.23	347.63
女性人口	Female	万人	10 000 persons	327.42	337.00
市区人口	Urban Area	万人	10 000 persons	205.78	218.38
就业	**Employment**				
社会从业人员	Employment	万人	10 000 persons	352.8	374.2
#单位从业人员	Employed Persons in Units	万人	10 000 persons	103.2	111.6
经济总量	**Gross Economic Amount**				
全市生产总值(当年价)	GDP(at current price)	亿元	100 million yuan	180.77	631.45
第一产业增加值	Primary Industry	亿元	100 million yuan	39.26	112.53
第二产业增加值	Secondary Industry	亿元	100 million yuan	86.76	294.43
第三产业增加值	Tertiary Industry	亿元	100 million yuan	54.75	224.49
人均生产总值	Per Capita GDP	元	yuan	2 714	9 089
农林牧渔业总产值(当年价)	Gross Output Value of Farming, Forestry, Animal Husbandry and Fishery (at current price)	亿元	100 million yuan	57.99	192.38
工业总产值(当年价)	Gross Industrial Output Value (at current price)	亿元	100 million yuan	357.18	941.26

注:1. 单位从业人员2004年以前为职工人数(不含私营企业)。
2. 规模以上固定资产投资数据2003年以前为城镇以上统计范围。
3. 2002年以前地方财政一般预算收支数据为地方财政收支口径。

Note: 1. Before 2004, the data of employed persons in units refers to the number of staff and workers (excluding private enterprises).
2. Before 2003, the data of investment in fixed assets above designated size refers to urban investment.
3. Before 2002, the data of general budgetaty revenue and expenditure of local government finance refers to revenue and expenditure of local government finance.

2000	2005	2006	2007	2008	2009	2010	2011
706.65	740.91	749.38	757.99	761.56	762.92	763.64	766.36
357.74	374.03	377.99	381.66	382.46	382.35	381.92	382.69
348.91	366.87	371.39	376.33	379.10	380.56	381.72	383.67
234.60	265.43	270.99	275.55	276.25	275.47	275.50	277.09
397.6	471.0	490.1	505.8	513.8	525.7	540.3	551.2
118.3	224.3	243.2	249.8	254.1	260.5	269.4	275.9
1 191.25	2 687.46	3 183.18	3 750.16	4 401.56	4 853.87	5 666.19	6 615.60
140.85	178.33	183.95	203.59	223.40	230.25	276.99	306.38
555.21	1 392.02	1 666.96	1 934.52	2 234.83	2 420.14	2 758.62	3 150.72
495.19	1 117.10	1 332.28	1 612.05	1 943.33	2 203.48	2 630.58	3 158.50
16 009	33 085	38 608	44 964	52 266	57 251	65 827	75 563
248.33	320.51	339.61	342.99	400.85	408.61	483.18	535.93
1 940.83	5 001.78	5 918.81	7 430.64	8 946.73	10 255.62	11 614.83	13 277.96

1 -7 续表1
continued

指　标	Indicator	单　位	Unit	1990	1995
财政	**Government Finance**				
地方财政一般预算收入	General Budgetaty Revenue of Local Government Finance	亿元	100 million yuan	24.23	29.48
地方财政一般预算支出	General Budgetaty Expenditure of Local Government Finance	亿元	100 million yuan	13.39	37.70
规模以上固定资产投资总额	**Investment in Fixed Assets above Designated Size**	**亿元**	**100 million yuan**	**28.46**	**164.83**
社会消费品零售额	**Total Retail Sales of Consumer Goods**	**亿元**	**100 million yuan**	**65.83**	**237.68**
港口吞吐量	**Volume of Freight Handled in Ports**	**万吨**	**10 000 tons**	**3 068**	**5 165**
集装箱吞吐量	**Volume of Containers Handled**	**万吨**	**10 000 tons**		
民航货邮吞吐量	**Volume of Freight and Mail Handled in Civil Aviation**	**万吨**	**10 000 tons**	**0.20**	**2.10**
对外贸易	**Foreign Trade**				
外贸进出口总额(不含中央省公司)	Imports and Exports (excluding central and provincial companies)	亿美元	100 million USD	4.16	37.64
#出口总额	Exports	亿美元	100 million USD	3.35	24.51
教育、卫生、文化	**Education Public Health, Culture**				
小学在校学生数	Students Enrollment in Primary Schools	万人	10 000 persons	63.23	59.59
普通中学在校学生	Students Enrollment in Regular Secorndary Schools	万人	10 000 persons	29.62	37.23

2000	2005	2006	2007	2008	2009	2010	2011
80.01	176.34	225.77	292.58	342.44	376.99	452.61	566.14
87.87	203.06	236.79	321.18	369.41	433.58	532.39	658.06
242.68	**1 403.30**	**1 485.69**	**1 635.36**	**2 019.01**	**2 458.89**	**3 022.48**	**3 502.54**
428.29	**870.11**	**1 016.35**	**1 216.22**	**1 492.22**	**1 730.22**	**1 961.13**	**2 302.37**
8 661	**18 727**	**22 438**	**26 507**	**30 029**	**31 668**	**35 012**	**37 971**
212.0	**630.7**	**770.0**	**946.6**	**1 037.7**	**1 027.7**	**1 201.0**	**1 302.0**
4.84	**8.91**	**10.10**	**11.57**	**13.05**	**13.54**	**16.37**	**16.65**
108.31	304.55	365.57	436.05	521.59	439.86	561.49	712.63
61.14	175.88	216.45	267.76	314.62	269.22	333.51	400.56
53.49	47.98	48.39	48.48	47.72	46.50	46.27	47.95
39.85	39.11	36.52	36.04	37.39	37.74	38.00	37.32

1-7 续表 2
continued

指　　标	Indicator	单 位	Unit	1990	1995
高等学校在校学生	Students Enrollment in Institutions of Higher Education	万人	10 000 persons	1.54	2.49
小学专任教师	Full-time Teachers in Primary Schools	万人	10 000 persons	3.15	3.00
普通中学专任教师	Full-time Teachers in Regular Secorndary Schools	万人	10 000 persons	2.04	2.26
影剧院	Cinemas	个	unit	106	61
医生总数	Doctors	万人	10 000 persons	1.38	1.38
医院床位数	Hospital Beds	万张	10 000 beds	1.66	1.81
人民生活	**People's Living Conditions**				
在岗职工工资总额	Total Wage Bill of Employed Staff and Workers	亿元	100 million yuan	24.39	68.30
城市居民人均可支配收入	Per Capita Disposable Income of Urban Households	元	yuan	1 624	5 612
农民人均纯收入	Per Capita Net Income of Rural Households	元	yuan	952	2 225
城乡人民币储蓄存款余额	Savings Deposit of Urban and Rural Households	亿元	100 million yuan	65.59	268.79
物价指数	**Price Indexes**				
商品零售价格指数(以1950年价格为100)	Retail Price Index(1950 = 100)	%	%	269.7	536.2
居民消费价格指数(以1950年价格为100)	Consumer Price Index(1950 = 100)	%	%	269.7	587.3
#食品价格指数(以1950年价格为100)	Food Price Index(1950 = 100)	%	%	333.3	792.5

注:在岗职工工资总额2005年前统计范围为全部职工不含私营企业。

Note: Before 2005, the statistics range of total wage bill of employed staff and workers is all the staff and workers except those in private enterprises.

2000	2005	2006	2007	2008	2009	2010	2011
4.61	23.98	26.03	26.49	26.93	27.52	28.49	29.15
3.17	3.17	3.22	3.26	3.24	3.22	3.2	3.16
2.63	2.97	2.92	2.96	2.99	3.06	3.08	3.14
45	39	40	40	40	40	40	40
1.49	1.50	1.55	1.50	1.63	1.67	1.77	1.83
2.01	2.86	2.67	2.81	2.99	3.05	3.34	3.56
120.40	359.5	445.6	518.1	578.7	638.1	738	877.5
8 016	12 920	15 328	17 856	20 464	22 368	24 998	28 567
3 637	5 806	6 546	7 477	8 509	9 249	10 550	12 370
535.32	1 343.10	1 567.62	1 702.04	2 123.36	2 527.88	2 912.33	3 198.51
520.5	495.0	493.5	506.8	526.6	519.2	526.5	550.2
711.9	753.1	759.9	794.1	831.4	835.6	854.0	896.7
800.1	871.8	886.6	989.5	1 105.3	1 123.0	1 194.9	1 327.5

1－8 国民经济主要结构指标
COMPOSITION INDICATORS ON NATIONAL ECONOMY

指 标	Indicator	1990	1995	2000
社会从业人员	**Employment**			
产业结构	Industrial Composition			
第一产业	Primary Industry	44.4	41.5	36.4
第二产业	Secondary Industry	34.9	35.4	33.9
第三产业	Tertiary Industry	20.7	23.1	29.7
全市生产总值	**GDP**			
产业结构	Industrial Composition			
第一产业	Primary Industry	21.7	17.8	11.8
第二产业	Secondary Industry	48.0	46.6	46.6
第三产业	Tertiary Industry	30.3	35.6	41.6
农业	**Agriculture**			
农林牧渔业产值结构	Composition of Farming, Forestry, Animal Husbandry and Fishery			
#农业	Farming	65.8	53.1	45.0
林业	Forestry	2.4	1.4	0.8
牧业	Animal Husbandry	20.6	26.2	27.9
渔业	Fishery	11.3	19.3	26.4
工业	**Industy**			
轻重工业产值结构	Composition of Output Value of Light and Heavy Industry			
轻工业	Light Industry	57.6	59.3	64.1
重工业	Heavy Industry	42.4	40.7	35.9
固定资产投资	**Investment in Fixed Assets**			
投资结构	Composition of Investment			
生产性	Productive	74.0	56.1	54.0
非生产性	Non-productive	26.0	43.9	46.0

单位:%

2005	2006	2007	2008	2009	2010	2011
22.2	21.0	20.2	19.9	20.1	19.5	19.2
41.8	42.8	43.1	43.0	41.9	41.4	41.2
36.0	36.2	36.7	37.1	38.0	39.1	39.6
6.6	5.8	5.4	5.1	4.7	4.9	4.6
51.8	52.4	51.6	50.8	49.9	48.7	47.6
41.6	41.8	43.0	44.1	45.4	46.4	47.8
39.5	40.1	43.3	44.4	45.4	48.4	44.1
0.8	0.7	0.6	0.6	0.5	0.4	0.4
33.4	31.7	28.4	30.3	28.4	26.2	29.1
26.3	25.2	24.2	21.4	22.0	21.8	23.0
49.4	48.5	45.0	42.3	41.7	38.7	38.3
50.6	51.5	55.0	57.7	58.3	61.3	61.7
65.4	62.0	62.6	61.6	56.3	53.6	53.2
34.6	38.0	37.4	38.4	43.7	46.4	46.8

1-9 平均每天主要社会经济活动
SELECTED INDICATORS ON AVERAGE DAILY SOCIAL AND ECONOMIC ACTIVITIES

指　　标	Indicator	单位	Unit	1990	1995
全市生产总值	GDP	万元	10 000 yuan	4 952	17 300
工业总产值	Gross Industrial Output Value	万元	10 000 yuan	9 786	25 788
农林牧渔业总产值	Gross Output Value of Farming, Forestry, Animal Husbandry and Fishery	万元	10 000 yuan	1 589	5 271
主要工业产品产量	Output of Major Industrial Products				
发电量	Electricity	万千瓦时	10 000 kW · h	1 102	1 772
钢材	Rolled-steel	吨	ton	1 042	1 359
纱	Yarn	吨	ton	275	218
布	Cloth	万米	10 000 m	93	113
家用电冰箱	Refrigerator	台	unit	751	2 956
彩色电视机	Color TV set	台	unit	507	1 658
社会消费品零售总额	Total Retail Sales of Consumer Goods	万元	10 000 yuan	1 803	6 512
规模以上固定资产投资	Investment in Fixed Assets above Designated Size	万元	10 000 yuan	780	4 516
外贸进出口总额	Imports and Exports	万美元	10 000 USD		2 352
港口吞吐量	Volume of Freight Handled in Ports	万吨	10 000 tons	8.41	14.15

2000	2005	2006	2007	2008	2009	2010	2011
32 637	73 629	87 210	102 744	120 591	132 983	155 238	181 249
53 174	137 035	162 159	203 579	245 116	280 976	318 215	363 780
6 803	8 781	9 304	9 397	10 982	11 195	13 238	14 683
2 489	2 701	3 412	4 255	4 509	4 730	4 984	4 759
2 558	9 049	10 288	10 015	9 593	9 579	9 136	9 101
191	198	154	131	118	106	97	53
114	141	151	121	133	85	48	120
8 523	24 899	35 342	22 173	19 813	22 663	21 951	19 686
10 395	36 282	33 030	23 989	22 922	29 170	30 444	31 622
11 734	23 839	27 845	33 321	40 883	47 403	53 730	63 079
6 649	38 446	40 704	44 804	55 315	67 367	82 808	95 960
3 707	9 047	12 527	12 527	14 695	12 288	15 633	19 768
23.73	51.31	61.47	72.62	82.27	86.76	95.92	104.03

1－10 主要指标占全国全省比重(2011 年)

PERCENTAGE OF MAIN INDICATORS TO CHINA AND SHANDONG(2011)

指　标	Indicator	单位	Unit
一、生产总值	GDP	亿元	100 million yuan
第一产业	Primary Industry	亿元	100 million yuan
第二产业	Secondary Industry	亿元	100 million yuan
第三产业	Tertiary Industry	亿元	100 million yuan
二、主要工业产品产量	Output of Major Industrial Products		
纱	Yarn	万吨	10 000 tons
布	Cloth	亿米	100 million m
家用电冰箱	Refrigerator	万台	10 000 units
彩色电视机	Color TV Set	万部	10 000 units
发电量	Electricity	亿千瓦时	100 million kW · h
钢材	Rolled-steel	万吨	10 000 tons
水泥	Cement	万吨	10 000 tons
三、主要农产品产量	Output of Major Farm Products		
粮食	Grain	万吨	10 000 tons
油料	Oil Plants	万吨	10 000 tons
棉花	Cotton	万吨	10 000 tons
肉类产量	Meat	万吨	10 000 tons
水产品	Aquatic Products	万吨	10 000 tons
四、固定资产投资额	Investment in Fixed Assets	亿元	100 million yuan
五、社会消费品零售总额	Total Retail Sales of Consumer Goods	亿元	100 million yuan
六、高等学校在校学生	Students Enrollment of Institutions of Higher Education	万人	10 000 persons

注:1. 本表全国、全省均为公报数。
2. 青岛市主要工业产品产量数据为本地口径。

Note:1. The number of the country and the province in the table are obtained from the statistical report.
2. The output of main industrial products of qingdao are at local calibre.

全国 China	全省 Shandong	青岛市 Qingdao	青岛市占全国 比重(%) Qingdao/China	青岛市占全省 比重(%) Qingdao/Shandong
471 564	45 429.2	6 615.60	1.40	14.56
47 712	3 973.8	306.38	0.64	7.71
220 592	24 037.4	3 150.72	1.43	13.11
203 260	17 418.0	3 158.50	1.55	18.13
2 900	723.4	1.94	0.07	0.27
837	124.5	4.39	0.52	3.53
8 699.2	718.5	718.5	8.26	100.00
12 231.4	1 249.5	1 154.20	9.44	92.37
47 000.7	3 162.2	173.69	0.37	5.49
88 258.2	7 033.7	332.19	0.38	4.72
209 000	15 035.6	530.80	0.25	3.53
57 121	4 426.3	363	0.64	8.20
3 279	341	44.37	1.35	13.01
660	78.5	0.39	0.06	0.50
7 957	700.2	59.55	0.75	8.50
5 600	813.5	113.41	2.03	13.94
311 022	26 770	3 502.5	1.13	13.08
183 919	17 155.5	2 302.37	1.25	13.42
2 308.5	164.6	29.15	1.26	17.71

1－11 主要年份全市生产总值(按当年价格计算)

MAJOR YEAR'S GROSS DOMESTIC PRODUCT(AT CURRENT PRICE)

单位:亿元 (100 million yuan)

年 份 Year	全市生产总值 GDP	第一产业 Primary Industry	第二产业 Secondary Industry	#工 业 Industry	第三产业 Tertiary Industry	人均生产总值(元) Per Capita GDP (yuan)
1949	2.87	1.19	1.10	–	0.58	71
1952	6.74	1.76	3.25	2.95	1.73	163
1957	10.82	2.00	5.76	5.39	3.06	239
1962	9.69	1.11	4.68	4.27	3.90	205
1965	15.50	1.80	8.96	8.48	4.74	325
1970	23.23	3.15	14.46	13.86	5.62	451
1975	29.07	6.93	15.39	14.67	6.75	522
1978	38.43	8.73	20.25	19.15	9.45	663
1980	48.65	10.19	26.27	24.28	12.19	819
1985	82.28	21.29	37.55	34.03	23.44	1 311
1988	142.87	32.72	70.32	63.42	39.83	2 199
1989	159.68	30.79	82.03	74.33	46.86	2 426
1990	180.77	39.26	86.76	78.94	54.75	2 714
1991	205.65	43.04	98.94	89.64	63.67	3 053
1992	261.35	43.92	130.27	117.61	87.16	3 856
1993	371.90	62.20	183.35	164.35	126.35	5 455
1994	510.81	85.12	244.30	218.87	181.39	7 436
1995	631.45	112.53	294.43	263.98	224.49	9 089
1996	713.60	133.27	322.33	289.87	258.00	10 130
1997	802.59	117.47	378.25	342.80	306.87	11 235
1998	901.19	140.66	409.60	369.89	350.93	12 443
1999	1 018.97	138.19	468.67	424.15	412.11	13 884
2000	1 191.25	140.85	555.21	504.44	495.19	16 009
2001	1 368.55	144.35	643.44	582.99	580.76	18 128
2002	1 583.51	147.21	758.33	686.55	677.97	20 655
2003	1 869.44	148.92	923.76	832.31	796.76	23 986
2004	2 270.16	163.49	1 149.94	1 032.50	956.73	28 540
2005	2 687.46	178.33	1 392.02	1 259.06	1 117.10	33 085
2006	3 183.18	183.95	1 666.96	1 517.28	1 332.28	38 608
2007	3 750.16	203.59	1 934.52	1 766.28	1 612.05	44 964
2008	4 401.56	223.40	2 234.83	2 034.25	1 943.33	52 266
2009	4 853.87	230.25	2 420.14	2 174.43	2 203.48	57 251
2010	5 666.19	276.99	2 758.62	2 454.19	2 630.58	65 827
2011	6 615.60	306.38	3 150.72	2 794.56	3 158.50	75 563

注:1. 人均生产总值按常住人口计算 。

2. 自 2005 年起三次产业分类采用《国民经济行业分类》(GB/T4754-2002)标准。

3. 本表数据为第二次经济普查修订后数据。

Note:1. Per capita GDP are calculated at permanent population.

2. Three Industries are grouped by "Classification and Code of the Sectors of the National Economy"(GB / T4754-2002) since 2005.

3. Data in this form have been amended according to the results of the Second China Economic Census.

1－12 主要年份全市生产总值构成(以全市生产总值为100)

COMPOSITION OF MAJOR YEAR'S GROSS DOMESTIC PRODUCT(GROSS DOMESTIC PRODUCT＝100)

单位:%

年 份 Year	全市生产总值 GDP	第一产业 Primary Industry	第二产业 Secondary Industry	#工 业 Industry	第三产业 Tertiary Industry
1952	100	26.1	48.2	43.8	25.7
1957	100	18.5	53.3	49.8	28.2
1962	100	11.4	48.3	44.1	40.3
1965	100	11.6	57.8	54.7	30.6
1970	100	13.6	62.2	59.7	24.2
1975	100	23.9	52.9	50.5	23.2
1978	100	22.7	52.7	49.8	24.6
1980	100	21.0	54.0	49.9	25.1
1985	100	25.9	45.6	41.4	28.5
1988	100	22.9	49.2	44.4	27.9
1989	100	19.3	51.4	46.6	29.3
1990	100	21.7	48.0	43.7	30.3
1991	100	20.9	48.1	43.6	31.0
1992	100	16.8	49.8	45.0	33.4
1993	100	16.7	49.3	44.2	34.0
1994	100	16.7	47.8	42.8	35.5
1995	100	17.8	46.6	41.8	35.6
1996	100	18.7	45.2	40.6	36.2
1997	100	14.6	47.1	42.7	38.2
1998	100	15.6	45.5	41.0	38.9
1999	100	13.6	46.0	41.6	40.4
2000	100	11.8	46.6	42.3	41.6
2001	100	10.5	47.0	42.6	42.4
2002	100	9.3	47.9	43.4	42.8
2003	100	8.0	49.4	44.5	42.6
2004	100	7.2	50.7	45.5	42.1
2005	100	6.6	51.8	46.8	41.6
2006	100	5.8	52.4	47.7	41.8
2007	100	5.4	51.6	47.1	43.0
2008	100	5.1	50.8	46.2	44.1
2009	100	4.7	49.9	44.8	45.4
2010	100	4.9	48.7	43.3	46.4
2011	100	4.6	47.6	41.5	47.8

1－13 主要年份全市生产总值增长速度(以上年为100)

GROWTH RATE OF MAJOR YEAR'S GROSS DOMESTIC PRODUCT(PRECEDING YEAR＝100)

单位:%

年份 Year	全市生产总值 GDP	第一产业 Primary Industry	第二产业 Secondary Industry	第三产业 Tertiary Industry	人均生产总值 Per Capita GDP
1979	12.0	10.6	12.9	11.4	10.4
1980	10.4	4.3	13.1	10.3	9.4
1981	-2.0	-9.1	-2.4	4.7	-3.2
1982	4.1	5.5	-0.2	11.9	2.6
1983	16.9	42.8	9.3	12.7	15.3
1984	13.0	18.9	11.5	10.3	12.0
1985	9.9	5.4	5.8	21.3	9.3
1986	9.2	2.6	12.1	10.0	8.3
1987	12.0	3.6	16.0	12.0	10.6
1988	13.8	-0.3	21.5	11.2	12.1
1989	5.1	-0.8	4.6	9.9	3.8
1990	9.3	9.8	7.3	12.2	8.0
1991	10.6	9.9	11.0	10.5	9.4
1992	18.1	2.7	23.5	20.7	17.4
1993	22.4	20.5	21.1	25.6	21.7
1994	14.4	3.6	14.7	20.2	13.5
1995	12.0	10.9	12.1	12.4	10.8
1996	7.2	7.7	7.6	6.4	5.7
1997	11.5	-10.6	16.8	14.6	9.9
1998	12.9	17.6	11.3	13.4	11.3
1999	13.9	4.1	15.5	15.3	12.4
2000	15.2	6.5	16.4	16.4	13.6
2001	13.7	2.3	16.3	14.2	12.1
2002	14.5	3.2	16.9	14.6	12.7
2003	16.3	2.5	20.1	14.9	14.4
2004	16.7	2.7	20.3	15.2	14.3
2005	16.6	0.4	19.6	15.7	14.1
2006	15.3	0.9	16.8	15.8	13.6
2007	15.5	-2.6	15.3	18.3	14.2
2008	13.2	1.4	11.1	17.1	12.1
2009	12.2	3.0	12.8	12.5	11.4
2010	12.9	1.4	12.6	14.4	11.2
2011	11.7	5.0	11.6	12.4	9.8
1978－2011 平均每年增长 1978－2011 Average Increase Rate	12.3	5.3	13.0	13.8	11.0
1991－2011 平均每年增长 1991－2011 Average Increase Rate	14.1	4.2	15.3	15.2	12.6
1996－2011 平均每年增长 1996－2011 Average Increase Rate	13.7	2.7	15.0	14.4	12.8
2001－2011 平均每年增长 2001－2011 Average Increase Rate	14.4	1.8	15.7	15.0	12.7
2006－2011 平均每年增长 2006－2011 Average Increase Rate	13.5	1.5	13.3	15.0	12.1

1－14 分市、区生产总值(2011 年)
GROSS DOMESTIC PRODUCT BY REGION(2011)

单位:亿元(100 million yuan)

市、区名称	Region	地区生产总值 GDP	第一产业 Primary Industry	第二产业 Secondary Industry	#工　业 Industry	第三产业 Tertiary Industry
市南区	Shinan District	634.21		63.05	35.00	571.16
市北区	Shibei District	317.70		54.99	31.49	262.71
四方区	Sifang District	195.00		80.13	66.15	114.87
李沧区	Licang District	247.38	0.02	128.53	117.20	118.83
崂山区	Laoshan District	364.70	4.96	203.73	180.59	156.01
黄岛区	Huangdao District	1 174.61	4.21	750.12	700.13	420.28
城阳区	Chengyang District	812.68	14.41	493.59	460.07	304.68
即墨市	Jimo District	690.10	53.52	373.43	335.00	263.15
胶州市	Jiaozhou District	668.33	44.95	377.12	336.96	246.26
胶南市	Jiaonan District	648.51	48.86	381.86	344.32	217.79
平度市	Pingdu District	624.06	84.08	317.09	289.14	222.89
莱西市	Laixi District	472.52	49.77	234.52	205.95	188.23

注:1. 本表按当年价格计算。
2. 三次产业分类采用《国民经济行业分类》(GB/T4754-2002)标准 。

Note:1. The data are calculated at current price.
2. Three Industries are grouped by "Classification and Code of the Sectors of the National Economy"(GB/T4754-2002).

1-15 按支出法计算的全市生产总值(2011 年)

GROSS DOMESTIC PRODUCT BY EXPENDITURE APPROACH(2011)

单位:亿元(100 million yuan)

项　目	Item	2011	2010	2011 年为 2010 年% 2011/2010(%)
支出法计算的全市生产总值	**Gross Domestic Product by Expenditure Approach**	**6 615.60**	**5 666.19**	**111.7**
(一)最终消费	Final Consumption Expenditures	2 228.55	1 907.32	110.8
1.居民消费	Household Consumption Expenditures	1 676.91	1 428.88	111.2
农村居民	Rural Household	273.23	241.13	106.6
城镇居民	Urban Household	1 403.68	1 187.75	112.1
2.政府消费	Government Consumption Expenditures	551.64	478.44	109.7
(二)资本形成总额	Gross Capital Formation	3 590.37	2 967.71	113.6
1.固定资本形成总额	Gross Fixed Capital Formation	3 469.72	2 841.97	114.5
2.存货增加	Change in Inventories	120.65	125.74	93.3
(三)货物和服务净流出	Net Exports of Goods and Services	796.68	791.16	106.4

注:绝对额按当年价格计算,速度按可比价格计算。

Note:The absolute numbers are calculated at current price, their growth are calculated at constant price.

1 –16 全市生产总值构成(2011 年)
COMPOSITION OF GROSS DOMESTIC PRODUCT(2011)

指　标	Indicator	增加值(亿元) Added Value (100 million yuan)	2011 年为 2010 年% 2011/2010(%)
全市生产总值	**GDP**	**6 615.60**	**111.7**
第一产业	Primary Industry	306.38	105.0
农、林、牧、渔业	Farming, Forestry, A nimal Husbandry and Fishery	306.38	105.0
第二产业	Secondary Industry	3 150.72	111.6
工业	Industry	2 794.56	111.3
建筑业	Construction	356.16	113.5
第三产业	Tertiary Industry	3 158.50	112.4
交通运输、仓储和邮政业	Transport, Storage and Post	480.08	104.9
信息传输、计算机服务和软件业	Information Transmission, Computer Services and Software	134.82	109.8
批发和零售业	Wholesale and Retail Trade	775.27	118.7
住宿和餐饮业	Hotels and Catering Services	166.20	119.5
金融业	Financial Intermediation	323.42	127.1
房地产业	Real Estate	262.96	92.8
租赁和商务服务业	Leasing and Business Services	189.34	120.6
科学研究、技术服务和地质勘查业	Scientific Research, Technical Services and Geologic Prospecting	89.18	111.5
水利、环境和公共设施管理业	Management of Water Conservancy, Environment and Public Facilities	33.82	105.1
居民服务和其他服务业	Services to Households and Other Services	137.81	115.5
教育	Education	191.86	112.9
卫生、社会保障和社会福利业	Health, Social Security and Social Welfare	98.90	108.0
文化、体育和娱乐业	Culture, Sports and Entertainment	44.32	110.5
公共管理和社会组织	Public Management and Social Organization	230.52	108.8

注:表中绝对数按现行价格计算;相对数按可比价格计算。

Note:The absolute numbers are calculated at current price, the relative numbers are calculated at constant price.

主要统计指标解释

国内生产总值(GDP)　指按市场价格计算的一个国家(或地区)所有常住单位在一定时期内生产活动的最终成果。国内生产总值有三种表现形态,即价值形态、收入形态和产品形态。从价值形态看,它是所有常住单位在一定时期内生产的全部货物和服务价值超过同期中间投入的全部非固定资产货物和服务价值的差额,即所有常住单位的增加值之和;从收入形态看,它是所有常住单位在一定时期内创造并分配给常住单位和非常住单位的初次收入分配之和;从产品形态看,它是所有常住单位在一定时期内最终使用的货物和服务价值与货物和服务净出口价值之和。在实际核算中,国内生产总值有三种计算方法,即生产法、收入法和支出法。三种方法分别从不同的方面反映国内生产总值及其构成。对于一个地区来说,称为地区生产总值或地区 GDP。

人均 GDP　人均 GDP 是一定时期内 GDP 与同期人口平均数的比值。按照国际标准,人口平均数应该是同期平均常住人口。我国在核算制度中也规定,无论是国家还是地区,人口数都采用常住人口。国家统计局规定从 2004 年开始,过去采用户籍人口计算人均 GDP 的地区,作为过渡性措施,可在两年内同时计算两种口径的人均 GDP(数据后面必须注明是什么口径),两年后取消按户籍人口计算的人均 GDP。我市采用常住人口计算人均 GDP。

三次产业　是根据社会生产活动历史发展的顺序对产业结构的划分,产品直接取自自然界的部门称为第一产业,对初级产品进行再加工的部门称为第二产业,为生产和消费提供各种服务的部门称为第三产业。它是世界上通用的产业结构分类,但各国的划分不尽一致。我国的三次产业划分是:

第一产业:是指农业、林业、畜牧业、渔业和农林牧渔服务业。

第二产业:是指采矿业,制造业,电力、燃气及水的生产和供应业;建筑业。

第三产业:除第一、第二产业以外的其他行业。

支出法国内生产总值　是从最终使用角度反映一个国家(或地区)一定时期内生产活动最终成果的一种方法,包括最终消费支出,资本形成总额及货物和服务净出口三部分。对于地区,名称为"支出法地区生产总值"。

最终消费　指常住单位为满足物质、文化和精神生活的需要,从本国经济领土和国外购买的货物和服务的支出;不包括非常住单位在本国经济领土内的消费支出。最终消费分为居民消费和政府消费。

居民消费　指常住住户在一定时期内对货物和服务的全部最终消费支出。居民消费支出除了直接以货币形式购买货物和服务的消费之外,还包括以其他方式获得的货物和服务的消费支出,即所谓的虚拟消费支出。居民虚拟消费支出包括以下几种类型:单位以实物报酬及实物转移的形式提供给劳动者的货物和服务;住户生产并由本住户消费了的货物和服务,其中的服务仅指住户的自有住房服务和付酬的家庭雇员提供的家庭和个人服务;金融机构提供的金融媒介服务。

政府消费　指政府部门为全社会提供公共服务的消费支出和免费或以较低价格向居民住户提供的货物和服务的净支出。前者等于政府服务的产出价值减去政府单位所获得的经营收入的价值;后者等于政府部门免费或以较低价格向居民住户提供的货物和服务的市场价值减去向住户收取的价值。

资本形成总额　指常住单位在一定时期内获得的减去处置的固定资产和存货的净额,包括固定资本形成总额和存货增加。

固定资本形成总额　指常住单位在一定时期内获得的固定资产减处置的固定资产的价值总额。固定资产是通过生产活动生产出来的,且使用年限在一年以上、单位价值在规定标准以上的资产,不包括自然资产。分有形固定资产形成总额和无形固定资产形成总额。有形固定资产形成总额包括一定时期内完成的建筑工程、安装工程和设备工器具购置(减处置)价值,以及土地改良、新增役、种、奶、毛、娱乐用牲畜和新增经济林木价值。无形固定资产形成总额包括矿藏的勘探、计算机软件等获得减处置。

存货增加　指常住单位在一定时期内存货实物量变动的市场价值,即期末价值减期初价值的差额,再扣除当期由于价格变动而产生的持有收益。存货增加可以是正值,也可以是负值;正值表示存货上升,负值表示存货下降。它包括生产单位购进的原材料、燃料和储备物资等存货,以及生产单位生产的产成品、在制品和半成品等存货。

货物和服务净出口　指货物和服务出口减货物和服务进口的差额。出口包括常住单位向非常住单位出售或无偿转让的各种货物和服务的价值；进口包括常住单位从非常住单位购买或无偿得到的各种货物和服务的价值。由于服务活动的提供与使用同时发生，一般把常住单位从国外得到的服务作为进口，非常住单位从本国得到的服务作为出口。货物的出口和进口都按离岸价格计算。

气候　指地球与大气之间长期能量交换与质量交换所形成的一种自然环境状态，它是多种因素综合作用的结果。气候既是人类生活和生产的环境要素之一，又是供给人类生活和生产的重要资源。气温、降水、湿度等气象要素的多年平均值是用来描述一个地区气候状况的主要参数，而各种气象要素某年、某月的平均值（或总量）则可以反映出该时期天气气候状况的重要特征。

气温　指空气的温度，我国一般以摄氏度（℃）为单位表示。气象观测的温度表是放在离地面约 1.5 米处通风良好的百叶箱里测量的，因此，通常说的气温指的是离地面 1.5 米处百叶箱中的温度。其统计计算方法为：月平均气温是将全月各日的平均气温相加，除以该月的天数而得。

年平均气温是将 12 个月的月平均气温累加后除以 12 而得。

降水量　指从天空降落到地面的液态或固态（经融化后）水，未经蒸发、渗透、流失而在地面上积聚的深度。其统计计算方法为：月降水量是将全月各日的降水量累加而得。年降水量是将 12 个月的月降水量累加而得。

Explanatory Notes on Main Statistical Indicators

Gross Domestic Product (GDP)　refers to the final products at market prices producted by all resident units in a country (or a region) during a certain period of time. Gross domestic product is expressed in three different persperctives, namely value, income, and products respectively. GDP in its value perspective refers to the total value of all goods and services produced by all resident units during a certain period of time, minus the total value of input of goods and services of the nature of non-fixed assets; in other words, it is the sum of the value-added of all resident units. GDP from the perspective of products refers to the value of all goods and services for final consumption by all resident units minus the net exports of goods and services during a given period of time. In the practice of national accounting, gross domestic product is calculated from three approaches, namely production approach, income approach and expenditure approach, which reflect gross domestic product and its composition from different angles. For a certain region, it refers region gross product or region GDP.

Per Capita GDP　refers to the ratio of GDP in a certain term and average population in the same term. According to the international standard, average population should be average permanent population in the same term. In the account regulation, population of both the country and the region should be permanent population. In the after two yers since 2004, per capita GDP can be calculated at two coverage. i. e. at permanent population and household registered population (the note of coverage should follow the data.) The per capita GDP calculated with household registered population will be abolished after two years. Per capita GDP of Qingdao is calculated at permanent population.

Three Strata of Industries　has been classfied according to the historical sequence of development. Primary industry refers to extraction of natural resources; secondary industry involves processing of primary products; and tertiary industry provides services of various kinds for production and consumption. The above classification is universal although it varies to some extent form country to country. In China economic activities are categorized into the following three strata of industry:

Primary industry refers to farming, forestry, animal husbandryand fishery and services in support of these industries.

Secondary industry refers to mining and quarrying, manufacturing, production and supply of electricity, water and gas, and construction.

Tertiary industry refers to all other economic activities not included in primary or secondary industries.

GDP by Expenditure Approach　refers to the method of measuring the final results of production activities of a country (region) during a given period from the perspective of final use. It includes final consumption, total capital formation and net export of goods and services. It reflects use and composition of gross domestic product. For a certain region, it refers region gross product by expenditure approach.

Final Consumption refers to the total expenditure of resident units for purchases of goods and services from both the domestic economic territory and abroad to meet the needs of material, cultural and spiritual life. It does not include the expenditure of non-resident units on consumption in the economic territory of the country. The final consumption is broken down into household consumption and government consumption.

Household Consumption refers to the total expenditure of resident households on the final consumption of goods and services. In addition to the consumption of goods and services bought by the households directly with money, the household consumption also includes expenditure on goods and services obtained by the households in other ways, i. e. the so-called imputed consumption, which includes the following: (a) the goods and services provided to households by employers in the form of payment in kind and transfer in kind; (b) goods and services produced and consumed by the households themselves, in which the services refer to the owner-occupied housing and services offered by payed family employees; (c) financial intermediate services provided by financial institution.

Government Consumption refers to the consumption expenditure spent for the provision of public services provided by the government to the whole country and the net expenditure on the goods and services provided by the government to households free of charge or at reduced prices. The former equals to the output value of the government services minus the value of operating income obtained by the government departments. The latter equals to the market value of the goods and services provided by the government free of charge or at reduced prices to the households minus the value received by the government from the households.

Gross Capital Formation refers to the fixed assets acquired less disposal and the net value of inventory, thus including the gross fixed capital formation and charges in inventories.

Gross Fixed Capital Formation refers to the value of acquisitions less those disposals of fixed assets during a given period. Fixed assets are the assets produced through production activities with unit value above a specified amount and which could be used for over one year. Natural assets are not included. Gross fixed capital formation can be categorized into total tangible fixed capital formation and total intangible fixed capital formation. Total tangible fixed capital formation includes the value of the construction projects and installation projects completed and the equipment, apparatus and instruments purchased (less those disposed) as well as the value of land improved, the value of draught animals, breeding stock and animals for milk, for wool and for recreational purposes and the newly increased forest with economic value. Total intangible fixed capital formation includes the prospecting of minerals and the acquisition of computer software minus the disposal of them.

Charges in Inventories refers to the market value of the change in the physical volume of inventory of resident units during a given period, i. e. the difference between the values at the beginning and at the end of the period minus the gains due to the change in prices. The changes in inventories can have a positive or a negative value. A positive value indicates an increase in inventory while a negative value indicates a decrease in inventory. The inventory includes raw materials, fuels and reserve materials purchased by the production units as well as the inventory of finished products, semi-finished products and work-in-progress.

Net Export of Goods and Services refers to the exports of goods and services subtracting the imports of goods and services. Exports include the value of various goods and services sold or gratuitously transferred by resident units to non-resident units. Imports include the value of various goods and services purchased or gratuitously acquired resident units from non-resident units. Because the provision of services and the use of them happen simultaneously, the acquisition of services by resident units from abroad is usually treated as import while the acquisition of services by non-resident units in this country is usually treated as export. The exports and imports of goods are calculated at FOB.

Climate refers to the natural environmental status formed by the long-term exchange of energy and mass between the earth and the air, and is the results of interaction of many factors. Climate is both one of the environment factors and the important resources for the living and production activities of the human being. The average values across several years of meteorological factors such as temperature, rainfall and humidity are used as important parameters to describe the climate of a region, while the average values (or total values) of a given year or month of meteorological factors reflect the key characteristics of climate for that period of time.

Temperature refers to the air temperature. China uses centigrade as the unit. The thermometry used for weather observation is put in a breezy shutter, which is 1.5 meters high from the ground. Therefore, the commonly used temperature refers to the temperature in the breezy shutter 1.5 meters away from the ground. The calculation method is as follows:

Monthly average temperature is the summation of average daily temperature of one month divided by the actual days of that particular month.

Annual average temperature is the summation of monthly average of a year divided by 12 months.

Volume of Precipitation refers to the deepness of liquid state or solid state (thawed) water falling from the sky to the ground that has not been evaporated, infiltrated or run off. The calculation method is as follows:

Monthly precipitation is the summation of daily precipitation of a month.

Annual precipitation is the summation of 12 months precipitation of a year.

人　口 2

POPULATION

简要说明

一、本篇资料的主要内容

本篇资料主要反映了全市人口方面的基本情况，包括全市主要年份和12区(市)的户数、人口数、人口密度、土地面积数据、人口出生率、死亡率、自然增长率、计划生育等数据。另外还对建国以来开展的六次人口普查主要数据进行了比较。

二、本篇资料的来源

本篇资料分别来源于国家开展的人口普查、人口抽样调查和市公安局的户籍登记资料，由市统计局人口和社会科技统计处整理提供。

Brief Introduction

I. Main Content

Data in this chapter show the basic condition of population, such as the basic condition of 12 districts and county-level cities, household, population, density of population, birth rate, death rate, natural growth rate and family planning situation. Furthermore, relevant figures obtained from the six national population censuses have been compared.

II. Source of Data

Data in this chapter are from national population censuses, national sample survey. Some are derived from household registration provided by Qingdao Municipal Bureau of Public Security. The data are compiled by the Division of Population and Science & Technology of Qingdao Municipal Bureau of Statistics.

2-1 主要年份全市总人口数
MAJOR YEAR'S TOTAL POPULATION

单位:人(person)

年 份 Year	总人口 Total Population	按性别分 Grouped by Sex		平均人口 Average Population
		男 Male	女 Female	
1949	4 056 550	1 997 293	2 059 257	4 054 431
1952	4 233 586	2 125 392	2 108 194	4 203 428
1957	4 822 756	2 424 729	2 398 027	4 773 862
1962	4 627 432	2 319 658	2 307 774	4 578 313
1965	4 901 670	2 461 629	2 440 041	4 859 712
1970	5 391 852	2 720 633	2 671 219	5 337 282
1975	5 742 206	2 904 347	2 837 859	5 717 456
1978	5 853 321	2 959 800	2 893 521	5 841 638
1980	5 961 129	3 015 357	2 945 772	5 937 187
1985	6 267 223	3 185 409	3 081 814	6 253 157
1988	6 516 920	3 319 534	3 197 386	6 474 541
1989	6 571 597	3 348 454	3 223 143	6 544 259
1990	6 666 482	3 392 253	3 274 229	6 619 040
1991	6 709 277	3 411 776	3 297 501	6 687 880
1992	6 731 072	3 420 886	3 310 186	6 720 175
1993	6 753 497	3 431 149	3 322 348	6 742 285
1994	6 785 291	3 446 019	3 339 272	6 769 394
1995	6 846 346	3 476 300	3 370 046	6 815 819
1996	6 902 677	3 502 600	3 400 077	6 874 512
1997	6 954 391	3 527 588	3 426 803	6 928 534
1998	6 995 666	3 545 403	3 450 263	6 975 029
1999	7 029 707	3 561 061	3 468 646	7 012 687
2000	7 066 481	3 577 367	3 489 114	7 048 094
2001	7 104 875	3 595 652	3 509 223	7 085 678
2002	7 156 537	3 619 778	3 536 759	7 130 706
2003	7 206 806	3 644 032	3 562 774	7 181 672
2004	7 311 228	3 692 991	3 618 237	7 259 017
2005	7 409 052	3 740 309	3 668 743	7 360 140
2006	7 493 812	3 779 891	3 713 921	7 451 432
2007	7 579 910	3 816 620	3 763 290	7 536 861
2008	7 615 647	3 824 665	3 790 982	7 597 779
2009	7 629 161	3 823 534	3 805 627	7 622 404
2010	7 636 392	3 819 240	3 817 152	7 632 777
2011	7 663 612	3 826 931	3 836 681	7 650 002

2-2 主要年份全市户数、人口数、人口密度
MAJOR YEAR'S HOUSEHOLDS, POPULATION AND DENSITY OF POPULATION

年份 Year	总户数(万户) Total Households (10000 households)		总人口(万人) Total Population (10000 persons)		平均每户人口(人) Average Persons Per Household(person)		人口密度(人/平方公里) Density of Population (person/sq. km)	
	全市 Whole Municipality	市区 Urban Area	全市 Whole Municipality	市区 Urban Area	全市 Whole Municipality	市区 Urban Area	全市 Whole Municipality	市区 Urban Area
1949	90.64	21.68	405.66	103.69	4.48	4.78	381	941
1952	93.96	22.70	423.36	107.62	4.51	4.74	397	977
1957	102.56	27.41	482.28	134.76	4.70	4.92	453	1 223
1962	106.11	29.29	462.74	137.86	4.36	4.71	434	1 251
1965	105.31	29.64	490.17	146.74	4.65	4.95	460	1 332
1970	113.07	32.14	539.19	150.81	4.77	4.69	506	1 369
1975	123.18	36.56	574.22	161.13	4.66	4.41	539	1 462
1978	131.27	40.08	585.33	168.00	4.46	4.19	549	1 525
1980	138.44	43.03	596.11	175.27	4.31	4.07	560	1 591
1985	157.06	53.43	626.72	190.87	3.99	3.57	588	1 732
1988	169.72	58.95	651.69	201.38	3.84	3.42	612	1 827
1989	177.47	61.57	657.16	203.63	3.70	3.31	617	1 848
1990	186.79	63.94	666.65	205.78	3.57	3.22	626	1 867
1991	192.46	67.15	670.93	207.22	3.49	3.09	630	1 880
1992	199.08	68.94	673.11	209.28	3.38	3.04	632	1 899
1993	201.36	70.13	675.35	212.06	3.35	3.02	634	1 924
1994	204.05	71.24	678.53	214.97	3.33	3.02	637	1 951
1995	208.13	72.53	684.63	218.38	3.29	3.01	643	1 982
1996	212.40	75.11	690.27	223.86	3.25	2.98	648	2 032
1997	215.12	76.39	695.44	227.22	3.23	2.97	653	2 062
1998	218.59	77.90	699.57	229.58	3.20	2.95	657	2 084
1999	222.61	79.27	702.97	231.94	3.16	2.93	660	2 105
2000	224.73	80.46	706.65	234.60	3.14	2.92	664	2 129
2001	227.43	81.41	710.49	237.60	3.12	2.92	667	2 156
2002	229.67	82.85	715.65	241.74	3.12	2.92	672	2 194
2003	232.26	84.15	720.68	246.77	3.10	2.93	677	2 240
2004	235.29	86.93	731.12	258.40	3.11	2.97	686	2 229
2005	237.35	87.99	740.91	265.43	3.12	3.02	695	2 290
2006	239.33	89.12	749.38	271.00	3.13	3.04	703	2 338
2007	241.55	90.21	757.99	275.55	3.14	3.05	711	2 377
2008	243.18	91.22	761.56	276.25	3.13	3.03	715	2 384
2009	244.74	92.15	762.92	275.47	3.12	2.99	676	1 873
2010	246.11	93.30	763.64	275.50	3.10	2.95	677	1 873
2011	247.94	94.69	766.36	277.09	3.09	2.93	679	1 884

2－3 第一、二、三、四、五、六次人口普查主要数据
MAIN DATA FROM THE SIX NATIONAL POPULATION CENSUSES

项　目	Item	第一次人口普查 1st National Population Census	第二次人口普查 2nd National Population Census	第三次人口普查 3rd National Population Census	第四次人口普查 4th National Population Census	第五次人口普查 5th National Population Census	第六次人口普查 6th National Population Census
一、总人口（万人）	**Total Population (10000 persons)**	**91.68**	**138.34**	**422.76**	**666.40**	**749.42**	**871.51**
按性别分	By Sex						
男（万人）	Male(10000 persons)	48.44	69.64	214.09	338.86	375.74	439.18
女（万人）	Female(10000 persons)	43.24	68.71	208.67	327.54	373.68	432.33
二、总户数（万户）	**Total Household (10000 households)**	**19.27**	**28.01**	**101.41**	**186.61**	**241.62**	**296.64**
家庭户（万户）	Family Household (10000 households)			101.09	185.56	232.70	282.43
平均家庭户规模(人)	Average Family Household Size(person)			4.07	3.49	2.97	2.79
三、民　族	**Ethnicity**						
民族个数（个）	Number of Ethnic Groups (unit)	14	16	25	41	51	53
汉族人口（万人）	Population of Han (10000 persons)	91.33	137.76	422.09	665.58	746.12	863.84
少数民族人口（万人）	Populaiton of Ethnic Minorities(10000 persons)	0.36	0.58	0.67	0.82	3.3	7.67
四、各种文化程度人口	**Popution with Various Education Attainments**						
大学（万人）	College(10000 persons)		1.51	3.62	12.39	41.64	129.54
高中（万人）	Senior Secondary School (10000 persons)		4.86	34.82	68.42	111.40	150.82
初中（万人）	Junior Secondary School (10000 persons)		13.72	102.28	195.10	281.91	334.22
小学（万人）	Primary School (10000 persons)		51.25	144.52	236.34	206.91	170.77

2-4 分市、区户数与人口数(2011 年底)
TOTAL HOUSEHOLDS AND POPULATION BY REGION(END OF 2011)

市、区名称	Region	户数(户) Households (household)	人口(人) Population (person)	按性别分 Grouped by Sex 男 Male	女 Female	平均人口(人) Average Population (person)
总　计	**Total**	**2 479 406**	**7 663 612**	**3 826 931**	**3 836 681**	**7 650 002**
市　区	Urban Area	946 894	2 770 929	1 370 488	1 400 441	2 762 979
市南区	Shinan District	171 299	548 467	268 381	280 086	549 295
市北区	Shibei District	186 052	494 844	244 195	250 649	491 766
四方区	Sifang District	135 323	372 070	187 632	184 438	373 544
李沧区	Licang District	115 617	309 744	153 925	155 819	307 394
崂山区	Laoshan District	77 127	249 130	123 140	125 990	245 474
黄岛区	Huangdao District	89 231	314 663	160 245	154 418	313 764
城阳区	Chengyang District	172 245	482 011	232 970	249 041	481 744
即墨市	Jimo	341 361	1 131 794	565 522	566 272	1 130 556
胶州市	Jiaozhou	249 270	807 140	402 848	404 292	805 102
胶南市	Jiaonan	267 437	841 222	423 145	418 077	840 212
平度市	Pingdu	423 884	1 376 204	694 838	681 366	1 375 255
莱西市	Laixi	250 560	736 323	370 090	366 233	735 899

2-5 分市、区土地面积、人口和人口密度(2011 年底)
LAND AREA, POPULATION AND DENSITY OF POPULATION BY REGION(END OF 2011)

市、区名称	Region	土地面积 Land Area 面积(平方公里) Area(sq. km)	比重(%) Percentage(%)	年末人口 Year-end Population 人口(人) Population(person)	比重(%) Percentage(%)	人口密度(人/平方公里) Density of Population (person/sq. km)
总　计	**Total**	**11 282**	**100.00**	**7 663 612**	**100.00**	**679**
市　区	Urban Area	1 471	13.03	2 770 929	36.15	1 884
即墨市	Jimo	1 921	17.03	1 131 794	14.77	589
胶州市	Jiaozhou	1 324	11.74	807 140	10.53	610
胶南市	Jiaonan	1 822	16.15	841 222	10.98	462
平度市	Pingdu	3 176	28.15	1 376 204	17.96	433
莱西市	Laixi	1 568	13.90	736 323	9.61	470

注：土地面积为第二次全国土地调查数据。

Note: Data on land area are based on the data of the Second China Land Census.

2-6 主要年份人口自然变动
MAJOR YEAR'S NATURAL CHANGE OF POPULATION

年份 Year	出生 Birth			死亡 Death			自然增长 Natural Growth		
	人数(万人) Population (10 000 persons)	出生率(‰) Birth Rate (‰)	#市区 Urban Area	人数(万人) Population (10 000 persons)	死亡率(‰) Death Rate (‰)	#市区 Urban Area	人数(万人) Population (10 000 persons)	增长率(‰) Natural Growth Rate(‰)	#市区 Urban Area
1949	11.62	28.66	31.86	6.10	15.03	11.25	5.52	13.62	20.61
1952	15.51	36.91	39.60	4.97	11.83	9.18	10.54	25.08	30.42
1957	17.82	37.34	42.40	6.38	13.37	8.82	11.44	23.97	33.58
1962	17.29	37.77	35.75	5.82	12.70	8.08	11.47	25.07	27.67
1965	17.63	36.28	27.18	4.66	9.59	5.61	12.97	26.69	21.57
1970	17.65	33.06	23.79	3.79	7.11	5.55	13.86	25.95	18.24
1975	10.55	18.45	17.52	3.95	6.90	5.67	6.60	11.55	11.85
1978	8.55	14.64	11.64	3.65	6.24	5.53	4.90	8.40	6.11
1980	8.00	13.48	11.28	3.77	6.35	5.73	4.23	7.13	5.55
1985	5.82	9.31	10.37	3.88	6.21	5.64	1.94	3.10	4.73
1988	10.22	15.79	15.39	4.17	6.44	5.29	6.05	9.35	10.10
1989	10.37	15.85	14.13	3.88	5.93	5.48	6.49	9.92	8.65
1990	11.44	17.28	11.68	4.35	6.58	5.78	7.09	10.70	5.90
1991	7.98	11.93	8.17	4.15	6.21	5.56	3.83	5.72	2.61
1992	6.17	9.18	8.65	4.54	6.75	6.14	1.63	2.43	2.51
1993	5.95	8.82	8.49	4.44	6.59	6.01	1.51	2.23	2.48
1994	6.92	10.22	8.66	4.71	6.96	6.40	2.21	3.26	2.26
1995	8.15	11.96	9.03	4.52	6.62	6.08	3.63	5.34	2.95
1996	8.40	12.21	8.98	4.83	7.03	6.38	3.57	5.18	2.60
1997	7.80	11.26	8.76	4.80	6.93	6.33	3.00	4.33	2.43
1998	7.51	10.77	8.62	4.68	6.71	6.12	2.83	4.06	2.50
1999	6.48	9.24	8.05	4.56	6.50	6.05	1.92	2.74	2.00
2000	7.31	10.38	9.25	4.95	7.02	6.33	2.37	3.36	2.92
2001	6.74	9.51	8.37	4.64	6.54	6.17	2.10	2.97	2.20
2002	7.54	10.57	9.24	4.74	6.65	6.12	2.80	3.92	3.12
2003	5.11	7.11	5.89	4.81	6.70	6.12	0.30	0.41	-0.23
2004	7.93	10.93	8.93	4.92	6.78	6.03	3.01	4.15	2.90
2005	7.55	10.26	7.84	4.81	6.54	6.10	2.74	3.72	1.74
2006	7.01	9.40	7.47	5.16	6.93	5.77	1.85	2.47	1.70
2007	7.65	10.15	9.38	4.76	6.32	5.84	2.89	3.83	3.54
2008	6.89	9.06	8.86	5.57	7.33	5.98	1.32	1.73	2.88
2009	6.30	8.27	8.40	5.14	6.75	5.82	1.16	1.52	2.58
2010	6.85	8.98	9.61	6.33	8.29	6.25	0.52	0.69	3.36
2011	6.58	8.60	9.31	5.55	7.26	6.05	1.03	1.34	3.26

2-7 分市、区人口出生率、死亡率、自然增长率(2011年底)

RATE OF BIRTH, DEATH AND NATURAL GROWTH IN POPULATION BY REGION(END OF 2011)

市、区名称	Region	出生 Birth		死亡 Death		自然增长 Natural Growth	
		人数(人) Population (person)	出生率(‰) Birth Rate (‰)	人数(人) Population (person)	死亡率(‰) Death Rate (‰)	人数(人) Population (person)	增长率(‰) Natural Growth Rate(‰)
总 计	**Total**	**65 793**	**8.60**	**55 537**	**7.26**	**10 256**	**1.34**
市 区	Urban Area	25 731	9.31	16 718	6.05	9 013	3.26
市南区	Shinan District	4 741	8.63	2 766	5.04	1 975	3.59
市北区	Shibei District	4 427	9.00	3 509	7.14	918	1.86
四方区	Sifang District	3 053	8.17	2 699	7.23	354	0.94
李沧区	Licang District	3 257	10.60	1 877	6.11	1 380	4.49
崂山区	Laoshan District	2 388	9.73	1 385	5.64	1 003	4.09
黄岛区	Huangdao District	3 496	11.14	1 270	4.05	2 226	7.09
城阳区	Chengyang District	4 369	9.07	3 212	6.67	1 157	2.40
即墨市	Jimo	8 528	7.54	8 716	7.71	-188	-0.17
胶州市	Jiaozhou	7 372	9.16	5 744	7.13	1 628	2.03
胶南市	Jiaonan	6 640	7.90	6 776	8.06	-136	-0.16
平度市	Pingdu	12 038	8.75	11 534	8.39	504	0.36
莱西市	Laixi	5 484	7.45	6 049	8.22	-565	-0.77

2-8 分市、区人口机械变动(2011年底)

MECHANICAL CHANGE OF POPULATION BY REGION(END OF 2011)

市、区名称	Region	迁入人数(人) Inflows(person)	迁出人数(人) Outflows(person)	增(+)、减(-) Increase(+), Decrease(-)
总 计	**Total**	**68 606**	**52 148**	**16 458**
市 区	Urban Area	42 927	35 966	6 961
市南区	Shinan District	11 334	12 493	-1 159
市北区	Shibei District	5 167	1 852	3 315
四方区	Sifang District	5 153	6 673	-1 520
李沧区	Licang District	3 095	1 126	1 969
崂山区	Laoshan District	5 426	1 339	4 087
黄岛区	Huangdao District	8 111	7 722	389
城阳区	Chengyang District	4 641	4 761	-120
即墨市	Jimo	5 370	2 830	2 540
胶州市	Jiaozhou	5 523	3 169	2 354
胶南市	Jiaonan	5 488	3 273	2 215
平度市	Pingdu	5 464	4 312	1 152
莱西市	Laixi	3 834	2 598	1 236

2－9 计划生育情况（1978－2011年）
FAMILY PLANNING SITUATION（1978－2011）

年 份 Year	已婚有生育能力的人数（人） Married and Fertile Persons（person）	节育人数（人） Persons under Birth Control（person）	节育率（%） Contraceptive Prevalence Rate（%）	四项手术人数（人） Persons Performed Four-operation（person）	#放环人数 Persons Set Rings
1978	694 292	571 077	82.25	125 913	68 475
1980	763 226	673 069	88.19	180 979	70 927
1985	1 017 649	929 284	91.32	146 742	67 234
1990	1 258 232	1 165 216	92.61	149 327	70 964
1991	1 319 722	1 219 795	92.43	153 970	77 406
1992	1 348 503	1 256 271	93.16	90 107	56 226
1993	1 380 717	1 271 884	92.12	76 783	45 492
1994	1 400 425	1 268 378	90.57	73 169	41 482
1995	1 427 442	1 285 264	90.04	84 099	52 716
1996	1 459 465	1 316 516	90.21	84 370	57 648
1997	1 482 204	1 340 399	90.43	76 579	55 285
1998	1 505 499	1 367 648	90.84	74 199	50 526
1999	1 523 471	1 378 131	90.46	73 663	44 976
2000	1 521 331	1 371 447	90.15	74 285	45 999
2001	1 514 274	1 360 543	89.85	70 205	43 601
2002	1 541 855	1 400 145	90.81	50 575	45 453
2003	1 518 448	1 354 917	89.23	57 458	47 953
2004	1 540 706	1 357 703	88.04	52 934	42 859
2005	1 590 476	1 417 755	89.14	58 097	49 716
2006	1 604 665	1 427 785	88.98	51 864	42 457
2007	1 595 390	1 426 787	89.43	50 074	41 198
2008	1 587 344	1 410 426	88.85	120 539	93 291
2009	1 623 969	1 418 178	87.33	111 084	100 193
2010	1 591 103	1 377 726	86.59	78 721	51 794
2011	1 581 231	1 355 808	85.74	70 823	48 210

2－10 分市、区计划生育情况（2011年）
FAMILY PLANNING SITUATION BY REGION（2011）

市、区名称	Region	计划生育率（%） Fertility Rate（%）	计划内出生（人） Birth within the Plan（person）		计划外出生（人） Birth without the Plan（person）		多胎（人） Third Birth and Above（person）
			一胎 First Birth	二胎 Second Birth	一胎 First Birth	二胎 Second Birth	
总　计	**Total**	**97.38**	**48 576**	**12 923**	**133**	**1 209**	**312**
市　区	Urban Area	97.91	21 982	2 647	31	455	40
市南区	Shinan District	97.56	4 941	304	11	111	9
市北区	Shibei District	97.62	3 634	223	4	84	6
四方区	Sifang District	98.04	2 795	159	2	53	4
李沧区	Licang District	97.84	2 662	143	6	52	4
崂山区	Laoshan District	98.55	1 886	296	1	30	1
黄岛区	Huangdao District	97.64	3 050	548	3	80	4
城阳区	Chengyang District	98.49	3 014	974	4	45	12
即墨市	Jimo	97.65	5 683	2 558	13	142	43
胶州市	Jiaozhou	97.62	4 387	1 683	13	105	30
胶南市	Jiaonan	97.79	4 606	1 752	7	105	32
平度市	Pingdu	95.83	8 010	3 124	51	295	139
莱西市	Laixi	97.07	3 908	1 159	18	107	28

主要统计指标解释

人口数 指一定时点、一定地区范围内有生命的个人总和。

出生率(又称粗出生率) 指在一定时期内(通常为一年)一定地区的出生人数与同期内平均人数(或期中人数)之比,用千分率表示。本资料中的出生率指年出生率,其计算公式为:

$$出生率=\frac{年出生人数}{年平均人数}\times 1000‰$$

式中:出生人数指活产婴儿,即胎儿脱离母体时(不管怀孕月数),有过呼吸或其他生命现象。

死亡率(又称粗死亡率) 指在一定时期内(通常为一年)一定地区的死亡人数与同期内平均人数(或期中人数)之比,用千分率表示。本资料中的死亡率指年死亡率,其计算公式为:

$$死亡率=\frac{年死亡人数}{年平均人数}\times 1000‰$$

人口自然增长率 指在一定时期内(通常为一年)人口自然增加数(出生人数减死亡人数)与该时期内平均人数(或期中人数)之比,用千分率表示。计算公式为:

$$人口自然增长率=\frac{本年出生人数-本年死亡人数}{年平均人数}\times 1000‰$$
$$=人口出生率-人口死亡率$$

Explanatory Notes on Main Statistical Indicators

Total Population refers to the total number of people alive at a certain point of time within a given area.

Birth Rate (or Crude Birth Rate) refers to the ratio of the number of births to the average population (or mid-period population) during a certain period of time (usually a year), expressed in ‰. Birth rate in the chapter refers to annual birth rate. The following formula is used:

Birth Rate = (Number of Births/Average Number of Population) ×1000‰

Number of births in the formula refers to live births, i. e. when a baby has breathed or showed any vital phenomena regardless of the length of pregnancy.

Annual average number of population is the average of the number of population at the beginning of the year and that at the end of the year. Sometimes it is substituted by the mid-year population.

Death Rate (or Crude Death Rate) refers to the ratio of the number of deaths to the average population (or mid-period population) during a certain period of time (usually a year), expressed in ‰. Death rate in the chapter refers to annual death rate. The following formula is used:

Death Rate = (Number of Deaths/Annual Average Number of Population) ×1000‰

Natural Growth Rate of Population refers to the ratio of natural increase in population (number of births minus number of deaths) in a certain period of time (usually a year) to the average population (or mid-period population) of the same period, expressed in ‰. The following formula is applied:

Natural Growth Rate of Population = [(Number of Births-Number of Deaths)/Average Number of Population] ×1000‰

Natural Growth Rate of Population = Birth Rate-Death Rate

从业人员及职工工资 3

EMPLOYMENT AND WAGES

简要说明

一、本篇资料的主要内容

本篇资料主要反映了全市从业人员和职工工资方面的基本情况，主要包括全市社会从业人数及各区（市）单位从业人数、在岗职工工资总额和平均工资等方面的资料。

二、本篇资料的来源

单位从业人员和职工工资来源于劳动统计年报，全市从业人员根据劳动统计年报、农村年报和市工商行政管理局、市人力资源和社会保障局、市交通委相关资料测算。由市统计局人口和社会科技统计处整理提供。

Brief Introduction

I. Main Content

Data in this chapter show the basic conditions of Qingdao's employment and wages, including the main data on labor statistics of employment, number of employment of the whole city and 12 district and county-level cities, total wage bill and average wage of staff and workers, etc.

II. Source of Data

Data on employment and wages are prepared according to the annual reports of labor statistics.Data on social employment are measured according to the annual reports of labor statistics,countryside statistics and related information from Industry & Commerce Administration Bureau,Human Resources & Social Security Bureau and Transportation Commision.

Data in this chapter are compiled by the Division of Population and Science & Technology of Qingdao Municipal Bureau of Statistics.

3－1 社会从业人数(1978－2011年)

SOCIAL EMPLOYMENT(1978－2011)

单位:万人(10 000 persons)

年　份 Year	合　计 Total	第一产业 Primary Industry	第二产业 Secondary Industry	第三产业 Tertiary Industry
1978	256.70	157.40	65.60	33.70
1979	265.60	156.10	72.20	37.30
1980	270.00	153.00	77.30	39.70
1981	278.90	153.60	82.10	43.20
1982	282.70	151.10	86.20	45.40
1983	289.60	156.50	85.00	48.10
1984	304.20	149.10	97.70	57.40
1985	315.30	149.20	104.40	61.70
1986	326.40	149.70	112.10	64.60
1987	334.80	149.90	120.20	64.70
1988	336.50	147.60	123.20	65.70
1989	344.20	152.50	122.10	69.60
1990	352.80	156.50	123.30	73.00
1991	361.20	161.90	124.30	75.00
1992	370.30	161.70	127.80	80.80
1993	365.70	160.50	128.80	76.40
1994	367.60	157.10	129.30	81.20
1995	374.20	155.40	132.40	86.40
1996	381.50	152.20	137.10	92.20
1997	388.70	155.30	138.10	95.30
1998	393.10	154.80	138.60	99.70
1999	396.10	150.30	142.00	103.80
2000	397.60	144.70	134.91	117.99
2001	400.50	133.90	142.30	124.30
2002	413.31	121.38	153.85	138.08
2003	438.96	119.91	163.93	155.12
2004	458.81	113.98	180.63	164.20
2005	471.03	104.48	196.80	169.75
2006	490.10	102.97	209.83	177.30
2007	505.80	102.30	217.80	185.70
2008	513.80	102.40	220.80	190.60
2009	525.71	105.65	220.33	199.73
2010	540.34	105.16	223.85	211.33
2011	551.18	106.02	227.08	218.08

3-2 主要年份全市单位从业人员人数

MAJOR YEAR'S NUMBER OF EMPLOYED PERSONS IN ALL UNITS OF THE CITY

单位:万人(10 000 persons)

年 份 Year	合 计 Total	#市 区 Urban Area	国有单位 State-owned Units	集体单位 Collective-owned Units	其他所有制单位 Other Ownership Units
1949	14.8	13.4	9.3	5.5	
1952	23.4	20.1	18.3	5.1	
1957	29.7	24.5	24.1	5.6	
1962	32.3	26.8	24.5	7.8	
1965	36.7	30.6	26.8	9.9	
1970	45.6	37.4	32.2	13.4	
1975	53.4	43.5	38.0	15.4	
1978	70.7	54.5	49.2	21.5	
1980	79.2	61.5	55.0	24.2	
1985	88.8	66.7	59.8	28.9	0.1
1988	98.2	70.0	66.7	31.2	0.3
1989	99.2	70.4	67.7	31.0	0.5
1990	103.2	70.6	69.5	32.9	0.8
1991	105.4	78.4	71.5	32.5	1.4
1992	108.2	80.4	73.6	32.8	1.8
1993	109.4	80.8	75.3	29.5	4.6
1994	110.1	80.2	72.4	28.3	9.4
1995	111.6	80.2	72.4	27.5	11.7
1996	118.4	81.1	71.6	26.0	20.8
1997	117.1	78.1	69.0	22.6	25.5
1998	116.2	75.6	64.2	19.0	33.0
1999	119.0	78.3	60.4	16.6	42.0
2000	118.3	76.6	57.6	14.2	46.5
2001	117.5	75.1	53.2	12.2	52.1
2002	119.1	75.2	49.5	10.3	59.3
2003	118.0	74.3	47.2	8.9	61.9
2004	207.1	111.1	43.7	18.0	145.4
2005	224.3	122.3	43.9	18.2	162.2
2006	243.2	133.7	41.7	16.2	185.3
2007	249.8	137.3	45.1	17.9	186.8
2008	254.1	140.9	44.4	15.4	194.3
2009	260.5	145.6	44.4	14.6	201.5
2010	269.4	151.1	44.6	15.1	209.7
2011	275.9	156.5	44.3	14.7	216.9

注:2004 年以前为城镇单位职工人数.

Note: Before 2004, the data refer to number of staff and workers in urban units.

3-3 全市单位国民经济各行业从业人员人数(2011年)

NUMBER OF EMPLOYED PERSONS IN ALL UNITS OF THE CITY BY SECTOR(2011)

单位:万人(10 000 persons)

		2011		2010	
		合计 Total	女性 Female	合计 Total	女性 Female
总　计	**Total**	**275.9**	**118.4**	**269.4**	**116.0**
1. 农、林、牧、渔业	Farming, Forestry, Animal Husbandry and Fishery	1.0	0.4	0.8	0.3
2. 采矿业	Mining	2.1	0.4	2.0	0.3
3. 制造业	Manufacturing	143.7	66.1	142.9	66.1
4. 电力、煤气及水的生产供应业	Production and Supply of Electricty, Gas and Water	17.3	3.5	16.1	3.4
5. 建筑业	Construction	2.7	0.7	2.5	0.7
6. 交通运输、仓储及邮政业	Transport, Storage and Post	12.1	3.5	11.7	3.2
7. 信息传输、计算机服务和软件业	Information Transmission, Computer Services and Software	1.6	0.6	1.5	0.5
8. 批发和零售业	Wholesale and Retail Trade	28.0	12.5	27.3	12.1
9. 住宿和餐饮业	Hotels and Catering Services	8.3	4.6	8.0	4.4
10. 金融业	Financial Intermediation	5.1	2.8	4.8	2.7
11. 房地产业	Real Estate	5.9	2.0	5.4	1.9
12. 租赁和商务服务业	Leasing and Business Services	10.4	4.5	10.2	4.4
13. 科学研究、技术服务和地质勘察业	Scientific Research, Technical Services and Geologic Prospecting	3.0	1.3	2.8	1.2
14. 水利、环境和公共设施管理业	Management of Water Conservancy, Environment and Public Facilities	2.5	0.8	2.3	0.8
15. 居民服务和其他服务业	Services to Households and Other Services	3.0	1.1	2.8	0.9
16. 教育	Education	13.7	7.4	13.3	7.1
17. 卫生、社会保障和社会福利业	Health, Social Security and Social Welfare	5.2	3.4	5.0	3.2
18. 文化、体育和娱乐业	Culture, Sports and Entertainment	2.3	0.7	2.2	0.7
19. 公共管理和社会组织	Public Management and Social Organization	8.0	2.1	7.8	2.1
20. 国际组织	International Organization				

3-4 全市单位分市、区国民经济各部门从业人员人数(2011年)
NUMBER OF EMPLOYED PERSONS IN ALL UNITS OF THE CITY BY REGION AND SECTOR (2011)

市、区名称	Region	合计 Total	农林牧渔业 Farming, Forestry, Animal Husbandry and Fishery	采矿业 Mining	制造业 Manufacturing	电力燃气和水生产供应业 Production and Supply of Electricty, Gas and Water	建筑业 Construction
总　计	**Total**	**275.9**	**1.0**	**2.1**	**143.7**	**2.7**	**17.3**
#崂山区	Laoshan District	16.8			7.0	0.1	0.8
黄岛区	Huangdao District	22.6			12.6	0.2	2.6
城阳区	Chengyang District	36.3	0.1	0.1	27.3	0.1	1.5
即墨市	Jimo	31.8	0.2		23.3	0.1	2.2
胶州市	Jiaozhou	29.8	0.2		20.6	0.1	3.7
胶南市	Jiaonan	20.7		0.3	14.9	0.2	0.9
平度市	Pingdu	18.1	0.2	1.1	12.0	0.2	0.7
莱西市	Laixi	18.9	0.1	0.3	13.0	0.2	1.2

3-4 续表
Continued

市、区名称	Region	金融业 Financial Intermediation	房地产业 Real Estate	租赁和商务服务业 Leasing and Business Services	科学研究技术服务和地质勘察业 Scientific Research, Technical Services and Geologic Prospecting	水利环境和公共设施管理业 Management of Water Conservancy, Environment and Public Facilities
总　计	**Total**	**5.1**	**5.9**	**10.4**	**3.0**	**2.5**
#崂山区	Laoshan District	0.1	0.9	0.5	0.4	0.2
黄岛区	Huangdao District	0.1	0.3	0.7	0.4	0.1
城阳区	Chengyang District	0.1	0.8	0.8	0.3	0.2
即墨市	Jimo	0.3	0.4	0.3		0.1
胶州市	Jiaozhou	0.3	0.4	0.3	0.1	0.2
胶南市	Jiaonan	0.2	0.3	0.1	0.2	0.1
平度市	Pingdu	0.2	0.3			0.1
莱西市	Laixi	0.1	0.1	0.1	0.1	0.1

单位:万人(10 000 persons)

交通运输仓储及邮政业 Transport, Storage and Post	信息传输计算机服务软件业 Information Transmission, Computer Services and Software	批发和零售业 Wholesale and Retail Trade	住宿和餐饮业 Hotels and Catering Services
12.1	**1.6**	**28.0**	**8.3**
0.5	0.3	3.4	1.1
0.9	0.1	1.8	0.6
0.9	0.2	1.4	0.5
0.2	0.1	1.3	0.4
0.2	0.1	1.0	0.3
0.2		0.9	0.4
0.1		0.5	0.1
0.1	0.1	1.1	0.4

单位:万人(10 000 persons)

居民服务其他服务业 Services to Households and Other Services	教育 Education	卫生社会保障和社会福利业 Health, Social Security and Social Welfare	文化体育和娱乐业 Culture, Sports and Entertainment	公共管理和社会组织 Public Management and Social Organization	国际组织 International Organization
3.0	**13.7**	**5.2**	**2.3**	**8.0**	
0.2	0.6	0.1	0.1	0.5	
0.1	1.3	0.2	0.1	0.5	
0.3	1.0	0.2		0.5	
	1.4	0.4	0.1	1.0	
0.1	1.2	0.4		0.6	
	1.1	0.3		0.6	
	1.4	0.4	0.1	0.7	
	0.8	0.4		0.7	

3-5 全市单位分市、区全部从业人员人数(2011 年底)

NUMBER OF EMPLOYED PERSONS IN ALL UNITS OF THE CITY BY REGION(END OF 2011)

单位:万人(10 000 persons)

市、区名称	Region	年末人数 Year-end Population	国有单位 State-owned Units	集体单位 Collective-owned Units	其他经济类型单位 Others
总　计	**Total**	**275.9**	**44.3**	**14.7**	**216.9**
市　区	Urban Area	156.6	27.8	6.8	122.0
#崂山区	Laoshan District	16.8	1.6	1.7	13.5
黄岛区	Huangdao District	22.6	2.3	0.4	19.9
城阳区	Chengyang District	36.3	2.5	2.4	31.4
即墨市	Jimo	31.8	3.2	1.8	26.8
胶州市	Jiaozhou	29.8	5.0	2.1	22.7
胶南市	Jiaonan	20.7	2.7	1.5	16.5
平度市	Pingdu	18.1	3.0	1.1	14.0
莱西市	Laixi	18.9	2.6	1.4	14.9

3－6 全市在岗职工工资总额、平均工资(1978－2011年)

TOTAL WAGE BILL AND AVERAGE WAGE OF EMPLOYED STAFF AND WORKERS(1978－2011)

年 份 Year	工资总额(亿元) Total Wage Bill(100 million yuan)		平均工资(元) Average Wage(yuan)	
	全社会单位 All Units	其中:非私营单位 of which:Non-private Units	全社会单位 All Units	其中:非私营单位 of which:Non-private Units
1978		4.0		584
1979		4.8		662
1980		6.0		782
1981		6.3		778
1982		6.6		785
1983		6.9		809
1984		9.0		1 041
1985		9.6		1 103
1986		11.8		1 311
1987		14.2		1 519
1988		18.0		1 862
1989		20.7		2 120
1990		24.4		2 400
1991		26.4		2 553
1992		31.8		2 970
1993		40.4		3 694
1994		59.5		5 455
1995		68.3		6 164
1996		78.2		6 640
1997		82.5		7 030
1998		87.2		7 518
1999		100.1		8 405
2000		120.4		10 072
2001		135.8		11 426
2002		153.8		12 839
2003	225.6	160.3	12 597	15 335
2004	280.5	193.4	13 932	17 190
2005	359.5	242.8	16 015	20 022
2006	445.6	292.0	18 574	23 457
2007	518.1	338.6	21 419	27 083
2008	578.7	371.9	23 296	30 233
2009	638.1	393.2	25 396	33 258
2010	738.0	446.8	28 549	37 805
2011	877.5	522.0	32 763	43 077

注:2003年以前为职工工资总额、平均工资。

Note:The data before 2003 refer to the total wage bill and average wage of staff and workers.

3-7 全市在岗职工工资总额、平均工资指数(1978-2011年)

INDEXES OF TOTAL WAGE BILL AND AVERAGE WAGE OF EMPLOYED STAFF AND WORKERS(1978-2011)

年份 Year	工资总额指数 Total Wage Bill Indexes		平均工资指数 Average Wage Indexes	
	全社会单位 All Units	其中:非私营单位 of which:Non-private Units	全社会单位 All Units	其中:非私营单位 of which:Non-private Units
1978		120.80		104.66
1979		119.53		113.36
1980		123.95		118.13
1981		106.71		99.49
1982		103.80		100.90
1983		104.14		103.06
1984		130.64		128.68
1985		107.11		105.96
1986		123.22		118.86
1987		120.10		115.87
1988		126.48		122.58
1989		115.29		113.86
1990		117.66		113.21
1991		108.28		106.38
1992		120.26		116.33
1993		127.09		124.38
1994		147.46		147.67
1995		114.76		113.00
1996		114.54		107.72
1997		105.50		105.87
1998		105.64		106.94
1999		114.81		111.80
2000		120.29		119.83
2001		112.77		113.44
2002		113.31		112.37
2003		108.84		110.30
2004	124.34	120.65	110.60	112.10
2005	128.16	125.54	114.95	116.47
2006	123.95	120.26	115.98	117.16
2007	116.27	115.96	115.32	115.46
2008	111.70	109.83	108.76	111.63
2009	110.26	105.73	109.01	110.01
2010	115.66	113.63	112.42	113.67
2011	118.90	116.83	114.76	113.95

注:2004年以前为职工工资总额、平均工资指数。

Note:The data before 2004 refer to the indexes of total wage bill and average wage of staff and workers.

3－8 分行业在岗职工平均工资(2011 年)

AVERAGE WAGE OF EMPLOYED STAFF AND WORKERS BY SECTOR(2011)

行 业	Sector	非私营单位(元) Non-private Units (yuan)	私营单位(元) Private Units (yuan)
总 计	**Total**	**43 077**	**23 950**
农、林、牧、渔业	Farming, Forestry, Animal Husbandry and Fishery	30 437	23 023
采矿业	Mining	27 986	23 819
制造业	Manufacturing	33 280	23 606
电力、煤气及水的生产供应业	Production and Supply of Electricty, Gas and Water	57 652	27 271
建筑业	Construction	42 830	24 880
交通运输、仓储及邮政业	Transport, Storage and Post	48 961	23 252
信息传输、计算机服务和软件业	Information Transmission, Computer Services and Software	76 140	28 448
批发和零售业	Wholesale and Retail Trade	34 774	23 779
住宿和餐饮业	Hotels and Catering Services	30 257	23 962
金融业	Financial Intermediation	133 293	
房地产业	Real Estate	43 394	27 744
租赁和商务服务业	Leasing and Business Services	40 670	24 292
科学研究、技术服务和地质勘察业	Scientific Research, Technical Services and Geologic Prospecting	60 745	27 138
水利、环境和公共设施管理业	Management of Water Conservancy, Environment and Public Facilities	35 244	24 394
居民服务和其他服务业	Services to Households and Other Services	35 197	22 296
教育	Education	58 184	22 657
卫生、社会保障和社会福利业	Health, Social Security and Social Welfare	49 525	22 404
文化、体育和娱乐业	Culture, Sports and Entertainment	53 409	24 626
公共管理和社会组织	Public Management and Social Organization	67 637	

3-9 分市、区在岗职工工资总额(2011年)

TOTAL WAGE BILL OF EMPLOYED STAFF AND WORKERS BY REGION(2011)

单位:亿元(100 million yuan)

市、区名称	Region	合计 Total	国有单位 State-owned Units	集体单位 Collective-owned Units	其他所有制单位 Other Ownership Units
总　计	**Total**	**877.5**	**217.6**	**37.8**	**622.1**
#崂山区	Laoshan District	56.0	11.7	4.8	39.5
黄岛区	Huangdao District	82.2	13.3	1.3	67.6
城阳区	Chengyang District	106.8	13.8	6.7	86.3
即墨市	Jimo	94.3	15.1	4.1	75.1
胶州市	Jiaozhou	82.1	16.0	4.5	61.6
胶南市	Jiaonan	57.0	14.7	3.1	39.2
平度市	Pingdu	48.9	13.9	2.7	32.3
莱西市	Laixi	53.1	10.9	2.8	39.4

3-10 分市、区在岗职工平均工资(2011年)

AVERAGE WAGE OF EMPLOYED STAFF AND WORKERS BY REGION(2011)

单位:元/年(yuan/year)

市、区名称	Region	合计 Total	国有单位 State-owned Units	集体单位 Collective-owned Units	其他所有制单位 Other Ownership Units
总　计	**Total**	**32 763**	**59 340**	**27 217**	**28 561**
#崂山区	Laoshan District	35 483	74 142	31 995	30 450
黄岛区	Huangdao District	36 223	66 288	29 710	31 912
城阳区	Chengyang District	30 094	69 552	24 561	27 998
即墨市	Jimo	31 201	49 586	27 983	28 203
胶州市	Jiaozhou	29 183	53 544	29 188	24 731
胶南市	Jiaonan	27 935	56 938	24 281	22 362
平度市	Pingdu	24 362	47 029	22 378	20 817
莱西市	Laixi	25 738	42 815	25 641	23 202

主要统计指标解释

社会从业人员 指从事一定社会劳动并取得劳动报酬或经营收入的全部劳动力。这一指标反映了一定时期内全部劳动力资源的实际利用情况,是研究我国基本国情国力的重要指标。各单位的从业人员是指在各级国家机关、政党机关、社会团体及企业、事业单位中工作,并取得劳动报酬的全部人员。包括在岗职工、再就业的离退休人员、民办教师以及在各单位工作的外方人员和港、澳、台方人员等。

职工 指在内资(国有、集体、股份合作、联营、有限责任公司、股份有限公司)单位、港澳台商投资单位和外商投资单位及其附属机构工作,并由其支付工资的在岗人员以及不在岗但劳动关系仍在本单位的离岗人员。

在岗职工 指在本单位工作并由单位支付工资的人员,以及有工作岗位,但由于学习、病伤产假等原因暂未工作,仍由单位支付工资的人员。

职工工资总额 指各单位在一定时期内直接支付给本单位全部职工的劳动报酬总额,即在岗职工工资总额和离岗职工生活费两部分。工资总额的计算原则应以直接支付给职工的全部劳动报酬为根据。各单位支付给职工的劳动报酬以及其他根据有关规定支付的工资,不论是计入成本的还是不计入成本的,不论是按国家规定列入计征奖金税项目的,还是未列入计征奖金税项目的,不论是以货币形式支付的还是以实物形式支付的,均包括在工资总额内。

职工平均工资 指各单位一定时期内平均每人所得的工资。它表明一定时期职工工资收入的高低程度,是反映职工工资水平的主要指标。

全社会单位 包括:国有经济、集体经济、联营经济、股份制经济、外商和港、澳、台投资经济、私营经济、其他内资。

非私营单位 包括:国有经济、集体经济、联营经济、股份制经济、外商和港、澳、台投资经济。

Explanatory Notes on Main Statistical Indicators

Social Employment refers to the persons who are engaged in social working and receive remuneration payment or earn business income. This indicator reflects the actual utilization of total labour force during a certain period of time and is often used for the research on China's economic situation and national power. Persons Employed in Various Units refers to all the persons working in government agencies of various levels, political and party organizations, social organizations, enterprises and institutions, and receiving wages or other forms of payment. They include fully-employed staff and workers, re-employed retirees, teachers in schools run by the local people, foreigners and Chinese compatriots from Hong Kong, Macao, and Taiwan working in various units.

Staff and Workers refer to persons working in, and receive payment from units of state ownership, collective ownership, joint ownership, share holding ownership, foreign ownership, and ownership by entrepreneurs from Hong Kong, Macao, and Taiwan, and other types of ownership and their affiliated units.

Employed Staff and Workers refers to persons who work in, and receive wages from their working units, as well as persons who have their work posts, but are temporarily absent from work for reasons of study or on sick, injury or maternal leave and still receive wages from their working units.

Total Wage Bill refer to the total remuneration payment to staff and workers in various units during a certain period of time. The calculation of total wages is based on the total remuneration payment to the staff and workers. Therefore, all the wages and salaries and other payments to staff and workers are included in the total wages regardless of their sources, category, and forms (in kind or cash). (Total wages of staff and workers in this yearbook include only total wages of fully employed staff and workers, excluding the living allowances distributed to those who have left their working units while keeping their labour contract/employment relation unchanged).

Average Wage refers to the average wage in money terms per person during a certain period of time for staff and workers in enterprises, institutions, and government agencies, which reflects the general level of wage income during a certain period of time.

All Units include state ownership, collective ownership, joint ownership, share holding ownership, foreign ownership, ownership by entrepreneurs from Hong Kong, Macao and Taiwan, private ownership, and domestic ownership.

Non-private Units include state ownership, collective ownership, joint ownership, share holding ownership, foreign ownership, and ownership by entrepreneurs from Hong Kong, Macao and Taiwan.

固定资产投资 4

INVESTMENT IN FIXED ASSETS

简要说明

一、本篇资料的主要内容

本篇资料主要反映了全市固定资产投资及房地产开发方面的情况，主要包括固定资产投资的规模、结构、资金来源和房地产开发投资、施竣工及销售情况等方面的资料。

二、本篇资料的来源

本篇资料来源于固定资产投资及房地产开发投资统计年报，由市统计局固定资产投资统计处整理提供。

Brief Introduction

I. Main Content

Data in this chapter show the basic conditions of investment in fixed assets and real estate development of the whole city, mainly including the total investment in fixed assets, the structure of investment, the resources of investment and investment in real estate development, construction, completion, sales, etc.

II. Source of Data

Data in this chapter are based on the annual report on investment in fixed assets and real estate development, and provided by the Division of Investment and Construction Statistics of Qingdao Municipal Bureau of Statistics.

4-1 主要年份固定资产投资
MAJOR YEAR'S INVESTMENT IN FIXED ASSETS

单位:万元(10 000 yuan)

年 份 Year	规模以上固定资产投资总额 Investment in Fixed Assets above Designated Size	按用途分 Grouped by Use 生产性投资 Productive Investment	非生产性投资 Non-Productive Investment	#住宅投资 Investment in Residential Buildings
1949	16	12	4	3
1952	3 097	1 368	1 729	1 007
1957	5 923	3 947	1 976	1 151
1962	2 747	2 049	698	192
1965	5 481	4 155	1 326	375
1970	6 100	5 813	287	154
1975	15 839	13 548	2 381	1 064
1978	29 660	23 499	6 161	3 203
1980	47 499	33 865	13 634	9 335
1985	107 421	60 643	73 424	19 058
1989	262 214	190 950	71 264	26 592
1990	284 576	210 453	74 123	38 898
1991	349 031	256 633	92 398	51 898
1992	583 068	420 748	162 320	83 844
1993	953 274	511 684	441 590	162 419
1994	1 329 716	728 532	601 184	324 094
1995	1 648 281	925 194	723 087	390 206
1996	1 610 562	972 398	638 164	285 412
1997	1 611 902	932 207	679 695	278 951
1998	1 909 711	1 125 821	783 890	316 999
1999	2 205 891	1 246 328	959 563	421 151
2000	2 426 820	1 311 538	1 115 282	470 963
2001	2 934 728	1 487 762	1 446 966	729 181
2002	3 683 623	1 962 588	1 721 035	765 030
2003	5 475 526	3 023 930	2 451 596	1 038 304
2004	9 845 646	6 336 279	3 509 367	1 608 738
2005	14 032 960	9 172 206	4 860 754	1 841 644
2006	14 856 894	9 214 578	5 642 316	2 222 733
2007	16 353 636	10 231 673	6 121 963	2 720 970
2008	20 190 098	12 443 179	7 746 919	3 315 538
2009	24 588 889	13 852 653	10 736 236	3 831 976
2010	30 224 785	16 207 885	14 016 900	5 609 189
2011	35 025 382	18 622 819	16 402 563	5 707 625

注:1. 规模以上固定资产投资数据2003年以前为城镇以上统计范围。
2. 因2004年以来数据有调整,故表中数据不可比。

Note:1. The data of investment above designated size refer to investment above city and town level before 2003.
2. The data since 2004 are not comparable with other data because of the adjustment.

4 -1 续表
continued

单位:万元(10 000 yuan)

年份 Year	按构成分 Grouped by Composition of Funds			按资金来源分 Grouped by Sources of Funds			
	建筑安装工程 Construction and Installation	设备工器具购置 Purchase of Equipment and Instruments	其他费用 Others	国家投资 State Investment	国内贷款 Domestic Loans	利用外资 Foreign Investment	自筹及其他 Self-raising Fund and Others
1949	11	3	2	16			
1952	2 146	870	81	1 512			1 585
1957	2 853	2 773	297	3 816			2 107
1962	1 631	984	132	2 205			542
1965	3 346	1 859	276	4 451			1 030
1970	3 136	2 835	129	2 721			3 379
1975	7 489	8 133	217	9 378	1 362		5 099
1978	19 968	9 124	568	16 828	1 601		11 231
1980	30 993	15 541	965	10 371	12 925	1 420	22 783
1985	64 665	35 100	7 656	17 377	35 888	1 136	53 020
1989	141 821	95 333	17 269	38 747	79 999	25 081	114 939
1990	167 731	91 305	25 540	24 687	91 895	23 688	144 306
1991	196 212	108 929	43 890	22 615	131 676	38 325	156 415
1992	304 060	208 384	70 624	22 660	213 217	89 130	258 061
1993	600 011	225 555	127 708	23 736	208 672	94 469	626 397
1994	842 809	272 126	214 781	26 062	318 334	221 265	764 055
1995	1 020 484	385 934	241 863	25 683	379 198	328 124	915 276
1996	929 735	458 284	222 543	35 639	444 443	310 722	819 758
1997	875 057	485 122	251 723	27 928	297 089	363 789	923 096
1998	1 034 500	574 852	300 359	67 762	491 812	170 709	1 179 428
1999	1 456 473	459 596	289 822	128 603	584 120	145 589	1 347 579
2000	1 476 397	652 640	297 783	75 978	489 697	164 175	1 806 238
2001	1 781 235	744 549	408 944	93 491	620 562	217 526	2 157 787
2002	2 328 492	796 685	558 446	78 775	719 677	411 704	2 831 288
2003	3 544 790	1 133 333	797 403	127 861	989 178	722 644	4 237 643
2004	6 413 046	2 312 139	1 120 461	85 549	1 100 297	1 016 145	8 245 272
2005	8 949 231	3 141 732	1 941 997	136 632	1 250 343	1 850 921	11 540 604
2006	8 818 614	3 668 191	2 370 089	391 315	2 126 523	1 662 897	11 856 506
2007	9 981 666	4 171 878	2 200 092	215 649	2 427 031	1 788 056	13 109 824
2008	11 795 435	5 907 195	2 487 468	322 484	3 309 471	1 951 468	15 855 082
2009	14 911 874	5 869 214	3 807 801	778 090	4 217 265	1 593 287	21 555 685
2010	18 725 922	6 362 880	5 135 983	1 305 737	5 881 886	2 135 736	27 898 294
2011	22 865 421	7 521 441	4 638 520	1 640 702	5 871 709	1 766 278	33 579 182

4-2 主要年份固定资产投资构成(以投资总额为100)
COMPOSITION OF MAJOR YEAR'S INVESTMENT IN FIXED ASSETS(TOTAL INVESTMENT = 100)

年 份 Year	按用途分 Grouped by Use		
	生产性投资 Productive Investment	非生产性投资 Non-Productive Investment	#住宅投资占非生产性比重 Percentage of Investment in Residential Buildings to Non-Productive Investment
1949	75.00	25.00	75.00
1952	44.17	55.83	58.24
1957	66.64	33.36	58.25
1962	74.59	25.41	27.51
1965	75.81	24.19	28.28
1970	95.30	4.70	53.66
1975	84.97	15.03	44.69
1978	79.23	20.77	51.99
1980	71.30	28.70	68.47
1985	56.45	43.55	40.74
1989	72.82	27.18	37.30
1990	73.95	26.05	52.50
1991	73.53	26.47	56.17
1992	72.16	27.84	51.65
1993	53.68	46.32	36.78
1994	54.79	45.21	53.91
1995	56.10	43.90	54.00
1996	60.40	39.60	44.70
1997	57.80	42.20	41.00
1998	59.00	41.00	16.60
1999	56.50	43.50	19.10
2000	54.00	46.00	19.40
2001	50.70	49.30	50.40
2002	53.30	46.70	44.50
2003	55.20	44.80	42.40
2004	64.40	35.60	45.80
2005	65.40	34.60	37.90
2006	62.00	38.00	39.40
2007	62.60	37.40	44.40
2008	61.60	38.40	42.80
2009	56.30	43.70	35.70
2010	53.62	46.38	40.02
2011	53.17	46.83	34.80

4-2 续表

continued

年 份 Year	按构成分 Grouped by Composition of Funds 建筑安装工程 Construction and Installation	设备工器具购置 Purchase of Equipment and Instruction	其他费用 Others	按资金来源分 Grouped by Sources of Funds 国家投资 State Investment	国内贷款 Domestic Loans	利用外资 Foreign Investment	自筹及其他 Self-raising Fund and Others
1949	68.75	18.75	12.5	100			
1952	69.29	28.09	2.62	48.82			51.18
1957	48.17	46.82	5.01	64.43			35.57
1962	59.37	35.82	4.81	80.27			19.73
1965	61.05	33.92	5.03	81.21			18.79
1970	51.41	46.48	2.11	44.61			55.39
1975	47.28	51.35	1.37	59.21	8.60		32.19
1978	67.32	30.76	1.92	56.74	5.40		37.86
1980	65.25	32.72	2.03	21.83	27.21	2.99	47.97
1985	60.20	32.68	7.12	16.18	33.41	1.06	49.35
1989	54.08	36.36	6.59	14.78	30.51	9.56	45.15
1990	58.94	32.08	8.98	8.68	32.29	8.32	50.71
1991	56.22	31.21	12.57	6.48	37.73	10.98	44.81
1992	52.15	35.74	12.11	3.89	36.56	15.29	44.26
1993	62.94	23.66	13.40	2.49	21.89	9.91	65.71
1994	63.38	20.46	16.16	1.96	23.94	16.64	57.46
1995	61.9	23.4	14.7	1.6	23.0	19.9	55.5
1996	57.7	28.5	13.8	2.2	27.6	19.3	50.9
1997	54.3	30.1	15.6	1.7	18.4	22.6	57.3
1998	54.2	20.8	15.7	3.5	25.8	8.9	61.8
1999	66.0	20.8	13.2	5.8	26.5	6.6	61.1
2000	60.8	26.9	12.3	3.1	20.2	6.8	74.4
2001	60.7	25.4	13.9	3.0	20.1	7.0	69.9
2002	63.2	21.6	15.2	1.9	17.8	10.2	70.1
2003	64.7	20.7	14.6	2.1	16.3	11.9	69.7
2004	65.1	23.5	11.4	0.8	10.6	9.7	78.9
2005	63.8	22.4	13.8	0.9	8.5	12.5	78.1
2006	59.4	24.7	15.9	2.4	13.3	10.4	73.9
2007	61.0	25.5	13.5	1.2	13.8	10.2	74.8
2008	58.4	29.3	12.3	1.5	15.4	9.1	74.0
2009	60.6	23.9	15.5	2.8	15.0	5.6	76.6
2010	62.0	21.0	17.0	3.5	15.8	5.7	75.0
2011	65.3	21.5	13.2	3.8	13.7	4.1	78.4

4 -3 按三次产业分规模以上固定资产投资(2011 年)
INVESTMENT IN FIXED ASSETS ABOVE DESIGNATED SIZE BY THREE STRATA OF INDUSTRY(2011)

单位:万元(10 000 yuan)

指　标	Indicator	2011 年
总　计	**Total**	**35 025 382**
第一产业	Primary Industry	422 567
第二产业	Secondary Industry	14 759 651
#工业	Industry	14 001 842
第三产业	Tertiary Industry	19 843 164

4 -4 分市、区固定资产投资额(2011 年)
INVESTMENT IN FIXED ASSETS BY REGION(2011)

单位:万元(10 000 yuan)

市、区名称	Region	规模以上固定资产投资额 Investment in Fixed Assets above Designated Size	#房地产开发 Investment in Real Estate Development
总　计	**Total**	**35 025 382**	**7 827 193**
市　区	Urban Area	15 909 555	6 310 838
#崂山区	Laoshan District	1 263 640	823 491
黄岛区	Huangdao District	4 426 759	918 659
城阳区	Chengyang District	4 360 176	848 620
即墨市	Jimo	4 186 637	344 949
胶州市	Jiaozhou	4 240 128	429 553
胶南市	Jiaonan	4 139 994	436 546
平度市	Pingdu	3 500 340	210 026
莱西市	Laixi	3 048 728	95 281

4-5 规模以上固定资产投资(2011年)

INVESTMENT IN FIXED ASSETS ABOVE DESIGNATED SIZE(2011)

单位:万元(10 000 yuan)

项目	Item	合计 Total	#房地产开发 Investment in Real Estate Development
一、本年施工项目(个)	**Projects Under Construction This Year(unit)**	**4 522**	
#本年新开工(个)	of which:Newly Started(unit)	2 681	
二、本年建成投产项目(个)	**Projects Completed and Put into Use This Year(unit)**	**3 502**	
三、本年完成投资	**Investment Completed This Year**	**35 025 382**	**7 827 193**
1.按构成分	Grouped by Composition		
#建筑工程	Construction Projects	20 640 823	4 663 846
安装工程	Installation Projects	2 224 598	682 153
设备工器具购置	Purchase of Equipment and Instruments	7 521 441	30 787
#用于更新的设备	Equipment Used in Updates	1 204 451	
2.按建设性质分	Grouped by Type of Construction		
#新　建	New Construction	16 833 248	
扩　建	Expansion	2 999 647	
改　建	Reconstruction	6 170 518	
3.按隶属关系分	Grouped by Subordination Relation		
中央单位	Central Units	943 740	237 022
地方单位	Local Units	34 081 642	7 590 171
4.按国民经济行业分	Grouped by Economic Sector		
(1)农、林、牧、渔业	Farming,Forestry,Animal Husbandry and Fishery	422 567	
农　业	Farming	148 138	
林　业	Forestry	34 613	
畜牧业	Animal Husbandry	86 612	
渔　业	Fishery	75 285	
农、林、牧、渔服务业	Farming,Forestry,Animal Husbandry and Fishery Services	77 919	
(2)采矿业	Mining	106 645	
煤炭开采和洗选业	Mining and Washing of Coal		
石油和天然气开采业	Extraction of Petroleum and Natural Gas		
黑色金属矿采选业	Mining of Ferrous Metal Ores	18 000	
有色金属矿采选业	Mining of Non-ferrous Metal Ores	15 513	
非金属矿采选业	Mining and Processing of Nonmetal Ores	73 132	
其他采矿业	Mining of Other Ores		

4－5 续表1
continued

单位:万元(10 000 yuan)

项　　目	Item	合计 Total	#房地产开发 Investment in Real Estate Development
(3)制造业	Manufacturing	13 246 154	
农副食品加工业	Processing of Food from Agricultural Products	1 126 317	
食品制造业	Manufacture of Foods	276 409	
饮料制造业	Manufacture of Beverage	137 323	
烟草加工业	Manufacture of Tobacco		
纺织业	Manufacture of Textile	463 810	
纺织服装、鞋、帽制造业	Manufacture of Textile Wearing Apparel, Footware, and Caps	547 774	
皮革、毛皮、羽毛(绒)及其制品业	Manufacture of Leather, Fur, Feather & Its Products	184 741	
木材加工及木、竹、藤、棕、草制品业	Processing of Timbers, Manufacture of Wood, Bamboo, Rattan, Palm, and Straw Products	163 765	
家具制造业	Manufacture of Furniture	205 145	
造纸及纸制品业	Manufacture of Paper and Paper Products	216 113	
印刷业和记录媒介的复制	Printing, Reproduction of Recording Media	141 301	
文教体育用品制造业	Manufacture of Articles for Culture, Education and Sport Activity	117 777	
石油加工、炼焦及核燃料加工业	Processing of Petroleum, Coking, Processing of Nucleus Fuel	175 950	
化学原料及化学制品制造业	Manufacture of Chemical Raw Material and Chemical Products	523 757	
医药制造业	Manufacture of Medicines	271 534	
化学纤维制造业	Manufacture of Chemical Fiber	28 467	
橡胶制品业	Manufacture of Rubber	388 536	
塑料制品业	Manufacture of Plastic	360 629	
非金属矿物制品业	Manufacture of Non-metallic Mineral Products	787 217	
黑色金属冶炼及压延加工业	Smelting and Pressing of Ferrous Metals	144 409	
有色金属冶炼及压延加工业	Smelting and Pressing of Non-ferrous Metals	83 605	
金属制品业	Manufacture of Metal Products	1 279 525	
通用设备制造业	Manufacture of General Purpose Machinery	1 488 996	
专用设备制造业	Manufacture of Special Purpose Machinery	962 780	
交通运输设备制造业	Manufacture of Transport Equipment	1 659 820	
电气机械及器材制造业	Manufacture of Electrical Machinery & Equipment	852 811	

4 -5 续表 2
continued

单位:万元(10 000 yuan)

项　　目	Item	合计 Total	#房地产开发 Investment in Real Estate Development
通信设备、计算机及其他电子设备制造业	Manufacture of Communication Equipment, Computer and Other Electronic Equipment	295 417	
仪器仪表及文化、办公用机械制造业	Manufacture of Measuring Instrument and Machinery for Cultural Activity & Office Work	98 367	
工艺品及其他制造业	Manufacture of Artwork, Other Manufacture	251 159	
废旧资源和废旧材料回收加工业	Recycling and Disposal of Waste	12 700	
(4)电力、燃气及水的生产和供应业	Production and Supply of Electricity, Gas and Water	649 043	
电力、热力的生产和供应业	Production and Supply of Electric Power and Heat Power	383 950	
燃气生产和供应业	Production and Supply of Gas	105 318	
水的生产和供应业	Production and Supply of Water	159 775	
(5)建筑业	Construction	757 809	
(6)交通运输、仓储及邮政业	Transport, Storage and Post	3 062 975	
铁路运输业	Railway Transport	204 565	
道路运输业	Road Transport	651 676	
城市公共交通业	Urban Public Transport	239 860	
水上运输业	Water Transport	1 430 050	
航空运输业	Air Transport	15 607	
(7)信息传输、计算机服务和软件业	Information Transmission, Computer Services and Software	83 618	
(8)批发和零售业	Wholesale and Retail Trade	1 070 709	
(9)住宿和餐饮业	Hotels and Catering Services	1 293 684	
(10)金融业	Financial Intermediation	55 557	
(11)房地产业	Real Estate	9 747 626	7 827 193

4-5 续表3
continued

单位:万元(10 000 yuan)

项　目	Item	合计 Total	#房地产开发 Investment in Real Estate Development
(12)租赁和商务服务业	Leasing and Business Services	495 682	
(13)科学研究、技术服务和地质勘察业	Scientific Research, Technical Service and Geologic Prospecting	183 305	
(14)水利、环境和公共设施管理业	Management of Water Conservancy, Environment and Public Facilities	1 872 018	
水利管理业	Management of Water Conservancy	95 918	
环境管理业	Environmental Management	361 210	
公共设施管理业	Management of Public Facilities	1 414 890	
(15)居民服务和其他服务业	Services to Households and Other Services	106 973	
居民服务业	Services to Households	86 849	
其他服务业	Other Services	20 124	
(16)教育	Education	237 366	
(17)卫生、社会保障和社会福利业	Health, Social Security and Social Welfare	177 784	
卫生	Health	170 239	
(18)文化、体育和娱乐业	Culture, Sports and Entertainment	702 892	
新闻出版业	Journalism and Publishing Activities		
广播、电视、体育和音像业	Broadcasting, Movies, Televisions and Audiovisual Activities	9 491	
文化艺术业	Cultural and Art Activities	32 714	
体育	Sports Activities	51 220	
娱乐业	Entertainment	609 467	
(19)公共管理和社会组织	Public Management and Social Organization	752 975	
国家机构	Government Agencies	226 365	
群众团体、社会团体和宗教组织	Non-Governmental Institutions, Social Organizations and Religion Organizations	13 890	
基层群众自治组织	Local People Self-government Organization	508 289	
(20)国际组织	International Organization		

4-5 续表 4
continued

单位：万元(10 000 yuan)

项　目	Item	合计 Total	#房地产开发 Investment in Real Estate Development
四、本年新增固定资产	**Newly Increased Fixed Assets This Year**	**23 409 549**	**2 924 611**
(1)农、林、牧、渔业	Farming, Forestry, Animal Husbandry and Fishery	368 462	
(2)采矿业	Mining	85 589	
(3)制造业	Manufacturing	10 376 877	
(4)电力、燃气及水的生产和供应业	Construction	580 633	
(5)建筑业	Production and Supply of Electricty, Gas and Water	459 766	
(6)交通运输、仓储和邮政业	Transport, Storage and Post	1 564 755	
(7)信息传输、计算机服务和软件业	Information Transmission, Computer Services and Software	53 211	
(8)批发和零售业	Wholesale and Retail Trade	875 212	
(9)住宿和餐饮业	Hotels and Catering Services	854 086	
(10)金融业	Financial Intermediation	50 424	
(11)房地产业	Real Estate	4 140 084	2 924 611
(12)租赁和商务服务业	Leasing and Business Services	187 568	
(13)科学研究、技术服务和地质勘察业	Scientific Research, Technical Services and Geologic Prospecting	103 998	
(14)水利、环境和公共设施管理业	Management of Water Conservancy, Environment and Public Facilities	2 449 327	
(15)居民服务和其他服务业	Services to Households and Other Services	101 607	
(16)教育	Education	142 610	
(17)卫生、社会保障和社会福利业	Health, Social Security and Social Welfare	173 436	
(18)文化、体育和娱乐业	Culture, Sports and Entertainment	125 502	
(19)公共管理和社会组织	Public Management and Social Organization	716 402	
(20)国际组织	International Organization		
五、本年资金来源合计	**Total Funds This Year**	**48 074 762**	**17 323 384**
上年末结余资金	Balance of Last Year	5 216 891	4 378 985
本年资金来源小计	Sub-total Funds This Year	42 857 871	12 944 399
国家预算内资金	State Budget	1 646 768	6 066
国内贷款	Domestic Loans	5 871 709	3 216 291
债券	State Treasury Bond	21 000	
利用外资	Foreign Investment	1 766 278	151 704
自筹资金	Self-raising Funds	27 788 869	4 372 865
其他资金来源	Others	5 769 313	5 203 539

4-6 主要年份房地产开发投资
MAJOR YEAR'S INVESTMENT IN REAL ESTATE DEVELOPMENT

单位：万元、万平方米（10 000 yuan，10 000 sq. m）

年 份 Year	房地产开发投资额 Investment in Real Estate Development	房屋施工面积 Floor Space Under Construction	房屋竣工面积 Floor Space Completed	房屋实际销售面积 Floor Space of Buildings Sold	房屋实际销售额 Sale of Buildings
1995	562 861	1 008	240	103	185 384
1996	455 765	748	203	80	125 150
1997	426 570	675	237	113	216 311
1998	438 059	742	259	178	351 805
1999	629 717	900	474	240	430 123
2000	675 142	1 047	352	301	550 401
2001	925 153	1 374	532	406	802 364
2002	1 036 476	1 417	537	427	933 031
2003	1 277 969	1 765	552	469	1 121 885
2004	1 626 965	2 101	635	516	1 530 964
2005	2 238 370	2 363	811	740	2 666 738
2006	2 683 631	2 751	654	719	3 054 907
2007	3 223 547	3 224	641	833	4 333 566
2008	3 805 652	3 773	672	770	3 924 175
2009	4 594 829	4 310	814	1 262	7 036 744
2010	6 024 387	5 058	1 020	1 360	8 952 942
2011	7 827 193	5 693	925	1 026	7 702 379

4 -7 房地产开发投资情况(2011 年)
INVESTMENT IN REAL ESTATE DEVELOPMENT(2011)

单位:万元(10 000 yuan)

指标名称	Indicator	合计 Total	按经济类型分 Grouped by Economic Types		
			国有经济 State-owned	集体经济 Collective-owned	其他经济 Others
本年完成投资额	**Investment Completed This Year**	**7 827 193**	**773 892**	**191 628**	**6 861 673**
1. 住宅	Residential Buildings	5 707 625	557 067	131 024	5 019 534
2. 办公楼	Office Buildings	283 021	32 886	3 200	246 935
3. 商业营业用房	Houses for Business Use	1 006 017	64 860	30 092	911 065
4. 其他	Others	830 530	119 079	27 312	684 139

4 -7 续表(2011 年)
continued

单位:万元(10 000 yuan)

指标名称	Indicator	按资质等级分 Grouped by Qualification Criteria					
		一级 First Grade	二级 Second Grade	三级 Third Grade	四级 Fourth Grade	暂定 Provisional	其他 Others
本年完成投资额	**Investment Completed This Year**	**483 028**	**767 801**	**860 841**	**146 862**	**4 990 085**	**578 576**
1. 住宅	Residential Buildings	380 367	601 232	673 417	103 640	3 479 438	469 531
2. 办公楼	Office Buildings	3 490	12 970	13 443	7 509	237 473	8 136
3. 商业营业用房	Houses for Business Use	22 997	80 576	96 059	27 408	701 298	77 679
4. 其他	Others	76 174	73 023	77 922	8 305	571 876	23 230

4-8 房地产施工、竣工面积及竣工价值(2011 年)
FLOOR SPACE UNDER CONSTRUCTION AND COMPLETED AND COMPLETED VALUE OF REAL ESTATE(2011)

单位:万平方米(10 000 sq. m)

施工、竣工房屋面积及竣工价值	Indicator	施工面积 Floor Space Under Construction	#新开工 Newly Started	竣工面积 Floor Space Completed	竣工房屋价值(万元) Completed Value (10 000 yuan)
房屋建筑面积总计	**Floor Space of Buildings**	**5 693**	**1 813**	**925**	**2 438 708**
住　宅	Residential Buildings	4 004	1 316	672	1 732 773
其中:经济适用房	of which: Economically Affordable Housing	208	40	52	
办公楼	Office Buildings	184	54	21	92 759
商业营业用房	Houses for Business Use	754	219	125	369 093
其　他	Others	751	224	107	244 083

4-9 商品房屋销售情况(2011 年)
BASIC STATISTICS ON SALES OF COMMERCIALIZED BUILDINGS(2011)

单位:万平方米(10 000 sq. m)

商品房屋销售情况	Sales and Rental of Commercialized Buildings	实际销售 Actual Sales	实际销售额(万元) Actual Sales Volume (10 000 yuan)	待售面积 Area for Sale
房屋面积总计	**Floor Space of Buildings**	**1 026**	**7 702 379**	**236**
住　宅	Residential Buildings	916	6 572 014	126
其中:经济适用房	of which: Economically Affordable Housing			
办公楼	Office Buildings	16	186 500	16
商业营业用房	Houses for Business Use	67	800 521	75
其　他	Others	27	143 344	19

主要统计指标解释

固定资产投资 是以货币形式表现的在一定时期内全社会建造和购置固定资产的工作量以及与此有关的费用的总称。该指标是反映固定资产投资规模、结构和发展速度的综合性指标,又是观察工程进度和考核投资效果的重要依据。全社会固定资产投资按登记注册类型可分为国有、集体、个体、联营、股份制、外商、港澳台商、其他等。

城镇固定资产投资 是指城镇各种登记注册类型的企业、事业、行政单位及个体户进行的计划总投资(或实际需要总投资)500万元及500万元以上的建设项目投资、房地产开发投资、城镇和工矿区私人建房投资。县城及以上区域内发生的投资,县及县以上各级政府及主管部门直接领导、管理的建设项目和企业事业单位的投资均为城镇固定资产投资。

固定资产投资 包括城镇、农村500万元以上投资项目。

房地产开发投资 指各种登记注册类型的房地产开发公司、商品房建设公司及其他房地产开发法人单位和附属于其他法人单位实际从事房地产开发或经营活动的单位统一开发的包括统代建、拆迁还建的住宅、厂房、仓库、饭店、宾馆、度假村、写字楼、办公楼等房屋建筑物和配套的服务设施,土地开发工程(如道路、给水、排水、供电、供热、通讯、平整场地等基础设施工程)的投资;不包括单纯的土地交易活动。

固定资产投资的资金来源 根据固定资产投资的资金来源不同,分为国家预算内资金、国内贷款、利用外资、自筹资金和其他资金。

固定资产投资按国民经济行业分 根据建设项目建成投产后的主要产品或主要用途及社会经济活动性质来确定国民经济行业。一般情况下,一个建设项目或一个企业、事业单位只能属于一种国民经济行业。

固定资产投资按建设性质分 建设项目的性质一般分为新建、扩建、改建和技术改造、迁建、恢复。

固定资产投资按构成分 固定资产投资活动按其工作内容和实现方式分为建筑安装工程,设备、工具、器具购置,其他费用三个部分。

施工项目 指报告期内进行过建筑或安装施工活动的项目。凡是报告期内施过工的建设项目,不论施工时间长短,均作为施工项目统计。

新增生产能力(或工程效益) 指通过固定资产投资活动而增加的设计能力(或工程效益),它是以实物形态表现的固定资产投资成果。

新增生产能力(或工程效益)一般有以下几种表现形式:

(1)以建设项目或单项工程建成后的年产能力表示,如煤炭开采,石油开采等。

(2) 以建设项目或单项工程建成后处理原料的能力表示,如选矿工程的年处理矿石能力,城市污水处理能力等。

(3)以新增加的主要设备的数量或容量表示,如新增棉布织机、电机组容量等。

(4)用建筑物容积、容量、面积、长度表示,如新建公路、水库容量、学校学生席位等。

房屋施工面积 是指报告期内施工的全部房屋建筑面积。包括本期新开工的面积和上期开工跨入本期继续施工的房屋面积,以及上期已停缓建在本期恢复施工的房屋面积。本期竣工和本期施工后又停缓建的房屋,其建筑面积仍计入本期房屋施工面积中。

房屋竣工面积 是指在报告期内房屋建筑按照设计要求全部完工,达到住人和使用条件,经验收鉴定合格(或达到竣工验收标准),正式移交使用单位的各栋房屋建筑面积的总和。

新增固定资产 又称交付使用的固定资产,是指已经完成建造和购置过程,并已交付生产或使用单位的固定资产价值。新增固定资产是表示固定资产投资成果的价值量指标,也是反映建设进度、计算固定资产投资效果的必要数据。

固定资产交付使用率 指一定时期新增固定资产与同期完成投资额的比率。该指标是反映固定资产动用速度,衡量建设过程中宏观投资效果的综合指标。由于新增固定资产是较长时期内形成的结果，而投资额则是当年完成的，因此，该指标一般适宜于反映较长时期内固定资产的动用情况。

Explanatory Notes on Main Statistical Indicators

Investment in Fixed Assets referss to the volume of activities in construction and purchases of fixed assets and related fees, expressed in monetary terms. It is a comprehensive indicator which shows the size, structure and growth of the investment in fixed assets, providing basis for observing the progress of construction projects and evaluating results of investment. Total investment in fixed assets in the whole country includes, by type of ownership, the investment by the state-owned units, collective units, individuals, joint ownership units, share-holding units, as well as investment by businessmen from foreign countries and from Hong Kong, Macau and Taiwan, and by other units.

Urban Investment in Fixed Assets refers to construction projects involving a total planned (or required) investment of 5,000,000 yuan and over by urban enterprises and institutions of various types of ownership, by administrative units and by individuals, investment in real estate development, and housing investment by individuals in urban areas and in industrial and mining areas. In other words, all investments that take place in county towns and urban areas, investment in construction projects under the direct leadership and management of government agencies at and above county levels and investments by enterprises and institutions at and above county levels are covered in urban investment in fixed assets.

Investment in Fixed Assets includes construction projects involving an urban or rural investment of 5,000,000 yuan and over.

Investment in Real Estate Development refers to the investment by the real estate development companies, commercial buildings construction companies and other real estate development units of various types of ownership in the construction of house buildings, such as residential buildings, factory buildings, warehouses, hotels, guesthouses, holiday villages, office buildings, and the complementary service facilities and land development projects, such as roads, water supply, water drainage, power supply, heating, telecommunications, land leveling and other projects of infrastructure. It excludes the activities in pure land transactions.

Sources of Funds for Investment in Fixed Assets include fund from state budget, domestic loans, foreign investment, self-raised funds, and others depending on the source of investment.

Investment in Fixed Assets by Sector The classification of construction projects by sector is determined by the major products or the purpose of the projects when they are put into production or use, and by the nature of their social economic activities. In general, one project or one enterprise or institution can only be classified into one sector.

Investment in Fixed Assets by Type of Construction The construction projects in general can be classified, by the type of construction, into new construction, expansion, reconstruction and technical transformation, moving and restoration. However, investment by type of construction is not applied to investment by real-estate development units, investment in rural areas and investment in housing by urban individuals.

Investment in Fixed Assets by Structure By their contents, investment activities are classified into 3 categories, i. e. construction and installation, purchase of equipment and instrument, and other expenses.

Projects under Construction refer to projects with construction and installation activities undertaken in the reference period. All projects that have construction activities undertaken during the reference period are reported as projects under construction irrespective of the length of construction work.

Newly Increased Production Capacity (or Project Efficiency) efers to the increase of designed capacity (or project efficiency) through investment in fixed assets, which reflects the accomplishment of investment in fixed assets in kind.

The newly increased production capacity (project efficiency) are usually expressed in one of the following forms:

(1) output of products, i. e. the output that the project can produce during a given period (usually a year). For instance, the capacity in coal mining is expressed in 10,000 tons/year, the capacity in producing chemical pesticides expressed in ton/year, the capacity in producing tractors in tractor/year, etc. For some chemical products where the effective contents differ significantly, the production capacity is expressed as the designed effective content equivalent, such as in the case of sulphuric acid, soda ash, caustic soda, etc;

(2) raw materials processing capacity, i. e. the volume of raw materials that could be processed by the project per day (or per hour), such as tons of materials processed per day by a sugar refining project or edible vegetable oil project, or tons of urban sewage processed per day;

(3) number or capacity of major equipment increased, such as number of cotton or silk looms increased, wool spindles increased, or capacity (in kilowatts) of power generators increased; and

(4) physical measures (volume, capacity, area, and length) of construction, which is typical for non-industrial projects, for instance, the length of railways put into operation, the length of highways, the capacity of reservoirs, the capacity of warehouses, the floor space of housing projects, capacity for new students in schools or beds in hospitals, areas under new irrigation project, etc.

Floor Space of Buildings under Construction refers to total floor space of all buildings under construction during the reference period, including floor space of newly started buildings during the reference period, floor space of construction extended from the previous period to the current period, and floor space of construction suspended during the previous period and resumed in the current period. Floor space of construction completed in the current period, and floor space of construction started and then suspended in the current period are also included in the floor space under construction of the current year.

Floor Space of Buildings Completed refers to the floor space of all buildings completed in the reference period, which have been appraised and accepted (or come up to the designed standards) and have been transferred to the owners for use.

Newly Increased Fixed Assets refer to the newly increased value of fixed assets, constructed or purchased, that have been transferred to the investors. This is an indicator that demonstrates the results of investment in fixed assets in monetary terms, and an important indicator to reflect the speed of construction and to calculate the efficiency of investment.

Rate of Projects of Fixed Assets Completed and Put into Operation refers to the ratio of the newly increased fixed assets to the total investment made in the same period. This is a comprehensive indicator reflecting the speed of the employment of fixed assets and the investment efficiency at the macro-level. As the newly increase fixed assets is the result of a long period while the investment is completed in the current year, this indicator is expected to be used to reflect the employment of fixed assets over a long period of time.

对外经济贸易 5
FOREIGN TRADE

简要说明

一、本篇资料的主要内容

本篇资料主要反映了全市外经外贸和外资企业的基本情况，主要包括外贸进出口、利用外资、外商投资企业生产经营状况等方面的资料。

二、本篇资料的来源

1、口岸进出口数据来源于市口岸办。

2、进出口、利用外资等资料来源于市商务局。

3、外商投资企业经营情况数据来源于全国外商投资企业联合年检。

本篇资料由市统计局外经贸易统计处整理提供。

Brief Introduction

I. Main Content

Data in this chapter show the basic conditions of foreign trade and foreign-funded enterprises, mainly including imports and exports, utilization of foreign capitals, production and operation condition of foreign-funded enterprises, etc.

II. Source of Data

（1）Data on imports and exports of Qingdao port are provided by Office of Qingdao Port Administration.

（2）Data on imports & exports and utilization of foreign capitals are provided by Qingdao Municipal Commerce Bureau.

（3）Data on production and operation condition of foreign-funded enterprises are based on the National Union Annual Inspection of foreign-funded enterprises.

Data in this chapter are prepared and compiled by the Division of Trade and External Economic Relations Statistics of Qingdao Municipal Bureau of Statistics.

5-1 青岛口岸进出口总额(1985-2011年)

TOTAL VALUE OF IMPORTS AND EXPORTS OF QINGDAO PORT(1985-2011)

单位:万美元(10000 USD)

年份 Year	青岛口岸进出口总额 Total Value of Imports and Exports of Qingdao Port	出口 Exports	进口 Imports
1985	414 448	234 652	179 796
1986	382 840	191 926	190 914
1987	445 090	259 458	185 632
1988	474 516	259 176	215 340
1989	506 152	268 397	237 755
1990	477 117	304 011	173 106
1991	519 273	332 949	186 324
1992	581 495	350 163	231 332
1993	678 013	360 297	317 716
1994	888 574	510 760	377 814
1995	1 307 508	705 245	602 263
1996	1 391 323	760 566	629 757
1997	1 542 284	936 142	609 142
1998	1 463 718	933 392	530 326
1999	1 696 514	1 063 768	632 746
2000	2 520 420	1 423 266	1 097 154
2001	2 797 085	1 636 888	1 160 197
2002	3 128 048	1 889 612	1 238 436
2003	4 088 096	2 366 046	1 722 050
2004	5 677 570	3 197 697	2 479 873
2005	6 932 944	3 959 947	2 972 997
2006	8 019 198	4 495 731	3 523 467
2007	9 257 099	5 263 539	3 993 560
2008	11 558 079	5 953 501	5 604 578
2009	9 049 699	4 694 832	4 354 867
2010	11 912 702	5 988 254	5 924 448
2011	15 095 088	7 294 226	7 800 862

5-2 进出口总额(1988-2011年)

TOTAL VALUE OF IMPORTS AND EXPORTS(1988-2011)

单位:万美元(10000 USD)

年 份 Year	进出口总额(含中央、省驻青公司) Total Value of Imports and Exports (including central and provincial companies)	出口 Exports	进口 Imports	进出口总额(不含中央、省驻青公司) Total Value of Imports and Exports (excluding central and provincial companies)	出口 Exports	进口 Imports
1988				28 097	21 731	6 366
1989				39 327	27 797	11 530
1990				41 649	33 529	8 120
1991				54 624	44 746	9 878
1992				88 600	66 291	22 309
1993	517 643	346 288	171 355	139 048	100 201	38 847
1994	633 213	434 102	199 111	234 978	164 135	70 843
1995	858 560	536 386	322 174	376 372	245 072	131 300
1996	863 521	516 317	347 204	461 950	287 123	174 827
1997	916 269	579 261	377 008	521 967	338 535	183 432
1998	882 042	573 020	309 022	595 826	382 657	213 169
1999	1 009 885	631 072	378 813	775 565	446 260	329 305
2000	1 353 222	826 891	526 331	1 083 133	611 426	471 707
2001	1 541 564	950 160	591 404	1 235 781	712 024	523 757
2002	1 692 567	1 057 141	635 426	1 409 598	850 420	559 178
2003	2 065 912	1 239 199	826 713	1 784 556	1 035 528	749 028
2004	2 698 781	1 578 167	1 120 614	2 433 188	1 391 171	1 042 017
2005	3 302 230	1 942 242	1 359 988	3 045 542	1 758 834	1 286 708
2006	3 911 543	2 346 552	1 564 991	3 655 737	2 164 541	1 491 196
2007	4 572 534	2 831 004	1 741 530	4 360 499	2 677 596	1 682 903
2008	5 363 659	3 262 476	2 101 183	5 215 886	3 146 246	2 069 640
2009	4 485 115	2 729 865	1 755 250	4 398 639	2 692 197	1 706 442
2010	5 705 963	3 391 560	2 314 403	5 614 928	3 335 141	2 279 787
2011	7 215 217	4 061 309	3 153 908	7 126 310	4 005 572	3 120 738

5-3 分国别(地区)外贸出口总额(含中央、省驻青公司)

TOTLA VALUE OF EXPORTS BY COUNTRIES OR REGIONS
(INCLUDING CENTRAL AND PROVINCIAL COMPANIES)

单位:万美元(10000 USD)

国别(地区)	Country(Region)	2011	2010	2011年比2010年±% 2011/2010(±%)
总　计	**Total**	**4 061 309**	**3 391 560**	**19.7**
亚洲	Asia	1 753 142	1 437 002	22.0
香港	Hong Kong	133 258	115 675	15.2
日本	Japan	624 570	522 216	19.6
韩国	Korea	403 167	352 419	14.4
台湾	Taiwan	58 696	40 648	44.4
非洲	Africa	194 246	166 735	16.5
南非	South Africa	30 690	23 865	28.6
欧洲	Europe	912 546	740 703	23.2
欧盟	EU	812 701	663 971	22.4
南美洲	South America	295 762	233 251	26.8
北美洲	North America	820 259	746 369	9.9
美国	United States	736 447	665 264	10.7
大洋洲	Oceanica	84 844	67 230	26.2
澳大利亚	Australia	72 464	56 924	27.3

5-4 分国别(地区)外贸出口总额(不含中央、省驻青公司)

TOTLA VALUE OF EXPORTS BY COUNTRIES OR REGIONS
(EXCLUDING CENTRAL AND PROVINCIAL COMPANIES)

单位:万美元(10000 USD)

国别(地区)	Country(Region)	2011	2010	2011年比2010年±% 2011/2010(±%)
总　计	**Total**	**4 005 572**	**3 324 661**	**20.5**
亚洲	Asia	1 732 346	1 415 315	22.4
香港	Hong Kong	132 809	114 986	15.5
日本	Japan	617 597	514 236	20.1
韩国	Korea	400 679	348 417	15.0
台湾	Taiwan	58 555	40 551	44.4
非洲	Africa	191 415	160 718	19.1
南非	South Africa	30 396	23 274	30.6
欧洲	Europe	899 704	722 654	24.5
欧盟	EU	802 739	646 849	24.1
南美洲	South America	291 482	228 793	27.4
北美洲	North America	806 046	730 776	10.3
美国	United States	724 770	652 358	11.1
大洋洲	Oceanica	84 148	66 154	27.2
澳大利亚	Australia	71 919	56 187	28.0

5-5 外贸出口商品分类(不含中央、省驻青公司)

EXPORT COMMODITIES BY CATEGORY(EXCLUDING CENTRAL AND PROVINCIAL COMPANIES)

单位:万美元(10000 USD)

项　目	Item	2011	2010	2011年比2010年±% 2011/2010(±%)
合　计	**Total**	**4 005 572**	**3 324 661**	**20.5**
按企业性质划分	By Enterprises Nature			
国有企业	State-owned Enterprises	437 893	383 319	14.2
外商投资企业	Foreign Funded Enterprises	1 933 109	1 677 959	15.2
其他企业	Other Enterprises	1 634 570	1 263 383	29.4
按贸易方式划分	By Customs Regime			
一般贸易	Ordinary Trade	2 006 116	1 579 481	27.0
加工贸易	Processing Trade	1 805 399	1 560 759	15.7
其他贸易	Others	194 057	184 421	5.2
按大类商品划分	By Category of Commodities			
纺织服装	Textile Garments	770 462	645 974	19.3
农产品	Agricultural Products	497 816	385 729	29.1
机电产品	Mechanical and Electrical Products	1 514 806	1 294 530	17.0
高新技术产品	High-tech Products	370 028	318 825	16.1

5-6 主要出口商品总值(不含中央、省驻青公司)

TOTAL VALUE OF MAJOR EXPORT COMMODITIES(EXCLUDING CENTRAL AND PROVINCIAL COMPANIES)

单位:万美元(10000 USD)

商品名称	Name	2011	2010	2011年比2010年±% 2011/2010(±%)
服装	Garments	512 872	424 563	20.8
运输工具	Transport Tools	439 791	310 806	41.5
机械设备	Machinery and Equipment	438 084	351 029	24.8
电器及电子类产品	Electric Appliance and Electronic Products	366 201	385 069	-4.9
纺织品	Textile Products	257 590	221 488	16.3
计算机与通信技术	Computer and Communication Technology	233 827	277 375	-15.7
金属制品	Metal Products	182 836	152 873	19.6
轮胎	Tyre	168 697	115 230	46.4
水海产品	Aquatic and Seawater Products	152 745	120 083	27.2
鞋类	Shoes	101 681	92 019	10.5
蔬菜	Vegetables	93 718	80 514	16.4
钢材	Rolled Steel	69 151	52 268	32.3
箱包	Luggage and Bags	67 164	62 536	7.4
电话机	Telephone Sets	66 788	89 408	-25.3
家具及其零件	Furniture	66 764	65 583	1.8
汽车零件	Parts of Motor Vehicles	50 400	39 905	26.3
塑料制品	Plastic Articles	40 078	28 304	41.6
游戏机	Game Console	25 846	40 638	-36.4
空调	Air Conditioner	21 038	18 818	11.8
铁合金	Ferroalloy	8 196	16 591	-50.6

5-7 利用外资情况(1990-2011年)
UTILIZATION OF FOREIGN CAPITAL(1990-2011)

项　目	Item	单位	Unit	1990	1995
批准企业(项目)个数	**Number of Enterprises (Projects) Approved**	**个**	**unit**	**167**	**1 148**
一、外商直接投资	Foreign Direct Investments	个	unit	64	718
中外合资企业	Sino-foreign Joint Ventures	个	unit	40	260
中外合作企业	Sino-foreign Cooperative Enterprises	个	unit	7	45
外商独资企业	Foreign-owned Enterprises	个	unit	17	412
其它	Others	个	unit		1
二、外商其他投资	Other Foreign Investments	个	unit	103	430
合同外资金额	**Total Amount of Contracted Foreign Investment**	**万美元**	**10000 USD**	**8 137**	**165 402**
一、外商直接投资	Foreign Direct Investments	万美元	10000 USD	6 900	1 467 343
中外合资企业	Sino-foreign Joint Ventures	万美元	10000 USD	3 265	52 118
中外合作企业	Sino-foreign Cooperative Enterprises	万美元	10000 USD	346	14 774
外商独资企业	Foreign-owned Enterprises	万美元	10000 USD	3 289	79 842
其它	Others	万美元	10000 USD		
二、外商其他投资	Other Foreign Investments	万美元	10000 USD	1 237	18 668
实际利用外资金额	**Total Amount of Foreign Investment Actually Utilized**	**万美元**	**10000 USD**	**7 770**	**86 573**
一、外商直接投资	Foreign Direct Investments	万美元	10000 USD	4 839	70 310
中外合资企业	Sino-foreign Joint Ventures	万美元	10000 USD	4 161	22 640
中外合作企业	Sino-foreign Cooperative Enterprises	万美元	10000 USD	19	2 671
外商独资企业	Foreign-owned Enterprises	万美元	10000 USD	659	44 999
其它	Others	万美元	10000 USD		
二、外商其他投资	Other Foreign Investments	万美元	10000 USD	2 931	16 263

单位:万美元(10000 USD)

2000	2005	2006	2007	2008	2009	2010	2011
1 132	**2 530**	**1 397**	**1 068**	**640**	**647**	**731**	**707**
1 128	2 530	1 397	1 068	640	647	731	707
303	274	267	165	99	99	153	158
57	18	13	11	4	2	4	4
76	2 236	1 117	892	537	545	574	544
1	2				1		1
4							
269 081	**954 486**	**311 697**	**382 500**	**304 505**	**271 504**	**475 723**	**528 501**
266 221	954 486	311 697	382 500	304 505	271 504	475 723	528 501
69 889	112 777	31 368	51 821	81 796	61 734	124 148	142 535
26 835	17 588	6 883	13 878	367	4 531	9 179	15 173
169 370	813 485	273 446	316 187	221 759	204 187	341 977	369 425
127	10 636		614	583	1 052	419	1 368
2 860							
128 171	**365 625**	**365 815**	**380 652**	**264 295**	**186 397**	**284 281**	**363 350**
126 132	365 625	365 815	380 652	264 295	186 397	284 281	363 350
39 224	77 636	49 240	46 370	43 810	46 856	84 920	100 699
3 886	5 654	7 123	15 490	2 945	3 971	3 567	2 759
82 992	280 130	309 452	318 578	217 540	135 026	194 500	255 763
30	2 205		214		544	1 294	4 129
2 039							

5-8 外商直接投资项目数和投资额(2011 年)

NUMBER OF PROJECTS AND TOTAL AMOUNT OF FOREIGN DIRECT INVESTMENT(2011)

项　目	Item	批准企业项目数（个）Number of Projects Approved (unit)	合同外资金额（万美元）Total Amount of Contracted Foreign Investment(10000 USD)	实际利用外资金额(万美元) Total Amount of Foreign Investment Actually Utilized(10000 USD)
外商直接投资	**Foreign Direct Investments**	**707**	**528 501**	**363 350**
一、按投资方式分	**Grouped by Investment Form**			
中外合资企业	Sino-foreign Joint Ventures	158	142 535	100 699
中外合作企业	Sino-foreign Cooperative Enterprises	4	15 173	2 759
外商独资企业	Foreign-owned Enterprises	544	369 425	255 763
二、按行业分	**Grouped by Sector**			
#农、林、牧、渔业	Farming, Forestry, Animal Husbandry and Fishery	26	18 173	12 656
制造业	Manufacturing	313	227 776	140 767
电力、燃气及水的生产和供应业	Production and Supply of Electricity, Gas and Water	4	11 094	4 671
建筑业	Construction	11	14 960	9 944
交通运输、仓储和邮政业	Transport, Storage and Post	14	12 044	17 556
批发和零售业	Wholesale and Retail Trades	221	75 536	29 646
住宿和餐饮业	Hotels and Catering Services	10	1 609	1 944
房地产业	Real Estate	14	114 192	121 294
租赁和商务服务业	Leasing and Business Services	58	18 266	11 267
三、按主要国别(地区)分	**Grouped by Countries(Regions)**			
#韩国	Korea	217	42 142	38 828
香港	Hong Kong	242	340 299	209 370
日本	Japan	61	26 037	19 657
美国	United States	28	20 190	6 078
台湾省	Taiwan	36	29 964	10 318
英属维尔京群岛	Virgin Islands	8	19 201	19 432
新加坡	Singapore	18	10 527	14 738

5-9 外商投资企业生产经营状况(2011 年)
PRODUCTION AND OPERATION CONDITION OF FOREIGN-FUNDED ENTERPRISES(2011)

项目	Item	单位	Unit	总计 Total	中外合资企业 Sino-foreign Joint Ventures	中外合作企业 Sino-foreign Cooperative Enterprises	外商独资企业 Foreign-owned Enterprises
实有企业数	Number of Enterprises	个	unit	6 901	1 067	89	4 245
#亏损企业	of which: Loss-making Enterprises	个	unit	3 956	509	51	2 614
主营业务收入	Revenue from Principal Business	万元	10000 yuan	30 414 617	8 240 702	372 679	11 013 487
从业人员	Employment	人	person	661 334	122 921	10 943	389 446
#外籍人员	of which: Foreign Employees	人	person	8 859	563	40	7 491
企业资产总计	Total Assets	万元	10000 yuan	37 452 033	11 225 335	673 028	11 071 773
#流动资产合计	of which: Total Current Assets	万元	10000 yuan	25 165 079	7 700 114	470 200	6 665 278
固定资产合计	Total Fixed Assets	万元	10000 yuan	12 286 956	3 525 221	202 829	4 406 497
负债合计	Total Liabilities	万元	10000 yuan	22 558 820	7 685 115	462 985	5 889 619
所有者权益	Owners' Equity	万元	10000 yuan	14 744 197	3 521 654	207 722	5 137 395
费用总额	Total Expenses	万元	10000 yuan	3 691 976	821 802	52 213	1 410 080
利润总额	Total Profits	万元	10000 yuan	1 282 182	591 645	12 434	164 961
税金总额	Total Taxes	万元	10000 yuan	1 593 184	548 391	11 764	488 639
R&D 研发经费支出	Expenditure for R&D	万元	10000 yuan	83 823	28 373	1 242	15 012

5-9 续表
continued

项　目	Item	单位	Unit
实有企业数	Number of Enterprises	个	unit
#亏损企业	of which: Loss-making Enterprises	个	unit
主营业务收入	Revenue from Principal Business	万元	10000 yuan
从业人员	Employment	人	person
#外籍人员	of which: Foreign Employees	人	person
企业资产总计	Total Assets	万元	10000 yuan
#流动资产合计	of which: Total Current Assets	万元	10000 yuan
固定资产合计	Total Fixed Assets	万元	10000 yuan
负债合计	Total Liabilities	万元	10000 yuan
所有者权益	Owners' Equity	万元	10000 yuan
费用总额	Total Expenses	万元	10000 yuan
利润总额	Total Profits	万元	10000 yuan
税金总额	Total Taxes	万元	10000 yuan
R&D 研发经费支出	Expenditure for R&D	万元	10000 yuan

港澳台与大陆合资经营企业 Hong Kong, Macao and Taiwan and Mainland Joint Ventures	港澳台与大陆合作经营企业 Hong Kong, Macao and Taiwan and Mainland Cooperative Enterprises	港澳台独资企业 Hong Kong, Macao and Taiwan Funded Enterprises	中外股份制 Sino-foreign Stock Enterprises
579	48	862	11
300	27	452	3
5 103 705	1 519 033	2 766 396	1 398 615
67 034	5 160	57 139	8 691
132	5	605	23
6 993 207	1 119 403	4 707 831	1 661 456
5 387 105	850 242	3 221 042	871 100
1 606 105	269 162	1 486 786	790 357
4 716 214	768 325	2 448 539	588 024
2 214 672	349 451	2 239 872	1 073 433
705 303	47 080	358 544	296 953
220 137	64 113	96 385	132 506
254 529	36 548	122 487	130 827
34 389		2 153	2 655

5－10 分行业外商投资企业生产经营状况（2011 年）
PRODUCTION AND OPERATION CONDITION OF FOREIGN-FUNDED ENTERPRISES BY SECTOR(2011)

行　业	Sector
农、林、牧、渔业	Farming, Forestry, Animal Husbandry and Fishery
其中：农业	of which: Farming
采矿业	Mining
制造业	Manufacturing
其中：农副食品加工业	Processing of Food from Agricultural Products
食品制造业	Manufacture of Foods
饮料制造业	Manufacture of Beverage
纺织业	Manufacture of Textile
纺织服装、鞋、帽制造业	Manufacture of Textile Wearing Apparel, Footware, and Caps
皮革、皮衣、羽毛（绒）及其制造品业	Manufacture of Leather, Fur, Feather & Its Products
家具制造业	Manufacture of Furniture
造纸及纸制品业	Manufacture of Paper and Paper Products
文教体育用品制造业	Manufacture of Articles for Culture, Education and Sport Activity
化学原料及化学制品制造业	Manufacture of Chemical Raw Material and Chemical Products
医药制造业	Manufacture of Medicines
橡胶制品业	Manufacture of Rubber
塑料制品业	Manufacture of Plastic
黑色金属冶炼及压延加工业	Smelting and Pressing of Ferrous Metals
有色金属冶炼及压延加工业	Smelting and Pressing of Non-ferrous Metals
金属制品业	Manufacture of Metal Products
通用设备制造业	Manufacture of General Purpose Machinery
专业设备制造业	Manufacture of Special Purpose Machinery
交通运输设备制造业	Manufacture of Transport Equipment
电气机械及器材制造业	Manufacture of Electrical Machinery & Equipment
通信设备、计算机及其他电子设备	Manufacture of Communication Equipment, Computer and Other Electronic Equipment
工艺品及其他制造业	Manufacture of Artwork and Other Manufacture
电力、燃气及水的生产和供应业	Production and Supply of Electricity, Gas and Water
建筑业	Construction
交通运输、仓储和邮政业	Transport, Storage and Post
信息传输、计算服务和软件业	Information Transmission, Computer Services and Software
批发与零售业	Wholesale and Retail Trades
其中：批发业	Wholesale Trade
零售业	Retail Trade
住宿和餐饮业	Hotels and Catering Services
其中：住宿业	Hotels
餐饮业	Catering Service
房地产业	Real Estate
租赁和商务服务	Leasing and Business Services
科学研究、技术服务与地质勘查业	Scientific Research, Technical Service and Geologic Prospecting
水利、环境和公共设施管理业	Management of Water Conservancy, Environment and Public Facilities
居民服务和其他服务业	Services to Households and Other Services
教育	Education
卫生、社会保障和社会福利业	Health, Social Security and Social Welfare
文化、体育和娱乐业	Culture, Sports and Entertainment

主营业务收入(万元) Revenue from Principal Business (10000 yuan)	税金总额 (万元) Total Taxes (10000 yuan)	利润总额 (万元) Total Profits (10000 yuan)	从业人员 (人) Employment (person)
39 674	408	-1 713	2 447
10 167	69	191	934
13 409	1 276	2 421	404
24 714 657	1 238 903	995 819	593 152
1 958 326	33 173	33 029	38 690
970 254	57 294	6 270	19 154
1 266 127	131 785	108 439	5 618
1 001 081	25 460	9 073	32 539
1 616 884	35 417	-5 693	129 224
408 068	11 565	-1 593	38 152
196 153	4 285	-938	10 868
251 308	9 390	3 310	5 304
356 399	8 238	1 303	22 165
1 910 872	218 316	62 123	13 635
110 894	6 627	6 305	3 029
471 375	23 001	16 467	12 340
520 909	21 368	20 314	17 268
905 251	43 944	6 306	2 747
915 020	14 607	-4 207	3 157
1 716 453	42 188	88 816	33 207
1 522 517	110 961	130 331	23 185
781 581	54 228	34 691	14 151
1 609 336	130 411	181 475	25 849
1 758 953	60 494	142 327	20 492
2 908 460	115 451	92 133	62 612
709 739	24 895	12 512	40 580
117 799	6 423	14 799	1 534
16 062	1 867	1 516	479
785 118	51 093	127 654	10 030
31 063	5 890	12 759	1 760
3 003 734	118 417	-24 774	24 843
2 433 824	86 890	-29 950	18 409
569 909	31 527	5 176	6 434
230 259	24 300	14 835	15 346
37 149	6 238	-5 656	3 557
193 110	18 063	20 491	11 789
1 239 517	134 718	146 942	3 953
112 956	1 994	-10 652	2 071
26 849	2 620	2 167	1 279
11 001	205	-1 227	384
66 312	4 245	3 021	3 040
3 510	293	-553	157
144	5	-10	7
1 823	388	-929	386

5-11 分国别(地区)外商投资企业生产经营状况(2011 年)

PRODUCTION AND OPERATION CONDITION OF FOREIGN-FUNDED ENTERPRISES BY COUNTRIES(REGIONS)(2011)

国别(地区)	Country(Region)	主营业务收入(万元) Revenue from Principal Business (10000 yuan)	税金总额(万元) Total Taxes (10000 yuan)	利润总额(万元) Total Profits (10000 yuan)	从业人员(人) Employment (person)
按投资国别、地区分组	**Grouped by Countries and Regions**				
1、亚洲	Asia	23 071 785	1 136 831	676 885	522 468
#香港	Hong Kong	10 033 659	512 801	479 304	120 028
澳门	Macao	9 002	275	-1 544	253
台湾	Taiwan	503 051	20 426	7 653	13 905
印度尼西亚	Indonesia	19 772	235	-494	155
日本	Japan	3 315 757	135 192	98 514	92 116
马来西亚	Malaysia	70 657	520	-929	1 077
菲律宾	Philippines	37 451	610	2 334	432
新加坡	Singapore	1 920 779	189 102	27 097	8 093
韩国	Korea	6 226 420	260 903	-25 288	275 310
泰国	Thailand	50 839	578	-1 349	793
2、非洲	Africa	617 790	83 325	229 505	8 759
3、欧洲	Europe	2 247 524	155 100	183 333	46 746
#比利时	Belgium	93	10	-78	32
丹麦	Denmark	51 136	15 385	22 783	1 345
英国	United Kingdom	370 814	16 466	18 840	9 583
德国	Germany	350 541	36 760	62 458	6 073
法国	France	218 308	9 492	14 500	3 585
爱尔兰	Ireland	11	3	-31	11
意大利	Italy	233 874	11 243	16 046	5 112
卢森堡	Luxemburg	48 024	2 162	409	239
荷兰	Netherlands	420 150	30 167	21 839	11 295
希腊	Greece	271		-69	13
葡萄牙	Portugal	15 527	1 345	-3 963	112
西班牙	Spain	13 786	614	-789	475
芬兰	Finland			-12	1
瑞士	Switzerland	184 151	13 052	15 163	1 679
4、拉丁美洲	Latin America	2 110 011	101 397	111 734	25 241
#英属维尔京群岛	Virgin Islands(E)	1 905 062	85 031	77 520	22 795
5、北美洲	North America	1 874 533	91 563	54 697	50 132
#加拿大	Canada	164 434	4 092	2 357	5 530
美国	United States	1 499 137	85 441	52 737	37 865
6、大洋洲	Oceanica	489 747	24 822	25 713	7 927
#澳大利亚	Australia	187 201	11 842	7 616	3 799
新西兰	New Zealand	138 671	935	8 231	343

5－12 分市、区外商投资企业生产经营状况(2011年)

PRODUCTION AND OPERATION CONDITION OF FOREIGN-FUNDED ENTERPRISES BY REGION(2011)

单位:万元(10 000 yuan)

市、区名称	Region	资产总计 Total Assets	#流动资产合计 Total Current Assets	固定资产合计 Total Fixed Assets
合　计	**Total**	**37 452 033**	**25 165 079**	**12 286 956**
市　区	Urban Area	26 564 741	17 914 266	8 650 473
#崂山区	Laoshan District	4 792 007	3 842 487	949 521
黄岛区	Huangdao District	8 114 404	4 376 175	3 738 229
城阳区	Chengyang District	6 315 415	4 724 576	1 590 838
即墨市	Jimo	3 098 615	2 148 690	949 926
胶州市	Jiaozhou	2 754 777	1 896 421	858 358
胶南市	Jiaonan	2 062 027	1 385 031	676 995
平度市	Pingdu	1 490 693	960 955	529 739
莱西市	Laixi	1 219 936	662 694	557 243
高新区	High-tech Zone	261 244	197 023	64 222

5－12 续表1

continued

单位:万元(10 000 yuan)

市、区名称	Region	负债合计 Total Liabilities	流动负债合计 Total Current Liabilities	长期负债合计 Total Long-term Liabilities	所有者权益合计 Total Owners' Equity
合　计	**Total**	**22 558 820**	**19 885 475**	**2 673 345**	**14 744 197**
市　区	Urban Area	16 352 836	14 203 457	2 149 378	10 127 498
#崂山区	Laoshan District	3 356 545	2 911 073	445 472	1 392 368
黄岛区	Huangdao District	4 623 874	4 148 557	475 317	3 464 866
城阳区	Chengyang District	4 131 634	3 738 491	393 143	2 176 250
即墨市	Jimo	1 701 325	1 595 105	106 221	1 391 438
胶州市	Jiaozhou	1 625 332	1 503 529	121 803	1 100 438
胶南市	Jiaonan	1 267 441	1 109 020	158 420	792 225
平度市	Pingdu	714 029	679 123	34 906	777 166
莱西市	Laixi	688 402	610 481	77 921	503 645
高新区	High-tech Zone	209 457	184 761	24 696	51 788

5－12 续表2
continued

单位:万元(10 000 yuan)

市、区名称	Region	主营业务收入 Revenue from Principal Business	主营业务成本 Cost of Principal Business	费用总额 Total Expenses	利润总额 Total Profits
合　计	**Total**	**30 414 617**	**25 515 536**	**3 691 976**	**1 282 182**
市　区	Urban Area	21 557 863	17 865 504	2 651 928	1 089 748
#崂山区	Laoshan District	4 380 127	3 437 340	649 260	260 851
黄岛区	Huangdao District	6 469 664	5 530 817	619 431	388 961
城阳区	Chengyang District	5 268 697	4 456 095	570 807	197 183
即墨市	Jimo	2 410 585	2 036 915	246 086	68 498
胶州市	Jiaozhou	2 416 876	2 103 764	242 517	81 514
胶南市	Jiaonan	1 389 594	1 163 540	228 944	2 361
平度市	Pingdu	1 376 125	1 238 214	162 397	22 382
莱西市	Laixi	1 083 317	966 428	125 079	14 186
高新区	High-tech Zone	180 257	141 171	35 026	3 493

5－12 续表3
continued

单位:万元(10 000 yuan)

市、区名称	Region	税金总额 Total Taxes	从业人员(人) Employment(person)	研发经费 Expenditure for R&D	单位数量(个) Number of Company (unit)
合　计	**Total**	**1 593 184**	**661 334**	**83 823**	**6 901**
市　区	Urban Area	1 237 110	342 957	69 091	4 131
#崂山区	Laoshan District	256 119	37 852	42 734	387
黄岛区	Huangdao District	423 026	80 825	17 679	831
城阳区	Chengyang District	243 409	161 361	7 487	1 897
即墨市	Jimo	81 891	100 734	1 326	799
胶州市	Jiaozhou	105 567	88 157	2 610	736
胶南市	Jiaonan	65 226	42 625	1 707	382
平度市	Pingdu	59 389	41 579	8 040	494
莱西市	Laixi	33 986	44 537	1 048	346
高新区	High-tech Zone	10 015	745		13

主要统计指标解释

批准企业(项目)个数 是指外商直接投资中批准设立的外商投资企业个数、批准的合作开发项目个数。

合同外资金额 是指批准外商投资企业的合同、章程中规定的外国投资者认缴的出资额和企业投资总额内的应由外方投资者以自己的境外自有资金直接向企业提供的贷款。包括新批准企业合同外资和原有企业的增资减资,增资减资不对企业(项目)个数进行调整。

实际使用外资金额 是指合同外资金额的实际执行金额。

外商直接投资 是指外国企业和经济组织或个人(包括华侨、港澳台胞以及我国在境外注册的企业)按我国有关政策、法规,用现汇、实物、技术等在我国境内开办外商独资企业、与我国境内的企业或经济组织共同举办中外合资经营企业、合作经营企业或合作开发资源的投资(包括外商投资收益的再投资)以及经政府有关部门批准的项目投资总额内,企业从境外借入的资金。

外商其它投资 是指除外商直接投资以外其他方式吸收的外资。

进出口总额 指实际进出我国国境的货物总金额。包括对外贸易实际进出口货物,来料加工装配进出口货物,国家间、联合国及国际组织无偿援助物资和赠送品,华侨、港澳台同胞和外籍华人捐赠品,租赁期满归承租人所有的租赁货物,进料加工进出口货物,边境地方贸易及边境地区小额贸易进出口货物(边民互市贸易除外),中外合资企业、中外合作经营企业、外商独资经营企业进出口货物和公用物品,到、离岸价格在规定限额以上的进出口货样和广告品(无商业价值、无使用价值和免费提供出口的除外),从保税仓库提取在中国境内销售的进口货物,以及其他进出口货物。

Explanatory Notes on Main Statistical Indicators

Enterprises(Projects) Permitted refers to number of foreign invested enterprises and developed projects under cooperation through the permission.

Contracted Foreign Investment refers to expenditure promised by the foreign investor and loan stemed from broad innate fund of the foreign investor, according to the contract and regulation approved of enterprise invested by foreigner.

Actual Utilization of Foreign Investment refers to actual usage of contracted foreign investment, including cash, investment in kind and incorporeal agreed by the both sides as part of the investment, such as services and technology.

Foreign Direct Investment refers to the investments by foreign enterprises and economic organizations or individuals(including overseas Chinese, compatriots from Hong dong, Macao and Taiwan, and Chinese enterprises registered abroad), following the relevant policies and laws of China, for the establishment of ventures and cooperative enterprises or cooperative exploration of resources with enterprises or economic organizations in China, lt includes the reinvestment of thc foreign`entrepreneurs with the profits gained from the investment and the funds that enterprises borrow from aboard in the total investment of projects which are approved by the relevant department of the government.

Other Investment by Foreign Entrepreneurs refers to all forms of utilization of foreign capitals other than foreign direct investment.

Total Imports and Exports refers to the real value of commodities imported into and exported from the boundary of China. They include the actual imports and exports through foreign trade, imported and exported goods under the processing and assembling trades and materials, supplies and gifts as aid given gratis between governments and by the United Nations and other international organizations, and contributions donated by overseas Chinese, compatriots in Hong Kong and Macao and Chinese with foreign citizenship, leasing commodities owned by tenant at the expiration of leasing period, the imported and exported commodities processed with imported materials, commodities trading in border areas (excluding mutual exchange goods), the imported and exported commodities and articles for public use of the Sino-foreign joint ventures, cooperative enterprises and ventures exclusively with foreign own investment. Also included are import or export of samples and advertising goods for whose CIF or FOB value are beyond the permitted ceiling (excluding goods of no trading or use value and free commodities for export), imported goods sold in China from bonded warehouses and other imported or exported goods.

能源消耗 6

CONSUMPTION OF ENERGY

简要说明

一、本篇资料的主要内容

本篇资料主要反映了全市规模以上工业主要能源消费与库存情况，主要包括规模以上工业主要能源消费与库存、规模以上工业主要能源分行业消费量、重点耗能工业企业能源加工转换、规模以上工业主要能源工业消费量等方面的资料。

二、本篇资料的来源

本篇资料来源于规模以上工业能源统计年报，由市统计局工业（能源）统计处整理提供。

Brief Introduction

I. Main Content

Data in this chapter show the consumption and stock of major energy of industry above designated size, including consumption and stock of major energy of industry above designated size, major energy consumption of industry above designated size grouped by sector, energy conversion of major energy-consuming industrial enterprises and major energy consumption of industry above designated size, etc.

II. Source of Data

Data in this chapter are based on the annual report of energy consumed by industrial enterprises above designated size. The data are provided by the Division of Industry (Energy) Statistics of Qingdao Municipal Bureau of Statistics.

6－1 规模以上工业主要能源消费与库存(2011 年)

CONSUMPTION AND STOCK OF MAJOR ENERGY OF INDUSTRY ABOVE DESIGNATED SIZE(2011)

名称	Name	计算单位	Unit	年初库存 Stock at Year-beginning	本年消费 Consumption in the Year	#工业 Industry	#非工业 Non-industry	年末库存 Stock at Year-end
原煤	Raw Coal	吨	ton	1 499 494.21	16 604 993.84	16 543 544.98	61 448.86	2 007 056.50
焦炭	Coke	吨	ton	54 954.90	1 442 806.47	1 442 728.90	77.57	66 170.15
焦炉煤气	Coking Gas	万立方米	10 000 cu. m		6 508.38	6 498.01	10.38	
高炉煤气	Blast Furnace Gas	万立方米	10 000 cu. m		12 497.16	12 497.16		
原油	Crude Oil	吨	ton	489 463.97	12 900 419.32	12 900 386.92	32.40	450 367.04
汽油	Petrol	吨	ton	623.64	202 431.86	168 113.53	34 318.34	738.27
煤油	Kerosene	吨	ton	30.59	3 264.34	2 350.14	914.21	1.00
柴油	Diesel Oil	吨	ton	1 828.47	137 743.85	122 397.29	15 346.56	1 957.14
燃料油	Fuel Oil	吨	ton	13 879.10	695 275.71	694 819.36	456.35	28 094.82
液化石油气	Liquefied Petroleum Gas	吨	ton	766.30	114 396.01	113 761.49	634.48	654.80
炼厂干气	Refinery Dry Gas	吨	ton		417 626.00	417 626.00		
热力	Heat	百万千焦	million kJ		31 961 207.66	31 098 496.49	862 711.16	
电力	Electricity	万千瓦时	10 000 kW · h		2 076 493.14	2 045 912.23	30 580.84	

补充资料:2011 年综合能源消费量 1636.5 万吨标准煤。

Note: In 2011, comprehensive energy consumption is 16.365 million tons SCE.

6-2 规模以上工业主要能源分行业消费量(2011年)

MAJOR ENERGY CONSUMPTION OF INDUSTRY ABOVE DESIGNATED SIZE BY SECTOR (2011)

名称	Name	原煤(吨) Raw Coal (ton)	焦炭(吨) Coke (ton)	焦炉煤气(万立方米) Coking Gas (10 000 cu. m)	原油(吨) Crude Oil (ton)	汽油(吨) Petrol (ton)
总计	**Total**	**16 604 993.84**	**1 442 806.47**	**6 508.38**	**12 900 419.32**	**202 431.86**
采掘业	Mining	46 827.14				1 796.61
制造业	Manufacturing	5 438 147.27	1 442 806.47	6 508.38	12 900 419.32	197 346.44
电力煤气及水生产供应业	Production and Supply of Electricity, Gas and Water	11 120 019.43				3 288.81

6-2 续表

continued

名称	Name	煤油(吨) Kerosene (ton)	柴油(吨) Diesel Oil (ton)	燃料油(吨) Fuel Oil (ton)	液化石油气(吨) Liquefied Petroleum Gas (ton)	热力(百万千焦) Heat (million kJ)	电力(万千瓦时) Electricity (10 000 kW·h)
总计	**Total**	**3 264.34**	**137 743.85**	**695 275.71**	**114 396.01**	**31 961 207.66**	**2 076 493.14**
采掘业	Mining		2 935.04				17 207.98
制造业	Manufacturing	3 264.34	131 814.21	693 520.21	114 393.74	29 820 088.88	1 733 082.19
电力煤气及水生产供应业	Production and Supply of Electricity, Gas and Water		2 994.60	1 755.50	2.27	2 141 118.78	326 202.97

6-3 重点耗能工业企业能源加工转换(2011年)

ENERGY CONVERSION OF MAJOR ENERGY-CONSUMING INDUSTRIAL ENTERPRISES(2011)

名称	Name	单位	Unit	工业生产能源消费合计 Total Energy Consumption	#加工转换投入 Conversion Input	火电 Thermal Power	供热 Heating	炼油 Petrolume Refining	制气 Gas Production	能源加工转换产出 Conversion Output of Energy
原煤	Raw Coal	吨	ton	12 892 360.73	12 175 835.33	7 966 236.79	4 209 598.54			
洗精煤	Dressing Coal	吨	ton	1 142 978.48	1 142 978.48				580 689.48	
煤制品	Coal Products	吨	ton							
焦炭	Coke	吨	ton	1 372 606.00						851 457.43
其他焦化产品	Other Coking Products	吨	ton	105 792.90						26 397.95
焦炉煤气	Coking Gas	万立方米	10 000 cu. m							9 136.69
高炉煤气	Blast Furnace Gas	万立方米	10 000 cu. m	12 497.16	12 497.16		12 497.16			
原油	Raw Oil	吨	ton	12 762 890.00	12 754 580.00			12 754 580.00		
汽油	Petrol	吨	ton	650.21						3 164 203.57
煤油	Kerosene	吨	ton	1.97						502 674.00
柴油	Diesel Oil	吨	ton	7 652.66						5 150 560.90
燃料油	Fuel Oil	吨	ton	637 011.20	636 188.70	1 415.00	205.00	634 568.70		166 227.00
液化石油气	Liquefied Petroleum Gas	吨	ton	1 635.44						960 024.00
炼厂干气	Refinery Dry Gas	吨	ton	417 626.00	29 473.00	2 947.00	26 526.00			427 178.00
其他石油制品	Other Petroleum Products	吨	ton	602 399.53	551 229.66	47 467.14		503 762.52		1 547 037.86
热力	Heat	百万千焦	million kJ	17 844 473.70						75 921 471.86
电力	Electricity	万千瓦时	10 000 kW · h	508 126.11						1 825 750.02
其他燃料	Other Fuel	吨标准煤	ton SCE							
能源合计	**Total**	**吨标准煤**	**ton SCE**	**33 527 565.37**	**29 676 278.91**	**5 532 249.94**	**3 259 064.24**	**19 833 005.36**	**522 620.53**	**25 088 107.03**

6-4 规模以上工业主要能源工业消费量(2011年)
MAJOR ENERGY CONSUMPTION OF INDUSTRY ABOVE DESIGNATED SIZE(2011)

行业	Sector	原煤 (吨) Raw Coal (ton)
总　计	**Total**	**16 604 993.84**
黑色金属矿采选业	Mining of Ferrous Metal Ores	3 664.00
有色金属矿采选业	Mining of Non-ferrous Metal Ores	
非金属矿采选业	Mining and Processing of Nonmetal Ores	43 163.14
其他采矿选业	Mining of Other Ores	
农副食品加工业	Processing of Food from Agricultural Products	238 201.27
食品制造业	Manufacture of Foods	72 458.94
饮料制造业	Manufacture of Beverage	84 890.59
烟草制品业	Manufacture of Tobacco	
纺织业	Manufacture of Textile	243 554.14
纺织服装、鞋、帽制造业	Manufacture of Textile Wearing Apparel, Footware, and Caps	159 471.14
皮革、毛皮、羽毛(绒)及其制品业	Manufacture of Leather, Fur, Feather & Its Products	100 010.99
木材加工及木、竹、藤、棕、草制品业	Processing of Timbers, Manufacture of Wood, Bamboo, Rattan, Palm, and Straw Products	21 591.67
家具制造业	Manufacture of Furniture	53 665.33
造纸及纸制品业	Manufacture of Paper and Paper Products	177 449.39
印刷业、记录媒介的复制	Printing, Reproduction of Recording Media	42 633.29
文教体育用品制造业	Manufacture of Articles for Culture, Education and Sport Activity	41 889.58
石油加工、炼焦及核燃料加工业	Processing of Petroleum, Coking, Processing of Nucleus Fuel	4 438.00
化学原料及化学制品制造业	Manufacture of Chemical Raw Material and Chemical Products	1 195 756.19
医药制造业	Manufacture of Medicines	14 590.73
化学纤维制造业	Manufacture of Chemical Fiber	3 146.70
橡胶制品业	Manufacture of Rubber	480 562.69
塑料制品业	Manufacture of Plastic	85 098.28
非金属矿物制品业	Manufacture of Non-metallic Mineral Products	471 886.28
黑色金属冶炼及压延加工业	Smelting and Pressing of Ferrous Metals	588 469.89
有色金属冶炼及压延加工业	Smelting and Pressing of Non-ferrous Metals	25 519.97
金属制品业	Manufacture of Metal Products	144 592.02
通用设备制造业	Manufacture of General Purpose Machinery	445 231.72
专用设备制造业	Manufacture of Special Purpose Machinery	161 899.80
交通运输设备制造业	Manufacture of Transport Equipment	174 958.29
电气机械及器材制造业	Manufacture of Electrical Machinery & Equipment	288 306.68
通信设备、计算机及其他电子设备制造业	Manufacture of Communication Equipment, Computer and Other Electronic Equipment	46 373.58
仪器仪表及文化、办公用机械制造业	Manufacture of Measuring Instrument and Machinery for Cultural Activity & Office Work	13 480.01
工艺品及其他制造业	Manufacture of Artwork, Other Manufacture	57 040.11
废弃资源和废旧材料回收加工	Recycling and Disposal of Waste	980.00
电力、热力的生产和供应业	Production and Supply of Electric Power and Heat Power	10 955 617.43
燃气生产和供应业	Production and Supply of Gas	164 373.00
水的生产和供应业	Production and Supply of Water	29.00

洗精煤 (吨) Dressing Coal(ton)	其他洗煤 (吨) Other Dressing Coal(ton)	煤制品 (吨) Coal Products (ton)	焦炭 (吨) Coke (ton)
1 265 055.96	**2 169.66**	**11 648.25**	**1 442 806.47**
7 932.00		1 990.19	689.97
334.43		1 758.59	
		100.82	1 481.00
14.93	14.21	98.94	
			70.00
		965.00	
			74.26
	4.52	2.18	
108 656.00		1 062.44	
		884.71	
	11.80		686.00
	1 554.71	1 547.47	680.00
5 110.00	560.00	101.00	10.94
562 289.00			1 372 606.00
	24.42		467.64
19.07			47 285.30
		1 527.00	6 671.02
11.05		1 609.91	11 983.79
			5.76
			5.00
			89.79
580 689.48			

6-4 续表1
continued

行业	Sector	焦炉煤气（万立方米）Coking Gas (10 000 cu. m)
总　计	**Total**	**6 508.38**
黑色金属矿采选业	Mining of Ferrous Metal Ores	
有色金属矿采选业	Mining of Non-ferrous Metal Ores	
非金属矿采选业	Mining and Processing of Nonmetal Ores	
其他采矿选业	Mining of Other Ores	
农副食品加工业	Processing of Food from Agricultural Products	
食品制造业	Manufacture of Foods	0.70
饮料制造业	Manufacture of Beverage	
烟草制品业	Manufacture of Tobacco	
纺织业	Manufacture of Textile	19.84
纺织服装、鞋、帽制造业	Manufacture of Textile Wearing Apparel, Footware, and Caps	
皮革、毛皮、羽毛(绒)及其制品业	Manufacture of Leather, Fur, Feather & Its Products	
木材加工及木、竹、藤、棕、草制品业	Processing of Timbers, Manufacture of Wood, Bamboo, Rattan, Palm, and Straw Products	
家具制造业	Manufacture of Furniture	
造纸及纸制品业	Manufacture of Paper and Paper Products	
印刷业、记录媒介的复制	Printing, Reproduction of Recording Media	
文教体育用品制造业	Manufacture of Articles for Culture, Education and Sport Activity	
石油加工、炼焦及核燃料加工业	Processing of Petroleum, Coking, Processing of Nucleus Fuel	
化学原料及化学制品制造业	Manufacture of Chemical Raw Material and Chemical Products	5 298.60
医药制造业	Manufacture of Medicines	
化学纤维制造业	Manufacture of Chemical Fiber	
橡胶制品业	Manufacture of Rubber	
塑料制品业	Manufacture of Plastic	
非金属矿物制品业	Manufacture of Non-metallic Mineral Products	160.29
黑色金属冶炼及压延加工业	Smelting and Pressing of Ferrous Metals	
有色金属冶炼及压延加工业	Smelting and Pressing of Non-ferrous Metals	
金属制品业	Manufacture of Metal Products	
通用设备制造业	Manufacture of General Purpose Machinery	
专用设备制造业	Manufacture of Special Purpose Machinery	
交通运输设备制造业	Manufacture of Transport Equipment	1 028.95
电气机械及器材制造业	Manufacture of Electrical Machinery & Equipment	
通信设备、计算机及其他电子设备制造业	Manufacture of Communication Equipment, Computer and Other Electronic Equipment	
仪器仪表及文化、办公用机械制造业	Manufacture of Measuring Instrument and Machinery for Cultural Activity & Office Work	
工艺品及其他制造业	Manufacture of Artwork, Other Manufacture	
废弃资源和废旧材料回收加工	Recycling and Disposal of Waste	
电力、热力的生产和供应业	Production and Supply of Electric Power and Heat Power	
燃气生产和供应业	Production and Supply of Gas	
水的生产和供应业	Production and Supply of Water	

高炉煤气 (万立方米) Blast Furnace Gas (10 000 cu. m)	原油 (吨) Crude Oil(ton)	汽油 (吨) Petrol (ton)	煤油 (吨) Kerosene (ton)
12 497.16	**12 900 419.32**	**202 431.86**	**3 264.34**
		1 150.21	
		646.40	
	165.90	25 336.59	470.53
		3 810.66	320.37
		1 057.24	
		166.61	
		8 594.53	59.75
	76.49	11 355.54	90.77
	16.14	8 389.27	242.69
		1 066.37	5.12
	9.90	5 653.58	
	7.50	3 323.27	25.10
		2 133.66	15.00
		3 761.50	3.00
	12 900 046.23	249.18	36.92
		7 990.84	44.64
		574.34	
		1 049.28	
	25.00	6 364.63	12.00
		6 423.49	
	15.00	10 395.26	358.80
12 497.16		596.46	
		1 923.36	403.75
		14 888.36	9.37
	1.60	20 796.72	153.37
		16 483.66	833.39
	43.56	9 155.76	61.36
		11 054.88	32.62
	12.00	6 595.87	13.00
		1 647.40	24.00
		6 421.88	48.79
		86.25	
		2 347.67	
		326.70	
		614.44	

6-4 续表2
continued

行业	Sector	柴油（吨）Diesel Oil（ton）
总　　计	**Total**	**137 743.85**
黑色金属矿采选业	Mining of Ferrous Metal Ores	1 845.04
有色金属矿采选业	Mining of Non-ferrous Metal Ores	
非金属矿采选业	Mining and Processing of Nonmetal Ores	1 090.00
其他采矿选业	Mining of Other Ores	
农副食品加工业	Processing of Food from Agricultural Products	10 051.38
食品制造业	Manufacture of Foods	3 809.17
饮料制造业	Manufacture of Beverage	1 246.19
烟草制品业	Manufacture of Tobacco	20.81
纺织业	Manufacture of Textile	5 743.23
纺织服装、鞋、帽制造业	Manufacture of Textile Wearing Apparel, Footware, and Caps	5 851.56
皮革、毛皮、羽毛(绒)及其制品业	Manufacture of Leather, Fur, Feather & Its Products	3 707.36
木材加工及木、竹、藤、棕、草制品业	Processing of Timbers, Manufacture of Wood, Bamboo, Rattan, Palm, and Straw Products	516.95
家具制造业	Manufacture of Furniture	1 429.96
造纸及纸制品业	Manufacture of Paper and Paper Products	2 552.78
印刷业、记录媒介的复制	Printing, Reproduction of Recording Media	892.44
文教体育用品制造业	Manufacture of Articles for Culture, Education and Sport Activity	1 548.59
石油加工、炼焦及核燃料加工业	Processing of Petroleum, Coking, Processing of Nucleus Fuel	216.35
化学原料及化学制品制造业	Manufacture of Chemical Raw Material and Chemical Products	6 333.48
医药制造业	Manufacture of Medicines	2 508.79
化学纤维制造业	Manufacture of Chemical Fiber	26.25
橡胶制品业	Manufacture of Rubber	3 473.86
塑料制品业	Manufacture of Plastic	5 149.64
非金属矿物制品业	Manufacture of Non-metallic Mineral Products	21 771.29
黑色金属冶炼及压延加工业	Smelting and Pressing of Ferrous Metals	4 828.15
有色金属冶炼及压延加工业	Smelting and Pressing of Non-ferrous Metals	1 357.20
金属制品业	Manufacture of Metal Products	6 622.84
通用设备制造业	Manufacture of General Purpose Machinery	12 215.11
专用设备制造业	Manufacture of Special Purpose Machinery	5 689.27
交通运输设备制造业	Manufacture of Transport Equipment	14 294.15
电气机械及器材制造业	Manufacture of Electrical Machinery & Equipment	4 285.17
通信设备、计算机及其他电子设备制造业	Manufacture of Communication Equipment, Computer and Other Electronic Equipment	2 668.05
仪器仪表及文化、办公用机械制造业	Manufacture of Measuring Instrument and Machinery for Cultural Activity & Office Work	553.76
工艺品及其他制造业	Manufacture of Artwork, Other Manufacture	2 362.85
废弃资源和废旧材料回收加工	Recycling and Disposal of Waste	87.58
电力、热力的生产和供应业	Production and Supply of Electric Power and Heat Power	2 148.18
燃气生产和供应业	Production and Supply of Gas	562.36
水的生产和供应业	Production and Supply of Water	284.06

燃料油 （吨） Fuel Oil （ton）	液化石油气 （吨）Liquefied Petroleum Gas（ton）	炼厂干气 （吨） Refinery Dry Gas（ton）
695 275.71	**114 396.01**	**417 626.00**
75.77	452.40	
432.10	365.80	
	320.00	
6 311.15		
234.73	25.07	
3 128.31	8.00	
346.99		
42.90		
1 760.89	62.05	
635 304.53		417 626.00
1 473.80	101 159.80	
16.23		
5 533.50		
348.21	0.90	
37 141.66	22.90	
	1 225.12	
	99.66	
64.98	463.20	
359.81	138.31	
203.29		
668.20	4 690.01	
44.28	4 509.70	
9.35	848.75	
19.53	2.07	
1 755.50	2.27	

6 -4 续表 3
continued

行业	Sector	其他油制品（吨）Other Petroleum Products(ton)
总　计	**Total**	**607 410.70**
黑色金属矿采选业	Mining of Ferrous Metal Ores	
有色金属矿采选业	Mining of Non-ferrous Metal Ores	
非金属矿采选业	Mining and Processing of Nonmetal Ores	
其他采矿选业	Mining of Other Ores	
农副食品加工业	Processing of Food from Agricultural Products	
食品制造业	Manufacture of Foods	798.00
饮料制造业	Manufacture of Beverage	
烟草制品业	Manufacture of Tobacco	
纺织业	Manufacture of Textile	1.75
纺织服装、鞋、帽制造业	Manufacture of Textile Wearing Apparel, Footware, and Caps	
皮革、毛皮、羽毛(绒)及其制品业	Manufacture of Leather, Fur, Feather & Its Products	
木材加工及木、竹、藤、棕、草制品业	Processing of Timbers, Manufacture of Wood, Bamboo, Rattan, Palm, and Straw Products	
家具制造业	Manufacture of Furniture	
造纸及纸制品业	Manufacture of Paper and Paper Products	
印刷业、记录媒介的复制	Printing, Reproduction of Recording Media	
文教体育用品制造业	Manufacture of Articles for Culture, Education and Sport Activity	
石油加工、炼焦及核燃料加工业	Processing of Petroleum, Coking, Processing of Nucleus Fuel	595 982.80
化学原料及化学制品制造业	Manufacture of Chemical Raw Material and Chemical Products	10 026.81
医药制造业	Manufacture of Medicines	
化学纤维制造业	Manufacture of Chemical Fiber	
橡胶制品业	Manufacture of Rubber	
塑料制品业	Manufacture of Plastic	3.90
非金属矿物制品业	Manufacture of Non-metallic Mineral Products	
黑色金属冶炼及压延加工业	Smelting and Pressing of Ferrous Metals	
有色金属冶炼及压延加工业	Smelting and Pressing of Non-ferrous Metals	
金属制品业	Manufacture of Metal Products	
通用设备制造业	Manufacture of General Purpose Machinery	31.92
专用设备制造业	Manufacture of Special Purpose Machinery	
交通运输设备制造业	Manufacture of Transport Equipment	10.75
电气机械及器材制造业	Manufacture of Electrical Machinery & Equipment	
通信设备、计算机及其他电子设备制造业	Manufacture of Communication Equipment, Computer and Other Electronic Equipment	
仪器仪表及文化、办公用机械制造业	Manufacture of Measuring Instrument and Machinery for Cultural Activity & Office Work	
工艺品及其他制造业	Manufacture of Artwork, Other Manufacture	
废弃资源和废旧材料回收加工	Recycling and Disposal of Waste	
电力、热力的生产和供应业	Production and Supply of Electric Power and Heat Power	
燃气生产和供应业	Production and Supply of Gas	554.77
水的生产和供应业	Production and Supply of Water	

热　力 （百万千焦） Heat (million kJ)	电　力 （万千瓦时） Electricity (10 000 kW · h)	其他燃料 （吨标准煤） Other Fuel (ton SCE)
31 961 207.66	**2 076 493.14**	**371.00**
	6 182.57	
	11 025.41	
1 162 605.72	114 015.76	
446 621.43	33 157.19	
2 032 647.89	20 966.34	
257 510.00	4 263.71	
3 757 812.62	80 664.45	
374 108.77	42 058.82	371.00
357 494.57	30 263.45	
	5 005.73	
2 234.00	13 381.09	
1 376 579.00	30 357.30	
44 796.00	11 910.91	
11 953.82	12 393.90	
5 576 048.00	101 002.02	
10 473 205.05	177 535.75	
519 628.78	9 425.94	
30 905.12	12 689.77	
408 091.19	101 582.54	
76 620.15	53 074.62	
27 878.63	107 779.50	
88 131.83	175 734.45	
1 216.12	27 356.81	
161 073.00	72 729.17	
215 406.15	135 574.59	
90 590.33	50 034.83	
1 049 751.80	148 126.71	
993 112.12	92 919.71	
212 382.78	45 818.87	
	5 861.85	
71 684.01	17 250.07	
	146.34	
1 963 588.28	306 818.97	
177 530.50	5 847.20	
	13 536.80	

主要统计指标解释

工业企业能源消费量 工业企业能源消费包括工业企业在生产过程中作为燃料、动力、原料、辅助材料使用的能源以及工艺用能、非生产用能;作为能源加工转换企业,还要包括能源加工转换的投入量。工业企业能源消费量具体包括:

(1)用于本企业产品生产、工业性作业和其他生产性活动的能源。

(2)用于技术更新改造措施、新技术研究和新产品试制以及科学试验等方面的能源。

(3)用于经营维修、建筑及设备大修理、机电设备和交通运输工具等方面的能源。

(4)用于劳动保护的能源。

(5)其他非生产消费的能源。

不包括:

(1)由仓库发到车间,但在报告期最后一天没有消费的能源。这部分能源应在办理假退料手续后计入库存量。

(2)拨到外单位,委托外单位加工用的能源。

(3)调出本单位或借给外单位的能源。

工业生产能源消费 是指工业企业为进行工业生产活动所使用的能源。主要包括:

1. 用于本企业产品生产、工业性作业的能源,包括用作原料、材料、燃料、动力;作为能源加工转换企业,还包括用作加工转换的能源。

2. 产品生产过程中作为辅助材料使用的能源。

3. 生产工艺过程使用的能源。

4. 新技术研究、新产品试制、科学试验使用的能源。

5. 为了工业生产活动而在进行的各种修理过程中使用的能源。

6. 生产区内的劳动保护用能等。

Explanatory Notes on Main Statistical Indicators

Energy Consumption of Industrial Enterprises include energy in the production process as fuel, power, raw materials, supplementary materials, and for use of technology and non-production. As energy processing and conversion enterprises, also include energy processing and conversion of inputs. These specifically include: (1) Energy for the enterprise product, industrial production operations and other activities. (2) Energy for technical upgrading measures and new technology research and new product production and scientific experiments. (3) Energy for operation maintenance, construction and equipment overhaul, electrical and mechanical equipment and transport, and other aspects. (4) Energy for the protection of labor. (5) Energy for Other non-production and consumption. And these exclude: (1) Energy from the warehouse to the workshop, but out of consumption on the last day of the reporting period. This part of the energy should leave retreat materials handling procedures included stock. (2) Energy transferred to other units, entrusted with the processing. (3) Energy transferred out of the unit or loans to other units.

Energy Consumption for Industrial Production refers to energy for industrial enterprises in industrial production activities. These mainly include: 1. Energy for the enterprise products, industrial operations, including energy as raw materials, materials, fuels, and power. As energy processing and conversion enterprises, also include energy for processing and conversion. 2. Energy as supplementary material in product process. 3. Energy used in production process. 4. Energy for new technologies, new product production, and scientific experiment. 5. Energy in process of repairing for industrial production activities. 6. Energy for labor protection in production areas and so on.

财政、金融和保险业 7

GOVERNMENT FINANCE, FINANCIAL INTERMEDIATION AND INSURANCE

简要说明

一、本篇资料的主要内容

本篇资料主要反映了全市财政收支、金融和保险方面的情况，主要包括财政收入、财政支出、金融机构存贷款、保险业务开展等方面的资料。

二、本篇资料的来源

1、财政部分的资料来源于市财政局。

2、金融方面的资料来源于中国人民银行青岛市中心支行。

3、保险方面的资料来源于中国保险监督管理委员会青岛监管局。

本篇资料由市统计局国民经济核算处整理提供。

Brief Introduction

I. Main Content

Data in this chapter show the conditions of local government budgetary finance, banking and insurance,and securities, including government revenue and expenditure, deposits and loans of financial institutions and statistics on insurance companies.

II. Source of Data

（1）Data on local government finance are provided by Qingdao Municipal Finance Bureau.

（2）Data on banking are provided by Qingdao Branch of the People's Bank of China.

（3）Data on insurance are provide by China Insurance Regulatory Commission of Qingdao Bureau.

Data in this chapter are prepared and compiled by the Division of National Accounts of Qingdao Municipal Bureau of Statistics.

7－1 主要年份地方财政收支

MAJOR YEAR'S REVENUE AND EXPENDITURE OF LOCAL GOVERNMENT FINANCE

单位:万元(10 000 yuan)

年份 Year	财政收入 Revenue of Government Finance	财政支出 Expenditure of Government Finance
1949	1 527	306
1952	19 809	2 226
1957	29 875	3 556
1962	32 869	4 327
1965	47 682	6 280
1970	95 778	7 825
1975	90 220	11 966
1978	130 749	19 427
1980	124 835	20 064
1985	165 155	41 996
1988	201 206	93 931
1989	221 183	113 585
1990	242 303	133 875
1991	259 377	137 716
1992	275 589	155 696
1993	182 348	211 938
1994	227 490	277 331
1995	294 771	376 982
1996	379 674	469 569
1997	476 804	564 787
1998	580 434	678 575
1999	680 089	740 937
2000	800 120	878 702
2001	987 080	1 097 848
2002	1 006 616	1 243 880
2003	1 201 398	1 471 747
2004	1 305 136	1 646 214
2005	1 763 412	2 030 622
2006	2 257 663	2 367 875
2007	2 925 798	3 211 777
2008	3 424 359	3 694 111
2009	3 769 896	4 335 754
2010	4 526 138	5 323 888
2011	5 661 400	6 580 605

注:1. 1993 年以后实行新制度,财政收入数与历年不可比。
2. 2002 年以后,财政收入、支出为一般预算数。

Note: 1. Since 1993, new regulations have been adopted in calculating revenue of government finance, the figures are not comparable with those over the years.
2. Since 2002, revenue of government finance and expenditure of government finance refer to general budgetary revenue and expenditure.

7-2 分市、区地方财政一般预算收入(2011 年)

GENERAL BUDGETARY REVENUE OF LOCAL GOVERNMENT FINANCE BY REGION(2011)

单位:万元(10 000 yuan)

市、区名称	Region	财政一般预算收入 General Budgetaty Revenue of Government Finance	#增值税 Value-added Tax	营业税 Business Tax	企业所得税 Enterprise Income Tax
总　计	**Total**	**5 661 400**	**573 582**	**1 466 191**	**713 756**
市　区	Urban Area	1 924 815	213 038	457 665	252 510
#崂山区	Laoshan District	392 382	45 347	64 822	55 265
黄岛区	Huangdao District	446 921	57 297	86 620	57 278
城阳区	Chengyang District	292 567	34 948	58 712	36 830
即墨市	Jimo	361 046	41 358	66 069	33 451
胶州市	Jiaozhou	343 026	38 739	57 585	44 030
胶南市	Jiaonan	363 567	26 160	65 545	24 880
平度市	Pingdu	271 459	25 711	28 330	16 188
莱西市	Laixi	232 370	15 541	22 942	7 060
市本级	Municipal Level	2 165 117	213 035	768 055	335 637

7-2 续表

continued

单位:万元(10 000 yuan)

市、区名称	Region	个人所得税 Personal Income Tax	城市维护建设税 Urban Maintenance and Development Tax	基金预算收入 Funds Budgetary Revenue
总　计	**Total**	**220 854**	**307 199**	**6 265 147**
市　区	Urban Area	89 975	199 074	1 830 349
#崂山区	Laoshan District	16 179	63 586	413 509
黄岛区	Huangdao District	12 025	58 712	694 051
城阳区	Chengyang District	10 300	29 250	531 009
即墨市	Jimo	9 460	17 267	325 685
胶州市	Jiaozhou	9 839	16 102	719 667
胶南市	Jiaonan	7 183	13 268	508 461
平度市	Pingdu	5 686	9 982	4 173
莱西市	Laixi	8 362	6 041	4 029
市本级	Municipal Level	90 349	45 465	2 872 783

7 -3 分市、区地方财政一般预算支出(2011 年)

GENERAL BUDGETARY EXPENDITURE OF LOCAL FINANCE BY REGION(2011)

单位:万元(10 000 yuan)

市、区名称	Region	财政一般预算支出 General Budgetaty Expenditure of Government Finance	#一般公共服务支出 General Public Services	公共安全 Public Security	教育 Education	科学技术 Science and Technology	文化体育与传媒 Culture, Sport and Media
总　计	**Total**	**6 580 605**	**956 558**	**412 853**	**1 126 402**	**161 225**	**148 164**
市　区	Urban Area	2 049 445	316 314	73 248	437 177	83 164	25 163
#崂山区	Laoshan District	375 363	49 081	12 120	69 711	12 048	7 369
黄岛区	Huangdao District	432 045	61 348	13 242	62 537	24 830	6 574
城阳区	Chengyang District	341 600	56 921	9 820	89 817	19 268	3 567
即墨市	Jimo	483 926	116 612	15 543	125 773	2 012	10 268
胶州市	Jiaozhou	460 638	95 188	23 129	112 596	8 807	5 006
胶南市	Jiaonan	462 734	85 746	22 938	106 465	9 058	8 029
平度市	Pingdu	414 439	66 198	15 166	120 870	6 591	6 486
莱西市	Laixi	351 408	44 317	13 445	76 118	1 583	2 263
市本级	Municipal Level	2 358 015	232 183	249 384	147 403	50 010	90 949

7 -3 续表

continued

单位:万元(10 000 yuan)

市、区名称	Region	社会保障和就业 Social Security and Employment	医疗卫生 Health Care	环境保护 Environment Protection	城乡社区事务 Urban and Rural Community Affairs	农林水事务 Affairs of Agiculture, Forest and Irrigation	基金预算支出 Funds Budgetary Expenditure
总　计	**Total**	**478 186**	**296 155**	**104 021**	**973 981**	**381 197**	**6 302 743**
市　区	Urban Area	116 201	73 318	18 819	408 304	94 468	2 364 484
#崂山区	Laoshan District	12 313	11 102	843	82 882	31 666	372 345
黄岛区	Huangdao District	16 601	16 208	7 708	69 833	18 562	729 184
城阳区	Chengyang District	16 335	12 043	5 913	71 344	31 231	639 355
即墨市	Jimo	41 962	29 852	13 920	33 467	47 963	249 090
胶州市	Jiaozhou	29 602	25 662	5 715	39 994	50 069	742 816
胶南市	Jiaonan	26 952	23 090	10 864	67 627	54 080	506 680
平度市	Pingdu	48 987	39 706	4 263	38 414	47 019	11 247
莱西市	Laixi	22 787	25 198	2 935	9 833	35 150	25 731
市本级	Municipal Level	191 695	79 329	47 505	376 342	52 448	2 402 695

7-4 主要年份金融系统人民币存贷款(年末余额)

MAJOR YEAR'S DEPOSITS AND LOANS OF FINANCIAL INSTITUTIONS(YEAR-END BALANCE)

单位:万元(10 000 yuan)

年份 Year	存款合计 Total Deposits	#企业存款 Deposits by Enterprises	储蓄存款 Savings Deposits	贷款合计 Total Loans
1949	693	239	28	278
1952	9 093	4 308	1 838	3 322
1957	10 372	3 359	4 037	30 690
1962	20 040	8 579	3 279	73 601
1965	27 331	11 830	6 347	64 555
1970	38 264	13 024	7 576	126 382
1975	60 622	22 568	15 637	207 006
1978	66 523	21 004	21 455	297 184
1980	120 644	38 105	38 609	379 666
1985	344 760	99 736	155 604	452 142
1988	754 442	206 541	366 483	955 351
1989	932 430	245 529	481 692	1 174 448
1990	1 235 562	321 542	655 895	1 535 751
1991	1 553 564	411 417	824 428	1 871 462
1992	2 076 667	612 868	1 044 165	2 352 449
1993	2 747 294	835 617	1 372 239	2 940 658
1994	3 769 019	1 399 110	1 918 734	3 610 564
1995	5 324 026	2 030 382	2 687 888	4 777 864
1996	6 991 289	2 630 958	3 499 219	5 941 281
1997	7 385 092	2 885 632	4 060 259	6 508 776
1998	8 183 471	3 018 063	4 591 012	7 239 231
1999	9 160 001	3 454 570	4 978 045	8 945 730
2000	10 560 624	4 386 316	5 353 215	9 564 293
2001	12 323 942	4 955 336	6 187 409	10 798 871
2002	15 225 733	5 819 655	7 449 408	13 044 792
2003	18 920 868	7 027 227	9 084 693	16 783 917
2004	22 462 592	7 924 690	10 894 941	18 472 613
2005	26 975 372	8 226 661	13 431 016	20 394 792
2006	32 453 583	10 144 296	15 676 197	25 779 442
2007	38 915 882	13 213 434	17 020 383	30 970 553
2008	47 353 803	14 641 948	21 233 637	37 483 209
2009	63 019 764	21 001 185	25 278 658	48 735 326
2010	76 592 065	27 271 963	29 123 256	58 862 263
2011	86 384 994	49 189 415	31 985 099	69 477 500

注:自2011年起,企业存款指标改为单位存款,口径与以前年度不一致。

Note: Since 2011, "Deposits by Corporate" has been used instead of "Deposits by Enterprises", and the caliber is different from the preoious year.

7-5 金融系统人民币存贷款(年末余额)

DEPOSITS AND LOANS OF FINANCIAL INSTITUTIONS(YEAR-END BALANCE)

单位:万元(10 000 yuan)

项目	Item	2011 年	比年初增减数 Incremental/Reductions Compared to the Beginning of the Year
一、存款总计	**Total Deposits**	**86 384 994**	**9 858 026**
单位存款	Deposits by Corporate	49 189 415	6 994 056
储蓄存款	Savings Deposits	31 985 099	2 915 745
二、贷款总计	**Total Loans**	**69 477 500**	**10 768 712**
短期贷款	Short-Term Loans	26 871 365	5 319 456
#个人贷款及透支	Personal Loans and Line	2 815 287	780 878
单位贷款及透支	Business Loans and Line	21 488 807	3 398 225
贸易融资	Trade Financing	2 516 535	1 164 977
中长期贷款	Medium&Long-term Loans	40 051 084	4 975 592
#个人贷款	Personal Loans	12 118 705	2 085 895
单位贷款	Business Loans	22 543 813	1 452 765
银团贷款	Syndicated Loans	4 143 222	1 236 262
贸易融资	Trade Financing	1 245 345	200 670
票据融资	Notes Financing	2 501 873	471 488

7-6 国内保险业务(1990-2011 年)
DOMESTIC INSURANCE BUSINESS(1990-2011)

项目	Item	1990	1995	2000	2005	2006
国内保险总值	**Total domestic insurance Value**	**4 392 323**	**11 256 080**	**38 357 485**	**91 691 581**	**119 396 881**
国内业务收入	Domestic Business Income	17 177	107 159	220 780	495 701	605 143
保费收入	Premium Income	12 085	81 976	218 714	495 701	605 143
财产险	Property Insurance	10 417	51 808	85 161	159 746	199 213
农业险	Agriculture Insurance	145	142	18	12	19
人身险	Personal Insurance	1 523	30 026	133 535	335 943	405 911
国内业务支出	**Domestic Business Expenditure**	**5 449**	**40 115**	**94 877**	**214 148**	**252 477**
1. 赔款支出	Claim Expenditure	4 735	32 105	62 275	111 385	131 321
财产险	Property Insurance	4 145	29 420	58 361	92 700	115 214
农业险	Agriculture Insurance	129	24	5	11	3
人身险	Personal Insurance	461	2 661	3 909	18 674	16 104
2. 给付支出	Mature Payment	509	7 652	27 955	32 739	63 144
3. 退保	Surrender	205	358	4 647	70 024	58 012

注:自 2011 年起,保险业实施新会计准则,保险统计各项指标口径发生变化,与以往年度不可比。

Note:Since 2011,new accounting standard has been used in insurance,indicators caliber of insurance statistics has been changed,and the data are not comparable with the previous year.

单位:万元(10 000 yuan)

2007	2008	2009	2010	2011
228 774 417	**276 989 344**	**293 519 697**	**309 244 255**	**380 829 634**
776 031	1 027 258	1 153 101	1 538 526	1 457 269
776 031	1 027 258	1 153 101	1 538 526	1 457 269
272 664	280 008	339 314	492 190	556 257
1 542	3 135	4 066	3 261	3 587
501 825	744 115	809 721	1 043 075	897 425
361 183	**423 743**	**476 377**	**497 832**	**463 751**
171 613	196 318	219 546	279 019	307 564
138 739	164 415	188 723	250 966	286 214
53	907	3 452	2 808	1 087
32 821	30 996	27 371	25 245	20 263
95 282	132 621	123 056	109 318	156 188
94 288	94 804	133 775	109 496	69 275

主要统计指标解释

财政收入 指国家财政参与社会产品分配所取得的收入,是实现国家职能的财力保证。财政收入所包括的内容几经变化,目前主要包括:

(1)税收收入:包括增值税、营业税、企业所得税、个人所得税、资源税、固定资产投资方向调节税、城市维护建设税、房产税、印花税、城镇土地使用税、土地增值税、车船税、耕地占用税、契税、烟叶税、其他税收收入。

(2)非税收入:包括专项收入、行政事业性收费收入、罚没收入、国有资本经营收入、国有资源有偿使用收入、其他收入。

财政支出 国家财政将筹集起来的资金进行分配使用,以满足经济建设和各项事业的需要,主要包括:

(1)一般公共服务支出:反映政府提供一般公共服务的支出。

(2)公共安全:反映政府维护社会公共安全方面的支出,有关事务包括武装警察、公安、国家安全、检察、法院、司法行政、监狱、劳教、国家保密、缉私警察等。

(3)教育支出:反映政府教育事务支出。有关具体教育事务包括教育行政管理、学前教育、小学教育、初中教育、普通高中教育、普通高等教育、初等职业教育、中专教育、技校教育、职业高中教育、高等职业教育、广播电视教育、留学生教育、特殊教育、干部继续教育、教育机关服务等。

(4)科学技术:反映政府用于科学技术方面的支出。

(5)文化体育与传媒:反映政府在文化、文物、体育、广播电视、新闻出版等方面的支出。

(6)社会保障和就业:反映政府在社会保障与就业方面的支出。有关事项包括社会保障与就业管理事务、民政管理事务、财政对社会保险基金的补助、补充全国社会保障基金、行政事业单位离退休、企业改革补助、就业补助、抚恤、退役安置、社会福利、残疾人事业、城市居民最低生活保障、其他城镇社会救济、农村社会救济、自然灾害生活补助、红十字事务等。

(7)医疗卫生支出:反映政府医疗卫生方面的支出。具体包括医疗卫生管理事务支出、医疗服务支出、医疗保障支出、疾病预防控制支出、卫生监督支出、妇幼保健支出、农村卫生支出等。

(8)环境保护:反映政府环境保护支出。具体包括:环境保护管理事务支出、环境监测与监察支出、污染治理支出、自然生态保护支出、天然林保护工程支出、退耕还林支出、风沙荒漠治理支出、退牧还草支出、已垦草原退耕还草支出。

(9)城乡社区事务:反映政府城乡社区事务支出。具体包括:城乡社区管理事务支出、城乡社区规划与管理支出、城乡社区公共设施支出、城乡社区住宅支出、城乡社区环境卫生支出、建设市场管理与监督支出等。

(10)农林水事务:反映政府农林水事务方面的支出。具体包括农业、林业、水利、扶贫支出、农业综合开发支出等。

存款 指企业、机关、团体或居民根据资金必须收回的原则,把货币资金存入银行或其他信贷机构保管并取得一定利息的一种信用活动形式。根据存款对象或性质的不同可划分为企业存款、财政存款、机关团体存款、基本建设存款、储蓄存款、农村存款、委托存款、其他存款等科目。它是银行信贷资金的主要来源。

贷款 指银行或其他信贷机构根据资金必须归还的原则,按一定利率,为企业、个人等提供资金的一种信用活动形式。我国银行贷款分为短期贷款、中期流动资金贷款、中长期贷款、信托贷款、融资租赁、委托贷款、票据融资、各项垫款等。

承保额 又叫保险金额,指保险人承担赔偿或者给付保险金责任的最高限额。

保费 指投保人为取得保险人在约定范围内所承担赔偿责任而支付给保险人的费用。

Explanatory Notes on Main Statistical Indicators

Government Revenue refers to the revenue of the government finance by means of participating in the distribution of the social products, which is the financial resources for ensuring the government to function. The contents of government revenue have been changed several times. Now it includes the following main items:

(1) Various tax revenues, including value added tax, business tax, enterprise income tax, personal income tax, resources tax, fixed assets investment direction regulating tax, tax on city maintenance and construction, real estate tax, stamp tax, tax on use of urban land, land value added tax, vehicle and vessel tax, tax on occupancy of cultivated land, property tax, tobacco leaf tax, and other tax revenues.

(2) Non-tax Revenues including special revenues, revenues from Administrative and institutional fees, penalty and confiscatory revenues , revenues from state-owned capital operationg, revenues from paid use of state-owned resources, and other revenues.

Government Expenditure refers to the distribution and use of the funds the government finance has raised, so as to meet the needs of economic construction and various causes. It includes the following main items:

(1) Expenditure for general public services: It reflects the expenditure from the government for general public services.

(2) Expenditure on public security: It reflects the expenditure from the government towards safeguarding the public security, including the related affairs of armed police, public security, state security, procuratorial administration, law court, judicial administration, jail , reeducation through labor, state confidentiality, anti-smuggling Patrol, etc.

(3) Expenditure on education: It reflects the expenditure from the government on education, including the related affairs of educational administration management, preschool education, primary education, junior secondary educate, regular senior secondary educate, regular higher education, primary vocational education, specialized secondary educate, technical educate, vocational senior secondary educate, vocational higher education, radio and television education, foreign student educate, special education, cadre continuing education, education institution services, etc.

(4) Expenditure on science and technology: It reflects the expenditure from the government on science and technology.

(5) Expenditure on culture, sport and media: It reflects the expenditure from the government on culture, cultural relics, sport, radio and television, publication, etc.

(6) Expenditure on social security and employment: It reflects the expenditure from the government on social security and employment, including the related affairs of management of social security and employment, civil administration, subsidies to social insurance funds, supplement to national social security funds, retirees of government agencies and institutions, subsidies to enterprises reform, subsidies to employment, pension, settling down demobilized servicemen, social security, disabled person administration, minimum living allowance in urban area, other social relief in urban area, social relief in rural area, subsidies to natural disaster, Red Cross business, etc.

(7) Expenditure on health care: It reflects the expenditure from the government on health care, including expenditure on management of health care, medical services, medical security, disease control and prevention, public health supervision, rural health care, etc.

(8) Expenditure on environment protection: It reflects the expenditure from the government on environment protection, including expenditure on management of environment protection, environment monitoring and supervisory, pollution government, natural ecological protection, project of natural forest protection, returning farmland to forest, sandstorm and wilderness government, returning grazing land to grassland, returning cultivated grassland to grassland, etc.

(9) Expenditure on urban and rural community affairs: It reflects the expenditure from the government on urban and rural community affairs, including expenditure on management of urban and rural community affairs, plan and management of urban and rural community, public utility of urban and rural community, residential buildings of urban and rural community, environmental sanitation of urban and rural community, management and supervision of markets construction, etc.

(10) Expenditure on agriculture, forest and irrigation: It reflects the expenditure from the government on agriculture, forest and irrigation, including expenditure on agriculture, forest, irrigation, poverty alleviation, comprehensive development of agriculture, etc.

Deposit is a form of credit by which enterprises, institutions, organizations or households can put money into banks and other credit institutions for safekeeping and interest earning under the principle of free withdrawal. According to different depositors, deposits are divided into enterprise deposits, treasury deposits, deposits of government agencies and organizations, capital construction deposits, savings deposits, rural saving deposits, entrusted deposits and other deposits. Deposits are major sources of the credit funds of banks.

Loan is a form of credit by which banks and other credit institutions provide funds at certain interest rate to enterprises and individuals in the light of the principle of unconditional repayment. Loans from Chinese banks include circulating capital loans, fixed assets loans, loans to urban and rural individuals engaged in industrial and commercial business and agricultural loans.

Amount Covered which also is known as amount Insured, refers to the maximum that the insurant will get for the claim of the case insured.

Premium is the fee paid by the insurant to the insurer to obtain the obligation of compensation from the insurance within the agreed terms.

物价 8

PRICE

简要说明

一、本篇资料的主要内容

本篇资料主要包括工业生产者出厂、工业生产者购进、固定资产投资、房地产、居民消费、商品零售等价格指数。

二、本篇资料的来源

1、工业生产者出厂、工业生产者购进、固定资产投资、房地产价格指数分别来源于生产、投资、房地产价格统计调查年报，由国家统计局青岛调查队生产投资价格调查处整理提供。

2、居民消费、商品零售价格指数来源于消费价格统计调查年报，由国家统计局青岛调查队消费价格调查处整理提供。

Brief Introduction

I. Main Content

Data in this chapter mainly include producer price indices for manufactured goods, purchasing price indices for industrial producers, price indices of investment in fixed assets, real estate price indices, consumer price indices and retail price indices.

II. Source of Data

(1) Data on producer price indices for manufactured goods, purchasing price indices for industrial producers, price indices of investment in fixed assets, real estate price indices are based on annual report of price survey on production, investment, real estate, and provided by the Division of Production Price Survey of Survey Office of the National Bureau of Statistics in Qingdao.

(2) Data on consumer price indices and retail price indices are based on annual report of consumer price survey, and provided by the Division of Consumer Price Survey of Survey Office of the National Bureau of Statistics in Qingdao.

8－1 主要年份居民消费和商品零售价格指数

MAJOR YEAR'S CONSUMER AND RETAIL PRICE INDEXES

（上年＝100）　　(preceding year＝100)

年份 Year	居民消费价格指数 Consumer Price Index	#食品类 Food	衣着类 Clothing	服务项目价格指数 Services Price Index	商品零售价格指数 Retail Price Index
1951	110.5	105.2	112.4		110.5
1952	99.8	99.6	98.7		99.8
1957	101.4	101.3	101.4	99.3	101.4
1962	102.6	102.0	100.2	99.9	102.6
1965	101.2	101.3	98.8	96.9	101.2
1970	98.9	99.7	100.0	99.5	98.9
1975	100.3	100.1	100.0	100.0	100.3
1978	100.5	100.2	99.8	100.0	100.5
1980	105.2	108.5	100.3	100.6	105.5
1985	110.4	115.2	102.3	102.7	110.9
1987	109.4	112.5	106.8	102.5	109.8
1988	120.7	125.2	117.3	118.3	120.9
1989	115.3	109.2	121.1	130.2	114.4
1990	104.5	103.4	103.4	118.8	103.6
1991	107.0	107.0	112.1	109.6	106.8
1992	111.4	115.1	108.6	119.9	110.8
1993	123.9	120.9	119.0	158.5	119.8
1994	126.9	135.2	130.1	117.9	122.8
1995	116.2	118.1	122.8	123.2	114.2
1996	112.6	110.1	104.3	130.4	106.0
1997	104.0	101.2	102.3	120.8	100.2
1998	100.0	93.7	94.5	136.2	94.9
1999	100.2	96.7	97.1	115.6	96.6
2000	103.3	100.0	108.3	112.0	99.7
2001	101.0	100.6	98.0	108.7	98.9
2002	98.9	97.8	100.2	101.0	99.5
2003	101.4	104.3	98.4	101.7	98.3
2004	102.1	104.0	103.6	104.7	99.0
2005	102.3	102.1	108.3	101.4	99.3
2006	100.9	101.7	99.4	100.8	99.7
2007	104.5	111.6	99.4	102.4	102.7
2008	104.7	111.7	103.9	99.8	103.9
2009	100.5	101.6	101.4	100.6	98.6
2010	102.2	106.4	101.0	100.4	101.4
2011	105.0	111.1	108.2	103.1	104.5

8－2 主要年份居民消费和商品零售价格指数(以1950年价格为100)

MAJOR YEAR'S CONSUMER AND RETAIL PRICE INDEXES (1950 = 100)

年份 Year	居民消费价格指数 Consumer Price Index	#食品类 Food	衣着类 Clothing	服务项目价格指数 Services Price Index	商品零售价格指数 Retail Price Index
1951	110.5	105.2	112.4		110.5
1952	110.3	104.8	110.9		110.3
1957	119.5	120.7	115.3	91.6	119.5
1962	127.4	128.8	115.1	94.2	127.4
1965	133.3	138.7	108.4	81.5	133.3
1970	129.0	137.6	110.3	76.8	129.0
1975	128.8	138.2	110.0	75.7	128.8
1978	129.1	138.7	109.8	75.7	129.1
1980	137.6	154.1	109.3	76.1	138.1
1985	160.8	196.1	103.8	80.5	162.5
1987	185.4	235.8	113.6	85.2	188.2
1988	223.8	295.2	133.2	100.8	227.6
1989	258.1	322.4	161.3	131.3	260.3
1990	269.7	333.3	166.8	155.9	269.7
1991	288.6	356.7	187.0	170.9	288.1
1992	321.5	410.5	203.1	204.9	319.2
1993	398.3	496.3	241.7	324.8	382.4
1994	505.4	671.1	314.4	382.9	469.5
1995	587.3	792.5	386.1	471.8	536.2
1996	661.3	872.6	402.7	615.2	568.4
1997	687.8	883.0	412.0	743.1	569.5
1998	687.8	827.4	389.3	1 012.1	540.5
1999	689.2	800.1	378.0	1 170.0	522.1
2000	711.9	800.1	409.4	1 310.4	520.5
2001	719.0	804.9	401.2	1 424.4	514.8
2002	711.1	787.2	402.0	1 438.7	512.2
2003	721.1	821.0	395.6	1 463.1	503.5
2004	736.2	853.9	409.8	1 531.9	498.5
2005	753.1	871.8	443.8	1 553.4	495.0
2006	759.9	886.6	441.2	1 565.8	493.5
2007	794.1	989.5	438.5	1 603.4	506.8
2008	831.4	1 105.3	455.6	1 600.2	526.6
2009	835.6	1 123.0	462.0	1 609.8	519.2
2010	854.0	1 194.9	466.6	1 616.2	526.5
2011	896.7	1 327.5	504.9	1 666.3	550.2

8－3 主要年份生产投资价格指数

MAJOR YEAR'S PRICE INDEXES FOR PRODUCTION AND INVESTMENT

(上年＝100)　　(preceding year＝100)

年份 Year	工业品出厂价格指数 Producer Price Indexes for Manufactured Goods	原材料、燃料、动力购进价格指数 Purchasing Price Indexes for Raw Material, Fuel and Power	房屋销售价格指数 Sales Price Indexes of Houses	房屋租赁价格指数 Renting Price Indexes of Houses	物业管理价格指数 Property Management Price Indexes	固定资产投资价格指数 Price Indexes for Investment in Fixed Assets
1990	104.33	108.64				
1991	101.68	108.10				
1992	105.46	107.13				
1993	115.49	126.91				
1994	121.62	120.30				
1995	112.70	114.25				
1996	103.81	103.25				
1997	100.22	101.93				
1998	94.96	92.77	100.1	94.0		
1999	96.93	95.88	103.7	104.3		
2000	101.89	106.81	102.3	95.8		
2001	98.00	97.81	104.1	107.0		
2002	97.37	96.78	107.6	94.4		
2003	100.97	106.51	114.6	99.4		
2004	102.92	113.62	115.2	98.6		105.8
2005	101.39	106.52	110.9	103.3	100.2	103.1
2006	101.08	105.80	106.9	110.1	99.8	102.6
2007	101.50	106.69	106.5	108.3	100.4	104.1
2008	105.33	115.91	105.1	106.5	102.1	111.0
2009	95.78	90.35	100.3	103.5	100.4	94.6
2010	103.75	112.21		103.0	100.5	104.9
2011	104.90	109.39				107.0

注：自2011年工业品出厂价格改为工业生产者出厂价格；主要原材料、燃料、动力购进价格改为工业生产者购进价格。

Note: Since 2011, "Producer Price Indexes for Industrial Producers" has been used in stead of "Producer Price Indexes for Manufactured Goods", "Purchasing Price Indexes for Industrial Producers" has been used in stead of "Purchasing Price Indexes for Raw Material, Fuel and Power".

8-4 工业品出厂价格指数
PRODUCER PRICE INDEXES FOR MANUFACTURED GOODS

(上年=100)　　(preceding year=100)

类　别	Item	1990	1995	2000	2005	2006	2007	2008	2009	2010	2011
总指数	**General Index**	**104.33**	**112.70**	**101.89**	**101.39**	**101.08**	**101.50**	**105.33**	**95.78**	**103.75**	**104.90**
其中:轻工业	Light Industry	106.19	115.33	98.50	99.78	99.58	100.97	102.93	97.21	100.80	103.46
重工业	Heavy Industry	102.06	108.61	105.62	104.32	103.94	102.49	109.17	93.45	107.57	105.89
其中:生产资料	**Means of Production**	**102.78**	**110.20**	**105.03**	**103.24**	**102.49**	**102.41**	**108.76**	**94.25**	**106.43**	**105.54**
采掘	Excavation	113.17	119.02	95.67	114.74	104.73	99.85	115.24	93.44	130.94	132.07
原料	Raw Materials	108.80	109.54	113.82	106.91	104.05	104.01	108.81	90.67	115.24	111.52
加工	Processing	99.71	110.29	97.58	101.45	101.86	101.91	108.59	95.34	103.50	103.49
生活资料	**Means of Livelihood**	**105.83**	**114.77**	**98.25**	**99.13**	**99.74**	**100.64**	**101.72**	**97.45**	**99.61**	**103.82**
食品	Food	108.04	116.48	96.59	98.80	101.52	106.55	108.42	98.21	105.06	109.71
衣着	Clothing	109.27	117.60	99.37	101.48	102.16	102.46	103.36	102.03	101.56	107.44
一般日用品	Articles for Daily Use	104.16	117.65	104.52	101.97	101.82	103.21	103.03	99.39	99.96	108.02
耐用消费品	Durable Consumer Goods	96.72	103.25	97.70	97.43	97.23	96.10	97.13	94.52	93.23	94.34

8－5 主要原材料、燃料、动力购进价格指数

PURCHASING PRICE INDEXES FOR RAW MATERIALS, FUELS AND POWER

(上年＝100)　　(preceding year＝100)

名　称	Item	1990	1995	2000	2005	2006	2007	2008	2009	2010	2011
总 指 数	**General Index**	**108.64**	**114.25**	**106.81**	**106.52**	**105.8**	**106.69**	**115.91**	**90.35**	**112.21**	**109.39**
燃料、动力类	Fuel and Power	97.94	109.96	113.82	117.34	117.17	103.14	126.19	90.53	115.43	111.29
黑色金属材料类	Ferrous Metals	113.94	97.00	102.66	107.84	95.83	109.61	122.19	82.38	111.97	113.08
#钢材	Rolled-steel		98.86	105.44	106.57	96.11	108.14	119.10	85.25	108.67	107.95
其他	Others		93.76	101.10	112.88	94.91	114.43	132.40	72.73	122.64	129.01
有色金属材料及电线类	Nonferrous Metals and Electric Wire	97.97	128.79	106.75	108.06	131.58	106.51	93.41	86.24	122.65	108.45
化工原料类	Raw Chemical Materials	98.35	129.93	106.9	112.47	99.71	111.09	123.00	87.66	111.04	113.79
木材及纸浆类	Timber and Paper Pulp	98.57	109.68	108.98	103.8	104.29	107.23	103.58	89.16	117.06	103.78
建筑材料及非金属矿类	Building Materials and Nonmetals	144.52	93.94	99.50	115.54	92.83	95.80	124.52	100.98	107.61	116.71
其他工业原材料及半成品	Other Industrial Raw Materials and Semi-finished Goods		97.04	105.32	97.87	103.33	104.43	109.65	92.70	106.41	103.31
农副产品	Agricultural Products	115.72	134.17	92.73	101.55	110.87	112.49	117.68	88.60	121.30	115.04
纺织原料类	Textile Materials	112.47	99.25	104.03	98.15	100.15	104.01	101.44	98.69	112.90	111.11

8-6 按工业行业分工业品出厂价格指数
PRODUCER PRICE INDEXES FOR MANUFACTURED GOODS BY SECTOR

(上年=100)

行　业	Sector	2000
工业品出厂价格指数	**Producer Price Indexes for Manufactured Goods**	**101.71**
煤炭开采和洗选业	Mining and Washing of Coal	
石油和天然气开采业	Extraction of Petroleum and Natural Gas	
黑色金属矿采选业	Mining of Ferrous Metal Ores	
有色金属矿采选业	Mining of Non-ferrous Metal Ores	
非金属矿采选业	Mining and Processing of Nonmetal Ores	106.09
其他采矿业	Mining of Other Ores	
农副食品加工业	Processing of Food from Agricultural Products	93.78
食品制造业	Manufacture of Foods	87.30
饮料制造业	Manufacture of Beverage	89.51
烟草制品业	Manufacture of Tobacco	100.00
纺织业	Manufacture of Textile	112.46
纺织服装、鞋、帽制造业	Manufacture of Textile Wearing Apparel, Footware, and Caps	
皮革、毛皮、羽毛(绒)及其制品业	Manufacture of Leather, Fur, Feather & Its Products	
木材加工及木、竹、藤、棕、草制品业	Processing of Timbers, Manufacture of Wood, Bamboo, Rattan, Palm, and Straw Products	
家具制造业	Manufacture of Furniture	100.03
造纸及纸制品业	Manufacture of Paper and Paper Products	101.82
印刷业和记录媒介的复制	Printing, Reproduction of Recording Media	
文教体育用品制造业	Manufacture of Articles for Culture, Education and Sport Activity	
石油加工、炼焦及核燃料加工业	Processing of Petroleum, Coking, Processing of Nucleus Fuel	139.69
化学原料及化学制品制造业	Manufacture of Chemical Raw Material and Chemical Products	116.25
医药制造业	Manufacture of Medicines	90.11
化学纤维制造业	Manufacture of Chemical Fiber	
橡胶制品业	Manufacture of Rubber	99.58
塑料制品业	Manufacture of Plastic	98.15
非金属矿物制品业	Manufacture of Non-metallic Mineral Products	102.93
黑色金属冶炼及压延加工业	Smelting and Pressing of Ferrous Metals	101.20
有色金属冶炼及压延加工业	Smelting and Pressing of Non-ferrous Metals	
金属制品业	Manufacture of Metal Products	
通用设备制造业	Manufacture of General Purpose Machinery	
专用设备制造业	Manufacture of Special Purpose Machinery	87.01
交通运输设备制造业	Manufacture of Transport Equipment	102.71
电气机械及器材制造业	Manufacture of Electrical Machinery & Equipment	103.81
通信设备、计算机及其他电子设备制造业	Manufacture of Communication Equipment, Computer and Other Electronic Equipment	101.91
仪器仪表及文化、办公用机械制造业	Manufacture of Measuring Instrument and Machinery for Cultural Activity & Office Work	107.28
工艺品及其他制造业	Manufacture of Artwork, Other Manufacture	
废弃资源和废旧材料回收加工业	Recycling and Disposal of Waste	
电力、热力的生产和供应业	Production and Supply of Electric Power and Heat Power	
燃气生产和供应业	Production and Supply of Gas	100.01
水的生产和供应业	Production and Supply of Water	94.46

(preceding year = 100)

2005	2006	2007	2008	2009	2010	2011
101.39	**101.08**	**101.50**	**105.33**	**95.78**	**103.75**	**104.90**
100.65	96.10	101.24	99.25	101.67	113.85	104.33
108.54	107.57	104.55	110.23	123.38	122.69	111.39
117.32	103.80	98.71	116.71	86.15	132.38	145.13
97.23	101.38	110.20	111.53	95.8	105.68	111.32
101.21	99.71	100.86	113.82	98.52	107.13	112.52
100.80	100.20	101.66	104.21	101.63	100.66	104.14
100.00	100.00	100.00	100.00	100.00	100.00	
101.64	100.67	100.71	104.01	100.22	105.39	105.09
102.56	103.20	102.83	102.20	99.51	101.82	105.42
99.38	101.63	103.44	100.52	100.56	100.70	102.95
101.46	98.54	102.47	102.03	100.54	101.41	108.13
104.29	99.84	100.13	106.09	100.47	100.01	101.11
106.98	98.92	102.91	111.51	91.37	104.01	105.71
100.60	101.11	106.56	115.27	107.72	94.71	110.06
100.25	100.60	100.12	103.39	100.3	102.21	99.65
113.93	112.84	110.56	118.02	83.82	124.23	114.95
107.20	96.74	102.84	107.31	86.37	113.85	114.60
102.19	98.65	102.45	103.67	99.71	101.52	107.33
107.79	98.92	101.82	95.98	78.75	114.01	123.72
99.82	103.49	104.21	105.44	101.5	101.59	118.21
103.37	100.33	102.40	103.38	92.05	99.92	108.76
101.18	100.96	102.80	108.40	98.21	104.13	108.15
101.93	97.31	111.16	133.12	79.23	115.41	110.90
100.22	128.45	103.03	91.81	85.30	125.88	108.26
108.47	93.02	102.83	112.00	100.08	98.83	102.19
103.58	102.09	102.21	108.50	100.32	98.87	100.79
103.47	100.15	101.87	102.69	104.70	100.91	101.69
100.98	99.44	100.50	101.65	98.51	99.63	99.22
102.28	106.64	101.74	100.34	97.15	100.53	103.10
84.90	88.78	87.30	93.92	89.41	91.49	84.65
105.75	100.44	100.78	98.75	101.55	102.46	101.77
105.95	104.84	105.02	104.07	98.39	98.37	100.94
104.92	103.25	100.00	103.10	104.95	101.17	101.49
105.85	104.33	101.61	104.29	91.66	112.18	107.34
120.28	127.90	100.41	99.90	99.83	100.05	100.15

8-7 固定资产投资价格指数
PRICE INDEXES FOR INVESTMENT IN FIXED ASSETS

(上年=100)　　(preceding year=100)

项目名称	Item	2004	2005	2006	2007	2008	2009	2010	2011
总　计	**Total**	**105.8**	**103.1**	**102.6**	**104.1**	**111.0**	**94.6**	**104.9**	**107.0**
建筑安装、装饰工程	Construction and Installation Project	109.3	103.7	103.5	105.4	115.5	92.1	107.5	110.1
其中:人工费	of which: Labor Cost	105.1	112.7	110.0	111.0	112.7	104.9	112.0	115.9
材料费	Materials Expenses	111.5	101.0	100.7	103.9	120.5	87.5	107.0	109.6
机械使用费	Expenses on Machinery Use	108.5	104.2	109.1	107.2	106.9	100.0	104.3	105.0
设备、工器具购置	Purchase of Equipment, Tools and Instruments	98.3	99.7	100.6	100.8	102.5	98.0	100.2	101.8
其他费用	Others	101.8	105.5	100.9	103.9	105.9	98.5	102.2	103.0

8-8 房地产价格指数(2011 年)
PRICE INDEXES FOR REAL ESTATE(2011)

(上年=100)　　(preceding year=100)

项目	Item	2011
新建住宅销售价格指数	**Sales Price Indexes of Newly Constructed Residential Buildings**	
一月	January	105.8
二月	February	104.6
三月	March	104.4
四月	April	104.1
五月	May	104.4
六月	June	104.6
七月	July	104.8
八月	August	104.6
九月	September	104.7
十月	October	101.6
十一月	November	101.2
十二月	December	100.5
二手住宅销售价格指数	**Sales Price Indexes of Second-hand Residential Buildings**	
一月	January	105.9
二月	February	105.9
三月	March	103.7
四月	April	102.7
五月	May	102.7
六月	June	103.1
七月	July	103.1
八月	August	102.9
九月	September	102.8
十月	October	101.5
十一月	November	100.6
十二月	December	98.8

8-9 居民消费价格分类指数(2011 年)
CONSUMER PRICE INDEXES BY CATEGORY(2011)

(上年=100)　(preceding year=100)

项　目	Item	指　数 Indexes
居民消费价格总指数	**Consumer Price Index**	**105.0**
非食品价格指数	Non-food Price Index	102.8
服务项目价格指数	Services Price Index	103.1
扣除鲜菜鲜果总指数	Price Index Without Fresh Vegetables and Fresh Fruits	105.1
消费品价格指数	Consumer Goods Price Index	105.8
一、食品	**Food**	**111.1**
1. 粮食	Grain	107.2
2. 淀粉及薯类	Starches and Tubers	109.0
3. 干豆类及豆制品	Beans and Bean Products	104.9
4. 油脂	Oil or Fat	108.4
5. 肉禽及其制品	Meat Poultry and Its Products	122.9
6. 蛋类	Eggs	110.6
7. 水产品	Aquatic Products	111.5
8. 菜	Vegetables	98.9
9. 调味品	Flavoring	112.2
10. 糖	Carbohydrate	108.0
11. 茶及饮料	Tea and Beverages	104.8
12. 干鲜瓜果类	Dried and Fresh Melons and Fruits	114.6
13. 糕点饼干面包	Cake,Biscuit and Bread	107.3
14. 液体乳及乳制品	Milk and Its Products	103.6
15. 在外用膳食品	Dining out	111.4
16. 其它食品及食品加工服务	Other Foods and Manufacturing Services	111.4
二、烟酒及用品	**Tobacco,Liquor and Articles**	**101.5**
1. 烟草	Tobacco	103.1
2. 酒	Liquor	100.1
3. 吸烟饮酒用品	Articles for Smoking and Drinking	

8 -9 续表
continued

项　目	Item	指　数 Indexes
三、衣着	**Clothing**	**108.2**
1. 服装	Garments	107.8
2. 衣着材料	Clothing Materials	122.8
3. 鞋袜帽	Footgear and Hats	108.9
4. 衣着加工服务	Clothing Manufacturing Services	106.2
四、家庭设备用品及维修服务	**Household Facilities, Articles and services**	**101.0**
1. 耐用消费品	Durable Consumer Goods	99.6
2. 室内装饰品	Interior Decorations	97.9
3. 床上用品	Bed Articles	109.3
4. 家庭日用杂品	Daily Use Household Articles	101.3
5. 家庭服务及加工维修服务	Household Services and Maintenance and Renovation	103.4
五、医疗保健和个人用品	**Health Care and Personal Articles**	**101.7**
1. 医疗保健	Health Care	101.4
2. 个人用品及服务	Personal Articles and Services	102.5
六、交通和通讯	**Transportation and Communication**	**100.6**
1. 交通	Transportation	101.8
2. 通讯	Communication	98.3
七、娱乐教育文化用品及服务	**Recreation, Education and Culture Articles and Services**	**100.7**
1. 文娱用耐用消费品及服务	Durable Consumer Goods for Cultural and Recreational Use and Services	97.6
2. 教育	Education	102.1
3. 文化娱乐用品	Cultural and Recreational Articles	98.7
4. 旅游及外出	Touring and Outing	101.6
八、居住	**Residence**	**103.5**
1. 建房及装修材料	Building and Building Decoration Materials	100.5
2. 租房	Renting	102.9
3. 自有住房	Private Housing	105.5
4. 水、电、燃料	Water, Electricity and Fuels	102.1

8－10 商品零售价格分类指数(2011 年)

RETAIL PRICE INDEXES BY CATEGORY(2011)

(上年=100)　　(preceding year=100)

项　目	Item	指　数 Indexes
商品零售价格总指数	**Retail Price Index**	**104.5**
一、食品	**Food**	**111.4**
1.粮食	Grain	106.0
2.淀粉及薯类	Starches and Tubers	109.0
3.干豆类及豆制品	Beans and Bean Products	105.2
4.油脂	Oil or Fat	108.3
5.肉禽及其制品	Meat Poultry and Its Products	122.5
6.蛋	Eggs	110.5
7.水产品	Aquatic Products	114.7
8.菜	Vegetables	98.9
9.调味品	Flavoring	111.5
10.糖	Carbohydrate	108.2
11.干鲜瓜果	Dried and Fresh Melons and Fruits	114.8
12.糕点饼干面包	Cake,Biscuit and Bread	107.3
13.液体乳及乳制品	Milk and Its Products	103.9
14.在外用膳食品	Dining out	111.9
15.其他食品	Other Foods	111.4
二、饮料、烟酒	**Beverages,Tobacco and Liquor**	**102.3**
1.茶及饮料	Tea and Beverages	104.8
2.烟草	Tobacco	103.1
3.酒	Liquor	100.2
三、服装、鞋帽类	**Clothing**	**108.1**
1.服装	Garments	107.8
2.鞋袜帽	Footgear and Hats	108.8
3.其他	Others	101.0
四、纺织品类	**Textiles**	**112.1**
1.衣着材料	Cotton Cloth	122.8
2.床上用品	Blend Cloth	110.3
五、家用电器及音像器材	**Household Appliances,Music and Video Equipment**	**96.9**
1.家庭设备	Household Facilities	97.7
2.文娱用耐用消费品	Durable Consumer Goods for Cultural and Recreational Use and Services	95.6
3.音像器材类	Music and Video Equipment	98.6

8－10 续表
continued

项　目	Item	指　数 Indexes
六、文化办公用品	**Culture and office Articles**	**99.1**
七、日用品	**Articles for Daily Use**	**100.9**
1. 日用百货	General Merchandise for Daily Use	101.7
2. 日用杂品	Miscellaneous for Daily Use	98.0
3. 洗涤用品	Cleaning Products	100.5
4. 其他日用品	Other Articles for Daily Use	102.0
八、体育娱乐用品	**Sports and Recreation Articles**	**99.6**
1. 体育用品	Sports Articles	98.9
2. 娱乐用品	Recreation Articles	100.0
九、交通、通信用品	**Transportation and Communication Appliances**	**93.4**
1. 交通运输机械	Transportation Machines	94.4
2. 通讯器材类	Communication Equipment	90.2
十、家具	**Furniture**	**103.7**
十一、化妆品类	**Cosmetics**	**103.0**
十二、金银珠宝类	**Gold, Silver and Jewelry**	**110.5**
十三、中西药品及医疗保健用品	**Traditional Chinese and Western Medicals and Health Care Articles**	**101.6**
1. 医疗器具及用品	Medical Apparatus and Articles	104.1
2. 中药材及中成药	Traditional Chinese Medicinal Materials and Medicines	108.0
3. 西药	Western Medicines	99.6
4. 保健器具及用品	Health Care Articles	101.8
十四、书报杂志及电子出版物	**Books, Newspapers, Magazines and Electronic Publications**	**99.5**
1. 教材及参考书	Teaching Material and Reference Books	104.5
2. 书报杂志	Books, Newspapers and Magazines	100.1
3. 电子音像制品	Electronic Music and Video Products	88.1
十五、燃料类	**Fuels**	**110.1**
1. 煤炭及制品类	Coal and Its Products	115.8
2. 石油及制品类	Petroleum and Its Products	109.5
十六、建筑材料及五金电料类	**Building Materials and Hardware**	**105.9**
1. 建筑装璜材料	Building Decoration Materials	105.4
2. 五金电料类	Hardware	106.6

主要统计指标解释

居民消费价格指数　是反映一定时期内城乡居民所购买的生活消费品价格和服务项目价格变动趋势和程度的相对数，是对城市居民消费价格指数和农村居民消费价格指数进行综合汇总计算的结果。该指数可以观察和分析消费品的零售价格和服务价格变动对城乡居民实际生活费支出的影响程度。

商品零售价格指数　是反映一定时期内城乡商品零售价格变动趋势和程度的相对数。商品零售价格的变动直接影响到城乡居民的生活支出和国家的财政收入，影响居民购买力和市场供需的平衡，影响到消费与积累的比例关系。因此，该指数可以从一个侧面对上述经济活动进行观察和分析。

工业生产者出厂价格指数　是反映一定时期内全部工业产品出厂价格总水平的变动趋势和程度的相对数，包括工业企业售给本企业以外所有单位的各种产品和直接售给居民用于生活消费的产品。该指数可以观察出厂价格变动对工业总产值及增加值的影响。

工业生产者购进价格指数　是反映工业企业作为生产投入，而从物资交易市场和能源、原材料生产企业购买原材料、燃料和动力产品时，所支付的价格水平变动趋势和程度的统计指标，是扣除工业企业物质消耗成本中的价格变动影响的重要依据。

房地产价格指数　是反映一定时期内房地产价格变动趋势和程度的相对数，包括新建住宅销售价格指数、二手住宅销售价格指数。

Explanatory Notes on Main Statistical Indicators

Consumer Price Indices　reflect the trend and degree of changes in prices of consumer goods and services purchased by urban and rural households during a given period. They are obtained by combining the Urban Consumer Price Indices and the Rural Consumer Price Indices. The Indices enable the observation and analysis of the degree of impact of the changes in the prices of retailed goods and services on the actual living expenses of urban and rural residents.

Retail Price Indices　reflect the trend and degree of change in retail prices of commodities during a given period. The change in retail prices of commodities directly affect the living expenditure of urban and rural residents, government revenue, purchasing power of residents and the equilibrium of market supply and demand, and the ratio of consumption to accumulation. Therefore, the retail price indices are useful to analyze the changes of the above economic activities.

Producer Price Indices for Industrial Producers　reflect the trend and degree of changes in general ex-factory prices of all industrial products during a given period, including sales of industrial products by an industrial enterprise to all units outside the enterprise, as well as sales of consumer goods to residents. It can be used to analyze the impact of ex-factory prices on gross output value and value-added of the industrial sector.

Purchasing Price Indices for Industrial Producers　reflect changes in the level and degree of prices paid by industrial enterprises when they purchase production input such as raw materials, fuels and power from the market or from other energy or raw materials producing enterprises. These indices provide important basis for measuring the material consumption of industrial enterprises after removing influence of price changes.

Price Indices for Real Estate　reflect the trend and degree of changes in prices of real estate during a given period, including sales price indices for newly constructed residential buildings and secondhand residential buildings.

9 人民生活

PEOPLE'S LIVING CONDITIONS

简要说明

一、本篇资料的主要内容

本篇资料主要反映了全市城市、农村居民的家庭收支、就业、居住、耐用消费品拥有量、生产和生活等方面的情况。

二、本篇资料的来源

1、本篇资料中城市居民家庭相关资料来源于城市住户调查年报，由国家统计局青岛调查队城镇住户调查处整理提供。

2、本篇资料中农村居民家庭相关资料来源于农村住户调查年报，由市统计局农村统计处（国家统计局青岛调查队农村调查处）整理提供。

3、人民生活基本情况由市统计局国民经济综合统计处加工整理。

Brief Introduction

I. Main Content

Data in this chapter show the basic conditions of the people's livelihood of the whole city, including income and expenditure of the households, employment, housing condition, consumption and possession of the major consumer goods, etc.

II. Source of Data

（1） Data on conditions of urban households are based on the annual report of sample survey on urban households and compiled by the Division of Urban Household Survey of Survey Office of the National Bureau of Statistics in Qingdao.

（2） Data on conditions of rural households are based on the annual report of sample survey on rural households and compiled by the Division of Countryside Statistics of Qingdao Municipal Bureau of Statistics （Division of Rural Household Survey of Survey Office of the National Bureau of Statistics in Qingdao）.

（3） Data on basic statistics on people's living conditions are compiled by the Division of Comprehensive Statistics of Qingdao Municipal Bureau of Statistics.

9-1 人民生活基本情况(1990-2011年)
BASIC STATISTICS ON PEOPLE'S LIVING CONDITIONS(1990-2011)

		单位	Unit	1990	1995	2000	2005	2006
一、城乡居民收入	**Income of Urban and Rural Households**							
城市居民年人均可支配收入	Annual Per Capita Disposable Income of Urban Households	元	yuan	1 624	5 612	8 016	12 920	15 328
农民年人均纯收入	Annual Per Capita Net Income of Rural Households	元	yuan	952	2 225	3 637	5 806	6 546
二、城乡居民消费	**Expenditure of Urban and Rural Households**							
城市居民人均消费支出	Per Capita Consumption Expenditure of Urban Households	元	yuan	1 507	4 606	6 677	9 883	11 945
农村居民人均生活消费支出	Per Capita Consumption Expenditure of Rural Households	元	yuan	633	1 723	2 380	3 737	4 203
三、城市居民人均现住房建筑面积	**Per Capita Building Space in Urban Areas**	**平方米**	**sq. m**	**14.16**	**17.12**	**20.76**	**22.96**	**23.73**
农村居民人均居住面积	Per Capita Living Space in Rural Areas	平方米	sq. m	19.60	23.03	25.88	29.54	30.82
四、城乡居民人民币储蓄余额	**Savings Deposit of Urban and Rural Households at Year-end (RMB)**	**亿元**	**100 million yuan**	**65.59**	**268.79**	**535.32**	**1 343.10**	**1 567.62**
人均人民币储蓄余额	Per Capita Savings Deposit at Year-end (RMB)	元	yuan	984	3 926	7 575	18 248	21 038
五、学龄儿童入学率	**Attendance Rate of School Age Children**	**%**	**%**	**99.84**	**99.82**	**99.99**	**99.99**	**99.99**
每万人口中大学在校学生	Students Enrollment of University Per 10000 Population	人	person	23	36	65	324	347
六、城市每百户拥有彩色电视机	**Color TV Per 100 Urban Households**	**台**	**set**	**68.00**	**100.00**	**120.00**	**118.25**	**124.5**
城市每百户拥有电冰箱	Refrigerators Per 100 Urban Households	台	set	62.00	89.00	94.30	94.50	98.5
七、每万人口拥有医疗床位	**Hospital Beds Per 10 000 Population**	**张**	**bed**	**35.3**	**36.9**	**34.5**	**41.3**	**38.3**
每万人口拥有医生	Doctors Per 10000 Population	人	person	20.6	20.2	21.0	20.3	20.6
八、城市每一就业者负担人数(包括本人)	**Number of Dependents Per Employee of Urban Household (including the employee himself or herself)**	**人**	**person**	**1.72**	**1.58**	**1.82**	**1.97**	**1.79**
农村每一就业者负担人数(包括本人)	Number of Dependents Per Employee of Rural Household (including the employee himself or herself)	人	person	1.60	1.41	1.33	1.33	1.34
九、农民、城市居民人均年收入对比	**Contrast of Rural and Urban Residents in Annual Per Capita Income**			**1:1.7**	**1:2.5**	**1:2.2**	**1:2.2**	**1:2.34**
农民、城市居民人均年生活费支出对比	Contrast of Rural and Urban Residents in Annual Per Capita Living Expenditure			1:2.4	1:2.7	1:2.8	1:2.6	1:2.84

注：1. 自2002年起城市居民年人均可支配收入为新口径。农民与城市居民人均年收入对比，农民以纯收入，城市居民以可支配收入计算。
2. 城乡居民住房面积分别根据城乡住户抽样调查取得。

Note: 1. Since 2002, new calibre has been adopted in per capita annual disposable income of urban households. The calculation of contrast of rural and urban residents in per capita annual income is using net income of rural residents and disposable income of urban residents.
2. Figures relating to floor space among urban and rural dwellers were based on a survey.

9-1 续表
continued

		单位	Unit	2007	2008	2009	2010	2011
一、城乡居民收入	**Income of Urban and Rural Households**							
城市居民年人均可支配收入	Annual Per Capita Disposable Income of Urban Households	元	yuan	17 856	20 464	22 368	24 998	28 567
农民年人均纯收入	Annual Per Capita Net Income of Rural Households	元	yuan	7 477	8 509	9 249	10 550	12 370
二、城乡居民消费	**Expenditure of Urban and Rural Households**							
城市居民人均消费支出	Per Capita Consumption Expenditure of Urban Households	元	yuan	13 376	14 999	16 080	17 531	19 297
农村居民人均生活消费支出	Per Capita Consumption Expenditure of Rural Households	元	yuan	4 736	5 303	5 832	6 662	7 661
三、城市居民人均现住房建筑面积	**Per Capita Building Space in Urban Areas**	**平方米**	**sq. m**	**23.71**	**26.83**	**26.71**	**27.42**	**27.67**
农村居民人均居住面积	Per Capita Living Space in Rural Areas	平方米	sq. m	30.95	30.73	31.39	30.97	31.73
四、城乡居民人民币储蓄余额	**Savings Deposit of Urban and Rural Households at Year-end (RMB)**	**亿元**	**100 million yuan**	**1 702.04**	**2 123.36**	**2 527.87**	**2 912.33**	**3 198.51**
人均人民币储蓄余额	Per Capita Savings Deposit at Year-end (RMB)	元	yuan	22 455	27 882	33 134	38 137	41 736
五、学龄儿童入学率	**Attendance Rate of School Age Children**	**%**	**%**	**99.99**	**99.99**	**99.99**	**99.99**	**99.99**
每万人口中大学在校学生	Students Enrollment of University Per 10000 Population	人	person	349	354	361	373	380
六、城市每百户拥有彩色电视机	**Color TV Per 100 Urban Households**	**台**	**set**	**121.84**	**116.00**	**117.50**	**118.50**	**117.25**
城市每百户拥有电冰箱	Refrigerators Per 100 Urban Households	台	set	106.70	102.75	105.00	106.75	108.25
七、每万人口拥有医疗床位	**Hospital Beds Per 10 000 Population**	**张**	**bed**	**39.7**	**42.5**	**43.0**	**47.2**	**52.2**
每万人口拥有医生	Doctors Per 10000 Population	人	person	19.8	21.4	21.9	23.2	23.9
八、城市每一就业者负担人数(包括本人)	**Number of Dependents Per Employee of Urban Household (including the employee himself or herself)**	**人**	**person**	**1.79**	**1.77**	**1.73**	**1.75**	**1.71**
农村每一就业者负担人数(包括本人)	Number of Dependents Per Employee of Rural Household (including the employee himself or herself)	人	person	1.33	1.33	1.34	1.33	1.48
九、农民、城市居民人均年收入对比	**Contrast of Rural and Urban Residents in Annual Per Capita Income**			**1:2.39**	**1:2.41**	**1:2.42**	**1:2.37**	**1:2.31**
农民、城市居民人均年生活费支出对比	Contrast of Rural and Urban Residents in Annual Per Capita Living Expenditure			1:2.82	1:2.83	1:2.76	1:2.63	1:2.52

9-2 城市居民家庭收支情况（2011 年）

BASIC CONDITIONS ON INCOME AND EXPENDITURE OF URBAN HOUSEHOLDS(2011)

单位：元(yuan)

指标名称	Name	2011	2010	2011 年比 2010 年增长(±%) 2011/2010(±%)
人均家庭总收入	**Per Capita Total Income of Household**	**31 492**	**27 283**	**15.4**
其中：人均可支配收入	of which: Per Capita Disposable Income	28 567	24 998	14.3
(一)工资性收入	Income from Wages and Salaries	20 100	17 512	14.8
(二)经营性净收入	Net Income from Household Operations	2 710	2 204	23.0
(三)财产性收入	Income from Properties	1 055	836	26.1
(四)转移性收入	Income from Transfers	7 627	6 731	13.3
人均消费性支出	**Per Capita Consumption Expenditure**	**19 297**	**17 531**	**10.1**
(一)食品	Food	7 241	6 553	10.5
(二)衣着	Clothing	2 593	2 188	18.5
(三)居住	Residence	1 783	1 640	8.8
(四)家庭设备用品及服务	Household Facilities, Articles and Services	1 139	1 221	-6.8
(五)医疗保健	Health Care and Medical Services	1 085	1 049	3.4
(六)交通和通讯	Transportation and Communication	2 901	2 584	12.3
(七)教育文化娱乐服务	Education, Cultural and Recreation Services	1 930	1 748	10.4
(八)其他商品和服务	Other Goods and Services	626	548	14.2

9－3 城市居民家庭基本情况（2011 年）

BASIC CONDITIONS OF URBAN HOUSEHOLDS(2011)

项目	Item	单位	Unit
调查户数	Number of Households Surveyed	户	household
平均每户人口数	Average Household Size	人	person
户均有收入者人数	Average Number of Persons Having Income Per Household	人	person
户均就业人口数	Average Number of Employed Persons Per Household	人	person
#国有经济单位职工人数	Working in State-owned Units	人	person
集体经济单位职工人数	Working in Collective-owned Units	人	person
聘留离退休人员数	Number of Retired Persons Employed Again	人	person
户均离退休人数	Average Number of Retired Persons Per Household	人	person
户均其他有收入者人数	Average Number of Other Persons Having Income Per Household	人	person
户均无收入者人数	Average Number of Persons Having No Income Per Household	人	person
平均每人期初手存现金	Per Capita Cash on Hand Term-beginning	元	yuan
平均每人每年家庭总收入	Per Capita Annual Income	元	yuan
#平均每人每年可支配收入	Per Capita Annual Disposable Income	元	yuan
平均每人每年出售财物收入	Per Capita Annual Income of Selling Properties	元	yuan
平均每人每年借贷收入	Per Capita Annual Savings and Lending Income	元	yuan
平均每人每年家庭总支出	Per Capita Annual Expenditure	元	yuan
#平均每人每年消费支出	Per Capita Annual Consumption Expenditure	元	yuan
平均每人每年储蓄借贷支出	Per Capita Annual Savings and Lending Expenditure	元	yuan
平均每人期末手存现金	Per Capita Cash on Hand Term-end	元	yuan
平均每一就业者负担人口(包括本人)	Number of Dependents Per Employee(including the employee himself or herself)	人	person

全市平均 Average	最低收入户 Lowest Income Households	低收入户 Low Income Households	较低收入户 Lower Middle Income Households
400	40	40	80
2.81	3.13	3.00	2.96
2.28	2.15	2.35	2.41
1.64	1.86	1.65	1.70
0.65	0.44	0.45	0.72
0.18	0.16	0.26	0.17
0.03		0.03	0.02
0.62	0.27	0.65	0.66
0.02	0.02	0.05	0.05
0.53	0.97	0.65	0.56
1 430.80	965.86	1 072.44	1 172.89
31 491.68	14 188.82	18 672.76	22 972.5
28 567.49	11 433.94	16 610.02	20 280.52
392.34	1.29	1.20	56.27
13 010.2	13 239.24	10 524.87	12 077.7
25 460.59	18 347.73	16 633.34	20 867.33
19 296.56	11 457.97	13 908.05	15 728.57
17 926.54	9 576.37	12 488.24	13 722.56
2 871.77	824.64	989.50	1 549.43
1.71	1.68	1.82	1.74

9－3 续表
continued

项　目	Item	单位	Unit
调查户数	Number of Households Surveyed	户	household
平均每户人口数	Average Household Size	人	person
户均有收入者人数	Average Number of Persons Having Income Per Household	人	person
户均就业人口数	Average Number of Employed Persons Per Household	人	person
#国有经济单位职工人数	Working in State-owned Units	人	person
集体经济单位职工人数	Working in Collective-owned Units	人	person
聘留离退休人员数	Number of Retired Persons Employed Again	人	person
户均离退休人数	Average Number of Retired Persons Per Household	人	person
户均其他有收入者人数	Average Number of Other Persons Having Income Per Household	人	person
户均无收入者人数	Average Number of Persons Having No Income Per Household	人	person
平均每人期初手存现金	Per Capita Cash on Hand Term-beginning	元	yuan
平均每人每年家庭总收入	Per Capita Annual Income	元	yuan
#平均每人每年可支配收入	Per Capita Annual Disposable Income	元	yuan
平均每人每年出售财物收入	Per Capita Annual Income of Selling Properties	元	yuan
平均每人每年借贷收入	Per Capita Annual Savings and Lending Income	元	yuan
平均每人每年家庭总支出	Per Capita Annual Expenditure	元	yuan
#平均每人每年消费支出	Per Capita Annual Consumption Expenditure	元	yuan
平均每人每年储蓄借贷支出	Per Capita Annual Savings and Lending Expenditure	元	yuan
平均每人期末手存现金	Per Capita Cash on Hand Term-end	元	yuan
平均每一就业者负担人口(包括本人)	Number of Dependents Per Employee(including the employee himself or herself)	人	person

中间收入户 Middle Income Households	较高收入户 Upper Middle Income Households	高收入户 High Income Households	最高收入户 Highest Income Households
80	80	40	40
2.77	2.65	2.71	2.50
2.23	2.26	2.35	2.18
1.67	1.64	1.53	1.29
0.54	0.77	0.64	0.91
0.24	0.21	0.08	0.03
0.01	0.02	0.08	0.05
0.55	0.61	0.79	0.89
0.01	0.01	0.03	
0.54	0.38	0.37	0.31
1 618.58	1 227.73	1 810.28	2 621.70
28 820.22	35 039.31	45 311.08	73 568.10
25 474.77	32 329.94	41 731.91	70 015.94
2.38	79.79	2.11	4 224.39
10 853.85	12 547.21	15 608.56	21 143.82
23 151.28	27 814.01	30 995.54	50 782.05
18 162.80	23 719.66	22 497.12	34 144.16
15 461.38	17 025.63	27 506.88	42 764.42
2 899.79	3 774.19	3 989.36	8 017.89
1.66	1.62	1.77	1.94

9－4 农村居民家庭基本情况(1990－2011 年)
BASIC CONDITIONS OF RURAL HOUSEHOLDS(1990－2011)

项　目	Item
调查户数(户)	**Number of Households Surveyed(household)**
常住人口(人)	Number of Permanent Residents(person)
平均每户常住人口(人)	Average Number of Permanent Residents Per Household(person)
平均每户整半劳力(人)	Average Number of Full/Semi Labour Force Per Household(person)
平均每个劳动力负担人口(含本人)(人)	Average Number of Dependents Per Labour Force(including the labour force himself or herself)(person)
总收入(元)	**Total Income(yuan)**
工资性收入	Income from Wages and Salaries
家庭经营收入	Income from Household Operations
财产性收入	Income from Properties
转移性收入	Income from Transfers
现金收入(元)	**Cash Income(yuan)**
工资性收入	Income from Wages and Salaries
家庭经营收入	Income from Household Operations
财产性收入	Income from Properties
转移性收入	Income from Transfers
总支出(元)	**Total Expenditure(yuan)**
家庭经营费用支出	Expenditure for Household Operations
购置生产性固定资产	Purchase of Productive Fixed Assets
税费支出	Taxes and Fees
生活消费支出	Expenditure on Household Consumption
转移性和财产性支出	Expenditure on Properties and Transfers
现金支出(元)	**Cash Expenditure(yuan)**
家庭经营费用支出	Expenditure for Household Operations
购买生产性固定资产	Purchase of Productive Fixed Assets
税费支出	Taxes and Fees
生活消费支出	Expenditure on Household Consumption
转移性和财产性支出	Expenditure on Properties and Transfers
平均每人年纯收入(元)	**Per Capita Annual Net Income(yuan)**
工资性收入	Income from Wages and Salaries
家庭经营纯收入	Income from Household Operations
财产性收入	Income from Properties
转移性收入	Income from Transfers

1990	1995	2000	2005	2006	2007	2008	2009	2010	2011
2 300	**770**	**820**	**860**	**900**	**900**	**900**	**900**	**900**	**680**
9 598	2 919	2 856	2 964	3 073	3 066	3 077	3 069	3 061	2 263
4.17	3.79	3.48	3.45	3.41	3.41	3.42	3.41	3.40	3.33
2.60	2.69	2.61	2.59	2.58	2.58	2.59	2.56	2.58	2.37
1.60	1.41	1.33	1.33	1.32	1.32	1.32	1.33	1.32	1.40
1 398	**3 516**	**5 394**	**8 370**	**9 464**	**10 881**	**12 381**	**13 299**	**14 993**	**17 156**
267	816	1 481	2 402	2 783	3 178	3 518	3 820	4 361	5 418
1 095	2 600	3 802	5 565	6 297	7 230	8 257	8 778	9 840	10 840
36	42	32	236	192	226	293	334	364	281
	58	79	167	192	247	314	367	427	617
1 087	**2 126**	**4 554**	**7 403**	**8 633**	**10 188**	**11 487**	**12 668**	**14 090**	**15 589**
267	816	1 479	2 400	2 775	3 177	3 512	3 819	4 361	5 367
784	1 207	2 428	4 603	5 460	6 544	7 395	8 203	8 882	9 420
	31	24	233	212	226	270	288	425	222
36	72	135	167	186	241	309	358	422	580
1 104	**3 093**	**4 223**	**6 363**	**7 198**	**8 144**	**9 144**	**9 871**	**11 031**	**13 192**
349	1 127	1 536	2 244	2 560	2 937	3 401	3 570	3 931	4 222
21	59	144	192	148	121	98	108	104	280
74	98	103	27	14	12	9	9	7	8
633	1 723	2 380	3 737	4 203	4 736	5 303	5 832	6 662	7 661
27	86	60	162	271	333	329	351	327	1 019
1 004	**2 377**	**3 883**	**5 700**	**6 737**	**7 851**	**8 771**	**9 474**	**10 655**	**12 779**
224	539	941	1 833	2 279	2 809	3 245	3 482	3 812	4 095
20	59	144	192	148	121	98	108	104	280
66	98	96	27	13	9	9	8	6	8
494	1 295	2 080	3 486	4 026	4 575	5 088	5 524	6 406	7 389
34	78	117	162	269	332	329	351	327	1 006
952	**2 225**	**3 637**	**5 806**	**6 546**	**7 477**	**8 509**	**9 249**	**10 550**	**12 370**
267	816	1 481	2 402	2 783	3 178	3 518	3 820	4 361	5 418
655	1 320	2 059	3 026	3 406	3 859	4 419	4 775	5 453	6 122
	42	32	236	192	226	293	334	364	281
30	47	65	142	165	214	280	319	372	549

9-5 城市住户每百户家庭主要耐用品拥有量（1980-2011年）

OWNERSHIP OF MAJOR DURABLE CONSUMER GOODS PER 100 URBAN HOUSEHOLDS(1980-2011)

年份 Year	家用电脑（台）Computer (set)	钢琴（架）Piano (set)	空调器（台）Air Conditioner (set)	淋浴热水器（台）Water Heater (set)	洗衣机（台）Washing Machine (set)	电冰箱（台）Refrigerator (set)	家用汽车（辆）Automobile (unit)	彩色电视机（台）Color TV (set)	移动电话（部）Cell Phone (unit)	照相机（架）Camera (set)
1980										2.0
1981					12.0			1.0		2.0
1982					22.0			2.0		4.0
1983					27.0	1.0		6.0		6.0
1984					30.0	2.0		8.0		8.0
1985					35.5	3.5		17.5		13.5
1986					40.0	4.5		24.5		15.0
1987					51.5	18.0		33.5		17.5
1988					60.5	33.0		47.0		20.5
1989					67.0	50.0		59.0		22.0
1990					66.0	62.0		68.0		26.0
1991					70.0	76.0		82.0		33.0
1992		1.0		12.5	72.5	83.0		81.0		38.5
1993		2.0	0.5	18.0	82.5	85.5		87.5		49.5
1994		4.0	1.0	17.0	81.0	88.5		92.0		51.0
1995		4.0	3.0	33.5	81.5	89.0		100.0		60.5
1996		4.5	6.5	39.5	83.0	91.5		105.0		63.0
1997	1.0	4.5	9.0	46.5	83.0	93.0		110.5	2.5	63.0
1998	8.3	5.3	16.5	53.0	83.0	91.8		110.8	6.8	69.4
1999	10.5	3.8	21.8	61.3	83.0	93.5		117.3	15.0	68.5
2000	19.3	2.0	24.5	65.8	83.3	94.3		120.0	30.3	69.5
2001	20.0	2.3	24.3	65.8	84.0	92.8		127.5	36.0	68.5
2002	31.5	2.3	38.3	75.3	89.3	93.0	0.5	123.3	80.0	72.8
2003	40.8	3.3	47.5	76.3	90.5	92.8	0.3	124.8	105.5	70.0
2004	46.0	3.0	55.0	79.0	92.5	92.5	2.0	123.5	128.0	68.3
2005	55.0	4.3	69.3	83.8	91.8	94.8	3.8	118.3	152.8	72.3
2006	71.3	7.8	89.3	88.0	97.3	98.5	6.3	124.5	187.0	81.8
2007	75.4	7.4	98.3	93.3	99.8	106.7	7.9	121.8	193.8	82.9
2008	75.0	5.0	93.8	90.3	94.5	102.8	12.8	116.0	190.8	67.0
2009	81.8	6.5	98.3	90.5	96.3	105.0	18.0	117.5	199.0	70.8
2010	86.0	7.5	99.3	90.8	97.3	106.8	20.3	118.5	207.5	71.0
2011	95.0	8.0	103.0	91.5	98.0	108.3	22.0	117.3	218.8	76.5

9-6 城市居民家庭居住情况
HOUSING CONDITIONS OF URBAN HOUSEHOLDS

类别	Category	2005	2006	2007	2008	2009	2010	2011
现住房总建筑面积(平方米/人)	**Floor Space of Houses (sq. m/person)**	**22.96**	**23.73**	**23.71**	**26.83**	**26.71**	**27.42**	**27.67**
房屋产权(合计)	**Housing Property**	**100.00**	**100.00**	**100.00**	**100.00**	**100.00**	**100.00**	**100.00**
租赁公房(%)	Leasehold of Public Housing(%)	11.00	11.00	7.50	2.25	1.75	2.00	5.25
租赁私房(%)	Leasehold of Private Housing(%)	1.75	2.00	2.25	3.75	3.25	3.00	2.25
原有私房(%)	Original Private Housing(%)	17.50	14.00	3.75	12.00	14.25	14.00	9.50
房改私房(%)	Private Housing After Housing Reform(%)	59.25	52.25	53.75	53.25	51.00	52.25	49.50
商品房(%)	Condominium(%)	10.00	20.00	32.00	27.75	29.00	27.75	32.00
其它(%)	Others(%)	0.50	0.75	0.75	1.00	0.75	1.00	1.50
住宅建筑式样(合计)	**Style of Residential Building**	**100.00**	**100.00**	**100.00**	**100.00**	**100.00**	**100.00**	**100.00**
单栋住宅(%)	Monomer House(%)	1.75	1.75	0.25	2.50	3.00	2.75	0.75
四居室(%)	Four Bedrooms Department(%)	1.50	2.00	3.50	1.00	1.75	2.75	3.75
三居室(%)	Three Bedrooms Department(%)	16.75	19.75	20.00	26.00	25.75	26.50	29.00
二居室(%)	Two Bedrooms Department(%)	64.75	63.25	60.50	55.75	55.25	53.75	51.75
一居室(%)	One Bedroom Department(%)	5.75	5.75	3.25	2.25	2.25	2.25	3.00
普通楼房(%)	Ordinary Building(%)	5.75	5.25	9.50	10.00	8.00	8.00	9.75

9 -6 续表
continued

类　别	Category	2005	2006	2007	2008	2009	2010	2011
平房及其它(%)	Bungalow and Others(%)	3.75	2.25	3.00	2.50	4.00	4.00	2.00
卫生设备(合计)	**Sanitary Equipment**	**100.00**	**100.00**	**100.00**	**100.00**	**100.00**	**100.00**	**100.00**
无卫生设备(%)	No Sanitary Equipment(%)			0.25	0.25			
有厕所浴室(%)	Having Toilet and Bathroom(%)	89.00	92.75	92.50	89.00	89.75	89.75	90.75
有厕所无浴室(%)	Having Toilet but No Bathroom(%)	6.50	3.25	3.25	8.75	8.25	8.00	5.75
公用(%)	Public Sanitary Equipment(%)	4.50	4.00	4.00	2.00	2.00	2.25	3.50
取暖设备(合计)	**Heating Equipment**	**100.00**	**100.00**	**100.00**	**100.00**	**100.00**	**100.00**	**100.00**
无取暖设备(%)	No Heating Equipment(%)	2.75	2.50	3.25	6.00	2.75	2.75	2.75
空调设备(%)	Having Air Conditioner(%)	41.75	43.25	35.25	24.00	25.50	25.50	22.00
暖气(%)	Having Heater(%)	36.00	43.50	46.25	57.50	60.75	62.00	68.00
其它(%)	Others(%)	19.50	10.75	15.25	12.50	11.00	9.75	7.25
炊用燃料使用情况(合计)	**Conditions of Cooking Fuel**	**100.00**	**100.00**	**100.00**	**100.00**	**100.00**	**100.00**	**100.00**
管道煤气(%)	Tap Gas(%)	55.00	61.00	61.25	58.50	61.50	61.75	67.50
液化石油气(%)	Liquid Natural Gas(%)	42.75	36.50	37.25	36.75	35.50	36.25	31.00
煤(%)	Coal(%)	2.25	2.00	0.75	4.50	2.75	1.75	1.25
其他(%)	Others(%)		0.50	0.75	0.25	0.25	0.25	0.25

9-7 城市居民家庭消费构成
COMPOSITION OF URBAN HOUSEHOLDS CONSUMPTION

项目	Item	2011		2010	
		年人均支出金额(元) Per Capita Annual Expenditure(yuan)	占消费支出的比重(%) Percentage to Consumption Expenditure(%)	年人均支出金额(元) Per Capita Annual Expenditure(yuan)	占消费支出的比重(%) Percentage to Consumption Expenditure(%)
消费支出	**Consumption Expenditure**	**19 296.56**	**100.0**	**17 531.05**	**100.0**
一、食　品	**Food**	**7 240.95**	**37.5**	**6 553.27**	**37.4**
#1. 粮　食	Grain	415.84	2.2	377.38	2.2
2. 油　脂	Oil or Fat	165.97	0.9	148.77	0.8
3. 肉禽及其制品	Meat, Poultry and Processed Products	1 231.74	6.4	1 025.45	5.8
4. 蛋　类	Eggs	197.28	1.0	173.11	1.0
5. 水产品	Aquatic Products	926.96	4.8	923.28	5.3
6. 菜　类	Vegetables	637.65	3.3	593.29	3.4
7. 烟　草	Tobacco	248.59	1.3	270.44	1.5
8. 酒和饮料	Liquor and Beverages	647.31	3.4	592.20	3.4
9. 干鲜果品	Dried and Fresh Melons and Fruits	758.03	3.9	637.28	3.6
10. 奶及奶制品	Milk and Its Products	342.03	1.8	316.35	1.8
二、衣　着	**Clothing**	**2 592.52**	**13.4**	**2 188.08**	**12.5**
#1. 服装	Garments	1 830.37	9.5	1 539.47	8.8
2. 衣着材料	Clothing Materials	14.90	0.1	10.01	0.1
三、家庭设备用品及服务	**Household Facilities, Articles and Services**	**1 138.59**	**5.9**	**1 221.12**	**7.0**
#日用耐用消费品	Daily Use Durable Consumer Goods	399.11	2.1	576.69	3.3
四、医疗保健	**Health Care and Medical Sevices**	**1 084.56**	**5.6**	**1 048.76**	**6.0**
五、交通与通讯	**Transportation and Communication**	**2 901.06**	**15.0**	**2 584.23**	**14.7**
六、娱乐教育文化服务	**Education, Cultural and Recreation Services**	**1 930.02**	**10.0**	**1 748.14**	**10.0**
1. 文化娱乐用品	Cultural and Recreational Articles	587.33	3.0	493.49	2.8
2. 文化娱乐服务	Cultural and Recreational Services	551.00	2.9	445.00	2.5
3. 教育	Education	791.69	4.1	809.65	4.6
七、居住	**Residence**	**1 783.37**	**9.2**	**1 639.71**	**9.4**
八、杂项商品与服务	**Miscellaneous Goods and Services**	**625.50**	**3.2**	**547.74**	**3.1**

9-8 城市居民家庭年人均消费支出（2011 年）
PER CAPITA ANNUAL CONSUMPTION EXPENDITURE OF URBAN HOUSEHOLDS (2011)

项　目	Item	全市平均 Average	最低收入户 Lowest Income Households	低收入户 Low Income Households
一、食品	**Food**	**7 240.95**	**4 922.75**	**6 381.17**
(一)粮油类	Grain and Oil	690.34	615.20	720.79
1. 粮食	Grain	415.84	349.82	424.60
2. 淀粉及薯类	Starches and Tubers	46.68	43.29	47.40
3. 干豆类及豆制品	Beans and Bean Products	61.84	52.39	67.66
4. 油脂类	Oil or Fat	165.97	169.70	181.14
(二)肉禽蛋水产品类	Meat, Poultry, Eggs and Aquatic Products	2 355.98	1 677.07	2 393.25
1. 肉类	Meat	1 020.30	769.13	1 018.47
2. 禽类	Poultry	211.44	136.34	245.81
3. 蛋类	Eggs	197.28	158.25	198.81
4. 水产品类	Aquatic Products	926.96	613.35	930.16
(三)蔬菜类	Vegetables	637.65	493.37	622.11
1. 鲜菜	Fresh Vegetables	584.24	465.28	568.27
2. 干菜	Dried Vegetables	40.78	22.65	45.20
3. 菜制品	Vegetable Products	12.64	5.44	8.64
(四)调味品	Flavoring	88.36	70.71	69.87
(五)糖烟酒饮料类	Carbohydrate, Tobacco, Liquor and Beverages	956.36	554.40	689.21
1. 糖类	Carbohydrate	60.46	37.76	41.48
2. 烟草类	Tobacco	248.59	153.96	137.87
3. 酒类	Liquor	359.53	219.02	278.97
4. 饮料	Beverages	287.78	143.67	230.90
(六)干鲜瓜果类	Dried and Fresh Melons and Fruits	758.03	487.79	683.62
1. 鲜果	Fresh Fruits	484.69	295.40	431.98
2. 鲜瓜	Fresh Melons	43.73	26.77	38.01
(七)糕点、奶及奶制品	Cake, Milk and Its Products	512.80	312.35	358.70
1. 糕点	Cake	170.76	83.64	133.83
2. 奶及奶制品	Milk and Its Products	342.03	228.72	224.87
(八)其他食品	Other Foods	130.33	96.65	116.04
(九)饮食服务	Catering Services	1 111.11	615.20	727.59
1. 食品加工服务费	Manufacturing Services	3.41	0.41	0.03
2. 在外饮食	Dining Out	1 107.70	614.79	727.56
非食品类	**Non-food**	**12 055.61**	**6 535.22**	**7 526.88**
二、衣着	**Clothing**	**2 592.52**	**1 400.26**	**1 683.00**
(一)服装	Garments	1 830.37	942.41	1 141.16

单位:元(yuan)

较低收入户 Lower Middle Income Households	中间收入户 Middle Income Households	较高收入户 Upper Middle Income Households	高收入户 High Income Households	最高收入户 Highest Income Households
6 579.65	**7 808.70**	**7 831.52**	**8 715.86**	**8 681.27**
685.51	695.10	711.58	716.79	674.85
415.78	414.47	431.99	416.31	457.49
46.68	47.31	39.02	53.80	57.73
59.20	56.78	68.59	70.17	60.95
163.85	176.54	171.98	176.51	98.68
2 263.88	2 501.22	2 344.40	3 016.44	2 373.12
1 006.90	1 053.81	1 005.00	1 331.91	990.37
208.11	230.34	213.88	234.62	200.00
197.62	201.33	204.16	223.22	191.67
851.24	1 015.74	921.36	1 226.69	991.08
621.43	673.63	645.84	740.55	668.14
571.02	623.11	579.91	684.47	599.02
40.80	38.19	44.54	44.26	52.48
9.61	12.33	21.39	11.81	16.63
81.23	93.79	105.57	85.93	103.78
725.85	1 255.21	1 115.25	1 053.18	1 230.43
50.06	71.07	70.32	80.14	70.83
198.07	367.16	265.85	253.60	315.98
248.91	525.97	430.44	368.86	365.40
228.82	291.01	348.64	350.58	478.21
710.17	798.58	786.08	998.86	894.03
444.89	514.08	496.82	669.19	592.88
41.59	49.32	48.10	50.75	47.70
464.66	582.51	577.40	661.76	611.57
167.44	170.35	207.81	219.50	201.76
297.22	412.16	369.60	442.27	409.82
118.33	114.08	150.67	215.17	119.17
908.58	1 094.59	1 394.71	1 227.20	2 006.18
2.23	2.73	4.20	3.72	13.89
906.35	1 091.86	1 390.52	1 223.47	1 992.29
9 148.92	**10 354.10**	**15 888.14**	**13 781.26**	**25 462.89**
1 892.51	**2 988.54**	**2 980.37**	**3 461.05**	**4 251.24**
1 320.54	2 056.23	2 157.49	2 420.45	3 188.89

9-8 续表1
continued

项　　目	Item	全市平均 Average	最低收入户 Lowest Income Households	低收入户 Low Income Households
(二)衣着材料	Clothing Materials	14.90	11.32	4.09
(三)鞋类	Shoes	628.98	380.02	455.54
(四)其他衣着用品	Other Clothing Articles	109.33	62.58	71.71
(五)衣着加工服务费	Clothing Manufacturing Services	8.94	3.93	10.50
三、家庭设备用品及服务	**Household Facilities, Articles and Services**	**1 138.59**	**803.98**	**859.97**
(一)耐用消费品	Durable Consumer Goods	399.11	341.26	377.34
1.家具	Furniture	44.01	73.08	22.68
2.家庭设备	Household Facilities	355.10	268.18	354.65
(1)洗衣机	Washing Machine	32.50	45.27	52.94
(2)电冰箱	Household Refrigerator	50.60	23.19	60.54
(3)微波炉	Microwave Oven	8.86	6.40	3.36
(4)空调器	Air Conditioner	62.21	28.62	130.68
(5)淋浴热水器	Water Heater	19.29	9.73	21.42
(6)消毒碗柜	Sterilized Cabinet			
(7)洗碗机	Dishwasher	0.11		
(8)其他	Others	181.53	154.96	85.71
(二)室内装饰品	Interior Decorations	30.60	7.78	7.10
(三)床上用品	Bed Articles	117.07	35.93	64.36
(四)家庭日用杂品	Daily Use Household Articles	520.27	392.51	392.40
(五)家具材料	Furniture Materias	38.93	18.40	
(六)家庭服务	Household Services	32.60	8.10	18.78
1.家政服务	Household Management Services	16.08	2.64	0.21
2.加工维修服务费	Maintenance and Renovation Services	16.52	5.46	18.57
四、医疗保健	**Health Care and Medical Sevices**	**1 084.56**	**642.24**	**702.63**
(一)医疗器具	Medical Articles	7.98	1.00	13.12
(二)保健器具	Health Protection Articles	10.73	12.76	15.48
(三)药品费	Medicines	395.06	253.31	316.00
(四)滋补保健品	Health Protection Products	384.92	196.10	141.40
(五)医疗费	Medical Services	266.56	154.60	202.58
(六)其他	Others	19.30	24.48	14.04
五、交通和通讯	**Transportation and Communication**	**2 901.06**	**1 002.44**	**1 091.95**
(一)交通	Transportation	1 961.39	384.04	326.99
1.家庭交通工具	Traffic Instruments	1 038.83	14.48	0.51

单位:元(yuan)

较低收入户 Lower Middle Income Households	中间收入户 Middle Income Households	较高收入户 Upper Middle Income Households	高收入户 High Income Households	最高收入户 Highest Income Households
12.42	14.66	16.76	13.86	36.51
461.39	793.72	666.98	881.28	836.13
91.89	115.61	130.56	138.78	164.96
6.28	8.33	8.58	6.68	24.76
853.45	**1 108.32**	**1 491.57**	**1 264.40**	**1 769.88**
349.73	431.88	458.77	233.18	600.62
18.50	52.08	77.07	28.31	21.96
331.23	379.80	381.69	204.87	578.66
42.44	6.74	24.57		79.01
36.45	62.83	70.38	25.54	65.05
15.96	10.73		12.99	11.85
54.11	77.77	43.28	42.77	69.49
10.40	11.07	28.88	23.85	43.73
			1.20	
171.87	210.66	214.59	98.52	309.54
32.45	34.22	20.70	57.04	68.34
73.02	131.86	192.89	185.92	118.04
361.29	495.10	691.88	583.71	844.75
19.83	3.96	49.21	169.80	72.58
17.14	11.31	78.13	34.74	65.56
0.21	1.44	61.17	1.49	42.58
16.93	9.87	16.96	33.25	22.97
776.00	**787.22**	**1 668.03**	**1 580.29**	**1 732.75**
5.19		6.94	6.56	39.78
3.01	17.44	7.69	9.28	14.34
292.26	294.45	617.29	484.84	570.82
136.25	249.44	552.36	973.65	830.52
332.21	202.61	458.63	92.81	243.02
7.07	23.28	25.13	13.15	34.27
2 099.64	**1 794.59**	**4 925.51**	**2 996.81**	**7 520.39**
1 233.39	763.40	3 901.86	1 969.26	6 263.03
748.86	31.23	2 863.86	201.41	3 568.92

9 -8 续表2
continued

项　目	Item	全市平均 Average	最低收入户 Lowest Income Households	低收入户 Low Income Households
(1)摩托车	Motor	2.14		
(3)助力车	Motorbike	11.41	14.40	
(4)家用汽车	Automobile	1 019.44		
(5)其他交通工具	Other Traffic Instruments	5.83	0.08	0.51
2. 车辆用燃料及零配件	Fuels and Automobile Spare Parts	493.98	124.05	86.20
(1)燃料	Fuels	473.42	122.85	82.47
(2)零配件	Automobile Spare Parts	6.05		3.73
(3)其他	Others	14.52	1.20	
3. 交通工具服务支出	Expenditure on Traffic Instrument Services	143.61	43.20	13.16
(1)维修费	Mending Cost	36.04	19.60	1.30
(2)车辆使用税费	Vehicle Usage Tax	77.13	8.00	
(3)其它车辆使用费用	Other Cost of Vehicle Usage	30.44	15.60	11.86
4. 交通费	Traffic Expenses	284.97	202.31	227.12
(1)飞机	Air Plane	47.38	12.72	22.26
(2)火车	Train	33.98	11.85	33.09
(3)长途汽车	Long-distance Bus	20.56	10.17	15.62
(4)市内公共交通	Bus	105.49	117.52	109.42
(5)出租汽车费	Taxi	53.60	43.20	34.09
(6)其他交通费	Other Traffic Expenses	23.96	6.86	12.65
(二)通信	Communication	939.67	618.40	764.96
1. 通信工具	Communication Instruments	149.71	81.44	52.59
(1)电话机	Telephone	8.51	9.07	1.16
(2)移动电话	Cell Phone	140.32	72.37	51.43
(3)其他通信工具	Other Communication Instruments	0.88		
2. 通信服务	Communication Services	789.96	536.96	712.37
(1)电信费	Telecommunications	776.96	512.92	706.83
(2)邮费	Postage	4.28	1.02	0.86
(3)其他	Others	8.73	23.02	4.69
六、教育文化娱乐服务	**Education, Cultural and Recreation Services**	**1 930.02**	**1 188.53**	**1 513.69**
(一)文化娱乐用品	Cultural and Recreational Articles	587.33	291.54	363.59
1. 彩色电视机	Color TV Set	123.13	21.60	
2. 家用电脑	Computer	155.26	146.34	74.76
(1)整机电脑	Entire Computer	132.95	109.83	65.52

单位:元(yuan)

较低收入户 Lower Middle Income Households	中间收入户 Middle Income Households	较高收入户 Upper Middle Income Households	高收入户 High Income Households	最高收入户 Highest Income Households
		11.28		
	17.46	12.18	21.83	22.70
747.55		2 838.55	167.18	3 531.96
1.30	13.76	1.86	12.40	14.26
205.38	432.81	491.48	1 227.71	1 516.14
201.96	424.68	467.94	1 209.72	1 382.63
2.75	2.28	9.21		33.25
0.67	5.85	14.33	17.99	100.27
47.49	96.31	251.86	180.10	500.43
17.90	49.20	20.56	83.19	96.26
19.02	40.04	210.53	33.44	244.47
10.57	7.07	20.78	63.47	159.70
231.67	203.05	294.65	360.04	677.55
50.81	5.37	20.14	36.32	282.94
26.49	8.54	41.77	52.07	103.31
16.48	27.68	30.74	3.72	30.08
91.54	99.60	107.50	122.51	109.85
40.99	39.79	50.41	94.70	115.17
5.36	22.07	44.09	50.72	36.20
866.25	1 031.20	1 023.65	1 027.55	1 257.36
152.19	123.51	226.97	101.10	294.31
12.03	4.36	10.62	16.05	4.58
138.95	117.81	214.97	84.06	289.73
1.21	1.34	1.38	0.99	
714.07	907.69	796.68	926.46	963.04
707.95	894.73	791.35	909.07	925.93
1.06	1.99	0.93	13.26	23.30
5.06	10.97	4.40	4.12	13.82
1 587.19	**1 436.98**	**2 286.92**	**1 998.30**	**4 513.75**
639.53	516.41	847.92	633.32	650.61
171.41	140.90	233.71	56.93	74.28
162.04	129.30	217.25	202.52	118.88
135.90	111.62	199.24	178.49	90.28

9-8 续表3
continued

项　　目	Item	全市平均 Average	最低收入户 Lowest Income Households	低收入户 Low Income Households
(2)计算机外部设备	External Equipment	10.50	25.63	0.80
(3)各种零配件及耗材	Various Spare Parts	11.81	10.88	8.43
5.组合音响	Hi-Fi Stereo Component System	0.45		
7.摄像机	Pick-up Camera	1.72	3.60	
8.照相机	Camera	34.88	3.20	50.43
9.钢琴	Piano	28.47		101.19
10.其他中高档乐器	Other Medium and Top Grade Music Instruments	2.72		
11.健身器材	Body Building Equipment	6.47		
12.电子辞典	Electronic Dictionary	7.21		
13.音像制品及软件	Audio-visual Products and Software	3.35	2.37	6.70
14.体育用品	Sports Articles	5.23	1.51	9.46
15.书报杂志	Books,Newspapers and Magazines	65.97	23.44	51.11
16.纸张文具	Paper and Stationery Goods	22.35	15.41	26.09
17.其他文娱用品	Other Recreation and Culture Articles	130.13	74.07	43.84
(二)文化娱乐服务	Recreation and Culture Services	551.00	210.41	365.14
1.参观游览	Sightseeing	79.53	6.90	4.76
2.健身活动	Body Building Activities	17.85	21.68	
3.团体旅游	Team Tour	311.88	91.96	256.06
4.其它文娱活动	Other Recreation and Culture Activities	135.65	82.30	97.80
5.文娱用品修理服务费	Service Charges for Recreation and Culture Articles Mending	6.09	7.58	6.50
(三)教育	Education	791.69	686.58	784.97
1.教材	Teaching Material	51.06	39.39	29.15
(1)课本及参考书	Text Books and Reference Books	32.09	21.20	26.22
(2)教育软件	Teaching Software	4.94	16.00	1.10
(3)其它教材	Other Teaching Material	14.03	2.19	1.83
2.教育费用	Education Cost	740.63	647.19	755.82
(1)非义务教育学杂费	Tuition Fee for Non-compulsory Education	242.64	376.36	182.48
(2)义务教育学杂费	Tuition Fee for Compulsory Education	16.88	27.35	12.67
(3)托幼费	Child-care Fee	93.18	52.11	128.39
(4)成人教育费	Adult Education Expenses	56.38	9.44	86.69
(5)家教费	Family Education Expenses	40.76	17.66	43.60
(6)培训班	Training Fee	174.21	66.50	197.68

单位:元(yuan)

较低收入户 Lower Middle Income Households	中间收入户 Middle Income Households	较高收入户 Upper Middle Income Households	高收入户 High Income Households	最高收入户 Highest Income Households
19.54	5.58	8.06		8.75
6.61	12.10	9.95	24.04	19.85
			1.58	3.51
		6.93		
10.82	11.70	106.14		51.21
83.25				
12.72				
11.03	1.84	1.78	19.78	17.54
7.28	7.01	7.49		33.02
1.77	3.86	3.87	4.69	0.62
3.08	10.76	3.57	0.25	6.72
56.27	54.77	64.21	164.12	83.55
19.04	33.20	11.16	29.14	27.17
100.81	123.07	191.80	154.31	234.11
398.47	369.44	774.60	605.86	1 458.46
25.60	17.53	276.27	34.64	157.02
24.05	17.73	21.00	21.14	9.09
249.05	181.35	323.97	355.63	1 043.54
92.79	150.46	150.92	190.70	228.23
6.99	2.38	2.43	3.74	20.58
549.18	551.12	664.40	759.12	2 404.69
32.80	52.64	36.85	87.19	125.75
28.90	39.46	27.48	46.37	38.56
	4.49	2.75	10.85	6.91
3.90	8.69	6.61	29.97	80.28
516.39	498.48	627.55	671.93	2 278.94
170.29	163.16	194.61	122.37	744.75
24.42	10.31	9.50	2.23	37.38
78.96	68.36	5.02	215.63	253.36
45.93	17.04	143.14	35.65	27.86
29.62	17.19	67.31	57.31	71.81
114.39	193.84	146.42	218.87	399.31

9-8 续表4
continued

项目	Item	全市平均 Average	最低收入户 Lowest Income Households	低收入户 Low Income Households
(7)学校住宿费	Accommodation Expenses at School	17.60	36.61	53.13
(8)其他	Others	98.99	61.16	51.18
七、居住	**Residence**	**1 783.37**	**1 330.87**	**1 393.93**
(一)住房	Housing	331.34	102.50	143.65
1.租赁房房租	House Rental	27.05	5.74	5.06
2.住房装潢支出	Decoration Expenses	251.35	50.48	14.35
3.维修用建筑材料	Construction Material for Mending	23.25	26.24	0.51
4.其他	Others	29.69	20.04	123.73
(二)水电燃料及其他	Water, Electricity, Fuel and Others	1 330.12	1 150.04	1 200.85
1.水	Water	74.15	53.94	66.38
2.电	Electricity	387.57	311.63	362.83
3.燃料	Fuels	212.40	187.14	205.18
(1)煤炭	Coal	35.91	60.38	34.79
(2)液化石油气	Liquefied Petroleum Gas	36.26	44.83	60.98
(3)管道煤气	Pipeline Gas	137.58	81.84	109.40
(4)柴油	Diesel Oil	0.47		
(5)其他燃料	Other Fuels	2.17	0.08	
4.取暖费	Heating Fees	496.33	321.88	289.39
5.其他	Others	159.66	275.45	277.07
(三)居住服务费	Residence Service Charges	121.91	78.33	49.44
1.物业管理费	Property Management Fee	84.00	20.42	33.00
2.维修服务费	Mending Serivce Charges	12.52	36.91	2.38
3.其它	Others	25.39	21.00	14.05
八、杂项商品和服务	**Miscellaneous Goods and Services**	**625.50**	**166.88**	**281.69**
(一)杂项商品	Miscellaneous Goods	414.28	101.93	219.70
1.金银珠宝饰品	Gold, Silver and Jewellery	136.96	18.08	73.87
2.手表	Watch	12.58		1.21
3.理发美容用具	Haircut and Cosmetology Articles	8.06	4.32	3.90
4.化妆品	Cosmetics	174.70	67.83	72.18
5.其他杂品	Other Miscellaneous Goods	81.98	11.69	68.53
(二)服务	Services	211.23	64.96	61.99
1.旅馆住宿费	Accommodation Expenses at Inn	12.33	0.08	
2.理发洗澡费	Washing and Haircut Service Charges	56.50	36.81	39.34
3.美容费	Cosmetology Service Charges	45.63	6.56	20.12
4.其他服务	Others	96.76	21.51	2.52

单位:元(yuan)

较低收入户 Lower Middle Income Households	中间收入户 Middle Income Households	较高收入户 Upper Middle Income Households	高收入户 High Income Households	最高收入户 Highest Income Households
17.07	2.93	13.02	1.63	12.38
35.73	25.64	48.54	18.26	732.07
1 517.58	**1 681.23**	**1 632.81**	**1 594.77**	**4 277.64**
126.84	141.67	194.03	87.68	2 371.09
66.65	17.00	11.24		71.23
46.06	88.90	110.02	76.35	2 187.45
10.38	20.16	24.61	10.40	97.48
3.75	15.61	48.16	0.93	14.94
1 332.06	1 393.77	1 323.23	1 298.51	1 620.08
64.13	79.86	82.31	83.90	92.72
356.69	437.29	380.61	417.62	460.30
240.62	226.81	209.64	162.34	212.48
61.50	25.75	19.26	5.39	36.11
38.63	24.46	33.47	25.67	34.04
134.68	176.60	152.88	128.12	138.53
1.25		1.08		
4.56		2.95	3.16	3.80
414.73	588.02	512.86	582.11	834.96
255.89	61.79	137.81	52.54	19.61
58.68	145.80	115.55	208.58	286.47
32.88	105.30	72.32	184.64	220.23
10.78	3.49	13.33	5.11	24.93
15.02	37.01	29.91	18.84	41.32
422.54	**557.21**	**902.92**	**885.65**	**1 397.23**
305.22	387.54	580.22	560.77	858.53
108.58	121.50	219.70	92.70	340.20
14.30	11.74	28.29	12.98	5.38
7.01	8.58	11.51	10.14	9.41
113.62	163.33	214.81	330.50	354.00
61.71	82.39	105.91	114.45	149.55
117.31	169.67	322.70	324.88	538.70
1.36	10.87	4.69	33.72	66.87
42.05	56.66	79.33	55.44	89.27
55.60	55.52	20.57	130.26	41.01
18.31	46.63	218.11	105.46	341.54

9-9 城市居民家庭年人均购买主要商品(2011 年)

PER CAPITA ANNUAL PURCHASES OF MAJOR COMMODITIES OF URBAN HOUSEHOLDS (2011)

项　目	Item	单位	Unit	全市平均 Average	最低收入户 Lowest Income Households	低收入户 Low Income Households
大米	Rice	千克	kg	18.52	15.11	19.32
面粉	Flour	千克	kg	15.35	16.46	19.09
食用植物油	Edible Vegetable Oil	千克	kg	7.79	8.18	8.76
猪肉	Pork	千克	kg	18.99	16.48	19.25
牛肉	Beef	千克	kg	2.58	1.70	2.19
羊肉	Mutton	千克	kg	1.55	1.27	1.27
鸡	Chicken	千克	kg	5.01	4.25	5.68
鲜蛋	Fresh Eggs	千克	kg	19.25	16.18	19.46
鱼	Fish	千克	kg	12.27	10.17	12.12
虾	Shrimp	千克	kg	4.45	2.93	4.03
白酒	Liquor	千克	kg	1.89	1.78	2.30
果酒	Fruit Wine	千克	kg	0.43	0.21	0.38
啤酒	Beer	千克	kg	16.23	14.55	15.37
碳酸饮料	Carbonated Beverage	千克	kg	1.75	0.95	1.54
瓶装饮用水	Bottled Drinking Water	千克	kg	15.07	9.51	9.85
茶叶	Tea	千克	kg	0.88	0.56	0.93
鲜果	Fresh Fruits	千克	kg	59.36	41.37	56.80
鲜瓜	Fresh Melons	千克	kg	12.10	8.27	9.94
糕点	Cake	千克	kg	8.45	4.44	7.50
鲜乳品	Fresh Milk Products	千克	kg	22.45	17.57	18.27
奶粉	Milk Power	千克	kg	0.70	0.49	0.20
酸奶	Yoghurt	千克	kg	6.54	3.15	4.53
服装	Garments	件	piece	9.32	6.46	7.08
鞋类	Shoes	双	pair	3.53	2.77	3.38
水	Water	吨	ton	29.01	20.34	25.17
电	Electricity	度	watt-hour	698.37	533.72	658.64
煤炭	Coal	千克	kg	34.90	50.53	36.24
液化石油气	Liquefied Petroleum Gas	千克	kg	5.85	6.41	8.35
管道燃气	Pipeline Gas	立方米	cu. m	57.99	43.82	51.30

较低收入户 Lower Middle Income Households	中间收入户 Middle Income Households	较高收入户 Upper Middle Income Households	高收入户 High Income Households	最高收入户 Highest Income Households
18.4	19.57	17.98	20.09	19.27
17.07	16.16	11.67	13.73	13.08
8.03	7.82	8.22	8.29	3.91
19.73	19.24	17.83	23.10	17.44
2.43	2.81	2.55	3.00	3.62
1.28	1.82	1.24	2.31	2.09
4.53	6.43	4.51	4.38	4.9
19.14	19.54	20.01	21.89	17.96
11.99	13.5	11.32	15.27	11.73
3.83	4.49	6.12	5.52	3.53
1.48	2.41	2.11	1.15	1.75
0.26	0.73	0.5	0.25	0.54
14.83	20.25	18.39	15.67	9.62
1.46	1.87	2.06	2.67	1.80
11.24	26.38	9.45	15.32	24.28
0.83	0.94	0.98	0.93	0.92
56.39	61.39	60.88	75.67	66.99
12.54	13.84	12.05	13.25	13.37
8.21	8.10	10.15	10.90	9.70
19.52	26.60	24.85	24.37	24.14
0.30	0.84	1.07	1.41	0.65
5.34	9.19	6.82	7.86	8.15
7.81	9.53	11.27	10.13	13.74
3.10	3.96	3.62	3.91	4.18
25.44	31.46	31.71	33.41	37.28
634.39	799.66	690.98	760.84	832.69
60.86	23.86	21.08	4.64	38.18
6.17	5.11	5.13	3.68	7.07
56.56	72.03	60.83	53.66	54.35

9-10 每百户城市居民家庭年末耐用品拥有量
OWNERSHIP OF MAJOR DURABLE CONSUMER GOODS PER 100 URBAN HOUSEHOLDS AT YEAR-END

项　目	Item	单位	Unit	全市平均 Average	最低收入户 Lowest Income Households	低收入户 Low Income Households
摩托车	Motor	辆	unit	8.25	10.00	5.00
助力车	Motorbike	辆	unit	6.25	7.50	
家用汽车	Automobile	辆	unit	22.00	10.00	15.00
洗衣机	Washing Machine	台	set	98.00	92.50	97.50
电冰箱	Household Refrigerator	台	set	108.25	102.50	102.50
彩色电视机	Color TV Set	台	set	117.25	107.50	120.00
家用电脑	Computer	台	set	95.00	70.00	97.50
组合音响	Hi-Fi Stereo Component System	套	set	35.00	25.00	25.00
摄像机	Pickup Camera	架	set	25.25	5.00	7.50
照相机	Camera	架	set	76.50	60.00	60.00
钢琴	Piano	架	set	8.00	5.00	5.00
其他中高档乐器	Other Medium and Top Grade Music Instruments	件	unit	8.75	2.50	10.00
微波炉	Microwave Oven	台	set	81.50	55.00	80.00
空调器	Air Conditioner	台	set	103.00	82.50	90.00
淋浴热水器	Water Heater	台	set	91.50	85.00	87.50
消毒碗柜	Sterilized Cabinet	台	set	13.00		5.00
洗碗机	Dishwasher	台	set	3.25		
健身器材	Body Building Equipment	套	set	13.75	7.50	5.00
普通电话	Telephone	部	set	71.00	55.00	62.50
移动电话	Cell Phone	部	set	218.75	200.00	240.00

较低收入户 Lower Middle Income Households	中间收入户 Middle Income Households	较高收入户 Upper Middle Income Households	高收入户 High Income Households	最高收入户 Highest Income Households
8.75	10.00	10.00	2.50	7.50
3.75	7.50	8.75	7.50	7.50
20.00	18.75	17.50	40.00	42.50
98.75	96.25	95.00	105.00	105.00
107.50	101.25	112.50	117.50	117.50
112.50	120.00	117.50	117.50	127.50
97.50	97.50	100.00	92.50	100.00
28.75	41.25	40.00	50.00	30.00
18.75	32.50	32.50	47.50	25.00
72.50	85.00	72.50	90.00	95.00
3.75	13.75	8.75	7.50	10.00
3.75	15.00	10.00	5.00	12.50
77.50	85.00	88.75	87.50	90.00
100.00	101.25	102.50	117.50	132.50
86.25	91.25	93.75	97.50	102.50
10.00	13.75	12.50	15.00	37.50
2.50	2.50	6.25	10.00	10.00
6.25	17.50	10.00	15.00	42.50
68.75	73.75	75.00	77.50	80.00
233.75	227.50	203.75	225.00	192.50

9－11 分市、区农村住户基本情况(2011 年)

BASIC CONDITIONS OF RURAL HOUSEHOLDS BY REGION(2011)

指　标	Indicators	青岛市 Qingdao	#崂山区 Laoshan District
调查户数(户)	Number of Households Surveyed(household)	680	50
平均每户常住人口(人)	Average Number of Permanent Residents Per Household (person)	3.33	3.18
平均每户整半劳动力(人)	Average Number of Full/Semi Labour Force Per Household(person)	2.37	2.18
全年纯收入	Per Capita Annual Net Income	12 370	14 114
生活消费支出	Expenses on Household Consumption	7 661	10 214
1.食品消费支出	Food	2 803	4 467
2.衣着消费支出	Clothing	701	1 211
3.居住消费支出	Residence	1 328	1 188
4.家庭设备、用品消费支出	Household Facilities and Articles	510	830
5.交通和通讯消费支出	Transportation and Communication	1 135	1 171
6.文化教育、娱乐消费支出	Culture, Education and R ecreation	649	823
7.医疗保健消费支出	Health Care and Medical Services	391	351
8.其他商品和服务消费支出	Other Goods and Services	144	173
平均每户年内新建(购)房屋面积(平方米)	Floor Space Newly Built(Bought) Per Household in the Year(sq. m)	32.60	49.30
平均每户期末拥有住房面积(平方米)	Living Space Per Household at Year-end(sq. m)	0.60	

单位:元(yuan)

黄岛区 Huangdao District	城阳区 Chengyang District	即墨市 Jimo	胶州市 Jiaozhou	胶南市 Jiaonan	平度市 Pingdu	莱西市 Laixi
50	80	100	100	100	100	100
3.48	3.09	3.22	3.23	3.67	3.22	3.50
2.42	2.237 5	2.38	2.21	2.44	2.29	2.64
13 976	13 031	12 293	12 318	12 280	12 022	12 049
9 792	9 067	7 692	8 714	7 412	6 688	6 641
4 293	3 542	2 779	2 465	2 661	2 575	2 518
1 142	940	830	555	718	466	695
1 059	1 488	1 469	1 704	1 520	1 086	992
466	570	585	473	444	432	550
982	1 027	1 039	2 100	1 105	978	752
1 080	981	524	572	542	669	630
484	383	313	683	318	366	335
286	136	153	162	104	116	169
28.90	42.80	32.30	36.60	25.20	27.10	38.30
		1.70		0.90	0.30	

9－12 农村住户基本情况(1990－2011 年)

BASIC CONDITIONS OF RURAL HOUSEHOLDS(1990－2011)

项　目	Item	单位	Unit
调查户数	**Number of Households Surveyed**	**户**	**household**
常住人口	**Number of Permanent Residents**	**人**	**person**
一、平均每户常住人口	**Average Number of Permanent Residents Per Household**	**人**	**person**
1. 年龄结构	Age Distribution	人	person
(1)6 岁及以下	6 Year-old and Under	人	person
(2)7-15 岁	Between 7 and 15 Year-old	人	person
(3)16-60 岁	Between 16 and 60 Year-old	人	person
(4)61 岁及以上	61 Year-old and Above	人	person
2. 在校学生人数	Students Enrollment	人	person
其中:7-15 岁在校学生人数	of which:Between 7 and 15 Year-old	人	person
3. 平均每户整半劳动力	Average Number of Full/Semi Labour Force Per Household	人	person
(1)整劳动力	Full Labour Force	人	person
(2)半劳动力	Semi Labour Force	人	person
整半劳动力占常住人口的比重	Percentage of Full/Semi Labour Force to Permanent Residents	%	%
平均每个劳动力负担人口	Average Number of Dependents Per Labour Force	人	person
二、平均每百个劳动力中	**Among Per 100 Labour Force**		
文盲半文盲人数	Illiterate and Semiliterate	人	person
小学程度人数	Primary School	人	person
初中程度人数	Junior High School	人	person
高中程度人数	Senior High School	人	person
中专程度人数	Secondary School	人	person
大专程度人数	Junior College	人	person
三、经营耕地面积(人均)	**Area of Cultivated Land under Management(per capita)**	**亩**	**mu**
#承包耕地面积	Area of Cultivated Land Contracted	亩	mu
占经营耕地面积的比重	Percentage to Area of Cultivated Land under Management	%	%
四、平均每户年末生产性固定资产原值	**Productive Original Value of Fixed Assets Per Household(year-end)**	**元**	**yuan**
1. 役畜、产品畜	Draught Animal and Commodity Animal	元	yuan
2. 大中型铁木农具	Large and Medium Iron and Wooden Farm Tools	元	yuan
3. 农林牧渔业机械	Agricultural Machinery	元	yuan
4. 工业机械	Industrial Machinery	元	yuan
5. 运输机械	Transport Machinery	元	yuan
6. 生产用房	Buildings for Production	元	yuan
7. 其他	Others	元	yuan
五、平均每户年末拥有汽车	**Ownership of Automobiles Per Household(year-end)**	**辆**	**set**
大中型拖拉机	Large and Medium Tractors	台	set
小型和手扶拖拉机	Small and Walking Tractors	台	set

注:平均每百个劳动力中文化程度人数,2010 年及以前为整半劳动力文化程度,2011 年为就业劳动力文化程度。

Note:In the education attainment statistics among per 100 labour force,the labour force refers to full/semi labour force before 2010,and refers to employed labour force since 2011.

1990	1995	2000	2005	2006	2007	2008	2009	2010	2011
2 300	**770**	**820**	**860**	**900**	**900**	**900**	**900**	**900**	**680**
9 598	**2 919**	**2 856**	**2 964**	**3 073**	**3 066**	**3 077**	**3 069**	**3 061**	**2 263**
4.17	**3.79**	**3.48**	**3.45**	**3.41**	**3.41**	**3.42**	**3.41**	**3.40**	**3.33**
			0.15	0.15	0.14	0.12	0.12	0.11	0.15
			0.33	0.35	0.35	0.35	0.35	0.31	0.36
			2.74	2.50	2.69	2.71	2.69	2.70	2.50
			0.23	0.19	0.23	0.24	0.25	0.28	0.30
			0.60	0.60	0.59	0.60	0.60	0.58	0.56
			0.33	0.35	0.35	0.35	0.34	0.30	0.36
2.60	2.69	2.61	2.59	2.58	2.58	2.59	2.56	2.58	2.37
1.95	2.11	1.78	1.73	1.76	1.72	1.66	1.57	1.51	1.52
0.65	0.58	0.83	0.86	0.82	0.86	0.93	0.99	1.06	0.85
62.35	71.00	75.00	75.10	75.60	75.67	75.63	75.20	75.76	71.24
1.60	1.41	1.33	1.33	1.32	1.32	1.32	1.33	1.32	1.40
9.00	4.7	2.99	2.07	1.46	1.64	1.68	1.60	1.38	1.65
38.00	31.5	23.03	15.72	12.78	12.24	12.46	12.52	9.27	13.45
42.00	47.2	53.9	54.04	54.43	53.10	53.89	56.63	58.13	60.59
10.00	14.4	15.83	21.61	24.01	24.48	23.12	19.89	20.44	16.53
1.00	2.00	3.22	4.27	4.69	5.30	5.20	5.24	5.56	2.70
	0.20	1.03	2.29	2.62	3.23	3.65	4.12	4.61	5.07
1.62	**1.45**	**1.49**	**1.40**	**1.31**	**1.26**	**1.27**	**1.30**	**1.47**	**1.38**
1.39	1.39	1.47	1.40	1.31	1.26	1.27	1.30	1.30	1.30
85.80	95.90	98.95	100.00	100.00	100.00	100.00	100.00	88.44	94.20
1 081.1	**3 165.1**	**5 458.2**	**13 844.9**	**16 190.9**	**21 568.3**	**21 993**	**21 626**	**22 950**	**24 349**
207.8	530.0	477.5	1 102.8	871.3	1 263.5	1 320	1 358	1 333	1 037
92.8	163.5	276.7	216.6	274.8	435.0	299	265	293	140
410.3	1 105.8	2 370.2	3 204.3	2911.9	4 260.6	4 658	4 062	4 118	4 153
35.1	265.1	244.0	1 246.5	1758.9	1 898.9	1 710	1 718	2 008	2 633
175.7	662.4	765.5	1 623.3	1168.7	1 767.8	1 110	1 138	1 234	2 421
63.3	405.1	495.8	3 745.7	4479.1	7 247.3	7 079	6 372	7 238	8 042
96.2	33.2	828.5	314.7	482.0	738.9	774	858	819	1 112
	0.01	**0.03**	**0.04**	**0.05**	**0.07**	**0.06**	**0.07**	**0.08**	**0.09**
0.01	0.02	0.04	0.05	0.03	0.03	0.04	0.05	0.05	0.05
0.05	0.11	0.25	0.31	0.34	0.29	0.30	0.30	0.30	0.22

9－13 农村住户居住情况(2005－2011 年)

HOUSING CONDITIONS OF RURAL HOUSEHOLDS(2005－2011)

类 别	Category	单位	Unit
一、期末住房情况	**Housing Conditions at Term-end**		
(一)住房面积	Floor Space of Houses	平方米/人	sq. m/person
(二)住房价值	Value of Houses	元/平方米	yuan/sq. m
(三)住房类型	Type of Houses		
1. 楼房面积	Floor Space of Apartment	平方米/人	sq. m/person
2. 砖瓦平房面积	Floor Space of Brick Bungalow	平方米/人	sq. m/person
3. 其他	Others	平方米/人	sq. m/person
(四)住房结构	Structure of Houses		
1. 钢筋混泥土结构面积	Reinforced Concrete Structure	平方米/人	sq. m/person
2. 砖木结构面积	Brick and Wood Structure	平方米/人	sq. m/person
3. 其他	Others	平方米/人	sq. m/person
二、期内新建(购)住房情况	**Conditions of Houses Newly Built (Bought) This Term**		
(一)新建(购)住房面积	Floor Space of Houses Newly Built (Bought)	平方米/人	sq. m/person
(二)新建(购)住房价值	Value of Houses Newly Built (Bought)	元/平方米	yuan/sq. m
(三)新建(购)住房类型	Type of Houses Newly Built (Bought)		
1. 楼房面积	Floor Space of Apartment	平方米/人	sq. m/person
2. 砖瓦平房面积	Floor Space of Brick Bungalow	平方米/人	sq. m/person
3. 其他	Others	平方米/人	sq. m/person
(四)新建(购)住房结构	Structure of Newly Building Housing		
1. 钢筋混泥土结构面积	Reinforced Concrete Structure	平方米/人	sq. m/person
2. 砖木结构面积	Brick and Wood Structure	平方米/人	sq. m/person
3. 其他	Residental Buildings	平方米/人	sq. m/person

2005	2006	2007	2008	2009	2010	2011
29.54	30.82	30.95	30.73	31.39	32.06	31.73
394	537	676	732	750	880	1345
3.42	7.04	6.08	5.96	6.34	6.33	4.15
25.85	23.48	24.52	24.54	24.81	24.58	27.57
0.26	0.30	0.35	0.23	0.24	0.47	
6.53	7.94	5.37	6.05	6.71	6.57	5.26
23	22.77	25.47	24.58	24.56	24.71	26.47
	0.11	0.11	0.11	0.12	0.1	
0.99	0.72	0.23	0.3	0.43	0.16	0.55
521	549	545	708	930	1221	1199
0.29	0.38	0	0.07	0.11	0.08	0.16
0.70	0.34	0.23	0.23	0.32	0.08	0.39
0.67	0.42	0.08	0.11	0.18	0.08	0.20
0.31	0.3	0.15	0.19	0.25	0.08	0.35

9 -13 续表
continued

类　别	Category	单位	Unit
三、居住条件	**Living Condition**		
(一)住房卫生设备使用情况	Condition of Health Equipment		
1. 使用水冲式厕所的户数	Having Flushing Toilet	户/百户	household/100 households
2. 使用旱厕的户数	Having Old Toilet	户/百户	household/100 households
3. 无厕所的户数	No Toilet	户/百户	household/100 households
(二)取暖设备使用情况	Condition of Heating Equipment		
#1. 使用空调的户数	Having Air Conditioner	户/百户	household/100 households
2. 使用暖气的户数	Having Heater	户/百户	household/100 households
3. 使用火炕的户数	Having Kang	户/百户	household/100 households
4. 无取暖设备的户数	No Heating Equipment	户/百户	household/100 households
(三)炊事使用的主要能源	Major Source of Cooking		
1. 使用液化气的户数	Liquid Natural Gas	户/百户	household/100 households
2. 使用煤炭的户数	Coal	户/百户	household/100 households
3. 使用柴草的户数	Fuelwood	户/百户	household/100 households
4. 使用电的户数	Electricity	户/百户	household/100 households
5. 使用其他燃料的户数	Other Fuels	户/百户	household/100 households
(四)饮用水来源情况	Source of Drinking Water		
#1. 饮用自来水的户数	Tap Water	户/百户	household/100 households
2. 饮用深井水的户数	Deep Well Water	户/百户	household/100 households
3. 饮用浅井水的户数	Other Water	户/百户	household/100 households
(五)住宅外道路路面状况	Condition of Road Near Residential		
1. 水泥或柏油路面的户数	Cement or Asphalt	户/百户	household/100 households
2. 沙石或石板等硬质路面的户数	Stone, Sand and Gravel or Other Hard Materials	户/百户	household/100 households
3. 其他路面的户数	Others	户/百户	household/100 households

2005	2006	2007	2008	2009	2010	2011
40	42	45	46	46	46	51
60	58	55	54	54	54	49
7	8	6	7	6	6	9
23	18	21	22	22	22	19
70	73	71	69	69	69	60
						11
60	62	82	82	83	83	65
	1					
40	37	16	16	16	16	35
	1	1	1	1	1	
						1
77	85	92	95	95	95	94
21	15	7	5	5	5	5
1						2
54	40	54	62	71	75	81
32	53	42	34	25	22	13
13	7	5	4	3	3	6

9-14 农村住户人均总收入和纯收入(2011年)

PER CAPITA TOTAL INCOME AND NET INCOME OF RURAL HOUSEHOLDS (2011)

单位:元(yuan)

项 目	Item	金额 Sum
一、总收入	**Total Income**	**17 156**
(一)工资收入	Income from Wages and Salaries	5 418
1.在非企业组织中劳动得到收入	Gained from Non-enterprise Organization	545
2.在本乡地域内劳动得到收入	Gained in Local Area	3 421
(1)在企业中劳动得到收入	Gained From Enterprises	3 013
(2)在国家投资基建项目得到收入	Gained From Capital Construction Programs Invested by State	6
(3)提供其他劳务收入	Other Labour Services	402
3.外出从业得到收入	Gained from Out-city Enterprise by Permanent Person	1 452
(1)在乡外县内从业得到收入	Out of Countryside and in County	1 149
(2)在县外省内从业得到收入	Out of County and in Province	237
(3)在省外国内从业得到收入	Out of Province and in County	17
(4)在国外从业得到收入	From Abroad	50
(二)家庭经营收入	Income from Household Operations	10 840
1.第一产业收入	Primary Industry	7 266
(1)农业收入	Farming	4 425
(2)林业收入	Forestry	61
(3)牧业收入	Animal Husbandry	2 418
(4)渔业收入	Fishery	362
2.第二产业收入	Secondary Industry	1 705
(1)工业收入	Industry	1 440
(2)建筑业收入	Construction	265

9-14 续表
continued

单位:元(yuan)

项　目	Item	金额 Sum
3.第三产业收入	Tertiary Industry	1 869
(1)其他产品收入	Other Products	3
(2)第三产业服务性收入	Services of Tertiary Industry	1 866
①交通、运输和邮电业收入	Transport and Postal Services	467
②批发零售贸易、餐饮业收入	Wholesale,Retail Trade and Catering	917
③社会服务业收入	Social Services	290
④文教卫生业收入	Culture,Education and Health Care	47
⑤其他行业收入	Other Household Business	145
(三)财产性收入	Income from Properties	281
#1.利息	Interest	20
2.租金(包括农业机械)	Rental	94
3.土地征用补偿收入	Compensation for Land Requisition	
4.转让承包土地经营权收入	Making over Business Power of Land	20
5.其他投资收益	Others	89
(四)转移性收入	Income from Transfers	617
#1.家庭非常住人口寄回	Of which:Income from Outside City	
2.城市亲友赠送收入	Presentation from relatives and Friends	23
3.农村亲友赠送收入	From Outside The Country	69
4.退耕还林还草补贴收入	Subsidy For Giving back Cultivation to Forest or Grass	9
二、全年人均纯收入	**Per Capita Annual Net Income**	**12 370**

9-15 农村住户人均总支出(2011年)
PER CAPITA TOTAL EXPENDITURE OF RURAL HOUSEHOLDS (2011)

单位:元(yuan)

项目	Item	金额 Sum
总支出	**Total Expenditure**	**13 192**
(一)家庭经营费用支出	Expenditure for Household Operations	4 222
1.第一产业生产费用支出	Primary Industry	2 984
(1)农业生产费用支出	Farming	1 414
(2)林业生产费用支出	Forestry	40
(3)牧业生产费用支出	Animal Husbandry	1 383
(4)渔业生产费用支出	Fishery	146
2.第二产业生产费用支出	Secondary Industry	623
(1)工业生产费用支出	Industry	548
(2)建筑业生产费用支出	Construction	74
3.第三产业生产费用支出	Tertiary Industry	615
(1)交通、运输和邮电业生产费用支出	Transport, Postal and Telecommunication Services	150
(2)批发贸易餐饮业生产费用支出	Wholesale, Retail Trade and Catering	383
(3)社会服务业生产费用支出	Social Services	60
(4)文教卫生业生产费用支出	Culture, Education and Health Care	3
(5)其他行业生产费用支出	Other	19
(二)购置生产用固定资产支出	Purchase of Productive Fixed Assets	280
(三)建造生产性固定资产雇工支出	Employee for Building Productive Fixed Assets	1
(四)税费支出	Taxes and Fees	8
1.第一产业税	Primary Industry	
2.第二产业税	Secondary Industry	2
3.第三产业生产税	Tertiary Industry	5
4.其他各种收费	Other Various Payment	1

9－15 续表
continued

单位：元(yuan)

项　目	Item	金额 Sum
(五)生活消费支出	Expenditure on Household Consumption	7 661
1. 食品消费支出	Food	2 803
2. 衣着消费支出	Clothing	701
3. 居住消费支出	Residence	1 328
4. 家庭设备、用品消费支出	Household Facilities, Articles and Services	510
5. 交通通讯消费支出	Transportation and Communication	1 135
6. 文化教育、娱乐消费支出	Cultural, Education and Recreation	649
7. 医疗保健消费支出	Medicines and Medical Services	391
8. 其他商品和服务消费支出	Other Goods and Services	144
(六)财产性支出	Expenditure on Properties	3
1. 宅基地有偿使用费	Unfree Use of Land for Building House	3
2. 承包其他农户转让费	Expenditure for Making Over	
3. 其他	Others	1
(七)转移性支出	Expenditure on Transfers	1 016
1. 寄给带给家庭非常住人口	Expenditure to Outside City	
2. 赠送农村亲友	Presentation to Relatives and Friends in Rural Area	164
3. 赠送城市亲友	Presentation to Relatives and Friends in Urban Area	22

9-16 农村住户人均生活消费支出(2011年)

PER CAPITA EXPENDITURE ON HOUSEHOLD CONSUMPUTION OF RURAL HOUSEHOLDS (2011)

单位:元(yuan)

项目	Item	金额 Sum
生活消费支出	**Expenditure on Household Consumption**	**7 661**
(一)食品	Food	2 803
购买食品支出	Buying Food	2 528
食品消费服务性支出	Services of Food Consumption	275
(二)衣着	Clothing	701
购买衣着支出	Buying Clothing	700
衣着消费服务性支出	Services ofClothing Consumption	1
(三)居住	Residence	1 328
1. 购买居住消费品支出	Buying Residential Consumption	1 046
2. 居住消费服务性支出	Services for Residential Consumption	282
(四)家庭设备、用品及服务	Household Facilities, Articles and Services	510
1. 购买家庭设备、用品支出	Buying Household Facilities and Articles	496
2. 家庭设备服务消费支出	Services for Household Facilities	14
(五)交通和通讯	Transportation and Communication	1 135
1. 购买交通和通讯用品支出	Buying Traffic and Communications Articles	841
2. 交通和通讯服务消费支出	Services for Traffic and Communications	294
(六)文化教育、娱乐用品及服务	Culture, Education and Recreation Articles and Services	649
1. 购买文化教育、娱乐用品	Culture, Education and Recreation Articles	250
2. 教育服务消费	Services for Education	253
3. 文化体育、娱乐服务消费	Services for Culture, Sports and Recreation	145
(七)医疗保健	Health Care and Medical Services	391
1. 购买医疗保健用品	Buying Articles of Medicines and Medical Services	156
2. 医疗保健服务消费支出	Services for Health care	235
(八)其他商品和服务	Other Goods and Services	144
1. 购买其他商品支出	Goods	104
2. 其他消费服务支出	Services	40

9-17 农村住户人均年购买消费品情况
PER CAPITA ANNUAL PURCHASES OF MAJOR COMMODITIES OF RURAL HOUSEHOLDS

商品名称	Name	计量单位	Unit	数量 Amount
蔬菜	Vegetables	千克	kg	51.86
豆制品	Bean Products	千克	kg	1.01
猪肉	Pork	千克	kg	12.45
牛羊肉	Beef and Mutton	千克	kg	0.83
食糖	Carbohydrate	千克	kg	0.63
糕点	Cake	千克	kg	3.83
糖果	Sweet	千克	kg	1.25
卷烟	Cigarette	盒	case	25.67
酒	Liquor	千克	kg	17.72
#啤酒	Beer	千克	kg	11.87
茶叶	Tea	千克	kg	0.83
水果	Fruits	千克	kg	23.87
服装	Garments	件	piece	5.59
购买洗衣机	Washing Machine	台	unit	0.02
购买电风扇	Electric Fan	台	unit	0.02
购买电冰箱	Refrigerator	台	unit	0.02
购买手机	Cell Phone	部	unit	0.11
购买彩色电视机	Color TV Set	台	unit	0.02
购买照相机	Camera	只	unit	
购买家用计算机(电脑)	Computer	台	unit	0.02

注:抽样调查资料。
Note:The data is from sampling.

9－18 农村住户每百户家庭主要耐用品拥有量(1985－2011年)

OWNERSHIP OF MAJOR DURABLE CONSUMER GOODS PER 100 RURAL HOUSEHOLDS(1985－2011)

年份 Year	家用电脑（台）Computer（unit）	空调器（台）Air Conditioner（unit）	热水器（台）Water Heater（unit）	自行车（辆）Bicycle（unit）	洗衣机（台）Washing Machine（unit）	电冰箱（台）Household Refrigerator（unit）	彩色电视机（台）Color TV Set（unit）	移动电话（部）Cell Phone（unit）	照相机（架）Camera（unit）	家用汽车（辆）Automobile（unit）
1985				147	0.3		3		1	
1986				165	1.1	0.3	4.5		1	
1987				148	2.4	0.5	7		2	
1988				154	2.4	1	9		2	
1989				170	3	1	12		2	
1990				164	4	2	13		2	
1991				173	5	4	16		2	
1992				178	5	7	20		2	
1993				203	7	14	26		2	
1994				204	9	21	35		7	
1995				203	16	28	43		6	
1996				198	13	33	46		8	
1997				191	15	36	56		13	
1998				184	17	39	63		15	
1999				185	20	42	74		10	
2000				165	28	47	86		13	
2001				153	28	53	92		13	
2002				152	36	58	98		16	
2003	6	5	33	137	39	60	100	45	16	2
2004	8	8	39	142	48	68	105	68	21	2
2005	14	14	53	138	57	77	109	91	21	5
2006	17	15	54	116	63	87	112	114	14	7
2007	19	19	63	118	70	94	113	132	17	8
2008	25	23	68	124	76	97	114	148	19	9
2009	28	25	71	127	79	99	115	160	21	11
2010	34	30	75	128	82	102	117	170	21	12
2011	44	32	76	114	85	100	112	202	18	15

9－19 农村住户平均每百户购买生产资料和建筑材料(2011 年)
PURCHASES OF PRODUCTION MEANS AND CONSTRUCTION MATERIALPERS PER 100 RURAL HOUSEHOLDS(2011)

商品名称	Name	计量单位	Unit	数量 Amount	金额(元) Sum(yuan)
化肥	Chemical Fertilizer	千克	kg	67 698.47	213 254.13
饼肥	Cake Fertilizer	千克	kg	387.23	1 081.30
农药	Farm Pesticides	千克	kg	1 065.13	13 258.84
农用薄膜	Plastic Fim	千克	kg	2 007.35	19 979.69
生产用燃料(生产用柴油、汽油及用煤合并)	Fuels for Production	千克	kg	12 744.40	92 762.65
汽车	Automobile	辆	set	0.94	29 323.51
大中型拖拉机	Large and Medium Tractors	台	set		
小型和手扶拖拉机	Small and Walking Tractors	台	set	0.26	980.60
机动脱粒机	Motorized Thresher	台	set	0.87	232.29
胶轮大车	Cart with Rubber Tires	辆	set		
胶轮手推车	Trolley with Rubber Tires	辆	set		
抽水机	Water Pump	台	set		
水泵	Pump	台	set	3.86	2 534.90
役畜	Draught Animal	头	head	0.12	645.13
产品畜	Commodity Animal	头	head	0.52	638.64
水泥	Cement	千克	kg	8 012.59	3 274.94
木材	Wood	立方米	cu. m	9.31	663.49
维修房屋用木材	Wood for House Mending	立方米	cu. m		
钢材	Rolled Steel	千克	kg	734.17	4 094.77
玻璃	Glass	平方米	sq. m		
维修房屋用玻璃	Glass for Housing Mending	平方米	sq. m		
砖瓦	Brick and Tile	块	piece	7 374.96	7 860.00

注:抽样调查资料。
Note:The data is from sampling.

9-20 农村住户人均主要食品消费量(1990-2011年)

PER CAPITA CONSUMPTIONS OF MAJOR COMMODITIES OF RURAL HOUSEHOLDS(1990-2011)

项目	Item	单位	Unit	1990	1995	2000	2005
1.粮食	Grain	千克	kg	248.33	185.01	216.45	155.79
2.蔬菜	Vegetables	千克	kg	135.38	129.66	103.98	69.51
3.食用油	Edible Oil	千克	kg	6.56	7.54	9.03	6.01
(1)植物油	Vegetable Oil	千克	kg	5.75	7.36	8.93	5.95
(2)动物油	Animal Fats	千克	kg	0.81	0.18	0.07	0.06
4.肉类	Meat	千克	kg	9.22	9.62	12.36	23.53
(1)猪肉	Pork	千克	kg	8.55	9.08	11.85	12.82
(2)牛羊肉	Beef and Mutton	千克	kg	0.67	0.54	0.51	0.76
5.牛羊奶	Milk	千克	kg	0.09	0.62	1.79	8.29
6.家禽	Poultry	千克	kg	0.91	1.31	2.55	3.81
7.蛋类	Eggs	千克	kg	4.79	9.29	14.41	11.52
8.水产品	Aquatic Products	千克	kg	4.44	10.77	12.7	14.28
9.食糖	Carbohydrate	千克	kg	0.76	0.83	0.86	0.52
10.卷烟	Cigarette	盒	case	23.21	22.43	23.18	24.36
11.酒	Liquor	千克	kg	8.97	14.07	22.81	20.13
12.茶叶	Tea	千克	kg	0.43	0.61	0.06	0.51
13.糖果	Sweet	千克	kg	0.60	0.58	0.52	0.41
14.糕点	Cake	千克	kg	2.91	3.65	4.51	3.10
15.水果及水果制品	Fruits and Fruit Products	千克	kg	7.75	28.11	39.73	20.11

注:抽样调查资料。

Note:The data is from sampling.

9-20 续表
continued

2006	2007	2008	2009	2010	2011
144.16	116.52	133.16	141.91	127.63	133.03
68.81	56.79	59.21	58.78	55.51	71.00
6.05	5.36	6.03	6.58	6.31	7.56
6.04	5.33	6.01	6.55	6.29	7.55
0.01	0.04	0.02	0.03	0.03	0.01
25.32	26.05	23.93	25.86	26.33	23.97
13.86	12.87	11.92	12.73	12.04	12.45
1.00	1.13	0.92	1.04	1.00	0.83
14.87	14.4	12.12	10.51	11.8	10.26
2.08	2.75	2.7	2.48	2.19	2.52
12.75	11.03	12.25	12.78	11.26	10.10
18.2	17.89	20.46	22.06	23.72	17.88
0.63	0.74	0.75	0.61	0.79	0.63
26.94	26.63	25.61	26.78	26.96	25.67
21.86	20.56	19.41	20.21	19.47	17.92
0.6	0.65	0.76	0.64	0.88	0.83
0.50	0.53	0.17	0.76	0.78	1.25
3.63	3.89	0.81	3.88	2.13	3.83
24.25	22.5	22.16	21.88	21.16	24.31

主要统计指标解释

城市家庭人口 指居住在一起,经济上合在一起共同生活的家庭成员。凡计算为家庭人口的成员其全部收支都包括在本家庭中。

城市就业者负担人数 指家庭人口与就业人口之比。

城市居民家庭总收入、可支配收入 城市居民家庭总收入指生活在一起的所有家庭成员得到的工资性收入、经营净收入、财产性收入、转移性收入之和,不包括出售财务收入和借贷收入。城市居民家庭可支配收入 指家庭成员得到可用于最终消费支出和其他非义务性支出以及储蓄的总和,即居民家庭可以用来自由支配的收入。它是家庭总收入扣除交纳的个人所得税、个人交纳的社会保障费以及记账补贴后的收入。计算公式为:

可支配收入 = 家庭总收入 - 交纳个人所得税 - 个人交纳的社会保障支出 - 记账补贴

城市居民消费性支出 指被调查的城市居民家庭用于日常生活的全部支出,包括购买商品支出和文化生活、服务等支出。包括用于赠送的商品或服务。不包括罚没、丢失款和缴纳的各种税款(如个人所得税、牌照税、房产税等),也不包括个体劳动者生产经营过程中发生的各项费用。

农村居民家庭整、半劳动力整劳动力 指男子18周岁到50周岁,女子18周岁到45周岁;半劳动力指男子16周岁到17周岁,51周岁到60周岁;女子16周岁到17周岁,46周岁到55周岁,同时具有劳动能力的人。虽然在劳动年龄之内,但已丧失劳动能力的人,不应算为劳动力;超过劳动年龄,但能经常参加劳动,计入半劳动力数内。常住人口中的职工,若这些职工为劳动力,就包括在本户的整半劳动力中。

农村居民家庭总收入、纯收入农村居民家庭总收入 指调查期内农村住户和住户成员从各种来源渠道得到的收入总和。按收入的性质划分为工资性收入、家庭经营收入、财产性收入和转移性收入。农民人均纯收入指按人口平均的纯收入水平,反映的是一个地区或一个农户农村居民的平均收入水平。纯收入指农村住户当年从各个来源得到的总收入相应地扣除所发生的费用后的收入总和。纯收入主要用于再生产投入和当年生活消费支出,也可用于储蓄和各种非义务性支出。计算方法:

纯收入 = 总收入 - 家庭经营费用支出 - 税费支出 - 生产性固定资产折旧 - 赠送农村外部亲友支出

农村居民家庭生活消费支出 指农村常住居民家庭用于日常生活的全部开支,是反映和研究农民家庭实际生活消费水平高低的重要指标。

Explanatory Notes on Main Statistical Indicators

Population of Urban Households refer to members of the household living and sharing economically together. All income and expenditure of the population of the household are included in the income and expenditure of the household.

Number of Dependents per Urban Employee refers to the ratio between number of persons in urban households and the number of dependents.

Total Income and Disposable Income of Urban Households Total Income of Urban Households refers to the sum of wage income, net business income, income from properties, and income from transfers of members of the households, excluding income from selling of properties and income from borrowings. Disposable Income of Urban Households refers to the actual income at the disposal of members of the households which can be used for final consumption, other non-compulsory expenditure and savings. This equals to total income minus income tax, personal contribution to social security and sample household subsidy for keeping dairies. Following formula is used:

Disposable income = total income - income tax - personal contribution to social security - sample household subsidy for keeping dairies.

Consumption Expenditure of Urban Households refers to total expenditure of the sample households for consumption in daily life, including expenditure for various commodities and expenses for non-commodity items such as culture and service, including commodities and service give the other person as a present, but excluding fines and confiscation, loss, tax payments (such as income tax, real estates tax, etc,) and various expenses by individual laborers for business purposes.

Rural Full/Semi Labour Force Full labour force refers to persons capable of work, aged 18-50 for males and 18-45 for females. Semi labour force refers to persons capable of work, aged 16-17 and 51-60 for males and 16-17 and 46-55 for females. Persons at their working ages but not capable of work are not to be included as labour force. Persons not at working ages but participating regularly in work are included in semi labour force. For staff and workers as resident population of the household, they are included as full or semi labour force of the household if they are in the labour force.

Total Income and Net Income of Rural Households Total Income of Rural Households refers to the sum of income earned from various sources by the rural households and their members during the reference period, and is classified as income from wages and salaries, income from from household operations, income from properties and income from transfers.

Net Income of Rural Households refers to the total income of rural households from all sources minus all corresponding expenses. the formula for calculation is an follows:

Net income = total income household operation expenses taxes and fees depreciation of fixed assets for production subsidy for participating in household survey gifts to non rural relatives.

Consumption Expenditure of Rural Households refers to total expenses of rural households on daily life. This indicator is used to show the actual consumption level of peasants.

城市建设、环境保护 10

CITY CONSTRUCTION AND ENVIRONMENT PROTECTION

简要说明

一、本篇资料的主要内容

本篇资料主要反映了全市城市基础设施基本情况，包括市政设施、供水、供电、公共交通、园林绿化、燃气供热、城市环卫、环境保护及工业“三废”排放情况等方面的资料。

二、本篇资料的来源

1、本篇资料中市政设施、供水、公共交通、园林绿化、燃气供热、城市环卫相关资料来源于市建设委员会的城市建设统计年报，由市统计局固定资产投资统计处整理提供。

2、本篇资料中供电资料来源于青岛供电公司，由市统计局工业（能源）统计处整理提供。

3、本篇资料中环境保护、环境质量及工业“三废”排放情况来源于市环境保护局，由市统计局人口和社会科技统计处整理提供。

Brief Introduction

I. Main Content

Data in this chapter show the basic conditions of public facilities of the whole city, including urban construction and infrastructure, water supply, electricity supply, public communications, urban greenery, gas and heating, urban sanitation, environmental protection and discharge conditions of industrial waste water, waste gas and solid waste, etc.

II. Source of Data

（1）Data on conditions of urban construction and infrastructure, water supply, public communi-cations, urban greenery, gas and heating, urban sanitation are based on the annual report of city construction provided by Qingdao Municipal Construction Commission, and compiled by the Division of Investment and Construction Statistics of Qingdao Municipal Bureau of Statistics.

（2）Data on electricity supply are provided by Qingdao Power Corporation, and compiled by the Division of Industry Statistics of Qingdao Municipal Bureau of Statistics.

（3）Data on environmental protection, environmental conditions and discharge conditions of industrial waste water, waste gas and solid waste are provided by Qingdao Municipal Bureau of Environmental Protection ,and compiled by the Division of Population and Science & Technology of Qingdao Municipal Bureau of Statistics.

10 -1 主要年份城市建设和公用事业
MAJOR YEAR'S CITY CONSTRUCTION AND PUBLIC UTILITIES

年份 Year	建成区面积（平方公里）Developed Areas(sq. km)	年末道路长度（公里）Length of Roads at Year-end(km)	年末道路面积（万平方米）Area of Roads at Year-end (10000 sq. m)	公共汽车、电车线路网长度(公里) Network Length of Bus and Trolley Bus(km)
1949	27	243	206	26.4
1952	29	245	213	124.4
1957	36	248	217	232.3
1962	55	266	235	252.8
1965	57	266	235	308.1
1970	59	374	346	358.5
1975	63	392	355	389.3
1978	66	408	368	422.1
1980	72	408	377	474.1
1985	79	462	464	611.3
1987	81	578	575	581
1989	92.5	541	583	661
1990	94.3	667	786	777
1991	94.7	673	826	922
1992	95.4	683	840	988
1993	99.9	764	944	1 094
1994	103.9	811	985	1 372
1995	106	936	1 177	1 101
1996	110	991	1 339	1 211
1997	112	1 047	1 436	1 492
1998	114	1 106	1 436	1 859
1999	116	1 171	1 698	2 339
2000	119.1	1 192	1 789	2 711
2001	123	1 248	2 169	2 521
2002	133	1 426	2 594	896
2003	145.9	1 595	2 816	973
2004	154.8	1 755	3 254	1 185
2005	178.8	1 862	3 547	1 159
2006	227.5	3 160	5 218	1 362
2007	250.7	3 288	5 411	1 480
2008	267.1	3 318	5 596	1 470
2009	272.9	3 402	5 763	1 216
2010	282.3	3 409	5 893	1 383
2011	291.5	3 705	6 605	1 719

注:1. 自 2002 年起人均公共绿地面积按辖区内全部人口计算。

2. 2005 年以前所用园林绿地面积;公共绿地面积;人均公共绿地面积;公园、动物园个数;公园、动物园面积指标分别改为现在的绿地面积;公共绿地面积;人均公园绿地面积;公园个数;公园面积。

Note:1. Per capita public green areas is calculated at total population in the area under jurisdiction since 2002.

2. Before 2005, the corresponding indicators of greenbelt area, park greenbelt area, per capita park greenbelt area, coverage rate of greenbelt, number of parks and area of parks were greenland area, public greenbelt area, per capita public greenbelt area, coverage rate of green, number of parks and zoos, area of parks and zoos.

10 -1 续表1
continued

年 份 Year	自来水供水管道长度(公里) Length of Tap Water Pipelines (km)	全年供水总量(万立方米) Annual Volume of Tap Water Supply (10000 cu. m)	#全年售水量(万立方米) Annual Volume of Tap Water Sale (10000 cu. m)	#居民家庭用水 of which: Consumption for Residential Use	用水普及率(%) Coverage Rate of Population with Access to Tap Water(%)	排水管道长度(公里) Length of Sewage Pipes(km)	全年用电量(亿千瓦时) Annual Volume of Electricity Supply (100 million kW·h)	#居民生活用电 of which: Consumption for Residential Use
1949	308	721	456	331	89.0	200	0.88	0.14
1952	341	778	612	310	90.0	227	1.85	0.14
1957	412	1 392	1 296	606	93.0	273	2.61	0.26
1962	483	2 700	2 512	937	98.0	290	3.77	0.57
1965	500	3 220	2 979	929	98.0	295	5.92	0.68
1970	521	4 503	4 106	1 085	99.0	350	9.83	1.02
1975	564	6 726	6 302	1 950	99.0	361	12.41	1.43
1978	572	5 334	4 975	1 314	99.0	382	16.34	1.62
1980	588	8 224	7 874	2 577	99.0	394	21.48	2.78
1985	685	7 557	7 038	2 628	99.9	505	26.39	2.87
1987	749	10 716	9 155	3 691	99.9	569	34.15	4.01
1989	853	10 349	8 606	3 666	97.0	620	38.36	3.38
1990	873	11 896	10 211	4 270	96.9	645	41.08	4.32
1991	908	13 865	11 760	4 990	96.6	649	44.51	5.34
1992	1 035	16 385	13 070	5 931	96.5	672	51.78	6.84
1993	1 123	16 137	14 027	6 124	99.1	734	55.02	7.66
1994	1 124	17 367	14 716	6 405	100	811	60.74	8.78
1995	1 046	22 513	15 810	7 050	100	990	67.23	10.16
1996	1 182	23 277	16 566	7 731	100	1 051	72.87	12.23
1997	1 266	24 130	17 215	8 787	100	1 167	77.82	13.73
1998	1 390	23 845	17 271	9 115	100	1 210	79.65	14.28
1999	1 471	23 849	18 558	10 032	100	1 301	88.12	15.31
2000	1 524	25 414	20 642	11 405	100	1 460	106.80	16.00
2001	1 665	22 225	18 556	10 555	100	1 539	116.10	17.62
2002	1 781	27 662	21 684	10 129	100	1 641	131.44	18.31
2003	2 060	27 594	21 483	10 142	100	1 884	147.68	19.88
2004	2 566	30 877	23 864	11 695	100	2 002	167.95	23.63
2005	2 876	33 265	25 874	12 536	100	2 309	193.81	33.76
2006	3 984	30 524	25 572	10 682	100	3 994	215.35	34.87
2007	4 187	31 533	26 454	11 408	100	4 079	236.42	37.40
2008	4 642	32 675	27 396	11 301	100	4 229	250.07	40.31
2009	4 767	33 490	28 274	12 250	100	4 555	259.42	43.29
2010	4 926	34 909	29 617	12 524	100	4 708	292.97	49.50
2011	5 121	34 109	28 837	10 049	100	5 187	313.44	50.13

10－1 续表2

continued

年　份 Year	公共汽车、电车营运车辆(辆) Number of Bus and Trolley Bus under Operation(unit)	全年客运量(万人次) Annual Passenger Traffic(10000 person-times)	出租汽车(辆) Number of Taxi(unit)	使用液化气、煤气、天然气人数(万人) Population with Access to Gas(10000 persons)	液化气 Liquefied Petroleum	煤　气 Coal Gas	天然气 Natural Gas	液化气供气量(吨) Volume of Liquefied Petroleum Supply(ton)
1949	32	298						
1952	76	932						
1957	112	4 110						
1962	127	4 747						
1965	173	6 092						
1970	224	13 002						
1975	324	14 426		2	2			184.9
1978	409	27 351		17	17			3 246
1980	485	38 981	48	24	24			4 345
1985	621	48 852	219	42.1	42.1			10 619
1987	679	56 102	652	56.4	45.4	11.0		12 947
1989	751	63 212	782	62.5	47.5	15.0		14 503
1990	801	63 495	832	75.0	57.4	17.6		17 512
1991	1 372	67 552	1 070	76.2	57.4	18.8		17 963
1992	1 470	73 529	1828	82.8	62.0	20.8		19 565
1993	1 875	72 427	4 874	88.4	64.6	23.8		22 224
1994	1 850	78 231	5 806	103.6	77.4	26.2		24 684
1995	1 891	71 867	5 887	116.2	82.9	33.3		32 443
1996	2 012	49 077	6 660	126.0	88.0	38.0		40 651
1997	2 148	55 642	6 861	133.6	92.9	40.7		38 717
1998	2 184	51 042	7 469	146.8	97.8	49.0		45 381
1999	2 470	55 414	7 839	154.9	98.3	56.6		40 537
2000	3 141	59 879	7 933	164.1	93.3	70.8		46 951
2001	3 453	60 167	8 110	168.8	87.5	81.3		45 295
2002	3 681	61 713	8 376	224.2	133.8	90.4		60 123
2003	3 648	58 792	8 109	246.7	138.3	93.1	15.3	67 803
2004	3 848	66 463	8 144	258.4	140.6	78.8	39.0	58 548
2005	4 039	68 776	8 121	265.0	132.6	45.7	86.7	78 000
2006	4 167	73 726	8 146	271.0	112.5	49.5	109.0	97 343
2007	4 524	78 702	8 221	275.6	104.1	12.1	159.4	79 715
2008	4 701	82 460	9 241	276.3	91.9	10.5	173.9	81 987
2009	4 288	81 768	9 316	276.1	59.8	12.3	204.0	96 721
2010	4 664	85 251	9 539	276.3	36.7	12.6	227.0	80 073
2011	5 419	89 614	9 683	277.1	25.8	12.6	238.7	79 812

注：1990年以前公共营运车辆不包括系统外及个体。

Note: Vehicles not belonging to system and individual vehicles are not contained in public operating vehicles before 1990.

10－1 续表3

continued

年份 Year	煤气供气量（万立方米）Volume of Coal Gas Supply (10000 cu. m)	天然气供气量（万立方米）Volume of Natural Gas Supply (10000 cu. m)	燃气普及率（%）Coverage Rate of Population with Access to Gas(%)	绿地面积（公顷）Area of Green Areas (hectare)	公园绿地面积（公顷）Park Green Areas (hectare)	人均公园绿地面积（平方米）Per Capita Park Green Areas(sq. m)	建成区绿化覆盖率(%) Green Coverage Rate of Developed Areas(%)	公园（个）Number of Parks and Zoos(unit)	公园面积（公顷）Area of Parks and Zoos (hectare)
1949				133	42	0.7	4.9	3	43
1952				134	43	0.7	4.4	4	45
1957				245	132	1.7	6.9	10	122
1962				771	184	2.2	14.0	12	174
1965				777	184	2.1	13.7	12	174
1970				772	184	2.1	13.0	6	117
1975			2.3	465	162	1.8	7.6	5	134
1978			18.6	469	162	1.7	7.6	6	165
1980			24.5	625	206	2.1	10.4	6	152
1985			36.3	1 072	255	2.3	17.3	7	153
1987	491		47.0	1 790	427	3.6	21.8	20	372
1989	2 585		47.3	1 941	459	3.5	21.7	22	381
1990	3 073		56.2	2 120	492	3.7	22.8	26	404
1991	3 439		56.5	2 318	500	3.7	24.4	28	443
1992	3 824		60.0	2 471	515	3.7	25.9	28	417
1993	4 215		63.1	2 488	543	3.9	26.5	31	453
1994	4 116		63.1	2 866	572	4.0	27.9	31	463
1995	4 734		79.2	4 547	771	5.3	30.1	33	675
1996	5 447		83.9	4 679	836	5.6	30.4	33	675
1997	5 920		87.3	4 717	924	6.0	31.3	34	730
1998	5 959		92.5	6 812	1 047	6.6	35.0	35	775
1999	7 319		96.0	7 007	1 186	7.4	35.9	36	791
2000	9 567		98.0	7 439	1 423	8.5	37.0	37	790
2001	11 814		99.0	7 688	1 588	9.3	37.5	39	832
2002	13 500		99.5	7 967	1 791	8.1	36.4	43	926
2003	14 826	1 181	100	8 829	2 305	9.3	37.5	45	1 034
2004	15 503	2 710	100	10 047	2 842	11	38.0	48	1 421
2005	16 573	7 456	100	11 137	3 132	11.8	38.8	47	1 110
2006	9 821	13 876	100	11 756	3 198	11.8	39.2	47	1 188
2007	9 516	18 103	100	15 369	3 661	13.3	37.8	73	1 268
2008	8 691	21 780	100	15 630	4 014	14.5	41.5	77	1 815
2009	7 523	26 948	100	16 003	4 003	14.5	43.4	71	1 897
2010	9 153	35 681	100	16 619	4 027	14.6	43.38	72	1 917
2011	9 137	46 147	100	18 013	4 041	14.6	44.69	74	1 931

注：1. 自2002年起人均公共绿地面积按辖区内全部人口计算。

2. 2005年以前所用园林绿地面积；公共绿地面积；人均公共绿地面积；公园、动物园个数；公园、动物园面积指标分别改为现在的绿地面积；公共绿地面积；人均公园绿地面积；公园个数；公园面积。

Note: 1. Per capita public green areas is calculated at total population in the area under jurisdiction since 2002.

2. Before 2005, the corresponding indicators of greenbelt area, park greenbelt area, per capita park greenbelt area, coverage rate of greenbelt, number of parks and area of parks were greenland area, public greenbelt area, per capita public greenbelt area, coverage rate of green, number of parks and zoos, area of parks and zoos.

10－2 全年供电(2011 年)
ANNUAL ELECTRICITY SUPPLY(2011)

全年供电 项　　目	Item	单位	Unit	2011
发电设备总容量	Total Capacity of Generation Equipment	万千瓦	10000 kW	386.93
#青岛电厂	Qingdao Power Plant	万千瓦	10000 kW	120
黄岛电厂	Huangdao Power Plant	万千瓦	10000 kW	179
全年发电量	Annual Electricity Generation	亿千瓦时	100 million kW · h	184.43
#青岛电厂	Qingdao Power Plant	亿千瓦时	100 million kW · h	62.4
黄岛电厂	Huangdao Power Plant	亿千瓦时	100 million kW · h	96.83
全年实际用电量	Annual Electricity Consumption	亿千瓦时	100 million kW · h	313.44
#工业	Industrial Consumption	亿千瓦时	100 million kW · h	203.42
农业	Agricultural Consumption	亿千瓦时	100 million kW · h	5.22
生活	Residential Consumption	亿千瓦时	100 million kW · h	50.13
平均每日用电量	Average Daily Consumption	万千瓦时	10000 kW · h	8 587

10－3 分行业用电(2011 年)
ELECTRICITY CONSUMPTION BY SECTOR(2011)

单位:万千瓦时(10 000 kW · h)

行业	Sector	2011	2011 年比 2010 年增长(%) Growth Rate in 2011 over 2010(%)
全社会用电总计	**Total Electricity Consumption**	**3 134 403**	**6.99**
一、农、林、牧、渔业	Farming, Forestry, Animal Husbandryand Fishery	52 194	-19.90
二、工业	Industry	2 034 217	8.38
三、建筑业	Construction	47 672	12.75
四、交通运输、仓储和邮政业	Transport, Storage and Post	85 701	17.17
五、信息传输、计算机服务和软件业	Information Transmission, Computer Services and Software	21 229	12.91
六、商业、住宿和餐饮业	Trade, Hotels and Catering Services	123 499	7.00
七、金融、房地产、商务及居民服务业	Financial Intermediation, Real Estate and Business Services	142 069	18.88
八、公共事业及管理组织	Public Management and Social Organization	126 515	2.54
九、城乡居民生活用电	Household Consumption	501 307	1.27
城镇居民	Urban Area	305 435	-2.84
乡村居民	Rural Area	195 872	8.43

10－4 城市供水(2011 年)
URBAN WATER SUPPLY(2011)

项　目	Item	单位	Unit	2011
自来水供水管道长度	Length of Tap Water Pipelines	公里	km	5 121
综合生产能力	Synthesis Production Capacity	万立方米/日	10000 cu. m/day	124
全年供水总量	Annual Volume of Tap Water Supply	万立方米	10000 cu. m	34 109
#售水量	of which: Volume of Tap Water Sale	万立方米	10000 cu. m	28 837
#生产运营用水	of which: Consumption for Production Use	万立方米	10000 cu. m	11 898
公共服务用水	Consumption for Public Services Use	万立方米	10000 cu. m	6 497
居民家庭用水	Consumption for Residential Use	万立方米	10000 cu. m	10 049
其他用水	Consumption for Other Uses	万立方米	10000 cu. m	393
平均每日供水量	Daily Volume of Tap Water Supply	万立方米	10000 cu. m	93.45
#生产用	of which: Consumption for Production Use	万立方米	10000 cu. m	32.60
生活用	Consumption for Residential Use	万立方米	10000 cu. m	27.53
用水户数	Households with Access to Water	户	household	1 030 486
用水人口	Population with Access to water	万人	10000 persons	262.19
工业用水量重复利用率	Recycle Rate of Water for Industrial Use	%	%	85.59

10－5 城市公共交通(2011 年)
URBAN PUBLIC TRAFFIC(2011)

项　目	Item	单位	Unit	2011
公共汽车、电车线路网长度	Network Length of Bus and Trolley Bus	公里	km	1 719
公共汽车、电车营运车辆	Number of Bus and Trolley Bus under Operation	辆	unit	5 419
#汽车	Bus	辆	unit	5 283
电车	Trolley Bus	辆	unit	136
公共汽车、电车全年客运量	Annual Passenger Traffic of Bus and Trolley Bus	万人次	10000 person-times	89 614
公共汽车、电车平均每日客运量	Daily Passenger Traffic of Bus and Trolley Bus	万人	10000 persons	246
出租汽车数	Number of Taxi	辆	unit	9 683
轮渡运营船数	Number of Ferry Boat under Operation	艘	ship	38
轮渡客运总量	Passenger Traffic of Ferry Boat	万人次	10000 person-times	791.2
轮渡平均每日客运量	Daily Passenger Traffic of Ferry Boat	万人	10000 persons	2.17

10-6 城市供气(2011年)
URBAN GAS SUPPLY(2011)

项　目	Item	单位	Unit	2011
煤气供应总量	Volume of Coal Gas Supply	万立方米	10000 cu. m	9 137
#家庭用量	Household Consumption	万立方米	10000 cu. m	1 179
煤气用气户数	Households with Access to Coal Gas	户	household	45 031
#家庭用户	Household Users	户	household	44 944
液化石油气供应总量	Volume of Liquefied Petroleum Supply	吨	ton	79 812
#家庭用量	Household Consumption	吨	ton	30 741
液化石油气用气户数	Households with Access to Liquefied Petroleum	户	household	182 691
#家庭用户	Household Users	户	household	179 658
天然气供应总量	Volume of Natural Gas Supply	万立方米	10000 cu. m	46 147
#家庭用量	Household Consumption	万立方米	10000 cu. m	12 455
天然气用气户数	Households with Access to Natural Gas	户	household	910 927
#家庭用户	Household Users	户	household	906 927
燃气普及率	Coverage Rate of Population with Access to Gas	%	%	100

10-7 城市环境卫生(2011年)
URBAN ENVIRONMENTAL SANITATION(2011)

项　目	Item	单位	Unit	2011
市容环卫专用车辆总数	Number of Special Vehicles for Environmental Sanitation	辆	unit	807
生活垃圾清运量	Volume of Garbage Disposal	万吨	10000 tons	135
生活垃圾无害化处理厂(场)数	Number of Bio-safety Disposal Plant of Garbage	座	unit	2
生活垃圾无害化处理能力	Bio-safety Disposal Capacity of Garbage	吨/日	ton/day	4 070
生活垃圾无害化处理量	Bio-safety Disposal Volume of Garbage	万吨	10000 tons	135
道路清扫保洁面积	Area under Cleaning Program	万平方米	10000 sq. m	3 539
#机械化	of which: Mechanization	万平方米	10000 sq. m	1 363
粪便清运量	Volume of Excrement and Urine Disposal	万吨	10000 tons	11.57
粪便无害化处理量	Bio-safety Disposal Volume of Excrement and Urine	万吨	10000 tons	9.74
公共厕所	Public Toilets	个	unit	381

10 -8 城市道路、下水道及绿化(2011 年)

URBAN ROAD,SEWAGE AND GREEN(2011)

项　目	Item	单位	Unit	2011
道路	**Road**			
年末道路长度	Length of Roads at Year-end	公里	km	3 705
年末道路面积	Area of Roads at Year-end	万平方米	10000 sq. m	6 605
#人行道面积	of which:Area of Pavements	万平方米	10000 sq. m	1 420
排水管道长度	Length of Sewage Pipes	公里	km	5 187.42
园林绿化	**Greening**			
绿化覆盖面积	Area of Green Coverage Areas	公顷	hectare	19 883
绿地面积	Area of Green Areas	公顷	hectare	18 013
公园绿地面积	Area of Park Green Areas	公顷	hectare	4 041
公园数	Number of Parks and Zoos	个	unit	74
公园面积	Area of Parks and Zoos	公顷	hectare	1 931
游人量	Number of Tourists	万人次	10000 person-times	1 042.9
城市每人平均公园绿地面积	Per Capita Park Green Area	平方米	sq. m	14.58
建成区绿化覆盖率	Green Coverage Rate of Developed Areas	%	%	44.69

10－9 环境保护基本情况(2011 年)
BASIC CONDITIONS OF ENVIRONMENTAL PROTECTION(2011)

项　目	Item	单位	Unit	2011	2010	2011 年比 2010 年增(＋)减(－)% 2011 Compared to 2010(＋/－)
二氧化硫排放总量	Sulphur Dioxide Emission	吨	ton	102 837.75	103 451.18	－0.59
烟(粉)尘排放总量	Soot(Industrial Dust) Emission	吨	ton	42 390.32	45 986.64	－7.82
工业固体废物排放总量	Industrial Solid Wastes Discharged	吨	ton			
化学需氧量排放总量	Discharge Amount of Chemical Oxygen Demand	吨	ton	158 338.73	166 962.71	－5.17
氨氮排放总量	Discharge Amount of Ammonia and Nitrogen	吨	ton	13 231.17	14 473.92	－8.59
废水排放总量	Waste Water Discharged	万吨	10 000 tons	41 157.04	40 442.81	1.77

10－10 环境质量状况(2011 年)
ENVIRONMENT CONDITION(2011)

项　目	Item	单位	Unit	2011	2010	2011 年比 2010 年增(＋)减(－)% 2011 Compared to 2010(＋/－)
市区空气质量优良率	The Percentages of Excellent Or Good Air Quality of Urban Area	%	%	91.5	90.7	0.8
空气质量按功能区达标率	The Reaching Rate of Air Quality For Corresponding Functional Regions	%	%	100	100	0.00
近岸海域功能区达标率	The Reaching Rate of The Offshore Sea Water for Corresponding Functional Regions	%	%	84.4	87.5	－3.1
市区区域环境噪声平均等效声级	The Average Equivalent Sound Level of the Urban Regional Environmental Noise	分贝(A)	db(A)	53.7	53.5	0.37
市区道路交通噪声平均等效声级	The Average Equivalent Sound Level of the Urban Road Traffic Noise	分贝(A)	db(A)	68.1	68.5	－0.58

10－11 工业“三废”排放情况(2011 年)

DISCHARGE CONDITIONS OF INDUSTRIAL WASTE WATER, WASTE GAS AND SOLID WASTE(2011)

项　目	Item	单 位	Unit	2011	2010	2011 年比 2010 年增(+)减(-)% 2011 Compared to 2010(+/-)
工业废水排放总量	Industrial Waste Water Discharged	万吨	10000 tons	11 229.75	10 512	6.83
废水治理设施数	Number of Facilities for Treatment of Waste Water	套	set	486	460	5.65
废水治理设施处理能力	Capacity of Facilities for Treatment of Waste Water	万吨/日	10000 tons/day	112	108.47	3.25
进入城市污水处理厂量	Volume Handled by Sewage Treatment Plant	万吨	10000 tons	8 138.74	6 559.94	24.07
工业废水排放达标量	Industrial Waste Water Meeting Discharge Standards	万吨	10000 tons			
化学需氧量排放量	Discharge Amount of Chemical Oxygen Demand	吨	ton	7 621.28	7 362.84	3.51
氨氮排放量	Discharge Amount of Ammonia and Nitrogen	吨	ton	755.67	815.51	-7.34
工业废气排放总量	Industrial Waste Air Discharged	万标立方米	10000 cu. m	24 383 323	28 446 354.03	-14.28
废气治理设施数	Number of Facilities for Treatment of Waste Air	套	set	1 197	668	79.19
其中:脱硫设施数	of which: Desulphurization Facilities	套	set	298	319	-6.58
废气治理设施处理能力	Capacity of Facilities for Treatment of Waste Air	万标立方米/时	10000 cu. m/hr	8 562.45	6 878.9	24.47
其中:脱硫能力	of which: Desulphurization Capacity	万立方米/时	ton/hr	2 792.39		
二氧化硫去除量	Sulphur Dioxide Removed	吨	ton	173 459.02	180 579.58	-3.94
二氧化硫排放量	Sulphur Dioxide Emission	吨	ton	75 777.43	76 387.89	-0.80
其中:达标排放量	of which: Amount Meeting Discharge Standards	吨	ton			
烟(粉)尘排放量	Soot(Industrial Dust) Emission	吨	ton	26 845.17	29 856.7	-10.09
其中:达标排放量	of which: Amount Meeting Discharge Standards	吨	ton			
工业固体废物产生量	Industrial Solid Wastes Producted	万吨	10000 tons	891.38	923.11	-3.44
其中:危险废物	of which: Hazardous Wastes	吨	ton	35 996	39 414.38	-8.67
工业固体废物综合利用量	Industrial Solid Wastes Comprehensive Utilized	万吨	10000 tons	883.55	859.44	2.81
工业固体废物排放量	Industrial Solid Wastes Discharged	万吨	10000 tons			
其中:危险废物	of which: Hazardous Wastes	吨	ton			
污染治理项目完成投资	Investment in Treatment Projects of Pollution	万元	10000 yuan	10 219	3 109.20	228.67
污染治理项目数	Number of Treatment Projects of Pollution	个	item	25	24	4.17
当年竣工治理项目数	Number of Completed Treatment Projects in the Year	个	item	19	23	-17.39

主要统计指标解释

供水综合生产能力 指按供水设施取水、净化、送水、出厂输水干管等环节设计能力计算的综合生产能力。

年末供水管道长度 指从送水泵至用户水表之间所有管道的长度。不包括新安装尚未使用的管道。

用水普及率 指城市用水人口数与城市人口总数的比率。计算公式:

$$用水普及率=\frac{城市用水人口数}{城市人口总数}\times 100\%$$

全年供水总量 指报告期供水企业(单位)供出的全部水量。包括有效供水量和漏损水量。

全年供气总量 指全年燃气企业(单位)向用户供应的燃气数量。包括销售量和损失量。

用气普及率 指报告期末使用燃气的城市人口数与城市人口总数的比率。计算公式为:

$$用气普及率=\frac{城市用气人口数}{城市人口总数}\times 100\%$$

年末道路长度 指年末道路长度和与道路相通的广场、桥梁、隧道的长度,按车行道中心线计算。在统计时只统计路面宽度在3.5米(含3.5米)以上的各种铺装道路,包括开放型工业区和住宅区道路在内。

工业废气排放量 指报告期内企业厂区内燃料燃烧和生产工艺过程中产生的各种排入大气的含有污染物的气体的总量,以标准状态(273K,101325Pa)计算。

工业废水排放量 指经过企业厂区所有排放口排到企业外部的工业废水量。包括生产废水、外排的直接冷却水、超标排放的矿井地下水和与工业废水混排的厂区生活污水,不包括外排的间接冷却水(清污不分流的间接冷却水应计算在内)。

工业废水排放达标量 指各项指标都达到国家或地方排放标准的外排工业废水量,包括未经处理外排达标的和经过处理后外排达标的和两部分。国家排放标准见GB8978—88。

工业固体废物产生量 指企业在生产过程中产生的固体状、半固体状和高浓度液体状废弃物的总量,包括危险废物、冶炼废渣、粉煤灰、炉渣、煤矸渣、尾矿、放射性废物和其他废物等;不包括矿山开采的剥离废石和掘进废石(煤矸石和呈酸性或碱性的废石除外)酸性或碱性废石是指采掘的废石其流经水、雨淋水的pH值小于4或pH值大于10.5者。

工业粉尘排放量 指企业在生产工艺过程中排放的能在空气中悬浮一定时间的固体颗粒物排放量。如钢铁企业的耐火材料粉尘、焦化企业的筛焦系统粉尘、烧结机的粉尘、石灰窑的粉尘、建材企业的水泥粉尘等。不包括电厂排入大气的烟尘。

化学需氧量(COD) 测量有机和无机物质化学分解所消耗氧的质量浓度的水污染指数。

Explanatory Notes on Main Statistical Indicators

Production Capacity of Water Supply refers to the designed comprehensive production capacity of water facilities, covering the 4 links of water collection, purification, conveyance, and outflow through trunk pipelines.

Length of Water Supply Pipelines at the Year-end refers to the total length of all the pipelines between the water pumps and the user water meters, excluding pipelines newly installed but not used yet.

Coverage Rate of Urban Population with Access to Tap Water refers to the ratio of the urban population with access to tap water to the total urban population. The formula is:

Coverage rate of urban population with access to tap water = (Urban population with access to tap water)/(Urban population) × 100%

Annual Volume of Water Supply refers to the total volume of water supplied by water-works(units) during the reference period, including both the effective water supply and loss during the water supply.

Annual Volume of Gas Supply refers to the total volume of gas provided to users by gas-producing enterprises(units) in a year, including the volume sold and the volume lost.

Coverage Rate of Urban Population with Access to Gas refers to the ratio of the urban population with access to gas to the total urban population at the end of the reference period. The formula is:

Coverage rate of urban population with access to gas = (Urban population with access to gas/Urban population) × 100%

Length of Paved Roads at the Year-end refers to the length of roads with paved surface including squares bridges and tunnels connected with roads by the end of the year. Length of the roads is measured by the central lines for vehicles for paved roads with a width of 3.5 meters and over, including roads in open-ended factory compounds and residential quarters.

Industrial Waste Air Emission refers to discharge into atmosphere of waste air containing pollutants generated from fuel burning and production process in enterprises within a given period of time. It is calculated at standard status(273K, 101325Pa).

Waste Water Discharged by Industry refers to the volume of waste water discharged by industrial enterprises through all their outlets, including waste water from production process, directly cooled water, groundwater from mining wells which does not meet discharge standards and sewage from households mixed with waste water produced by industrial activities, but excluding indirectly cooled water discharged(It should be included if the discharge is not separated with waste water).

Industrial Waste Water Meeting Discharge Standards refers to volume of industrial waste water discharge which, with or without treatment, reaches national or local standards with regard to all pollutants. National Discharge standards see GB8978—88.

Industrial Solid Wastes Produced refers to total volume of solid, semi-solid and high concentration liquid residues produced by industrial enterprises from production process in a given period of time, including hazardous wastes, slag, coal ash, gangue, tailings, radioactive residues and other wastes, but excluding stones stripped or dug out in mining(gangue and acid or alkaline stones not included). A stone is acid or alkaline depending on the pH value of the water below 4 or above 10.5 when the stone is in, or soaked by, the water.

Industrial Dust Emission refers to volume of dust emitted by production process of enterprises and suspended in the air for a given period of time, including dust from refractory material of iron and steel works, dust from coke-screening systems and sintering machines of coke plants, dust from lime kilns and dust from cement production in building material enterprises, but excluding soot and dust emitted from power plants.

Chemical Oxygen Demand(COD) refers to index of water pollution measuring the mass concentration of oxygen consumed by the chemical breakdown of organic and inorganic matter.

11 农　业
AGRICULTURE

简要说明

一、本篇资料的主要内容

本篇资料主要反映了全市农业生产和农村经济的基本情况，主要包括农林牧渔业总产值、中间消耗、增加值、农村劳动力、耕地、主要农产品产量、农业机械年末拥有量、农业机械化和电气化以及农田水利建设等方面的资料。

二、本篇资料的来源

本篇资料来源于农村综合统计年报，由市统计局农村统计处（国家统计局青岛调查队农村调查处）整理提供。

Brief Introduction

I. Main Content

Data in this chapter show the basic conditions of agricultural production and rural economy, mainly including agricultural output, intermediate consumption, value added, rural labor force, cultivated land, output of main agricultural produces, agricultural machinery and electrification in rural areas and basic construction on irrigation and drainage.

II. Source of Data

Data in this chapter are based on the annual report of rural summary conditions, and compiled by the Division of Countryside Statistics of Qingdao Municipal Bureau of Statistics (Division of Rural Household Survey of Survey Office of the National Bureau of Statistics in Qingdao).

11－1 农村基本情况(1980－2011 年)
BASIC STATISTICS ON RURAL AREA(1980－2011)

项目	Item	单位	Unit	1980	1990	1995	2000	2005
一、乡村户数、人口、劳动力	**Rural Households, Population and Labor Force**							
乡村户数	Rural Households	万户	10000 households	110.56	133.73	145.71	148.20	151.06
乡村人口	Rural Population	万人	10000 persons	477.53	495.45	496.93	483.39	478.78
乡村劳动力	Rural Labor Force	万人	10000 persons	194.10	247.29	258.66	254.62	257.87
男劳动力	Male	万人	10000 persons	113.67	137.28	139.62	137.09	137.66
女劳动力	Female	万人	10000 persons	80.43	110.01	119.04	117.53	120.21
二、年末实有耕地面积	**Year-end Area of Cultivated Land**	**万公顷**	**10000 hectares**	**53.13**	**49.84**	**48.65**	**47.75**	**42.10**
三、农用机械总动力	**Total Agricultural Machinery Power**	**万千瓦**	**10000 kW**	**110.44**	**253.52**	**289.23**	**459.21**	**619.69**
拖拉机	Tractors	台	unit	24 278	55 363	56 391	126 981	163 032
农用汽车	Agricultural Automobiles	辆	unit	728	3 880	6 314	9 613	11 552
四、农村用电量	**Electricity Consumed in Rural Areas**	**万千瓦时**	**10000 kW·h**	**20 492**	**67 616**	**134 284**	**189 651**	**372 645**
五、农用化肥施用量(折纯)	**Consumption of Chemical Fertilizer (convert to pure amount)**	**万吨**	**10000 tons**	**12.06**	**20.47**	**31.45**	**32.53**	**33.01**
六、有效灌溉面积	**Irrigated Area**	**万公顷**	**10000 hectares**	**29.66**	**27.47**	**28.70**	**29.52**	**29.65**

11 -1 续表
continued

项目	Item	单位	Unit	2006	2007	2008	2009	2010	2011
一、乡村户数、人口、劳动力	**Rural Households, Population and Labor Force**								
乡村户数	Rural Households	万户	10000 households	151.10	151.19	151.75	152.37	154.92	154.91
乡村人口	Rural Population	万人	10000 persons	478.32	478.06	480.22	484.81	487.04	488.67
乡村劳动力	Rural Labor Force	万人	10000 persons	264.70	268.31	270.71	274.74	276.03	277.24
男劳动力	Male	万人	10000 persons	141.27	144.04	144.36	146.20	147.09	146.67
女劳动力	Female	万人	10000 persons	123.43	124.27	126.35	128.54	128.94	130.57
二、年末实有耕地面积	**Year-end Area of Cultivated Land**	**万公顷**	**10000 hectares**	**41.29**	**41.31**	**41.79**	**41.87**	**42.04**	**41.98**
三、农用机械总动力	**Total Agricultural Machinery Power**	**万千瓦**	**10000 kW**	**650.65**	**680.16**	**697.38**	**719.33**	**763.61**	**784.06**
拖拉机	Tractors	台	unit	171 155	173 326	176 156	180 171	200 208	202 022
农用汽车	Agricultural Automobiles	辆	unit	11 098	11 408	11 408	11 408		
四、农村用电量	**Electricity Consumed in Rural Areas**	**万千瓦时**	**10000 kW · h**	**413 762**	**425 715**	**424 292**	**426 306**	**426 819**	**431 646**
五、农用化肥施用量(折纯)	**Consumption of Chemical Fertilizer (convert to pure amount)**	**万吨**	**10000 tons**	**32.64**	**33.89**	**31.05**	**30.17**	**29.89**	**29.37**
六、有效灌溉面积	**Irrigated Area**	**万公顷**	**10000 hectares**	**30.31**	**30.58**	**31.39**	**32.27**	**32.90**	**33.17**

11－2 农村劳动力(1985－2011年)
RURAL LABOR FORCE(1985－2011)

单位:万人(10 000 persons)

年　份 Year	合　计 Total	农林牧渔业 Farming, Forestry, Animal Husbandry and Fishery	工　业 Industry	建 筑 业 Construction
1985	225.09	147.89	32.92	15.62
1988	238.93	146.00	44.46	17.51
1989	242.70	151.16	44.65	16.46
1990	247.29	155.20	44.48	16.17
1991	253.01	160.31	45.49	15.87
1992	258.23	160.04	47.00	17.25
1993	259.18	159.22	44.04	20.20
1994	258.34	155.74	43.70	21.52
1995	258.66	154.08	44.06	22.33
1996	256.34	151.10	43.08	21.80
1997	258.60	153.07	41.66	22.02
1998	258.50	152.79	40.79	21.68
1999	256.82	149.11	42.18	22.32
2000	254.62	143.59	42.76	22.99
2001	253.98	132.46	47.76	24.66
2002	254.08	119.98	53.66	26.52
2003	257.67	118.27	55.65	26.65
2004	258.91	112.05	60.32	28.36
2005	257.87	103.03	65.59	29.03
2006	264.70	102.28	71.46	28.16
2007	268.31	100.63	74.70	30.97
2008	270.71	100.90	74.82	30.87
2009	274.74	102.64	75.42	31.23
2010	276.04	102.45	76.32	32.10
2011	277.24	102.73	76.87	32.57

11 -2 续表
continued

单位:万人(10 000 persons)

年 份 Year	交通运输仓储和邮电业 Transport, Postal and Telecommunication Services	批发零售贸易、餐饮业 Wholesale and Retail Trades and Catering Services	金融保险业 Finance and Insurance	其他劳动力 Other Labor Force
1985	5.23	0.06	19.76	3.61
1988	5.89	0.09	20.40	4.58
1989	6.00	0.12	19.95	4.36
1990	6.11	0.12	20.71	4.50
1991	6.09	0.13	20.52	4.60
1992	7.02	0.16	21.74	5.02
1993	8.93	0.16	20.65	5.98
1994	6.48	10.10		20.80
1995	7.11	10.71		20.37
1996	7.33	11.78		21.25
1997	7.62	12.40		21.83
1998	8.02	13.32		21.90
1999	8.19	14.03		20.99
2000	8.39	16.10		20.79
2001	9.02	17.80		22.28
2002	10.00	20.07		23.85
2003	9.96	20.60		26.54
2004	10.20	24.08		22.96
2005	10.70	25.88		22.34
2006	11.66	25.31		24.37
2007	11.61	27.61		21.16
2008	11.06	28.76		22.09
2009	11.40	29.03		22.75
2010	11.78	28.85		22.01
2011	11.89	29.34		21.02

11-3 分市、区乡村户数、人口、劳动力(2011年)
RURAL HOUSEHOLDS, POPULATION AND LABOR FORCE BY REGION(2011)

市、区名称	Region	乡村户数(万户) Rural Households (10000 households)	乡村人口(万人) Rural Population (10000 persons)	乡村劳动力(万人) Labor Force of Village (10000 persons)	男劳动力 Male Laborer	女劳动力 Female Laborer	农林牧渔业 Farming, Forestry, Animal Husbandry and Fishery	#林牧渔业 Forestry, Animal Husbandry and Fishery
总　计	**Total**	**154.91**	**488.67**	**277.24**	**146.67**	**130.57**	**102.73**	**19.66**
市　区	Urban Area	25.67	72.95	39.74	20.95	18.79	6.08	2.75
#崂山区	Laoshan District	5.41	15.76	8.95	4.82	4.13	1.95	0.60
黄岛区	Huangdao District	5.05	16.52	9.30	4.91	4.39	1.10	0.72
城阳区	Chengyang District	15.21	40.67	21.49	11.22	10.27	3.03	1.43
即墨市	Jimo	29.67	96.32	56.16	29.54	26.62	17.00	2.91
胶州市	Jiaozhou	19.27	63.10	36.32	18.81	17.50	9.94	0.82
胶南市	Jiaonan	21.95	70.13	36.63	19.67	16.96	13.80	2.84
平度市	Pingdu	37.53	122.54	71.60	37.82	33.78	37.66	8.79
莱西市	Laixi	20.82	63.63	36.80	19.88	16.92	18.26	1.55

11-3 续表
continued

市、区名称	Region	工　业 Industry	建 筑 业 Construction	交通运输仓储和邮电业 Transportation, Storage, Postal and Telecommunications	批发零售贸易、餐饮业 Wholesale, Retail and Catering Business	其他劳动力 Other Labor Force
总　计	**Total**	**76.87**	**32.57**	**11.89**	**29.34**	**21.02**
市　区	Urban Area	15.46	5.26	2.56	5.54	4.11
#崂山区	Laoshan District	2.63	1.42	0.61	1.06	1.14
黄岛区	Huangdao District	3.25	1.88	0.66	1.22	0.93
城阳区	Chengyang District	9.58	1.96	1.29	3.26	2.04
即墨市	Jimo	20.79	6.12	2.12	5.70	4.03
胶州市	Jiaozhou	11.70	4.78	1.55	4.61	3.48
胶南市	Jiaonan	9.67	5.37	1.17	2.94	3.26
平度市	Pingdu	12.96	7.23	2.94	7.20	3.00
莱西市	Laixi	6.29	3.81	1.55	3.36	3.14

11－4 主要年份农、林、牧、渔业总产值(按现价计算)
MAJOR YEAR'S GROSS OUTPUT VALUE OF FARMING,FORESTRY, ANIMAL HUSBANDRY AND FISHERY(CURRENT PRICE)

单位:万元(10 000 yuan)

年 份 Year	农、林、牧、渔业总产值 Gross Output Value of Farming, Forestry, Animal Husbandry and Fishery	农业产值 Farming	林业产值 Forestry	牧业产值 Animal Husbandry	渔业产值 Fishery
1949	16 511	14 755	325	1 200	231
1952	24 428	21 353	479	1 888	708
1957	26 189	22 717	644	2 218	610
1962	15 356	13 257	230	1 243	626
1965	25 123	21 488	854	2 110	671
1970	44 078	36 889	1 851	3 817	1 521
1975	93 213	79 208	2 144	7 923	3 938
1978	121 497	94 397	3 112	17 293	6 695
1980	149 436	117 547	2 953	22 215	6 721
1985	299 139	215 729	8 986	53 894	20 530
1987	378 981	263 066	5 949	73 271	36 695
1989	463 952	303 679	19 134	91 885	49 254
1990	579 877	381 287	13 801	119 208	65 581
1991	664 779	417 111	12 875	144 909	89 884
1992	703 433	400 471	15 252	150 942	136 768
1993	989 763	509 601	20 845	232 143	227 174
1994	1 424 074	763 366	23 101	356 734	280 873
1995	1 923 771	1 021 413	26 765	503 999	371 594
1996	2 317 434	1 145 399	29 100	692 362	450 573
1997	2 047 712	939 922	24 052	578 443	505 295
1998	2 386 303	1 198 043	16 760	633 735	537 765
1999	2 382 320	1 169 596	17 122	618 020	577 582
2000	2 483 256	1 116 397	19 102	692 782	654 975
2001	2 615 228	1 135 816	20 433	758 313	700 666
2002	2 688 532	1 110 671	23 157	796 007	758 697
2003	2 759 692	1 062 576	36 183	859 915	801 018
2004	2 967 389	1 181 009	32 831	937 494	816 055
2005	3 205 057	1 265 695	25 246	1 070 831	843 285
2006	3 396 096	1 360 755	23 546	1 076 254	855 131
2007	3 429 877	1 483 733	20 842	975 032	830 479
2008	4 008 540	1 778 404	24 452	1 214 648	856 227
2009	4 086 146	1 856 753	22 264	1 160 558	898 608
2010	4 831 806	2 339 238	19 241	1 264 028	1 051 452
2011	5 359 343	2 365 300	19 237	1 560 108	1 232 720

11－5 分市、区农、林、牧、渔业总产值(2011 年,现价)

GROSS OUTPUT VALUE OF FARMING,FORESTRY,ANIMAL HUSBANDRY AND FISHERY BY REGION(2011,CURRENT PRICE)

单位:万元(10 000 yuan)

市、区名称	Region	农、林、牧、渔业总产值 Gross Output Value of Farming,Forestry,Animal Husbandry and Fishery	农 业 Farming	林 业 Forestry	牧 业 Animal Husbandry	渔 业 Fishery
总　计	**Total**	**5 359 343**	**2 365 300**	**19 237**	**1 560 108**	**1 232 720**
市　区	Urban Area	424 866	46 445	1 196	43 438	317 667
#崂山区	Laoshan District	89 620	8 314	179	5 362	67 165
黄岛区	Huangdao District	71 327	15 112	316	10 611	39 588
城阳区	Chengyang District	263 650	22 750	701	27 465	210 914
即墨市	Jimo	902 313	333 656	4 018	213 025	308 204
胶州市	Jiaozhou	750 333	298 675	3 583	212 340	208 859
胶南市	Jiaonan	851 848	253 803	2 748	192 133	371 544
平度市	Pingdu	1 516 019	998 129	4 380	464 605	13 905
莱西市	Laixi	913 964	434 592	3 312	434 567	12 541

注:本表按当年价格计算。

Note:Data in this form are calculated at current price.

11－6 农、林、牧、渔业增加值(2011 年)

VALUE-ADDED OF FARMING, FORESTRY, ANIMAL HUSBANDRY AND FISHERY(2011)

单位:万元(10 000 yuan)

		总 计 Total	农 业 Farming	#种植业 Planting	林 业 Forestry	牧 业 Animal Husbandry	渔 业 Fishery
总产值	**Gross Output Value**	**5 359 343**	**2 365 300**	**2 365 300**	**19 237**	**1 560 108**	**1 232 720**
中间消耗	**Intermediate Expenditure**	**2 295 563**	**834 496**	**834 496**	**8 974**	**886 909**	**480 643**
中间物质消耗	Intermediate Expenditure of Matter	1 694 207	680 440	680 440	6 289	618 966	334 861
对非农生产部门的劳动支出	Expenditure of Labor Services to Nonagricultural Production Development	601 356	154 056	154 056	2 685	267 943	145 782
增加值	**Added Value**	**3 063 780**	**1 530 804**	**1 530 804**	**10 263**	**673 199**	**752 077**

11－7 分市、区农、林、牧、渔业增加值(2011 年)

VALUE-ADDED OF FARMING, FORESTRY,
ANIMAL HUSBANDRY FISHERY BY REGION(2011)

单位:万元(10 000 yuan)

市、区名称	Region	增加值 Added Value	农 业 Farming	林 业 Forestry	牧 业 Animal Husbandry	渔 业 Fishery
总 计	**Total**	**3 063 780**	**1 530 804**	**10 263**	**673 199**	**752 077**
市 区	Urban Area	241 949	28 849	712	18 919	184 432
#崂山区	Laoshan District	49 622	5 283	98	2 804	36 872
黄岛区	Huangdao District	42 123	9 952	111	4 814	23 757
城阳区	Chengyang District	150 043	13 453	503	11 301	123 803
即墨市	Jimo	535 225	225 634	2 198	103 913	179 884
胶州市	Jiaozhou	449 490	198 658	1 992	89 968	144 312
胶南市	Jiaonan	488 633	158 858	956	85 503	226 985
平度市	Pingdu	850 808	650 790	2 840	170 709	8 469
莱西市	Laixi	497 675	268 015	1 565	204 187	7 995

11－8 主要年份耕地面积与播种面积
MAJOR YEAR'S CULTIVATED AND SOWN AREA

单位:万公顷(10 000 hectares)

年份 Year	年末实有耕地面积 Year－end Area of Cultivated Land	农作物播种面积 Sown Area of Farm Crops	#粮食作物 Grain Crops	经济作物 Economic Crops
1949	65.70	93.47	84.00	7.20
1952	67.87	97.53	85.07	10.80
1957	59.67	97.87	87.07	10.53
1962	59.67	81.47	72.53	5.80
1965	59.53	82.80	71.80	8.33
1970	57.47	80.73	68.27	10.07
1975	55.25	79.82	65.84	11.01
1978	53.53	77.60	63.60	10.40
1980	53.13	75.87	60.33	12.00
1985	50.53	78.27	57.33	15.73
1987	50.00	76.67	55.87	15.93
1989	49.88	74.78	54.28	16.06
1990	49.84	76.85	56.99	15.53
1991	49.64	76.98	56.89	15.69
1992	49.23	76.96	56.37	15.64
1993	49.00	77.75	56.22	15.71
1994	48.81	76.61	54.08	16.20
1995	48.65	76.54	53.71	15.65
1996	48.46	77.26	54.81	14.90
1997	48.46	75.04	52.32	14.40
1998	48.33	77.18	53.05	14.54
1999	48.10	77.56	50.61	13.24
2000	47.75	76.47	45.07	13.98
2001	46.74	73.69	41.91	14.54
2002	45.45	72.32	40.83	13.95
2003	42.69	67.82	36.05	14.50
2004	42.26	71.33	41.40	14.11
2005	42.10	75.02	49.93	11.89
2006	41.29	74.86	49.79	11.75
2007	41.31	72.79	47.56	12.11
2008	41.79	74.09	51.06	11.29
2009	41.87	75.00	52.92	11.34
2010	42.04	75.39	53.56	11.00
2011	41.98	75.7	54.56	10.69

11－9 分市、区耕地面积(2011 年)

AREA OF CULTIVATED LAND BY REGION(2011)

单位:公顷(hectare)

市、区名称	Region	年末耕地面积 Year-end Area of Cultivated Land	#旱田 Dry Farmland	当年增加的耕地 Area of Cultivated Land Increased in the Year	#新开荒地 Wasteland Newly Opened up
总　计	**Total**	**419 783**	**419 743**	**1 078**	**290**
市　区	Urban Area	6 967	6 967	103	48
#崂山区	Laoshan District	862	862	103	48
黄岛区	Huangdao District	2 103	2 103		
城阳区	Chengyang District	3 932	3 932		
即墨市	Jimo	72 976	72 976	344	176
胶州市	Jiaozhou	53 466	53 466		
胶南市	Jiaonan	52 214	52 174	293	3
平度市	Pingdu	163 052	163 052	267	35
莱西市	Laixi	71 108	71 108	71	28

11－9 续表

continued

单位:公顷(hectare)

市、区名称	Region	当年减少的耕地 Area of Cultivated Land Decreased in the Year	国家基建占地 Government Capital Construction	乡镇集体基建占地 Rural Capital Construction	农民个人建房占地 Private Building
总　计	**Total**	**1 738**	**549**	**207**	**14**
市　区	Urban Area	213	92	1	
#崂山区	Laoshan District	62	4	1	
黄岛区	Huangdao District	88	88		
城阳区	Chengyang District	63			
即墨市	Jimo	370	49	143	1
胶州市	Jiaozhou	448			
胶南市	Jiaonan	120	62	34	
平度市	Pingdu	470	336	19	13
莱西市	Laixi	117	10	10	

11－10 分市、区农作物播种面积(2011 年)
SOWN AREA OF FARM CROPS BY REGION(2011)

单位:公顷(hectare)

市、区名称	Region	总播种面积 Total Sown Area	粮　食 Grain	#夏　粮 Summer Crops	#小　麦 Wheat	秋　粮 Autumn Crops	谷　子 Cereal	玉　米 Corn
总　计	**Total**	**756 963**	**545 563**	**270 341**	**270 260**	**275 221**	**175**	**258 257**
市　区	Urban Area	12 120	8 117	4 029	4 029	4 088		3 181
#崂山区	Laoshan District	727	227			227		67
黄岛区	Huangdao District	2 813	1 455	501	501	954		793
城阳区	Chengyang District	8 510	6 435	3 528	3 528	2 907		2 321
即墨市	Jimo	121 828	90 318	40 807	40 807	49 511	60	45 293
胶州市	Jiaozhou	106 158	76 637	41 292	41 211	35 345	109	33 500
胶南市	Jiaonan	87 756	57 821	28 151	28 151	29 669	2	21 296
平度市	Pingdu	292 675	214 384	106 358	106 358	108 026	4	107 201
莱西市	Laixi	136 426	98 285	49 703	49 703	48 581		47 787

11－10 续表
continued

单位:公顷(hectare)

市、区名称	Region	高　粱 Jowar	地　瓜 Sweet Potato	大　豆 Soja	棉　花 Cotton	花　生 Peanut	烟　叶 Tobacco	蔬　菜 Vegetable
总　计	**Total**	**243**	**4 259**	**11 996**	**2 990**	**94 517**	**448**	**103 554**
市　区	Urban Area		275	633		1 095		2 600
#崂山区	Laoshan District		156	5		233		257
黄岛区	Huangdao District		67	93		832		300
城阳区	Chengyang District		52	535		30		1 973
即墨市	Jimo	91	2 027	1 959		20 000		10 592
胶州市	Jiaozhou	88	360	1 192		7 038		21 921
胶南市	Jiaonan	8	1 082	7 254		19 390	363	9 703
平度市	Pingdu	26	208	564	2 990	28 720	85	41 504
莱西市	Laixi	30	308	395		18 274		17 234

11－11 分市、区农作物总产量(2011 年)
OUTPUT OF FARM CROPS BY REGION(2011)

单位:吨(ton)

市、区名称	Region	粮　食 Grain	#夏　粮 Summer Crops	#小　麦 Wheat	秋　粮 Autumn Crops	谷　子 Cereal	玉　米 Corn	高　粱 Jowar
总　计	**Total**	**3 630 047**	**1 653 863**	**1 653 376**	**1 976 183**	**722**	**1 906 374**	**1 017**
市　区	Urban Area	42 779	16 804	16 804	25 975		22 442	
#崂山区	Laoshan District	1 599			1 599		380	
黄岛区	Huangdao District	9 034	2 330	2 330	6 704		5 827	
城阳区	Chengyang District	32 146	14 474	14 474	17 672		16 235	
即墨市	Jimo	551 032	223 732	223 732	327 300	241	305 729	334
胶州市	Jiaozhou	478 131	243 422	242 934	234 709	464	227 372	388
胶南市	Jiaonan	308 624	129 380	129 380	179 244	6	151 545	26
平度市	Pingdu	1 580 011	719 196	719 196	860 815	12	855 787	82
莱西市	Laixi	669 470	321 331	321 331	348 140		343 501	187

11－11 续表
continued

单位:吨(ton)

市、区名称	Region	地　瓜 Sweet Potato	大　豆 Soja	棉　花 Cotton	花　生 Peanut	烟　叶 Tobacco	蔬　菜 Vegetable
总　计	**Total**	**35 858**	**30 988**	**3 917**	**443 713**	**1 191**	**5 838 183**
市　区	Urban Area	2 213	1 317		4 149		106 763
#崂山区	Laoshan District	1 208	12		700		8 195
黄岛区	Huangdao District	627	246		3 369		12 483
城阳区	Chengyang District	378	1 059		80		82 785
即墨市	Jimo	15 536	5 216		85 470		644 405
胶州市	Jiaozhou	2 916	3 165		30 388		1 193 617
胶南市	Jiaonan	9 819	17 684		91 703	932	449 431
平度市	Pingdu	2 671	2 150	3 917	143 326	259	2 386 432
莱西市	Laixi	2 704	1 456		88 676		1 057 536

11－12 分市、区农作物播公顷单产量(2011 年)

OUTPUT OF FARM CROPS PER HECTARE BY REGION(2011)

单位:千克(kg)

市、区名称	Region	粮 食 Grain	#夏 粮 Summer Crops	#小 麦 Wheat	秋 粮 Autumn Crops	谷 子 Cereal	玉 米 Corn	高 粱 Jowar
总　计	**Total**	**6 654**	**6 117**	**6 117**	**7 181**	**4 133**	**7 382**	**4 187**
市　区	Urban Area	5 270	4 171	4 171	6 354		7 055	
#崂山区	Laoshan District	7 032			7 032		5 688	
黄岛区	Huangdao District	6 207	4 650	4 650	7 025		7 350	
城阳区	Chengyang District	4 995	4 103	4 103	6 080		6 996	
即墨市	Jimo	6 101	5 483	5 483	6 611	4 013	6 750	3 651
胶州市	Jiaozhou	6 239	5 895	5 895	6 641	4 239	6 788	4 406
胶南市	Jiaonan	5 337	4 596	4 596	6 042	3 615	7 116	3 390
平度市	Pingdu	7 370	6 762	6 762	7 968	3 201	7 983	3 177
莱西市	Laixi	6 812	6 465	6 465	7 166		7 188	6 240

11－12 续表

continued

单位:千克(kg)

市、区名称	Region	地 瓜 Sweet Potato	大 豆 Soja	棉 花 Cotton	花 生 Peanut	烟 叶 Tobacco	蔬 菜 Vegetable
总　计	**Total**	**8 420**	**2 583**	**1 310**	**4 695**	**2 657**	**56 378**
市　区	Urban Area	8 047	2 081		3 789		41 063
#崂山区	Laoshan District	7 757	2 400		3 005		31 832
黄岛区	Huangdao District	9 345	2 640		4 050		41 565
城阳区	Chengyang District	7 325	1 980		2 666		41 964
即墨市	Jimo	7 665	2 663		4 274		60 837
胶州市	Jiaozhou	8 100	2 655		4 317		54 450
胶南市	Jiaonan	9 075	2 438		4 730	2 567	46 320
平度市	Pingdu	12 855	3 813	1 310	4 991	3 044	57 500
莱西市	Laixi	8 790	3 690		4 853		61 365

11－13 主要年份农作物总产量
MAJOR YEAR'S OUTPUT OF FARM CROPS

单位：吨（ton）

年 份 Year	粮 食 Grain	#小 麦 Wheat	玉 米 Corn	棉 花 Cotton	花 生 Peanut	水 果 Fruit	蔬 菜 Vegetable
1949	723 190	158 815	25 810	1 280	71 080	9 955	356 015
1952	967 640	200 380	58 130	6 025	115 585	13 468	284 050
1957	921 920	210 690	141 540	3 520	90 445	18 869	625 220
1962	628 930	104 340	53 010	1 280	35 470	8 366	524 455
1965	917 635	180 610	135 595	6 090	88 390	16 034	465 850
1970	1 175 985	243 945	244 530	16 490	96 280	33 907	541 145
1975	1 899 540	430 135	420 095	15 390	98 495	59 206	693 970
1978	1 900 850	514 570	510 635	8 720	114 370	82 819	921 140
1980	2 164 415	520 045	819 930	19 630	160 670	80 840	996 565
1985	2 331 060	961 055	739 455	19 335	475 270	200 515	1 253 075
1987	2 626 029	996 165	1 030 926	13 819	394 296	249 655	1 489 250
1989	2 654 334	993 406	1 084 441	14 638	391 782	288 757	1 664 238
1990	2 998 246	1 265 157	1 210 687	17 490	413 636	292 366	1 786 041
1991	3 180 893	1 421 143	1 285 043	25 965	446 880	294 349	1 837 265
1992	2 675 641	1 235 755	981 490	8 160	321 145	341 415	2 030 327
1993	3 164 812	1 463 759	1 248 780	15 344	419 109	383 368	2 705 349
1994	3 106 562	1 392 977	1 252 952	8 326	494 827	423 024	3 002 318
1995	3 291 587	1 480 385	1 365 167	8 177	510 662	478 685	3 221 507
1996	3 390 033	1 513 479	1 466 668	4 001	486 574	505 711	3 405 056
1997	2 523 064	1 584 478	743 199	2 000	308 233	438 398	3 333 181
1998	3 469 821	1 627 261	1 484 182	4 159	546 786	529 592	4 036 992
1999	3 331 124	1 501 182	1 499 775	3 668	572 941	606 800	5 459 140
2000	2 780 481	1 353 445	1 169 649	2 077	534 174	651 591	6 649 322
2001	2 539 257	1 143 679	1 178 851	3 409	579 441	675 244	6 250 361
2002	2 383 802	1 085 936	1 094 731	3 755	557 714	579 703	6 847 570
2003	2 221 697	931 787	1 117 704	5 324	568 798	677 361	7 305 618
2004	2 650 952	1 301 791	1 202 063	7 216	580 290	748 516	6 720 886
2005	3 150 203	1 535 471	1 478 616	4 042	503 941	737 300	5 792 110
2006	3 039 266	1 548 928	1 372 166	3 954	471 853	827 755	6 051 239
2007	3 007 443	1 395 643	1 497 343	4 330	495 972	793 859	6 157 471
2008	3 336 643	1 620 734	1 620 910	4 173	471 447	806 815	6 118 876
2009	3 539 075	1 727 966	1 723 279	4 529	468 022	820 887	5 679 434
2010	3 514 081	1 646 745	1 795 187	3 952	441 443	803 092	5 807 761
2011	3 630 046	1 653 376	1 906 374	3 917	443 713	805 192	5 838 183

11－14 分市、区大牲畜头数(2011 年)
NUMBER OF LARGE LIVESTOCK BY REGION(2011)

单位:万头(10 000 head)

市、区名称	Region	年末大牲畜头数 Number of Large Livestock (year-end)	牛 Cattle and Buffaloes	#奶　牛 Cows	马 Horses	驴 Donkeys	骡 Mules
总　　计	**Total**	**27.64**	**27.59**	**11.86**	**0.02**	**0.03**	**0.01**
市　　区	Urban Area	0.62	0.62	0.61			
#崂山区	Laoshan District	0.02	0.02	0.02			
黄岛区	Huangdao District	0.03	0.03	0.02			
城阳区	Chengyang District	0.57	0.57	0.57			
即墨市	Jimo	2.83	2.83	1.58			
胶州市	Jiaozhou	3.42	3.41	0.55			
胶南市	Jiaonan	2.33	2.31	0.10		0.02	
平度市	Pingdu	6.54	6.53	0.55			
莱西市	Laixi	11.90	11.88	8.46	0.02		

11－15 分市、区猪、羊及家禽存养量(2011 年)
HOGS,SHEEP,GOATS AND POULTRY IN STOCK BY REGION(2011)

单位:万只(10 000 head)

市、区名称	Region	年末生猪存养量 Hogs in Stock (year-end)	年末羊存养量 Sheep and Goats in Stock (year-end)	#山　羊 Goats	绵　羊 Sheep	家　禽 Poultry
总　　计	**Total**	**217.82**	**19.17**	**15.58**	**3.58**	**5 780.02**
市　　区	Urban Area	6.44	0.30	0.30		230.31
#崂山区	Laoshan District	1.17	0.02	0.02		47.00
黄岛区	Huangdao District	1.08	0.12	0.12		9.79
城阳区	Chengyang District	4.20	0.16	0.16		173.52
即墨市	Jimo	27.99	1.16	0.84	0.32	1 008.31
胶州市	Jiaozhou	34.95	3.64	3.19	0.45	485.49
胶南市	Jiaonan	38.88	5.57	5.07	0.50	403.13
平度市	Pingdu	66.66	5.30	3.38	1.91	1 582.94
莱西市	Laixi	42.92	3.21	2.80	0.41	2 069.85

11－16 分市、区肉、蛋、奶产量(2011 年)
OUTPUT OF MEAT, EGGS AND MILK BY REGION(2011)

单位:万吨(10000 tons)

市、区名称	Region	肉类产量 Output of Meat	#猪肉 Pork	牛肉 Beef	羊肉 Mutton	禽肉 Poultry Meat	禽蛋 Poultry Eggs	牛羊奶 Milk
总　计	**Total**	**59.55**	**26.65**	**0.98**	**0.20**	**31.47**	**19.14**	**37.17**
市　区	Urban Area	1.34	0.79			0.54	1.76	1.79
#崂山区	Laoshan District	0.27	0.14			0.12	0.34	0.07
黄岛区	Huangdao District	0.16	0.12			0.03	0.06	0.07
城阳区	Chengyang District	0.92	0.53			0.39	1.36	1.65
即墨市	Jimo	7.68	3.58	0.11	0.01	3.96	4.91	4.67
胶州市	Jiaozhou	5.79	4.19	0.16	0.04	1.39	3.27	2.34
胶南市	Jiaonan	6.80	4.77	0.13	0.06	1.63	2.07	1.51
平度市	Pingdu	18.22	7.72	0.27	0.05	10.17	3.57	2.38
莱西市	Laixi	19.72	5.60	0.30	0.03	13.79	3.56	24.48

11－17 分市、区渔业养殖面积
AQUACULTURE AREA BY REGION

单位:公顷(hectare)

市、区名称	Region	2011 养殖面积 Aquaculture Area	2011 海水 Seawater	2011 淡水 Fresh Water	2010 养殖面积 Aquaculture Area	2010 海水 Seawater	2010 淡水 Fresh Water
总　计	**Total**	**54 857**	**38 743**	**16 114**	**56 283**	**40 101**	**16 182**
市　区	Urban Area	16 896	15 053	1 843	16 505	14 524	1 981
#崂山区	Laoshan District	1 568	1 568		1 544	1 544	
黄岛区	Huangdao District	3 482	3 400	82	3 187	2 972	215
城阳区	Chengyang District	11 846	10 085	1 761	11 774	10 008	1 766
即墨市	Jimo	13 253	12 079	1 174	13 907	12 733	1 174
胶州市	Jiaozhou	5 439	3 137	2 302	5 432	3 137	2 295
胶南市	Jiaonan	10 741	8 474	2 267	11 936	9 707	2 229
平度市	Pingdu	3 800		3 800	3 800		3 800
莱西市	Laixi	4 728		4 728	4 703		4 703

11-18 分市、区水产品总产量(2011 年)
OUTPUT OF AQUATIC PRODUCTS BY REGION(2011)

单位:吨(ton)

市、区名称	Region	水产品总产量 Output of Aquatic Products	#养殖产量 Aquaculture Outpu	鱼 类 Fish	甲壳类 Crust	贝 类 Shellfish	藻 类 Algae
总 计	**Total**	**1 134 080**	**867 080**	**225 406**	**81 424**	**756 069**	**15 358**
市 区	Urban Area	380 597	276 808	59 391	23 446	254 936	12 268
#崂山区	Laoshan District	70 009	27 055	14 867	11 794	24 853	3 768
黄岛区	Huangdao District	28 697	23 486	5 464	394	21 892	
城阳区	Chengyang District	281 891	226 267	39 060	11 258	208 191	8 500
即墨市	Jimo	296 893	231 845	20 739	30 939	236 699	
胶州市	Jiaozhou	128 498	96 490	37 186	8 466	81 361	
胶南市	Jiaonan	305 800	239 645	85 858	18 532	183 073	3 090
平度市	Pingdu	11 002	11 002	10 970	28		
莱西市	Laixi	11 290	11 290	11 262	13		

11-19 分市、区植树及造林面积(2011 年)
AREA OF FORESTATION AND AFFORESTATION BY REGION(2011)

市、区名称	Region	当年造林面积(公顷) Area of Afforestation in the Year(hectare)	育苗面积(公顷) Nursery Garden Area(hectare)	幼林抚育面积(公顷) Laid out Area of Young Trees(hectare)	成林抚育面积(公顷) Laid out Area of Grown-up Trees (hectare)	零星(四旁)植树(万株) Surrounding Tree Planting(10 000 trees)
总 计	**Total**	**9 247**	**932**	**11 744**	**24 959**	**813.7**
市 区	Urban Area	333	141	460	2 373	52.2
#崂山区	Laoshan District	53	8		1 333	0.2
黄岛区	Huangdao District	152	53	460	533	30.0
城阳区	Chengyang District	128	80		507	22.0
即墨市	Jimo	1 405	67	1 405	2 000	80.0
胶州市	Jiaozhou	1 520	10		467	80.0
胶南市	Jiaonan	1 540	142		3 352	318.5
平度市	Pingdu	2 780	371	6 678	6 926	125.0
莱西市	Laixi	1 669	201	3 201	9 841	158.0

11－20 分市、区果园面积、水果总产量(2011 年)

AREA OF ORCHARDS AND OUTPUT OF FRUITS BY REGION(2011)

单位:吨(ton)

市、区名称	Region	果园总面积(公顷) Area of Orchards (hectare)	水果总产量(吨) Output of Fruits(ton)	#苹果 Apple	梨 Pear	桃 Peach	葡萄 Grape	杏 Apricot	山楂 Hawthorn
总 计	**Total**	**30 315**	**805 192**	**541 804**	**71 606**	**80 308**	**72 160**	**5 053**	**4 764**
市 区	Urban Area	2 104	23 633	2 394	342	11 632	2 192	2 117	69
#崂山区	Laoshan District	545	7 129	1 227	175	3 378	6	904	12
黄岛区	Huangdao District	300	3 035	607	19	1 770	12	92	17
城阳区	Chengyang District	1 231	13 059	560	148	6 074	2 174	1 121	40
即墨市	Jimo	1 036	24 074	8 218	1 949	4 981	688	112	190
胶州市	Jiaozhou	3 731	58 162	22 870	6 548	19 950	5 368	1 953	90
胶南市	Jiaonan	5 648	142 033	119 206	8 411	10 561	449	218	371
平度市	Pingdu	9 893	339 342	239 491	13 158	26 431	47 535	622	1 380
莱西市	Laixi	7 902	217 948	149 625	41 199	6 754	15 928	31	2 664

11－21 分市、区茶园、桑园面积和茶叶、蚕茧产量(2011 年)

AREA OF TEA AND MULBERRY PLANTATIONS AND OUTPUT OF TEA AND SILKWORM COCOONS BY REGION(2011)

市、区名称	Region	茶园面积(公顷) Area of Tea Plantations(hectare)	茶叶产量(吨) Output of Tea(ton)	桑园面积(公顷) Area of Mulberry Plantations(hectare)	蚕茧产量(吨) Output of Silkworm Cocoons(ton)
总 计	**Total**	**4 324**	**1 971**		**1 338**
市 区	Urban Area	1 353	1 024		
#崂山区	Laoshan District	1 157	987		
黄岛区	Huangdao District	76	19		
城阳区	Chengyang District	120	18		
即墨市	Jimo	292	461		
胶州市	Jiaozhou				
胶南市	Jiaonan	2 657	479		424.00
平度市	Pingdu	23	6		639.87
莱西市	Laixi				273.96

11－22 主要年份主要农业机械拥有量
MAJOR YEAR'S OWNERSHIP OF AGRICULTURAL MACHINERY

年份 Year	农业机械总动力(万千瓦) Total Agricultural Machinery Power (10 000 kW)	农用拖拉机 Agricultural Tractors		大、中型机引农具(万台) Large and Medium Towing Farm Machinery(10 000 sets)	农用汽车(辆) Agricultural Automobiles (vehicle)	排灌机械 Drainage and Irrigation Machinery	
		混合台 set	千瓦 kW			台 set	万千瓦 10 000 kW
1949							
1952					1		
1957	0.22	59	2.2	0.01	2		
1962	2.47	254	11.47	0.06	13		
1965	3.49	296	13.2	0.08	15		
1970	10.40	602	7 963	0.07	12		
1975	43.94	6 447	103 476	0.48	90		
1978	75.45	15 576	309 287	1.02	261		
1980	110.44	24 278	502 731	1.72	728		
1985	174.76	33 097	506 217	1.71	2 645	67 794	54.92
1987	228.00	50 904	649 340	1.91	3 961	86 314	62.90
1989	241.00	53 556	661 400	1.96	3 982	93 437	70.46
1990	253.52	55 363	680 903	2.03	3 880	105 574	74.63
1991	250.58	57 404	691 332	2.20	3 706	134 900	73.77
1992	253.94	57 182	684 182	2.28	3 948	124 800	82.68
1993	261.24	56 335	678 161	2.34	4 378	144 460	78.96
1994	278.41	58 698	688 886	2.39	5 474	147 259	80.81
1995	289.23	56 391	657 025	2.28	6 314	138 625	73.98
1996	303.57	59 698	680 447	2.32	7 263	148 313	81.53
1997	326.72	66 841	744 424	2.42	8 085	155 629	88.09
1998	364.21	87 226	894 985	2.48	8 409	156 565	86.68
1999	411.44	105 743	1 075 907	3.06	9 363	170 875	96.20
2000	459.21	126 981	1 253 210	3.30	9 613	182 646	108.26
2001	496.27	141 409	1 394 114	4.33	10 212	178 437	104.18
2002	534.92	152 920	1 537 544	4.79	10 411	182 799	107.35
2003	560.94	160 676	1 666 185	5.07	11 201	192 930	109.44
2004	598.87	168 061	1 818 276	5.31	11 085	192 144	110.38
2005	619.69	163 032	1 757 177	5.66	11 552	188 689	112.16
2006	650.65	171 155	1 890 402	6.20	11 098	192 010	116.08
2007	680.16	173 326	1 958 047	6.57	11 408	195 050	118.22
2008	697.38	176 156	2 034 453	7.98	11 408	208 711	134.10
2009	719.33	180 171	2 266 697	8.60	11 408	207 648	133.99
2010	763.61	200 208	2 331 867	9.80		190 770	123.33
2011	784.06	202 022	2 649 283	9.77		189 834	127.16

11－23 主要年份农业机械化、用电量、化肥施用量

MAJOR YEAR'S MECHANIZATION, ELECTRICITY AND CHEMICAL FERTILIZER CONSUMPTION

年　份 Year	有效灌溉面积(公顷) Irrigated Area (hectare)	配套机电井(眼) Number of Electromechanical Well(well)	机耕面积(公顷) Area of Motorized Cultivation (hectare)	机播面积(公顷) Area of Motorized Planting (hectare)	机收面积(公顷) Area of Motorized Harvesting (hectare)	农村用电量(万千瓦时) Electricity Consumption in Rural Area (10 000 kW·h)	化肥施用量(折纯万吨) Chemical Fertilizer Consumption (convert to 10 000 tons)
1949	8 340						
1952	14 980						
1957	59 353		12 800	13			0.19
1962	55 213	191	65 680	927	927	55	0.10
1965	80 000	125	11 433	573	247	128	0.55
1970	147 613	3 947	143 700	2 527	133	1 208	1.76
1975	233 980	12 820	248 867	54 507	953	2 522	2.77
1978	276 660	21 017	329 213	178 533	15 060	13 975	3.64
1980	296 606	22 472	444 800	187 980	55 333	20 492	12.06
1985	302 647	42 925	366 786	148 433	56 447	41 524	11.66
1987	260 800	48 497	410 820	187 680	104 240	58 280	13.87
1989	267 440	61 570	540 413	208 527	107 320	62 859	17.91
1990	274 680	56 821	426 680	220 593	143 133	67 616	20.47
1991	281 500	58 987	431 293	254 266	192 946	81 200	22.53
1992	281 610	62 100	438 533	270 453	207 780	88 024	22.60
1993	284 080	63 954	439 300	260 287	225 807	102 501	28.04
1994	286 750	64 877	436 820	262 846	238 693	121 307	28.73
1995	287 020	64 651	435 213	271 707	250 267	134 284	31.45
1996	289 320	65 237	438 947	280 480	235 933	143 740	31.36
1997	292 130	66 783	442 213	308 267	266 147	150 971	28.99
1998	294 120	64 109	442 920	359 447	285 513	153 113	31.95
1999	294 790	64 734	440 967	396 180	286 367	169 337	32.58
2000	295 190	65 179	439 980	346 480	292 787	189 651	32.53
2001	296 980	65 547	436 576	382 870	265 730	228 069	31.73
2002	294 310	65 588	433 660	364 680	267 690	256 453	31.07
2003	292 410	65 406	415 790	404 980	256 600	299 425	31.89
2004	292 520	65 501	415 220	454 800	314 680	330 609	32.45
2005	296 450	65 303	409 610	493 240	367 740	372 644	33.01
2006	303 070	65 981	403 980	493 750	398 700	413 762	32.64
2007	305 760	66 400	400 480	499 590	429 630	425 715	33.89
2008	313 920	66 828	404 080	517 540	455 120	424 292	31.05
2009	322 710	67 027	404 080	538 220	481 176	426 306	30.17
2010	328 960	67 242		558 611	499 248	426 819	29.89
2011	331 690	62 104		567 947	547 108	431 646	29.37

11 -24 分市、区农业机械化和电气化(2011 年)
MECHANIZATION AND ELECTRIFICATION IN AGRICULTURE BY REGION(2011)

市、区名称	Region	机耕作业面积 Area of Motorized Cultivation		机播地面积 Area of Motorized Planting	
		面积(公顷) Area(hectare)	占播种面积比重(%) Percentage to Area of Cultivated Land(%)	面积(公顷) Area(hectare)	占播种面积比重(%) Percentage to Sown Area(%)
总　计	**Total**	**600 451**	**79.32**	**567 947**	**75.03**
市　区	Urban Area	9 068	74.82	6 860	56.60
#崂山区	Laoshan District				
黄岛区	Huangdao District	2 168	77.07		
城阳区	Chengyang District	6 900	81.08	6 860	80.61
即墨市	Jimo	114 772	94.21	107 852	88.53
胶州市	Jiaozhou	79 656	75.04	85 556	80.59
胶南市	Jiaonan	77 000	87.74	57 300	65.29
平度市	Pingdu	237 956	81.30	193 723	66.19
莱西市	Laixi	81 999	60.11	116 656	85.51

11 -24 续表
continued

市、区名称	Region	机收面积 Area of Motorized Harvesting		农村用电量(万千瓦小时) Electricity Consumed in Rural Areas(10 000 kW · h)
		面积(公顷) Area(hectare)	占播种面积比重(%) Percentage to Sown Area(%)	
总　计	**Total**	**547 108**	**72.28**	**431 646**
市　区	Urban Area	5 286	43.62	82 663
#崂山区	Laoshan District			15 563
黄岛区	Huangdao District	620	22.05	12 168
城阳区	Chengyang District	4 666	54.83	54 932
即墨市	Jimo	93 101	76.42	72 001
胶州市	Jiaozhou	76 944	72.48	95 240
胶南市	Jiaonan	47 500	54.13	35 884
平度市	Pingdu	222 364	75.98	105 903
莱西市	Laixi	101 913	74.70	39 954

11-25 分市、区农用化肥施用量(2011 年)

CONSUMPTION OF CHEMICAL FERTILIZERS BY REGION(2011)

单位:折纯吨(ton converted to pure amount)

市、区名称	Region	农用化肥施用量 Consumption of Chemical Fertilizers	氮 肥 Nitrogenous Fertilizer	磷 肥 Phosphate Fertilizer	钾 肥 Potash Fertilizer	复合肥 Compound Fertilizer	附:平均每公顷耕地施用化肥量(*) Annotation:Consumption of Chemical Fertilizer Per Hectare
总 计	**Total**	**293 689**	**60 248**	**14 579**	**21 892**	**196 968**	**700**
市 区	Urban Area	3 463	915	206	237	2 107	497
#崂山区	Laoshan District	923	214	68	62	580	1 071
黄岛区	Huangdao District	738	165	7	56	510	351
城阳区	Chengyang District	1 802	536	131	119	1 017	458
即墨市	Jimo	39 095	16 988	2 977	1 451	17 679	536
胶州市	Jiaozhou	36 618	7 260	980	5 250	23 128	685
胶南市	Jiaonan	38 108	11 436	3 508	5 406	17 758	730
平度市	Pingdu	121 803	12 047	2 934	9 264	97 558	747
莱西市	Laixi	54 601	11 602	3 975	285	38 740	768

注:(*)单位为[折纯千克] Note:The(*)mark refers to kilogram converted to pure amount.

11-26 分市、区农田水利(2011 年)

FARMLAND WATER CONSERVANCY BY REGION(2011)

市、区名称	Region	有效灌溉面积(公顷) Irrigated Area (hectare)	#机、电排灌面积 of which:Area with Motorized Irrigation Facilities	有效灌溉面积占耕地面积比重(%) Percentage of Irrigated Area to Area of Cultivated Land(%)	农业排灌机械拥有量(万台/万千瓦) Ownership of Drainage and Irrigation Machinery (10 000 sets/10 000 kW)	农用水泵(万台) Agricultural Pump (10 000 sets)	喷灌机械(套) Spraying Irrigation Machinery (set)	机电井数(眼) Number of Electromechanical Well (well)
总 计	**Total**	**331 690**	**308 510**	**79.01**	**18.98/127.16**	**14.19**	**87 958**	**72 301**
市 区	Urban Area	4 970	4 170	71.34	0.81/6.4	0.43	2 746	2 189
#崂山区	Laoshan District	710	710	82.37				319
黄岛区	Huangdao District	1 260	1 000	59.91	0.17/1.92	0.01	74	248
城阳区	Chengyang District	2 780	2 460	70.70	0.64/4.48	0.42	2 672	1 424
即墨市	Jimo	56 230	51 580	77.05	2.11/14.91	2.13	18 521	5 341
胶州市	Jiaozhou	40 000	34 650	74.81	1.33/10.32	0.81	13 650	7 063
胶南市	Jiaonan	44 650	30 850	85.51	0.58/4.72	1.20	8 600	6 269
平度市	Pingdu	127 580	132 430	78.24	12.45/80.5	7.36	18 076	37 728
莱西市	Laixi	58 260	54 830	81.93	1.71/10.32	2.27	26 365	13 711

11－27 分市、区主要农业机械拥有量(2011 年)
OWNERSHIP OF MAJOR AGRICULTURAL MACHINERY BY REGION(2011)

市、区名称	Region	农业机械总动力(万千瓦) Agricultural Machinery Power (10 000 kW)	平均每公顷耕地拥有量(千瓦) Power Per Hectare of Cultivated Land(kW)	大中型拖拉机 Large and Medium Tractors		小型拖拉机 Small Tractors	
				台 set	千瓦 kW	台 set	千瓦 kW
总　计	**Total**	**784.06**	**18.68**	**36 745**	**1 379 469**	**165 277**	**1 269 814**
市　区	Urban Area	47.21	67.77	551	17 905	1 990	12 148
#崂山区	Laoshan District						
黄岛区	Huangdao District	12.92	61.43	117	3 688	452	1 563
城阳区	Chengyang District	34.29	87.20	434	14 217	1 538	10 585
即墨市	Jimo	120.4	16.50	6 564	188 552	32 082	264 347
胶州市	Jiaozhou	109.70	20.52	4 387	237 594	17 877	139 100
胶南市	Jiaonan	71.74	13.74	3 348	94 895	43 158	301 550
平度市	Pingdu	309.7	18.99	16 970	679 835	34 010	306 090
莱西市	Laixi	125.31	17.62	4 925	160 688	36 160	246 579

11－27 续表 1
continued

市、区名称	Region	大、中、小播种机(部) Large, Medium and Small Seeders(set)	机引犁(部) Towing Ploughs(unit)	机引耙(部) Towing Rakes(unit)	脱粒机(部) Threshers (unit)
总　计	**Total**	**56 212**	**129 124**	**28 476**	**34 246**
市　区	Urban Area	772	1 205	207	
#崂山区	Laoshan District				
黄岛区	Huangdao District		5		
城阳区	Chengyang District	772	1 200	207	
即墨市	Jimo	11 749	19 952	1 665	6 574
胶州市	Jiaozhou	8 520	14 321	4 900	3 390
胶南市	Jiaonan	1 340	38 600	1 200	7 300
平度市	Pingdu	26 300	21 843	16 542	12 014
莱西市	Laixi	7 531	33 203	3 962	4 968

11－27 续表 2
continued

市、区名称	Region	粮食加工机械(台) Grain Processing Machinery(unit)	棉花加工机械(部) Cotton Processing Machinery(unit)	油料加工机械(部) Oil Processing Machinery(unit)	饲料粉碎机(部) Pulverizers (unit)
总　计	**Total**	**25 553**	**125**	**9 136**	**1 172**
市　区	Urban Area	1 617	17	690	21
#崂山区	Laoshan District				
黄岛区	Huangdao District	12		170	
城阳区	Chengyang District	1 605	17	520	21
即墨市	Jimo	3 259		1 472	80
胶州市	Jiaozhou	2 950		2 025	430
胶南市	Jiaonan	1 100		243	48
平度市	Pingdu	4 367	6	1 406	314
莱西市	Laixi	12 260	102	3 300	279

主要统计指标解释

农业总产值　是以货币表现的农、林、牧、渔业全部产品的总量，它反映一定时期内农业生产的总规模和总成果。

农、林、牧、渔业的统计范围是：

(1)农业包括农作物种植业和其他农业。

农作物种植业包括谷物、豆类、薯类、棉、油料、糖料、麻类、烟叶、蔬菜、药材、瓜类和其他农作物的种植，以及茶园、桑园、果园的生产经营。其他农业包括采集野生植物的果实、纤维、树胶、树脂、油料以及柴草、野生药材、菌类等及农民家庭兼营的商品性工业。

(2)林业包括林木的栽培(不包括茶园、桑园和果园的栽培、管理和收获等活动)、林产品的采集和村及村以下合作经济组织和农户的竹木采伐。

(3)牧业包括除渔业养殖以外的一切动物饲养和放牧，以及野生动物的捕猎和饲养。

(4)渔业包括水生动物和海藻类植物的养殖和捕捞。

粮食产量　指稻谷、小麦、玉米、高粱等谷物及薯类和豆类的全社会产量。包括国有经济经营的、集体统一经营的和农民家庭经营的粮食产量，还包括工矿企业办的农场和其他生产单位的产量。其产量计算方法，豆类按去豆荚后的干豆计算；薯类(包括甘薯和马铃薯，不包括芋头和木薯)按5公斤鲜薯折1公斤粮食计算。城市郊区作为蔬菜的薯类(如马铃薯等)按鲜品计算，并且不作粮食统计。其他粮食一律按脱粒后的原粮计算。

水产品产量　指人工养殖的水产品和天然生长的水产品的捕捞量. 包括海水的鱼类、虾蟹类、贝类和藻类以及内陆水域的鱼类、虾蟹类和贝类，不包括淡水生植物。

猪、牛、羊肉产量　指当年出栏并已屠宰、除去头蹄下水后带骨头肉(即胴体重)的重量。其统计范围为全社会。

农用化肥施用量　指本年内实际用于农业生产的化肥数量，包括氮肥、磷肥、钾肥和复合肥。化肥施用量要求按折纯量计算数量。折纯量是指把氮肥、磷肥、钾肥分别按含氮、含五氧化二磷、含氧化钾的百分之百成分进行折算后的数量。复合肥按其所含主要成分折算。

公式：折纯量 = 实物量 × 某种化肥有效成分含量的百分比

农业机械总动力　指用于农、林、牧、渔业生产的各种动力机械的动力总和。动力机械包括耕作、排灌、种植、植物保护、收获、农产品加工、运输、畜牧、渔业、农田水利等各种机械。不包括专门用于乡办工业、基本建设、非农业运输、科学试验和教学等非农业生产方面用的动力机械与作业机械的数量。

Explanatory Notes on Main Statistical Indicators

Gross Output Value of Agriculture　refers to the total volume of products of farming, forestry, animal husbandry, and fishery expressed in the monetary terms. It reflects the overall scale and achievements of agricultural production during a given period of time.

The scope of statistics on farming, forestry, animal husbandry, and fishery are as follows:

Farming includes cultivation of farm crops and other agricultural activities.

Cultivation of farm crops include cultivation of grain crops, legume crops, tuber-crops, cotton, oil-bearing crops, sugar crops, and cultivation and management of tea plantations, mulberry fields and orchards.

Other agricultural activities include harvesting wild fruits, fiber, tree gum, resin, oil-bearing plants, firewood, wild medicinal herbs, fungus, and rural-household commodity industries.

Forestry refers to planting trees of various kinds (excluding tea plantations, mulberry fields and orchards), collection of forestry products and cutting and felling of bamboo and trees by villages and other cooperative organizations under village level.

Animal husbandry refers to raising and grazing of all kinds of farm animals except fishing and aquatic cultivating, and hunting and rising of wild animals.

Fishery refers to cultivation and catching of fish and other aquatic products and cultivation and collection of seaweed and other aquatic plants.

Grain Output refers to the total output of rice, wheat, corn, sorghum, millet and other miscellaneous grains as well as tubers and bean in the whole country including grains produced by states farms, collective unit, industrial enterprises and mines, output of beans refers to dry beans without pods, the output of tubers (sweet potatoes and potatoes, excluding taros and cassava) was converted into that of grain at the ratio 5: 1, i. e. 5 kilograms of fresh tubers was equivalent to 1 kilogram of grain, tubers supplies as vegetable (such as potatoes) in cities and suburbs are calculated as fresh vegetables and their output is not included in the output of grain output of all other grains refers to husked grain.

Output of Aquatic Products refers to catches of both artificially cultured and naturally grown aquatic products, including fish, shrimps, crabs and shellfish in sea and inland water as well as seaweed. Freshwater plants are not included.

Output of Pork, Beef, and Mutton refers to the meat of slaughtered hogs, cattle, sheep and goats with head, feet, and offal taken away. Data refers to the production of the whole country.

Consumption of Chemical Fertilizers in Agriculture refers to the quantity of chemical fertilizers applied in agriculture in the year, including nitrogenous fertilizer, phosphate fertilizer, potash fertilizer, and compound fertilizer. The consumption of chemical fertilizers is required in calculation to convert the gross weight into weight containing 100% effective component (e. g. 100% nitrogen content in nitrogenous fertilizer, 100% phosphorous pent oxide contents in phosphate fertilizer, 100% potassium oxide contents in potash fertilizer). Compound fertilizer is converted with its major component. The formula is:

Volume of effective component = physical quantity x effective component of certain chemical fertilizer (%)

Total Power of Agriculture Machinery Refers to the total mechanical power of machinery used in farming forestry animal husbandry and fishery, including machines used for ploughing, irrigation and drainage, crop growing, plant protection, harvesting, farm product processing, transport, stock breeding, fishery and water conservancy, Machinery employed for non agricultural purposes such as township industry, capital construction, non-agricultural transport, scientific experiments and for teaching is excluded.

工 业 12

INDUSTRY

简要说明

一、本篇资料的主要内容

本篇资料主要反映了全市工业生产和基本效益情况，主要包括工业企业单位数、历年工业总产值、规模以上工业、国有控股工业、国有工业、集体工业、外商投资和港澳台投资工业、大中型工业企业的主要经济指标、相关的财务分析指标和主要工业产品产量等方面的内容。

二、本篇资料的来源

1、本篇中规模以上工业资料来源于工业统计年报，由市统计局工业（能源）统计处整理提供。

2、规模以下工业资料产值来源于抽样调查推算，工业单位数来源于第二次经济普查，由国家统计局青岛调查队工业与投资建筑业调查处整理提供。

Brief Introduction

I. Main Content

Data in this chapter show the basic condition of industrial production and benefit in Qingdao, mainly including the number of industrial enterprises, gross industrial output value and indices, the output of major industrial products and major economic and relevant financial indicators of industrial enterprises. Industrial enterprises include enterprises above designated size, state share-holding enterprises, state owned enterprises, collective owned enterprises, foreign funded enterprises, enterprises with funds from Hong Kong, Macao and Taiwan, large and medium sized enterprises.

II. Source of Data

（1）Data on industry above designated size are based on the annual report of industrial statistics, and prepared by the Division of Industry(Energy) Statistics of Qingdao Municipal Bureau of Statistics.

（2）Data on output value of industry below designated size are based on the sample survey, and data on number of enterprises are based on the Second China Economic Census. The Data are complied by the Division of Industry, Investment and Construction Survey of Survey Office of the National Bureau of Statistics in Qingdao.

12－1 规模以上工业企业单位数
NUMBER OF INDUSTRIAL ENTERPRISES ABOVE DESIGNATEO SIZE

单位:个(unit)

项　目	Item	1985	1990	1995	2000	2005
总　计	**Total**	**2 411**	**2 997**	**4 987**	**1 504**	**3 697**
一、按隶属关系分	**Grouped by Subordination**					
中央工业	Central Industry	24	16	102	18	26
省属工业	Provincial Industry	26	22	64	7	37
地方工业	Local Industry	2 361	2 959	4 821	1 479	3 634
二、按经济类型分	Grouped by Economic Types					
国有企业	State-owned	502	568	1 084	179	76
集体企业	Collective-owned	1 907	2 386	2 731	226	87
其他经济类型企业	Other Economic Types	2	43	1 172	1 099	3 534
#外商及港澳台商投资企业	Foreign Funded Enterprises and Enterprises with Funds from Hong Kong, Macao and Taiwan		35	1 027	593	1 658
三、按轻重工业分	Grouped by Light and Heavy Industries					
轻工业	Light Industry	1 398	1 730	2 858	891	1 942
重工业	Heavy Industry	1 013	1 267	2 129	613	1 755
四、按企业规模分	Grouped by Size of Enterprises					
大型企业	Large	26	42	89	202	51
中型企业	Medium	80	168	216	229	441
小型企业	Small	2 305	2 787	4 480	1 073	3 205
五、按行业分	Grouped by Sectors					
黑色金属矿采选业	Mining of Ferrous Metal Ores		4	6	1	2
有色金属矿采选业	Mining of Non-ferrous Metal Ores	2	7	9	7	5
非金属矿采选业	Mining and Processing of Nonmetal Ores	43	70	87	29	34
食品制造业	Manufacture of Foods	244	324	437	170	121
#粮食及饲料加工	Processing of Grain and Feed	62	57	60	27	
饮料制造业	Manufacture of Beverage	31	44	74	23	29
#饮料酒	Beverage Liquor	20	28	27	19	20

注：1. 规模以上工业企业为年主营业务收入2000万元及以上的工业法人企业。
2. 2010年以前为国有及年主营业务收入500万元以上的非国有工业企业。
3. 本表1998年以前为乡及乡以上工业企业单位数。

Note: 1. Industrial enterprises above designated size refers to industrial enterprises with revenue from principal business over 20 million yuan.
2. Before 2010, industrial enterprises above designated size refered to all the state-owned enterprises and non-state enterprises with revenue from principal business over 5 million yuan.
3. Before 1998, the number of industial enterprises refer to those at and above county level.

12－1 续表 1

项　　目	Item	2006	2007	2008	2009	2010	2011
总　计	**Total**	**4 567**	**5 032**	**5 628**	**5 895**	**5 674**	**4 727**
一、按隶属关系分	**Grouped by Subordination**						
中央工业	Central Industry	17	9	40	44	31	31
省属工业	Provincial Industry	33	34	28	25	25	17
地方工业	Local Industry	4 517	4 989	5 560	5 826	5 618	4 679
二、按经济类型分	Grouped by Economic Types						
国有企业	State-owned	74	63	65	163	61	147
集体企业	Collective-owned	72	72	61	59	53	31
其他经济类型企业	Other Economic Types	4 421	4 897	5 502	5 673	5 560	4 549
#外商及港澳台商投资企业	Foreign Funded Enterprises and Enterprises with Funds from Hong Kong, Macao and Taiwan	1 952	2 091	2 217	2 244	2 037	1 618
三、按轻重工业分	Grouped by Light and Heavy Industries						
轻工业	Light Industry	2 313	2 489	2 704	2 805	2 635	2 131
重工业	Heavy Industry	2 254	2 543	2 924	3 090	3 039	2 596
四、按企业规模分	Grouped by Size of Enterprises						
大型企业	Large	51	53	48	50	52	50
中型企业	Medium	469	489	519	502	525	516
小型企业	Small	4 047	4 490	5 061	5 343	5 097	4 161
五、按行业分	Grouped by Sectors						
黑色金属矿采选业	Mining of Ferrous Metal Ores	5	7	23	22	12	12
有色金属矿采选业	Mining of Non-ferrous Metal Ores	5	5	6	6	4	
非金属矿采选业	Mining and Processing of Nonmetal Ores	31	33	30	26	26	23
食品制造业	Manufacture of Foods	137	156	158	174	167	127
#粮食及饲料加工	Processing of Grain and Feed						
饮料制造业	Manufacture of Beverage	28	33	40	42	42	36
#饮料酒	Beverage Liquor	25					

12－1 续表2
continued

单位:个(unit)

项　目	Item	1985	1990	1995	2000	2005
烟草制品业	Manufacture of Tobacco	2	2	5	3	2
纺织业	Manufacture of Textile	169	225	330	132	300
纺织服装、鞋、帽制造业	Manufacture of Textile Wearing Apparel, Footware and Caps	171	194	322	95	272
皮革、毛皮、羽毛(绒)及其制品业	Manufacture of Leather, Fur, Feather and Related Products	56	64	161	64	167
木材加工制品业	Processing of Wood and Wood Products	71	89	116	19	40
家具制造业	Manufacture of Furniture	61	72	88	10	72
造纸及纸制品业	Manufacture of Paper and Paper Products	66	74	110	56	102
印刷业和记录媒介的复制	Printing, Reproduction of Recording Media	61	81	215	23	44
文教体育用品制造业	Manufacture of Articles For Culture, Education and Sport Activities	31	27	93	48	89
石油加工、炼焦及核燃料加工业	Processing of Petroleum, Coking, Processing of Nuclear Fuel	2	3	13	5	10
化学原料及制品	Manufacture of Raw Chemical Materials and Chemical Products	106	156	278	81	178
医药制造业	Manufacture of Medicines	16	14	39	20	30
化学纤维制造业	Manufacture of Chemical Fibers	2	4	26	15	14
橡胶制品业	Manufacture of Rubber	53	57	143	48	116
塑料制品业	Manufacture of Plastics	103	131	237	64	153
非金属矿物制品业	Manufacture of Non-metallic Mineral Products	230	245	275	62	161
黑色金属压延加工业	Smelting and Pressing of Ferrous Metals	11	13	31	15	41
有色金属压延加工业	Smelting and Pressing of Non-ferrous Metals	6	8	19	9	28
金属制品业	Manufacture of Metal Products	161	186	372	88	186
通用设备制造业	Manufacture of General Purpose Machinery	320	398	320	94	299
交通运输制造业	Manufacture of Transport Equipment	104	114	358	52	151
电气机械及器材制造业	Manufacture of Electrical Machinery and Equipment	86	96	211	79	214
通信设备、计算机及其他电子设备制造业	Manufacture of Communication Equipment, Computers and Other Electronic Equipment	32	31	79	34	123
仪器仪表及文化、办公用机械制造业	Manufacture of Measuring Instruments and Machinery for Cultural Activity and Office Work	28	33	70	20	40
水的生产和供应业	Production and Supply of Water	8	12	12	8	10
电力、热力的生产和供应业	Production and Supply of Electric Power and Heat Power	10	16	20	17	27
燃气生产和供应业	Production and Supply of Gas	1	4	3	2	5
其他工业	Other Industrial Sectors	46	48	209	63	166

12－1 续表3
continued

单位：个(unit)

项 目	Item	2006	2007	2008	2009	2010	2011
烟草制品业	Manufacture of Tobacco	2	2	2	2	1	1
纺织业	Manufacture of Textile	327	340	330	322	287	229
纺织服装、鞋、帽制造业	Manufacture of Textile Wearing Apparel, Footware and Caps	339	362	418	434	392	295
皮革、毛皮、羽毛(绒)及其制品业	Manufacture of Leather, Fur, Feather and Related Products	194	197	209	210	211	160
木材加工制品业	Processing of Wood and Wood Products	53	64	66	68	68	49
家具制造业	Manufacture of Furniture	103	119	130	133	117	97
造纸及纸制品业	Manufacture of Paper and Paper Products	128	126	133	133	138	101
印刷业和记录媒介的复制	Printing, Reproduction of Recording Media	59	63	74	79	92	58
文教体育用品制造业	Manufacture of Articles For Culture, Education and Sport Activities	91	97	96	99	90	75
石油加工、炼焦及核燃料加工业	Processing of Petroleum, Coking, Processing of Nuclear Fuel	6	7	7	9	8	7
化学原料及制品	Manufacture of Raw Chemical Materials and Chemical Products	233	261	276	275	262	231
医药制造业	Manufacture of Medicines	46	48	49	56	52	44
化学纤维制造业	Manufacture of Chemical Fibers	13	12	13	14	12	10
橡胶制品业	Manufacture of Rubber	170	183	211	214	196	187
塑料制品业	Manufacture of Plastics	179	199	227	234	233	169
非金属矿物制品业	Manufacture of Non-metallic Mineral Products	218	259	311	320	327	303
黑色金属压延加工业	Smelting and Pressing of Ferrous Metals	45	39	24	27	31	29
有色金属压延加工业	Smelting and Pressing of Non-ferrous Metals	40	40	41	40	35	34
金属制品业	Manufacture of Metal Products	250	271	347	376	361	294
通用设备制造业	Manufacture of General Purpose Machinery	397	473	535	592	597	521
交通运输制造业	Manufacture of Transport Equipment	194	217	264	290	296	263
电气机械及器材制造业	Manufacture of Electrical Machinery and Equipment	249	274	303	300	281	230
通信设备、计算机及其他电子设备制造业	Manufacture of Communication Equipment, Computers and Other Electronic Equipment	140	152	163	168	167	124
仪器仪表及文化、办公用机械制造业	Manufacture of Measuring Instruments and Machinery for Cultural Activity and Office Work	44	47	47	55	54	39
水的生产和供应业	Production and Supply of Water	10	10	13	14	14	11
电力、热力的生产和供应业	Production and Supply of Electric Power and Heat Power	32	34	36	39	38	36
燃气生产和供应业	Production and Supply of Gas	6	7	13	13	14	11
其他工业	Other Industrial Sectors	534	895	1 033	1 109	1 049	921

12 –2 分市、区全部工业企业单位数(2011 年)

NUMBER OF ALL INDUSTRIAL ENTERPRISES BY REGION(2011)

单位:个(unit)

市、区名称	Region	合计 Total	规模以上 Above Designated Size	按轻重工业分 Grouped by Light and Heavy Industries		按企业规模分 Grouped by Size of Enterprises		
				轻工业 Light Industry	重工业 Heavy Industry	大型企业 Large	中型企业 Medium	小型企业 Small
总　计	**Total**	**81 998**	**4 727**	**2 131**	**2 596**	**50**	**516**	**4 161**
市　区	Urban Area	18 665	1 094	425	669	33	225	836
#崂山区	Laoshan District	2 545	114	47	67	3	23	88
黄岛区	Huangdao District	3 254	269	56	213	8	64	197
城阳区	Chengyang District	8 258	502	248	254	11	85	406
即墨市	Jimo	13 683	652	365	287	5	77	570
胶州市	Jiaozhou	11 143	820	397	423	4	102	714
胶南市	Jiaonan	13 736	755	240	515	5	41	709
平度市	Pingdu	13 546	690	301	389	0	38	652
莱西市	Laixi	11 206	697	402	295	3	29	665
高新区	High-tech Zone	19	19	1	18		4	15

12 –2 续表

continued

单位:个(unit)

市、区名称	Region	按经济类型分 Grouped by Economic Types				规模以下 Below Designated Size	#个体 Individual
		国有企业 State-owned	集体企业 Collective-owned	其他经济 Others	#外资及港澳台商企业 Foreign Funded Enterprises and Enterprises with Funds from Hong Kong, Macao and Taiwan		
总　计	**Total**	**147**	**31**	**2 931**	**1 618**	**77 271**	**52 651**
市　区	Urban Area	98	8	399	589	17 571	7 920
#崂山区	Laoshan District	11	2	55	46	2 431	1 327
黄岛区	Huangdao District	28	2	86	153	2 985	1 604
城阳区	Chengyang District	10	1	175	316	7 756	3 433
即墨市	Jimo	9	3	411	229	13 031	8 573
胶州市	Jiaozhou	8	1	574	237	10 323	7 244
胶南市	Jiaonan	8	2	590	155	12 981	9 939
平度市	Pingdu	15	8	464	203	12 856	10 378
莱西市	Laixi	6	9	487	195	10 509	8 597
高新区	High-tech Zone	3		6	10		

注:规模以下工业单位数是 2008 年第二次经济普查数据。

Note:Data of the number of industrial enterprises below designated size are from the result of the Second Economic Census in 2008.

12 -3 历年全部工业总产值

GROSS INDUSTRIAL OUTPUT VALUE OVER THE YEARS

单位:万元(10 000 yuan)

年 份 Year	工业总产值 Gross Industrial Output Value	轻工业产值 Light Industry	重工业产值 Heavy Industry
1949	21 605	18 494	3 111
1950	34 010	28 720	5 290
1951	53 538	44 600	8 938
1952	84 295	69 258	15037
1953	115 222	74 716	40 506
1954	126 064	80 604	45 460
1955	118 935	86 956	31 979
1956	144 833	93 809	51 024
1957	142 920	101 202	41 718
1958	217 648	92 407	125 241
1959	282 610	84 376	198 234
1960	291 451	77 043	214 408
1962	120 738	64 233	56 505
1963	139 542	83 630	55 912
1964	177 273	108 884	68 389
1965	215 536	141 765	73 771
1966	252 896	152 304	100 592
1967	287 739	163 627	124 112
1968	299 814	175 791	123 489
1969	296 814	188 860	107 954
1970	345 212	202 903	142 309

注:本表按当年价格计算,1995 年开始工业总产值按新规定计算。

Note:The data in this form are calculated at current price. Since 1995, new regulations have been adopted in calculating gross industrial output value.

12 -3 续表 1
continued

单位:万元(10 000 yuan)

年　份 Year	工业总产值 Gross Industrial Output Value	轻工业产值 Light Industry	重工业产值 Heavy Industry
1971	365 770	216 172	149 598
1972	378 266	230 309	147 957
1973	377 943	245 371	132 572
1974	237 219	154 054	83 165
1975	402 541	261 418	141 123
1976	439 793	278 514	161 279
1977	490 669	296 728	193 941
1978	565 503	336 817	228 686
1979	625 227	379 276	245 951
1980	677 690	442 078	235 612
1981	707 434	479 954	227 480
1982	732 705	474 767	257 938
1983	816 793	513 759	303 034
1984	918 364	569 080	349 284
1985	1 113 891	699 524	414 367
1986	1 316 230	833 864	482 366
1987	1 703 830	1 065 873	637 957
1988	2 481 594	1 451 215	1 030 379
1989	3 191 643	1 857 019	1 334 624
1990	3 571 845	2 057 968	1 513 878

12 -3 续表 2
continued

单位:万元(10 000 yuan)

年 份	Year	工业总产值 Gross Industrial Output Value	轻工业产值 Light Industry	重工业产值 Heavy Industry
1991	1991	3 986 427	2 318 257	1 668 170
1992	1992	4 826 834	2 835 728	1 991 106
1993	1993	5 929 236	3 422 107	2 507 129
1994	1994	8 456 974	4 931 262	3 525 712
1995	1995	9 412 635	5 579 637	3 832 998
1996	1996	11 173 672	6 793 007	4 380 665
1997	1997	13 704 735	8 620 710	5 084 025
1998	1998	15 794 106	10 153 634	5 640 472
1999	1999	16 822 436	10 918 827	5 903 609
2000	2000	19 408 338	12 433 214	6 975 124
2001	2001	22 398 464	14 368 582	8 029 882
2002	2002	25 794 324	14 811 106	10 983 218
2003	2003	31 195 595	17 306 539	13 889 056
2004	2004	39 590 783	21 473 202	18 117 581
2005	2005	50 017 829	24 697 792	25 320 037
2006	2006	59 188 120	28 686 826	30 501 294
2007	2007	74 306 364	33 463 071	40 843 293
2008	2008	89 467 300	37 871 227	51 596 073
2009	2009	102 556 155	42 715 781	59 840 374
2010	2010	116 148 345	44 954 630	71 193 715
2011	2011	132 779 629	50 854 938	81 924 691
"一五"时期合计	"First Five-Year Plan" Period	647 974	437 287	210 687
"二五"时期合计	"Second Five-Year Plan" Period	1 077 075	388 406	688 669
1963-1965 年合计	1963-1965	532 351	334 279	198 072
"三五"时期合计	"Third Five-Year Plan" Period	1 481 941	883 485	598 456
"四五"时期合计	"Fourth Five-Year Plan" Period	1 761 739	1 107 324	654 415
"五五"时期合计	"Fifth Five-Year Plan" Period	2 798 882	1 733 413	1 065 469
"六五"时期合计	"Sixth Five-Year Plan" Period	4 289 187	2 737 084	1 552 103
"七五"时期合计	"Seventh Five-Year Plan" Period	12 265 142	7 265 939	4 999 204
"八五"时期合计	"Eighth Five-Year Plan" Period	32 612 106	19 087 323	13 524 783
"九五"时期合计	"Ninth Five-Year Plan" Period	76 903 287	48 919 392	27 983 895
"十五"时期合计	"Tenth Five-Year Plan" Period	168 996 995	92 657 221	76 339 774
"十一五"时期合计	"Eleventh Five-Year Plan" Period	175 336 465	73 641 456	101 695 009

12－4 分市、区全部工业总产值(2011 年)
GROSS INDUSTRIAL OUTPUT VALUE BY REGION(2011)

单位:万元(10 000 yuan)

市、区名称	Region	工业总产值 Gross Industrial Output Value	规模以上 Above Designated Size	#外商及港澳台商投资企业 Foreign Funded Enterprises and Enterprises with Funds from Hong Kong, Macao and Taiwan	规模以下 Below Designated Size
总　计	**Total**	**132 779 629**	**121 659 629**	**35 248 935**	**11 120 000**
市　区	Urban Area	63 678 000	60 190 200	18 064 520	3 487 800
#崂山区	Laoshan District	5 273 618	4 811 418	804 783	462 200
黄岛区	Huangdao District	28 435 612	27 804 312	8 513 871	631 300
城阳区	Chengyang District	17 350 812	15 600 212	6 601 814	1 750 600
即墨市	Jimo	17 412 575	15 498 175	5 766 983	1 914 400
胶州市	Jiaozhou	15 747 027	14 272 927	3 771 841	1 474 100
胶南市	Jiaonan	14 890 194	13 410 194	2 438 643	1 480 000
平度市	Pingdu	11 865 562	10 368 862	2 882 621	1 496 700
莱西市	Laixi	8 685 436	7 418 436	2 132 808	1 267 000
高新区	High-tech Zone	500 837	500 837	191 518	

注:高新区为北部园区口径.

Note: In this from, high-tech zone reffers to the northern pork.

12－5 分市、区规模以上工业总产值(2011 年)

GROSS INDUSTRIAL OUTPUT VALUE ABOVE DESIGNATED SIZE BY REGION(2011)

指 标	Indicator	总计 Total	市内四区 Four Districts in Urban Area	崂山区 Laoshan District	黄岛区 Huangdao District	城阳区 Chengyang District
总 计	**Total**	**121 659 629**	**11 974 258**	**4 811 418**	**27 804 312**	**15 600 212**
按隶属关系分	**Grouped by Subordination**					
中央	Centrality	14 570 345	4 275 635	340 068	6 368 969	3 206 112
省(自治区、直辖市)	Province(Autonomous Region, Municipality)	701 953	78 990	8 927	7 047	386 511
市(地级)	Municipality(local level)	18 462 218	5 169 556	2 721 549	6 736 431	1 253 528
县级市(区)	Municipality at County Level(District)	4 362 375	576 611	267 760	63 472	775 550
镇、街道	Town and Subdistrict Office	6 340 808	12 458	104 165	10 450	1 673 540
乡	Country	65 639				
其它	Others	77 156 292	1 861 009	1 368 950	14 617 943	8 304 971
按登记注册类型分	**Grouped by Status of Registration**					
国有经济	State-owned	28 414 277	8 799 716	457 821	13 505 524	3 187 493
集体经济	Collective-owned	7 009 938	55 586	2 354 831	2 966 162	349 595
其他经济	Others	86 235 414	3 118 955	1 998 766	11 332 626	12 063 124
#外资与港澳台企业	Foreign Funded Enterprises and Enterprises with Funds from Hong Kong, Macao and Taiwan	35 248 935	2 144 052	804 783	8 513 871	6 601 814
按轻重工业分	**Grouped by Light and Heavy Industries**					
轻工业	Light Industry	46 595 950	2 053 407	3 122 455	7 979 569	4 803 876
重工业	Heavy Industry	75 063 679	9 920 851	1 688 963	19 824 743	10 796 336
按企业规模分	**Grouped by Size of Enterprises**					
大型企业	Large	32 364 772	6 025 112	2 996 738	10 707 997	5 887 701
中型企业	Medium	35 835 823	4 690 412	1 129 143	13 119 577	4 848 820
小型企业	Small	53 459 035	1 258 734	685 538	3 976 738	4 863 690

单位:万元(10 000 yuan)

即墨市 Jimo	胶州市 Jiaozhou	胶南市 Jiaonan	平度市 Pingdu	莱西市 Laixi	高新区 High-tech Zone
15 498 175	**14 272 927**	**13 410 194**	**10 368 862**	**7 418 436**	**500 837**
	159 248	18 686	153 287	5 510	42 831
		16 157	55 522		148 800
434 604	439 874	1 129 602	481 854	74 605	20 616
1 008 323	235 250	754 698	422 451	258 260	
421 022	2 372 842	1 230 391	457 271	58 669	
	10 125			55 514	
13 634 226	11 055 589	10 260 660	8 798 476	6 965 878	288 590
423 637	248 508	828 330	601 043	152 174	210 031
66 009	378 085	398 251	360 971	80 447	
15 008 529	13 646 334	12 183 612	9 406 847	7 185 815	290 806
5 766 983	3 771 841	2 438 643	2 882 621	2 132 808	191 518
9 152 296	6 341 478	4 139 546	4 310 402	4 688 329	4 592
6 345 879	7 931 449	9 270 648	6 058 460	2 730 107	496 245
1 935 094	798 847	2 187 838	416 710	1 408 735	
3 602 298	3 837 481	1 594 542	1 593 993	1 163 310	256 247
9 960 783	9 636 599	9 627 814	8 358 159	4 846 391	244 590

12－5 续表
continued

指　标	Indicator	总计 Total	市内四区 Four Districts in Urban Area	崂山区 Laoshan District
按行业分	**Grouped by Industrial Sector**			
煤炭开采和洗选业	Mining and Washing of Coal			
石油和天然气开采业	Extraction of Petroleum and Natural Gas			
黑色金属矿采选业	Mining of Ferrous Metal Ores	155 331		
有色金属矿采选业	Mining of Non-ferrous Metal Ores			
非金属矿采选业	Mining and Processing of Nonmetal Ores	357 418		
其他采矿业	Mining of Other Ores			
农副食品加工业	Processing of Food from Agricultural Products	10 396 430	611 680	47 026
食品制造业	Manufacture of Foods	2 034 389	43 564	102 131
饮料制造业	Manufacture of Beverage	1 363 787	564 971	258 889
烟草制品业	Manufacture of Tobacco			
纺织业	Manufacture of Textile	4 657 163	200 600	6 209
纺织服装、鞋、帽制造业	Manufacture of Textile Wearing Apparel, Footware, and Caps	4 067 184	53 414	12 943
皮革、毛皮、羽毛(绒)及其制品业	Manufacture of Leather, Fur, Feather & Its Products	2 728 484	26 685	4 502
木材加工及木、竹、藤、棕、草制品业	Processing of Timbers, Manufacture of Wood, Bamboo, Rattan, Palm, and Straw Products	562 375		
家具制造业	Manufacture of Furniture	1 305 092	26 323	
造纸及纸制品业	Manufacture of Paper and Paper Products	1 584 094		40 538
印刷业和记录媒介的复制	Printing, Reproduction of Recording Media	775 690	136 847	
文教体育用品制造业	Manufacture of Articles for Culture, Education and Sport Activity	947 501	37 733	13 545
石油加工、炼焦及核燃料加工业	Processing of Petroleum, Coking, Processing of Nucleus Fuel	7 819 454	2 033 723	49 299
化学原料及化学制品制造业	Manufacture of Chemical Raw Material and Chemical Products	5 771 775	1 092 623	30 580
医药制造业	Manufacture of Medicines	798 126	38 217	133 505
化学纤维制造业	Manufacture of Chemical Fiber	155 909	39 568	
橡胶制品业	Manufacture of Rubber	4 615 773	33 036	21 266
塑料制品业	Manufacture of Plastic	2 130 568	84 428	51 288
非金属矿物制品业	Manufacture of Non-metallic Mineral Products	4 042 796	167 455	98 117
黑色金属冶炼及压延加工业	Smelting and Pressing of Ferrous Metals	4 560 335	2 835 634	
有色金属冶炼及压延加工业	Smelting and Pressing of Non-ferrous Metals	943 653		3 910
金属制品业	Manufacture of Metal Products	5 455 093	54 325	9 202
通用设备制造业	Manufacture of General Purpose Machinery	11 121 353	539 916	31 890
专用设备制造业	Manufacture of Special Purpose Machinery	5 529 913	97 433	217 910
交通运输设备制造业	Manufacture of Transport Equipment	13 538 042	2 211 343	149 533
电气机械及器材制造业	Manufacture of Electrical Machinery & Equipment	12 966 875	197 715	3 093 587
通信设备、计算机及其他电子设备制造业	Manufacture of Communication Equipment, Computer and Other Electronic Equipment	6 566 787	86 458	286 917
仪器仪表及文化、办公用机械制造业	Manufacture of Measuring Instrument and Machinery for Cultural Activity & Office Work	545 751	20 219	114 495
工艺品及其他制造业	Manufacture of Artwork, Other Manufacture	1 754 624	74 787	15 205
废弃资源和废旧材料回收加工业	Recycling and Disposal of Waste	26 780		
电力、热力的生产和供应业	Production and Supply of Electric Power and Heat Power	1 927 666	430 135	18 932
燃气生产和供应业	Production and Supply of Gas	352 619	182 791	
水的生产和供应业	Production and Supply of Water	100 799	52 635	

单位:万元(10 000 yuan)

黄岛区 Huangdao District	城阳区 Chengyang District	即墨市 Jimo	胶州市 Jiaozhou	胶南市 Jiaonan	平度市 Pingdu	莱西市 Laixi	高新区 High-tech Zone
					90 438	64 893	
		2 537			254 188	100 693	
780 010	1 585 578	889 618	1 365 821	669 518	1 814 505	2 628 083	4 592
130 231	205 943	48 302	343 437	618 635	231 808	310 339	
	1 594	134 861	20 784	205 907	129 646	47 135	
21 265	796 637	2 093 143	539 243	264 714	357 357	377 995	
81 791	621 203	1 658 685	775 735	371 381	198 626	293 406	
6 328	142 480	1 054 842	842 147	245 984	34 747	370 771	
22 129	16 904	32 479	231 761	52 726	138 112	68 265	
	297 686	54 151	609 593	134 141	125 225	57 974	
48 677	180 281	428 444	193 578	453 597	146 067	92 912	
	104 851	332 659	25 474	173 643	2 216		
40 484	232 348	275 768	132 071	56 867	60 847	97 839	
5 340 498	389 538	4 118	2 278				
1 838 029	265 935	486 889	598 646	614 132	421 707	366 633	56 602
77 024	168 076	106 441	118 966	90 093	17 816	47 988	
57 536		8 189	36 920	8 768		4 928	
1 148 000	209 986	515 823	187 233	1 582 248	603 239	295 607	19 333
295 227	318 051	294 608	409 472	280 002	147 981	224 246	25 263
530 081	400 496	115 793	559 472	379 483	1 015 077	776 823	
983 757	610 542	73 847	21 179	18 962		16 415	
159 843	104 962	95 643	188 159		391 136		
1 155 606	740 975	511 287	1 775 290	692 485	269 043	169 457	77 423
1 627 553	457 878	2 932 147	2 150 835	1 372 990	1 759 350	199 192	49 603
952 897	754 753	361 156	640 641	2 113 970	201 900	179 012	10 245
3 862 727	4 097 439	310 123	505 415	1 747 095	299 398	112 424	242 546
4 493 326	919 185	1 688 602	1 264 417	810 338	360 325	139 380	
3 643 191	1 281 329	395 683	77 305	91 668	627 837	65 708	10 691
4 221	130 021	29 089	48 042	68 220	107 097	19 808	4 539
39 726	170 620	307 661	423 963	188 432	380 084	154 147	
				12 351		14 429	
411 108	351 905	188 471	170 918	74 530	177 061	104 608	
36 687	39 487	57 115	10 438	11 121		14 981	
16 362	3 530	10 002	3 697	6 193	6 031	2 349	

12-6 规模以上工业企业主要指标(2011 年)
MAIN INDICATORS OF INDUSTRIAL ENTERPRISES ABOVE DESIGNATED SIZE(2011)

项 目	Indicator	企业单位数(个) Number of Enterprises (unit)
总 计	**Total**	**4 727**
按注册登记类型分	**Grouped by Status of Registration**	
国有及国有控股企业	State-owned and State-holding Enterprises	147
集体企业	Collective-owned Enterprises	31
股份有限公司	Share-holding Corporations Ltd	26
外商投资企业	Foreign Funded Enterprises	1 340
港澳台商投资企业	Invested by HongKong, Macao and Taiwan	278
按轻重工业分	**Grouped by Light and Heavy Industries**	
轻工业	Light Industry	2 131
重工业	Heavy Industry	2 596
按企业规模分	**Grouped by Size of Enterprises**	
大型企业	Large	50
中型企业	Medium	516
小型企业	Small	4 161
按所在地分	**Grouped by Location**	
市 区	Urban Area	1 094
#崂山区	Laoshan District	114
黄岛区	Huangdao District	269
城阳区	Chengyang District	502
即墨市	Jimo	652
胶州市	Jiaozhou	820
胶南市	Jiaonan	755
平度市	Pingdu	690
莱西市	Laixi	697
高新区	High-tech Zone	19
按行业分	**Grouped by Sector**	
煤炭开采和洗选业	Mining and Washing of Coal	
石油和天然气开采业	Extraction of Petroleum and Natural Gas	
黑色金属矿采选业	Mining of Ferrous Metal Ores	12
有色金属矿采选业	Mining of Non-ferrous Metal Ores	
非金属矿采选业	Mining and Processing of Nonmetal Ores	23
其他采矿业	Mining of Other Ores	

单位:万元(10 000 yuan)

工业总产值 Gross Industrial Output Value	资产合计 Total Assets	流动资产合计 Total Current Assets	固定资产净值 Net Value of Fixed Assets
121 659 629	**69 905 791**	**41 322 479**	**18 297 810**
28 414 278	22 585 180	12 169 855	6 486 519
7 009 938	6 617 249	5 151 054	524 231
357 308	119 080	57 493	43 927
28 790 047	18 422 166	11 141 632	4 896 593
6 458 888	3 345 229	2 177 708	826 825
46 595 950	26 193 020	16 631 637	5 512 924
75 063 679	43 712 771	24 690 842	12 784 886
32 364 772	27 389 346	18 109 095	5 351 517
35 835 823	22 772 645	12 617 275	6 611 933
53 459 035	19 743 800	10 596 108	6 334 360
61 824 427	46 750 589	29 465 014	10 377 561
8 587 912	8 823 783	6 763 700	880 195
22 218 760	14 155 528	7 644 107	4 522 430
15 600 212	10 993 673	7 463 728	2 169 239
15 450 004	5 093 323	2 533 843	1 574 695
13 912 601	6 504 776	3 627 542	1 389 433
12 601 173	4 560 344	2 117 468	2 203 343
9 952 152	3 327 838	1 797 532	1 206 690
7 418 436	2 964 472	1 389 879	1 332 370
500 837	704 449	391 202	213 719
155 331	22 031	7 196	12 434
357 418	61 231	29 645	22 489

12－6 续表1
continued

项　目	Indicator	主营业务收入 Revenue from Principal Business
总　计	**Total**	**121 079 425**
按注册登记类型分	**Grouped by Status of Registration**	
国有及国有控股企业	State-owned and State-holding Enterprises	31 811 661
集体企业	Collective-owned Enterprises	8 586 150
股份有限公司	Share-holding Corporations Ltd	328 908
外商投资企业	Foreign Funded Enterprises	27 521 319
港澳台商投资企业	Invested by HongKong Macao and Taiwan	6 119 055
按轻重工业分	**Grouped by Light and Heavy Industries**	
轻工业	Light Industry	48 752 402
重工业	Heavy Industry	72 327 023
按企业规模分	**Grouped by size of Enterprises**	
大型企业	Large	37 495 161
中型企业	Medium	34 008 934
小型企业	Small	49 575 330
按所在地分	**Grouped by Location**	
市　区	Urban Area	61 120 804
#崂山区	Laoshan District	5 657 783
黄岛区	Huangdao District	28 973 196
城阳区	Chengyang District	12 675 604
即墨市	Jimo	15 304 654
胶州市	Jiaozhou	13 627 476
胶南市	Jiaonan	12 983 606
平度市	Pingdu	10 280 611
莱西市	Laixi	7 274 370
高新区	High-tech Zone	487 904
按行业分	**Grouped by Sector**	
煤炭开采和洗选业	Mining and Washing of Coal	
石油和天然气开采业	Extraction of Petroleum and Natural Gas	
黑色金属矿采选业	Mining of Ferrous Metal Ores	155 222
有色金属矿采选业	Mining of Non-ferrous Metal Ores	
非金属矿采选业	Mining and Processing of Nonmetal Ores	321 961
其他采矿业	Mining of Other Ores	

单位:万元(10 000 yuan)

主营业务成本 Cost of Principal Business	主营业务税金及附加 Taxes and Extra Charges on Principal Business	利润总额 Total Profits	本年应交增值税 Value-added Tax Payable	全部从业人员年平均人数(人) Annual Average Employed Persons(person)
103 105 057	**1 946 836**	**6 461 064**	**3 307 003**	**1 098 209**
27 653 916	1 148 470	828 080	710 144	139 780
6 673 522	48 493	481 148	170 176	23 774
273 489	5 453	19 003	14 383	6 927
23 251 860	250 766	1 757 416	701 150	385 615
5 320 691	34 721	330 122	147 827	61 074
40 816 912	389 148	2 848 503	1 441 374	565 640
62 288 145	1 557 687	3 612 561	1 865 629	532 569
31 754 038	193 752	1 920 859	727 785	240 911
29 460 168	1 160 889	1 196 885	700 192	353 626
41 890 852	592 195	3 343 320	1 879 025	503 672
52 119 295	1 263 430	2 505 941	1 153 475	420 880
4 395 766	35 839	402 386	138 571	40 482
24 208 030	821 044	1 219 381	570 530	127 764
11 131 452	43 121	669 864	218 292	167 584
13 172 063	132 777	890 668	502 273	175 299
11 590 506	116 941	999 190	611 207	173 489
10 648 192	356 348	849 743	604 567	119 588
8 889 679	53 672	688 811	300 358	89 001
6 284 070	22 906	510 316	128 571	115 361
401 252	762	16 395	6 551	4 591
126 548	1 780	15 743	3 851	1 323
253 709	2 235	27 688	13 656	2 195

12 -6 续表2
continued

项 目	Indicator	企业单位数(个) Number of Enterprises (unit)
农副食品加工业	Processing of Food from Agricultural Products	444
食品制造业	Manufacture of Foods	127
饮料制造业	Manufacture of Beverage	36
烟草制品业	Manufacture of Tobacco	1
纺织业	Manufacture of Textile	229
纺织服装、鞋、帽制造业	Manufacture of Textile Wearing Apparel, Footware, and Caps	295
皮革、毛皮、羽毛(绒)及其制品业	Manufacture of Leather, Fur, Feather & Its Products	160
木材加工及木、竹、藤、棕、草制品业	Processing of Timbers, Manufacture of Wood, Bamboo, Rattan, Palm, and Straw Products	49
家具制造业	Manufacture of Furniture	97
造纸及纸制品业	Manufacture of Paper and Paper Products	101
印刷业和记录媒介的复制	Printing, Reproduction of Recording Media	58
文教体育用品制造业	Manufacture of Articles for Culture, Education and Sport Activity	75
石油加工、炼焦及核燃料加工业	Processing of Petroleum, Coking, Processing of Nucleus Fuel	7
化学原料及化学制品制造业	Manufacture of Chemical Raw Material and Chemical Products	231
医药制造业	Manufacture of Medicines	44
化学纤维制造业	Manufacture of Chemical Fiber	10
橡胶制品业	Manufacture of Rubber	187
塑料制品业	Manufacture of Plastic	169
非金属矿物制品业	Manufacture of Non-metallic Mineral Products	303
黑色金属冶炼及压延加工业	Smelting and Pressing of Ferrous Metals	29
有色金属冶炼及压延加工业	Smelting and Pressing of Non-ferrous Metals	34
金属制品业	Manufacture of Metal Products	294
通用设备制造业	Manufacture of General Purpose Machinery	521
专用设备制造业	Manufacture of Special Purpose Machinery	289
交通运输设备制造业	Manufacture of Transport Equipment	263
电气机械及器材制造业	Manufacture of Electrical Machinery & Equipment	230
通信设备、计算机及其他电子设备制造业	Manufacture of Communication Equipment, Computer and Other Electronic Equipment	124
仪器仪表及文化、办公用机械制造业	Manufacture of Measuring Instrument and Machinery for Cultural Activity & Office Work	39
工艺品及其他制造业	Manufacture of Artwork, Other Manufacture	185
废弃资源和废旧材料回收加工业	Recycling and Disposal of Waste	3
电力、热力的生产和供应业	Production and Supply of Electric Power and Heat Power	36
燃气生产和供应业	Production and Supply of Gas	11
水的生产和供应业	Production and Supply of Water	11

单位:万元(10 000 yuan)

工业总产值 Gross Industrial Output Value	资产合计 Total Assets	流动资产合计 Total Current Assets	固定资产净值 Net Value of Fixed Assets
10 396 430	3 686 173	2 227 838	1 018 555
2 034 389	1 358 575	919 555	316 944
1 363 787	1 764 229	585 100	258 052
4 657 163	1 921 433	1 183 168	563 894
4 067 184	1 776 205	1 090 726	475 514
2 728 484	763 307	444 546	228 679
562 375	151 390	77 515	45 481
1 305 092	461 562	258 262	141 146
1 584 094	602 524	313 730	193 251
775 690	387 626	187 045	151 403
947 501	433 019	261 801	120 747
7 819 454	2 693 013	995 479	1 270 620
5 771 775	3 936 451	2 006 096	1 417 537
798 126	744 330	339 517	203 721
155 909	132 546	79 583	40 357
4 615 773	2 754 928	1 593 316	858 426
2 130 568	960 949	548 051	291 129
4 042 796	2 252 123	1 272 158	717 028
4 560 335	1 680 367	1 019 427	533 257
943 653	285 256	134 087	99 155
5 455 093	3 110 325	1 635 607	763 738
11 121 353	4 388 045	2 454 147	1 224 207
5 529 913	2 844 842	1 745 344	703 139
13 538 042	12 644 645	8 322 615	2 679 437
12 966 875	9 918 829	7 284 277	1 094 146
6 566 787	3 649 779	2 759 564	550 732
545 751	298 929	206 207	50 943
1 754 624	638 440	357 572	220 436
26 780	5 519	1 696	3 824
1 927 666	2 439 324	680 498	1 421 844
352 619	664 769	175 564	305 881
100 799	473 075	125 550	299 667

12－6 续表 3

continued

项　目	Indicator	主营业务收入 Revenue from Principal Business
农副食品加工业	Processing of Food from Agricultural Products	9 730 289
食品制造业	Manufacture of Foods	2 005 911
饮料制造业	Manufacture of Beverage	1 980 902
烟草制品业	Manufacture of Tobacco	
纺织业	Manufacture of Textile	4 550 447
纺织服装、鞋、帽制造业	Manufacture of Textile Wearing Apparel, Footware, and Caps	3 844 732
皮革、毛皮、羽毛(绒)及其制品业	Manufacture of Leather, Fur, Feather & Its Products	2 575 949
木材加工及木、竹、藤、棕、草制品业	Processing of Timbers, Manufacture of Wood, Bamboo, Rattan, Palm, and Straw Products	537 405
家具制造业	Manufacture of Furniture	1 221 359
造纸及纸制品业	Manufacture of Paper and Paper Products	1 417 332
印刷业和记录媒介的复制	Printing, Reproduction of Recording Media	699 078
文教体育用品制造业	Manufacture of Articles for Culture, Education and Sport Activity	863 016
石油加工、炼焦及核燃料加工业	Processing of Petroleum, Coking, Processing of Nucleus Fuel	7 837 861
化学原料及化学制品制造业	Manufacture of Chemical Raw Material and Chemical Products	5 536 169
医药制造业	Manufacture of Medicines	719 509
化学纤维制造业	Manufacture of Chemical Fiber	148 468
橡胶制品业	Manufacture of Rubber	4 762 121
塑料制品业	Manufacture of Plastic	2 030 985
非金属矿物制品业	Manufacture of Non-metallic Mineral Products	3 819 202
黑色金属冶炼及压延加工业	Smelting and Pressing of Ferrous Metals	5 028 253
有色金属冶炼及压延加工业	Smelting and Pressing of Non-ferrous Metals	880 144
金属制品业	Manufacture of Metal Products	5 283 615
通用设备制造业	Manufacture of General Purpose Machinery	10 420 704
专用设备制造业	Manufacture of Special Purpose Machinery	4 878 512
交通运输设备制造业	Manufacture of Transport Equipment	13 053 228
电气机械及器材制造业	Manufacture of Electrical Machinery & Equipment	14 513 022
通信设备、计算机及其他电子设备制造业	Manufacture of Communication Equipment, Computer and Other Electronic Equipment	7 748 479
仪器仪表及文化、办公用机械制造业	Manufacture of Measuring Instrument and Machinery for Cultural Activity & Office Work	498 694
工艺品及其他制造业	Manufacture of Artwork, Other Manufacture	1 630 476
废弃资源和废旧材料回收加工业	Recycling and Disposal of Waste	24 505
电力、热力的生产和供应业	Production and Supply of Electric Power and Heat Power	2 005 607
燃气生产和供应业	Production and Supply of Gas	260 357
水的生产和供应业	Production and Supply of Water	95 914

单位:万元(10 000 yuan)

主营业务成本 Cost of Principal Business	主营业务税金及附加 Taxes and Extra Charges on Principal Business	利润总额 Total Profits	本年应交增值税 Value-added Tax Payable	全部从业人员年平均人数(人) Annual Average Employed Persons(person)
8 617 158	42 499	450 466	194 927	105 563
1 596 650	19 595	182 024	81 869	21 370
1 410 112	57 486	189 496	91 280	11 757
3 999 807	23 681	220 527	131 003	69 253
3 273 368	36 092	251 745	124 053	95 876
2 221 660	26 318	168 121	91 657	68 010
471 122	7 222	40 892	22 951	6 838
1 067 682	24 174	78 023	50 749	19 184
1 222 061	16 000	81 768	53 935	14 369
557 947	9 776	61 233	34 559	8 834
745 772	9 733	37 811	22 408	20 395
6 801 229	1 006 810	-157 813	149 043	3 135
4 854 164	34 514	326 620	127 679	40 382
472 770	6 739	108 724	43 740	9 908
130 735	1 414	4 719	3 950	1 661
4 133 311	47 154	258 061	103 818	43 474
1 714 432	16 803	110 497	78 277	26 382
3 216 356	31 695	288 064	127 838	36 439
4 822 926	5 341	25 298	50 612	13 819
795 191	3 854	57 986	23 007	4 985
4 511 276	43 900	338 457	174 305	48 269
8 638 089	112 292	688 514	331 077	88 835
3 965 184	87 865	327 436	199 643	47 379
10 888 044	129 350	973 100	337 965	88 791
11 731 372	75 959	796 482	304 160	82 117
6 772 390	31 261	359 403	194 950	55 727
389 392	5 265	52 077	17 738	7 234
1 382 820	19 009	115 308	62 322	31 153
20 088	231	2 441	533	177
2 005 966	5 807	37 930	43 022	16 317
184 752	4 341	23 414	11 190	3 116
110 978	642	5 330	5 236	3 944

12－7 按行业分国有及国有控股工业企业主要指标（2011 年）

MAIN INDICATORS OF STATE-OWNED AND STATE-HOLDING INDUSTRIAL ENTERPRISES BY INDUSTRIAL SECTOR(2011)

项　目	Indicator	企业单位数（个）Number of Enterprises(unit)
总　计	**Total**	**147**
煤炭开采和洗选业	Mining and Washing of Coal	
石油和天然气开采业	Extraction of Petroleum and Natural Gas	
黑色金属矿采选业	Mining of Ferrous Metal Ores	
有色金属矿采选业	Mining of Non-ferrous Metal Ores	
非金属矿采选业	Mining and Processing of Nonmetal Ores	1
其他采矿业	Mining of Other Ores	
农副食品加工业	Processing of Food from Agricultural Products	1
食品制造业	Manufacture of Foods	
饮料制造业	Manufacture of Beverage	6
烟草制品业	Manufacture of Tobacco	1
纺织业	Manufacture of Textile	1
纺织服装、鞋、帽制造业	Manufacture of Textile Wearing Apparel, Footware, and Caps	5
皮革、毛皮、羽毛(绒)及其制品业	Manufacture of Leather, Fur, Feather & Its Products	1
木材加工及木、竹、藤、棕、草制品业	Processing of Timbers, Manufacture of Wood, Bamboo, Rattan, Palm, and Straw Products	
家具制造业	Manufacture of Furniture	
造纸及纸制品业	Manufacture of Paper and Paper Products	1
印刷业和记录媒介的复制	Printing, Reproduction of Recording Media	
文教体育用品制造业	Manufacture of Articles for Culture, Education and Sport Activity	
石油加工、炼焦及核燃料加工业	Processing of Petroleum, Coking, Processing of Nucleus Fuel	4
化学原料及化学制品制造业	Manufacture of Chemical Raw Material and Chemical Products	17
医药制造业	Manufacture of Medicines	4
化学纤维制造业	Manufacture of Chemical Fiber	
橡胶制品业	Manufacture of Rubber	5
塑料制品业	Manufacture of Plastic	1
非金属矿物制品业	Manufacture of Non-metallic Mineral Products	9
黑色金属冶炼及压延加工业	Smelting and Pressing of Ferrous Metals	3
有色金属冶炼及压延加工业	Smelting and Pressing of Non-ferrous Metals	3
金属制品业	Manufacture of Metal Products	2
通用设备制造业	Manufacture of General Purpose Machinery	10
专用设备制造业	Manufacture of Special Purpose Machinery	4
交通运输设备制造业	Manufacture of Transport Equipment	25
电气机械及器材制造业	Manufacture of Electrical Machinery & Equipment	3
通信设备、计算机及其他电子设备制造业	Manufacture of Communication Equipment, Computer and Other Electronic Equipment	2
仪器仪表及文化、办公用机械制造业	Manufacture of Measuring Instrument and Machinery for Cultural Activity & Office Work	2
工艺品及其他制造业	Manufacture of Artwork, Other Manufacture	1
废弃资源和废旧材料回收加工业	Recycling and Disposal of Waste	
电力、热力的生产和供应业	Production and Supply of Electric Power and Heat Power	26
燃气生产和供应业	Production and Supply of Gas	1
水的生产和供应业	Production and Supply of Water	7

单位:万元(10 000 yuan)

工业总产值 Gross Industrial Output Value	资产合计 Total Assets	流动资产合计 Total Current Assets	固定资产净值 Net Value of Fixed Assets
28 414 278	**22 585 180**	**12 169 855**	**6 486 519**
6 022	6 524	2 431	1 991
22 279	10 938	838	9 905
896 756	1 554 864	488 531	170 354
12 974	7 171	5 600	1 047
32 477	47 827	35 769	11 077
17 059	10 173	6 585	2 139
149 717	82 066	40 618	28 334
3 481	12 902	6 366	1 057
7 763 759	2 650 960	973 586	1 268 113
736 234	840 128	370 719	252 833
114 994	213 252	78 758	25 018
710 701	963 188	635 472	221 132
41 326	45 132	26 469	17 546
147 367	162 281	107 907	31 399
3 132 076	1 295 275	765 558	411 283
55 522	61 882	13 769	43 610
284 965	71 140	55 277	8 770
275 210	372 974	209 410	103 260
676 382	284 042	225 502	48 483
8 082 975	8 181 546	5 195 172	1 776 303
629 612	463 381	294 600	46 419
2 892 731	2 072 162	1 769 984	177 796
8 950	5 174	4 200	634
8 386	9 872	6 219	1 902
1 484 415	2 276 477	625 589	1 363 886
140 303	445 055	116 916	178 332
87 606	438 794	108 013	283 897

12 -7 续表
continued

项　目	Indicator	主营业务收入 Revenue from Principal Business
总　计	**Total**	**31 811 661**
煤炭开采和洗选业	Mining and Washing of Coal	
石油和天然气开采业	Extraction of Petroleum and Natural Gas	
黑色金属矿采选业	Mining of Ferrous Metal Ores	
有色金属矿采选业	Mining of Non-ferrous Metal Ores	
非金属矿采选业	Mining and Processing of Nonmetal Ores	9 316
其他采矿业	Mining of Other Ores	
农副食品加工业	Processing of Food from Agricultural Products	21 648
食品制造业	Manufacture of Foods	
饮料制造业	Manufacture of Beverage	1 507 338
烟草制品业	Manufacture of Tobacco	
纺织业	Manufacture of Textile	20 881
纺织服装、鞋、帽制造业	Manufacture of Textile Wearing Apparel, Footware, and Caps	62 781
皮革、毛皮、羽毛(绒)及其制品业	Manufacture of Leather, Fur, Feather & Its Products	14 557
木材加工及木、竹、藤、棕、草制品业	Processing of Timbers, Manufacture of Wood, Bamboo, Rattan, Palm, and Straw Products	
家具制造业	Manufacture of Furniture	
造纸及纸制品业	Manufacture of Paper and Paper Products	126 193
印刷业和记录媒介的复制	Printing, Reproduction of Recording Media	4 042
文教体育用品制造业	Manufacture of Articles for Culture, Education and Sport Activity	
石油加工、炼焦及核燃料加工业	Processing of Petroleum, Coking, Processing of Nucleus Fuel	7 779 607
化学原料及化学制品制造业	Manufacture of Chemical Raw Material and Chemical Products	769 390
医药制造业	Manufacture of Medicines	115 376
化学纤维制造业	Manufacture of Chemical Fiber	
橡胶制品业	Manufacture of Rubber	997 249
塑料制品业	Manufacture of Plastic	36 341
非金属矿物制品业	Manufacture of Non-metallic Mineral Products	143 152
黑色金属冶炼及压延加工业	Smelting and Pressing of Ferrous Metals	4 076 361
有色金属冶炼及压延加工业	Smelting and Pressing of Non-ferrous Metals	55 737
金属制品业	Manufacture of Metal Products	258 629
通用设备制造业	Manufacture of General Purpose Machinery	298 587
专用设备制造业	Manufacture of Special Purpose Machinery	573 632
交通运输设备制造业	Manufacture of Transport Equipment	7 898 046
电气机械及器材制造业	Manufacture of Electrical Machinery & Equipment	947 531
通信设备、计算机及其他电子设备制造业	Manufacture of Communication Equipment, Computer and Other Electronic Equipment	4 309 643
仪器仪表及文化、办公用机械制造业	Manufacture of Measuring Instrument and Machinery for Cultural Activity & Office Work	7 169
工艺品及其他制造业	Manufacture of Artwork, Other Manufacture	8 386
废弃资源和废旧材料回收加工业	Recycling and Disposal of Waste	
电力、热力的生产和供应业	Production and Supply of Electric Power and Heat Power	1 667 021
燃气生产和供应业	Production and Supply of Gas	20 063
水的生产和供应业	Production and Supply of Water	82 983

单位:万元(10 000 yuan)

主营业务成本 Cost of Principal Business	主营业务税金及附加 Taxes and Extra Charges on Principal Business	利润总额 Total Profits	本年应交增值税 Value-added Tax Payable	全部从业人员年平均人数(人) Annual Average Employed Persons(person)
27 653 916	**1 148 470**	**828 080**	**710 144**	**139 781**
6 689	49	158	728	410
20 581		-54		96
1 036 064	51 184	160 706	70 521	6 017
19 177	37	-231	371	436
58 686	277	560	409	2 894
11 801	60	800	503	318
121 392	247	655	2 530	2 009
2 471	39	631	398	151
6 757 410	1 006 210	-163 785	146 784	2 781
682 034	2 385	14 158	15 976	10 089
80 367	858	5 693	6 741	2 329
950 384	1 990	-12 432	8 921	11 326
34 838		848	1 801	236
121 970	627	8 448	5 452	2 079
3 955 850	3 894	13 283	33 900	10 658
37 481	76	9 823	582	822
263 730	585	2 112	487	939
251 807	790	14 953	7 107	5 635
474 718	498	12 846	21 107	3 222
6 463 428	58 226	550 093	171 012	36 081
875 608	926	2 381	10 666	7 770
3 621 943	13 964	255 293	158 304	12 598
4 380	54	189	384	173
7 180	43	36	405	117
1 675 914	4 846	-40 096	40 107	15 051
16 124	1	-1 676	0	1 778
101 891	606	-7 310	4 951	3 766

12－8 按行业分规模以上外商投资和港澳台商投资工业企业主要指标（2011年）

MAIN INDICATORS OF FOREIGN FUNDED ENTERPRISES AND ENTERPRISES WITH FUNDS FROM HONG KONG, MACAO AND TAIWAN ABOVE DESIGNATED SIZE BY INDUSTRIAL SECTOR(2011)

项　目	Indicator	企业单位数(个) Number of Enterprises(unit)
总　计	**Total**	**1 618**
煤炭开采和洗选业	Mining and Washing of Coal	
石油和天然气开采业	Extraction of Petroleum and Natural Gas	
黑色金属矿采选业	Mining of Ferrous Metal Ores	1
有色金属矿采选业	Mining of Non-ferrous Metal Ores	
非金属矿采选业	Mining and Processing of Nonmetal Ores	4
其他采矿业	Mining of Other Ores	
农副食品加工业	Processing of Food from Agricultural Products	161
食品制造业	Manufacture of Foods	64
饮料制造业	Manufacture of Beverage	10
烟草制品业	Manufacture of Tobacco	
纺织业	Manufacture of Textile	90
纺织服装、鞋、帽制造业	Manufacture of Textile Wearing Apparel, Footware, and Caps	161
皮革、毛皮、羽毛(绒)及其制品业	Manufacture of Leather, Fur, Feather & Its Products	91
木材加工及木、竹、藤、棕、草制品业	Processing of Timbers, Manufacture of Wood, Bamboo, Rattan, Palm, and Straw Products	15
家具制造业	Manufacture of Furniture	29
造纸及纸制品业	Manufacture of Paper and Paper Products	33
印刷业和记录媒介的复制	Printing, Reproduction of Recording Media	12
文教体育用品制造业	Manufacture of Articles for Culture, Education and Sport Activity	52
石油加工、炼焦及核燃料加工业	Processing of Petroleum, Coking, Processing of Nucleus Fuel	1
化学原料及化学制品制造业	Manufacture of Chemical Raw Material and Chemical Products	76
医药制造业	Manufacture of Medicines	11
化学纤维制造业	Manufacture of Chemical Fiber	7
橡胶制品业	Manufacture of Rubber	39
塑料制品业	Manufacture of Plastic	65
非金属矿物制品业	Manufacture of Non-metallic Mineral Products	56
黑色金属冶炼及压延加工业	Smelting and Pressing of Ferrous Metals	10
有色金属冶炼及压延加工业	Smelting and Pressing of Non-ferrous Metals	6
金属制品业	Manufacture of Metal Products	76
通用设备制造业	Manufacture of General Purpose Machinery	125
专用设备制造业	Manufacture of Special Purpose Machinery	63
交通运输设备制造业	Manufacture of Transport Equipment	86
电气机械及器材制造业	Manufacture of Electrical Machinery & Equipment	75
通信设备、计算机及其他电子设备制造业	Manufacture of Communication Equipment, Computer and Other Electronic Equipment	85
仪器仪表及文化、办公用机械制造业	Manufacture of Measuring Instrument and Machinery for Cultural Activity & Office Work	13
工艺品及其他制造业	Manufacture of Artwork, Other Manufacture	93
废弃资源和废旧材料回收加工业	Recycling and Disposal of Waste	
电力、热力的生产和供应业	Production and Supply of Electric Power and Heat Power	1
燃气生产和供应业	Production and Supply of Gas	6
水的生产和供应业	Production and Supply of Water	1

单位:万元(10 000 yuan)

工业总产值 Gross Industrial Output Value	资产合计 Total Assets	流动资产合计 Total Current Assets	固定资产净值 Net Value of Fixed Assets
35 248 935	**21 767 395**	**13 319 340**	**5 723 418**
56 592	6 429	641	4 320
30 589	8 921	4 702	4 220
3 651 257	1 713 705	1 125 399	415 805
1 324 625	1 056 237	735 998	241 072
799 355	1 504 867	463 731	151 072
1 451 052	605 623	310 062	206 800
1 920 934	767 502	437 031	247 475
1 517 189	481 129	285 160	142 366
149 555	44 256	20 885	16 256
267 192	125 139	68 316	34 485
568 005	266 654	169 071	67 622
266 996	175 787	100 313	65 955
617 074	338 975	213 127	93 333
49 299	36 203	17 887	874
2 603 024	1 841 282	1 048 444	674 761
244 010	102 247	58 342	33 000
110 221	117 702	71 718	33 379
731 343	676 759	337 962	306 512
955 595	527 051	294 737	177 553
818 533	529 353	284 441	177 528
1 231 412	308 451	205 770	97 657
148 594	80 378	41 387	30 736
2 000 023	1 217 217	736 915	342 636
3 189 396	1 522 486	870 716	469 226
1 151 391	616 270	343 152	173 883
3 680 804	4 471 778	3 421 914	825 980
1 252 025	643 341	404 488	176 324
3 173 539	1 305 909	826 717	334 755
265 284	198 482	144 934	28 803
850 830	361 846	236 849	95 015
15 909	1 277	134	1 143
154 275	109 620	35 098	51 766
3 017	4 521	3 300	1 111

12－8 续表
continued

项　目	Indicator	主营业务收入 Revenue from Principal Business
总　计	**Total**	**33 640 374**
煤炭开采和洗选业	Mining and Washing of Coal	
石油和天然气开采业	Extraction of Petroleum and Natural Gas	
黑色金属矿采选业	Mining of Ferrous Metal Ores	58 592
有色金属矿采选业	Mining of Non-ferrous Metal Ores	
非金属矿采选业	Mining and Processing of Nonmetal Ores	29 964
其他采矿业	Mining of Other Ores	
农副食品加工业	Processing of Food from Agricultural Products	3 667 482
食品制造业	Manufacture of Foods	1 303 618
饮料制造业	Manufacture of Beverage	1 482 087
烟草制品业	Manufacture of Tobacco	
纺织业	Manufacture of Textile	1 388 557
纺织服装、鞋、帽制造业	Manufacture of Textile Wearing Apparel, Footware, and Caps	1 705 261
皮革、毛皮、羽毛(绒)及其制品业	Manufacture of Leather, Fur, Feather & Its Products	1 418 812
木材加工及木、竹、藤、棕、草制品业	Processing of Timbers, Manufacture of Wood, Bamboo, Rattan, Palm, and Straw Products	144 008
家具制造业	Manufacture of Furniture	264 615
造纸及纸制品业	Manufacture of Paper and Paper Products	471 123
印刷业和记录媒介的复制	Printing, Reproduction of Recording Media	224 059
文教体育用品制造业	Manufacture of Articles for Culture, Education and Sport Activity	562 876
石油加工、炼焦及核燃料加工业	Processing of Petroleum, Coking, Processing of Nucleus Fuel	50 585
化学原料及化学制品制造业	Manufacture of Chemical Raw Material and Chemical Products	2 552 885
医药制造业	Manufacture of Medicines	192 564
化学纤维制造业	Manufacture of Chemical Fiber	103 788
橡胶制品业	Manufacture of Rubber	725 222
塑料制品业	Manufacture of Plastic	901 747
非金属矿物制品业	Manufacture of Non-metallic Mineral Products	785 051
黑色金属冶炼及压延加工业	Smelting and Pressing of Ferrous Metals	752 808
有色金属冶炼及压延加工业	Smelting and Pressing of Non-ferrous Metals	130 333
金属制品业	Manufacture of Metal Products	2 078 978
通用设备制造业	Manufacture of General Purpose Machinery	3 012 098
专用设备制造业	Manufacture of Special Purpose Machinery	744 477
交通运输设备制造业	Manufacture of Transport Equipment	3 531 812
电气机械及器材制造业	Manufacture of Electrical Machinery & Equipment	1 141 500
通信设备、计算机及其他电子设备制造业	Manufacture of Communication Equipment, Computer and Other Electronic Equipment	2 964 031
仪器仪表及文化、办公用机械制造业	Manufacture of Measuring Instrument and Machinery for Cultural Activity & Office Work	242 413
工艺品及其他制造业	Manufacture of Artwork, Other Manufacture	808 017
废弃资源和废旧材料回收加工业	Recycling and Disposal of Waste	
电力、热力的生产和供应业	Production and Supply of Electric Power and Heat Power	15 034
燃气生产和供应业	Production and Supply of Gas	182 961
水的生产和供应业	Production and Supply of Water	3 017

单位:万元(10 000 yuan)

主营业务成本 Cost of Principal Business	主营业务 税金及附加 Taxes and Extra Charges on Principal Business	利润总额 Total Profits	本年应 交增值税 Value-added Tax Payable	全部从业人员 年平均人数(人) Annual Average Employed Persons(person)
28 572 550	**285 486**	**2 087 538**	**848 977**	**446 689**
45 891	585	6 420	949	296
20 126	45	2 249	855	176
3 229 335	18 011	122 920	61 613	39 486
1 007 098	12 912	132 708	53 334	12 889
1 015 958	38 375	154 809	71 855	5 370
1 207 548	6 315	61 951	37 022	24 160
1 451 294	15 021	88 637	47 819	58 483
1 247 248	15 464	57 395	36 644	51 474
132 118	771	7 101	4 704	1 395
241 264	3 230	14 688	9 474	6 208
424 981	4 315	20 334	14 722	5 306
178 240	2 798	20 424	9 267	4 015
493 360	7 273	20 113	14 073	17 505
37 757	557	5 388	1 770	259
2 257 534	14 925	157 486	37 343	11 465
155 716	837	9 159	7 357	2 148
91 169	308	1 980	922	1 494
612 529	6 180	38 778	15 629	10 770
772 110	5 627	38 005	27 625	14 474
681 552	2 641	57 164	18 609	7 388
695 198	293	1 503	8 079	1 835
122 921	725	6 536	1 382	785
1 809 540	6 237	100 382	46 369	21 010
2 483 769	24 172	224 826	95 306	24 895
628 346	6 758	34 816	21 394	11 361
2 864 462	63 443	497 416	109 864	28 185
935 010	6 070	35 202	32 567	19 927
2 751 756	12 356	74 147	23 317	37 684
175 814	502	32 002	7 269	4 028
670 084	4 520	43 467	21 258	21 426
10 524	105	1 954	1 082	77
119 889	4 102	17 182	9 374	694
2 409	16	396	133	21

12-9 按行业分大中型工业企业主要指标（2011 年）

MAIN INDICATORS OF LARGE AND MEDIUM-SIZED INDUSTRIAL ENTERPRISES BY INDUSTRIAL SECTOR(2011)

项　目	Indicator	企业单位数(个) Number of Enterprises(unit)
总　计	**Total**	**566**
煤炭开采和洗选业	Mining and Washing of Coal	
石油和天然气开采业	Extraction of Petroleum and Natural Gas	
黑色金属矿采选业	Mining of Ferrous Metal Ores	
有色金属矿采选业	Mining of Non-ferrous Metal Ores	
非金属矿采选业	Mining and Processing of Nonmetal Ores	2
其他采矿业	Mining of Other Ores	
农副食品加工业	Processing of Food from Agricultural Products	42
食品制造业	Manufacture of Foods	15
饮料制造业	Manufacture of Beverage	9
烟草制品业	Manufacture of Tobacco	
纺织业	Manufacture of Textile	26
纺织服装、鞋、帽制造业	Manufacture of Textile Wearing Apparel, Footware, and Caps	46
皮革、毛皮、羽毛(绒)及其制品业	Manufacture of Leather, Fur, Feather & Its Products	18
木材加工及木、竹、藤、棕、草制品业	Processing of Timbers, Manufacture of Wood, Bamboo, Rattan, Palm, and Straw Products	3
家具制造业	Manufacture of Furniture	8
造纸及纸制品业	Manufacture of Paper and Paper Products	4
印刷业和记录媒介的复制	Printing, Reproduction of Recording Media	8
文教体育用品制造业	Manufacture of Articles for Culture, Education and Sport Activity	10
石油加工、炼焦及核燃料加工业	Processing of Petroleum, Coking, Processing of Nucleus Fuel	3
化学原料及化学制品制造业	Manufacture of Chemical Raw Material and Chemical Products	26
医药制造业	Manufacture of Medicines	8
化学纤维制造业	Manufacture of Chemical Fiber	1
橡胶制品业	Manufacture of Rubber	20
塑料制品业	Manufacture of Plastic	19
非金属矿物制品业	Manufacture of Non-metallic Mineral Products	20
黑色金属冶炼及压延加工业	Smelting and Pressing of Ferrous Metals	3
有色金属冶炼及压延加工业	Smelting and Pressing of Non-ferrous Metals	4
金属制品业	Manufacture of Metal Products	34
通用设备制造业	Manufacture of General Purpose Machinery	55
专用设备制造业	Manufacture of Special Purpose Machinery	20
交通运输设备制造业	Manufacture of Transport Equipment	47
电气机械及器材制造业	Manufacture of Electrical Machinery & Equipment	37
通信设备、计算机及其他电子设备制造业	Manufacture of Communication Equipment, Computer and Other Electronic Equipment	33
仪器仪表及文化、办公用机械制造业	Manufacture of Measuring Instrument and Machinery for Cultural Activity & Office Work	6
工艺品及其他制造业	Manufacture of Artwork, Other Manufacture	19
废弃资源和废旧材料回收加工业	Recycling and Disposal of Waste	
电力、热力的生产和供应业	Production and Supply of Electric Power and Heat Power	16
燃气生产和供应业	Production and Supply of Gas	2
水的生产和供应业	Production and Supply of Water	2

单位:万元(10 000 yuan)

工业总产值 Gross Industrial Output Value	资产合计 Total Assets	流动资产合计 Total Current Assets	固定资产净值 Net Value of Fixed Assets
68 200 595	**50 161 991**	**30 726 370**	**11 963 450**
46 436	11 975	4 071	5 802
5 465 732	2 127 976	1 310 471	613 405
749 619	739 529	578 345	112 165
1 036 746	1 634 439	521 139	215 878
2 238 506	1 232 585	628 432	352 069
1 446 998	920 043	607 066	214 682
1 170 081	414 113	230 291	126 788
50 096	26 803	12 423	8 195
366 830	137 337	86 982	31 079
278 043	132 442	77 949	40 255
190 510	176 835	102 028	65 030
271 958	255 516	155 731	64 337
7 656 497	2 566 213	951 195	1 232 572
3 040 303	2 496 613	1 217 362	967 241
295 513	505 653	238 254	90 894
40 097	42 314	24 053	13 354
2 398 119	2 021 667	1 228 333	593 998
525 239	360 100	211 651	97 472
789 564	1 025 617	584 099	301 722
3 390 465	1 435 975	832 672	482 860
232 869	81 439	20 828	48 429
2 440 032	1 976 072	1 079 160	361 527
4 122 403	2 268 767	1 430 742	465 078
2 080 168	1 465 791	1 052 316	228 463
10 502 984	11 035 242	7 481 519	2 159 947
9 562 569	8 629 661	6 575 799	788 920
5 567 177	3 217 372	2 489 525	443 831
215 523	118 264	80 578	19 511
383 501	225 628	156 854	56 983
1 401 364	2 006 974	559 130	1 272 996
182 791	540 889	131 037	249 907
61 863	332 150	66 336	238 064

12－9 续表
continued

项　目	Indicator	主营业务收入 Revenue from Principal Business
总　计	**Total**	**71 504 095**
煤炭开采和洗选业	Mining and Washing of Coal	
石油和天然气开采业	Extraction of Petroleum and Natural Gas	
黑色金属矿采选业	Mining of Ferrous Metal Ores	
有色金属矿采选业	Mining of Non-ferrous Metal Ores	
非金属矿采选业	Mining and Processing of Nonmetal Ores	49 220
其他采矿业	Mining of Other Ores	
农副食品加工业	Processing of Food from Agricultural Products	4 906 113
食品制造业	Manufacture of Foods	791 912
饮料制造业	Manufacture of Beverage	1 676 799
烟草制品业	Manufacture of Tobacco	
纺织业	Manufacture of Textile	2 286 172
纺织服装、鞋、帽制造业	Manufacture of Textile Wearing Apparel, Footware, and Caps	1 454 608
皮革、毛皮、羽毛(绒)及其制品业	Manufacture of Leather, Fur, Feather & Its Products	1 126 423
木材加工及木、竹、藤、棕、草制品业	Processing of Timbers, Manufacture of Wood, Bamboo, Rattan, Palm, and Straw Products	48 605
家具制造业	Manufacture of Furniture	355 267
造纸及纸制品业	Manufacture of Paper and Paper Products	248 612
印刷业和记录媒介的复制	Printing, Reproduction of Recording Media	174 079
文教体育用品制造业	Manufacture of Articles for Culture, Education and Sport Activity	267 938
石油加工、炼焦及核燃料加工业	Processing of Petroleum, Coking, Processing of Nucleus Fuel	7 672 344
化学原料及化学制品制造业	Manufacture of Chemical Raw Material and Chemical Products	2 911 852
医药制造业	Manufacture of Medicines	289 942
化学纤维制造业	Manufacture of Chemical Fiber	36 944
橡胶制品业	Manufacture of Rubber	2 643 965
塑料制品业	Manufacture of Plastic	509 059
非金属矿物制品业	Manufacture of Non-metallic Mineral Products	722 037
黑色金属冶炼及压延加工业	Smelting and Pressing of Ferrous Metals	4 268 266
有色金属冶炼及压延加工业	Smelting and Pressing of Non-ferrous Metals	214 682
金属制品业	Manufacture of Metal Products	2 398 105
通用设备制造业	Manufacture of General Purpose Machinery	3 829 583
专用设备制造业	Manufacture of Special Purpose Machinery	1 718 339
交通运输设备制造业	Manufacture of Transport Equipment	10 331 617
电气机械及器材制造业	Manufacture of Electrical Machinery & Equipment	11 432 557
通信设备、计算机及其他电子设备制造业	Manufacture of Communication Equipment, Computer and Other Electronic Equipment	6 847 225
仪器仪表及文化、办公用机械制造业	Manufacture of Measuring Instrument and Machinery for Cultural Activity & Office Work	208 902
工艺品及其他制造业	Manufacture of Artwork, Other Manufacture	366 399
废弃资源和废旧材料回收加工业	Recycling and Disposal of Waste	
电力、热力的生产和供应业	Production and Supply of Electric Power and Heat Power	1 591 021
燃气生产和供应业	Production and Supply of Gas	62 462
水的生产和供应业	Production and Supply of Water	63 048

单位:万元(10 000 yuan)

主营业务成本 Cost of Principal Business	主营业务税金及附加 Taxes and Extra Charges on Principal Business	利润总额 Total Profits	本年应交增值税 Value-added Tax Payable	全部从业人员年平均人数(人) Annual Average Employed Persons (person)
61 214 205	**1 354 641**	**3 117 744**	**1 427 977**	**594 539**
35 026	447	5 524	1 295	813
4 417 250	14 277	102 834	41 271	59 763
566 481	4 055	99 360	34 064	7 489
1 172 602	51 022	167 070	77 480	8 534
2 042 337	5 283	79 930	49 032	41 720
1 220 849	10 635	93 006	31 944	46 935
983 168	9 070	65 885	21 431	35 767
43 765	2 173	2 920	3 761	2 178
317 398	7 313	11 464	8 526	8 121
231 257	566	4 670	6 372	3 391
131 910	1 933	17 283	7 473	3 580
240 932	5 840	3 306	8 082	7 574
6 653 492	1 005 235	-157 036	136 304	2 643
2 659 188	12 236	140 646	31 897	19 595
128 779	2 811	77 627	24 760	5 707
34 445	98	-889	505	503
2 351 875	4 581	107 835	21 382	24 826
435 332	1 684	13 338	13 899	9 711
634 402	7 126	56 113	22 522	12 499
4 148 355	3 574	9 660	33 671	11 482
193 146	1 487	19 364	5 167	1 911
2 099 724	6 617	150 980	50 964	23 771
3 228 187	26 084	234 280	69 270	37 418
1 380 245	11 345	99 101	63 081	18 879
8 588 745	75 779	777 566	224 642	63 719
9 097 329	51 713	599 306	207 955	58 625
5 988 058	23 936	315 255	169 515	43 883
158 642	643	28 359	8 226	3 359
317 037	1 695	17 447	8 532	10 942
1 581 836	4 790	-25 107	39 919	14 032
53 716	139	5 012	1 096	2 307
78 700	458	-4 364	3 942	2 862

12－10 按行业分规模以上工业企业主要经济效益指标（2011 年）

MAIN INDICATORS ON ECONOMIC BENEFIT OF INDUSTRIAL ENTERPRISES ABOVE DESIGNATED SIZE BY INDUSTRIAL SECTOR(2011)

行　业	Sector	总资产贡献率(%) Ratio of Total Assets to Industrial Output Value(%)
总　计	**Total**	**17.79**
按轻重工业分	**Grouped by Light and Heavy Industries**	
轻工业	Light Industry	18.67
重工业	Heavy Industry	17.26
按行业分	**Grouped by Sector**	
煤炭开采和洗选业	Mining and Washing of Coal	
石油和天然气开采业	Extraction of Petroleum and Natural Gas	
黑色金属矿采选业	Mining of Ferrous Metal Ores	97.82
有色金属矿采选业	Mining of Non-ferrous Metal Ores	
非金属矿采选业	Mining and Processing of Nonmetal Ores	71.88
其他采矿业	Mining of Other Ores	
农副食品加工业	Processing of Food from Agricultural Products	20.56
食品制造业	Manufacture of Foods	21.99
饮料制造业	Manufacture of Beverage	19.61
烟草制品业	Manufacture of Tobacco	
纺织业	Manufacture of Textile	20.77
纺织服装、鞋、帽制造业	Manufacture of Textile Wearing Apparel, Footware, and Caps	24.85
皮革、毛皮、羽毛(绒)及其制品业	Manufacture of Leather, Fur, Feather & Its Products	38.64
木材加工及木、竹、藤、棕、草制品业	Processing of Timbers, Manufacture of Wood, Bamboo, Rattan, Palm, and Straw Products	47.49
家具制造业	Manufacture of Furniture	34.75
造纸及纸制品业	Manufacture of Paper and Paper Products	26.46
印刷业和记录媒介的复制	Printing, Reproduction of Recording Media	28.62
文教体育用品制造业	Manufacture of Articles for Culture, Education and Sport Activity	16.88
石油加工、炼焦及核燃料加工业	Processing of Petroleum, Coking, Processing of Nucleus Fuel	39.25
化学原料及化学制品制造业	Manufacture of Chemical Raw Material and Chemical Products	14.12
医药制造业	Manufacture of Medicines	22.06
化学纤维制造业	Manufacture of Chemical Fiber	9.00
橡胶制品业	Manufacture of Rubber	16.16
塑料制品业	Manufacture of Plastic	22.62
非金属矿物制品业	Manufacture of Non-metallic Mineral Products	20.68
黑色金属冶炼及压延加工业	Smelting and Pressing of Ferrous Metals	8.18
有色金属冶炼及压延加工业	Smelting and Pressing of Non-ferrous Metals	32.11
金属制品业	Manufacture of Metal Products	19.03
通用设备制造业	Manufacture of General Purpose Machinery	26.96
专用设备制造业	Manufacture of Special Purpose Machinery	22.75
交通运输设备制造业	Manufacture of Transport Equipment	11.81
电气机械及器材制造业	Manufacture of Electrical Machinery & Equipment	12.16
通信设备、计算机及其他电子设备制造业	Manufacture of Communication Equipment, Computer and Other Electronic Equipment	16.13
仪器仪表及文化、办公用机械制造业	Manufacture of Measuring Instrument and Machinery for Cultural Activity & Office Work	25.66
工艺品及其他制造业	Manufacture of Artwork, Other Manufacture	31.40
废弃资源和废旧材料回收加工业	Recycling and Disposal of Waste	58.95
电力、热力的生产和供应业	Production and Supply of Electric Power and Heat Power	2.75
燃气生产和供应业	Production and Supply of Gas	6.91
水的生产和供应业	Production and Supply of Water	0.59

资产负债率 (%) Assets-Liability Ratio(%)	流动资产周转次数(次/年) Number of Times of Annualof Turnover Current Assets(time/year)	工业成本费用利润率(%) Ratio of Profits to Industrial Costs(%)	产品销售率 (%) Ratio of Sales to Output(%)
58.21	**2.97**	**5.63**	**98.40**
54.97	2.96	6.13	99.92
60.15	2.98	5.29	97.46
22.44	21.57	11.45	98.64
38.57	10.86	9.14	98.14
55.24	4.38	4.84	97.83
44	2.24	9.56	97.67
36.15	3.59	9.96	147.91
54.30	3.86	5.05	98.91
51.34	3.53	6.90	99.06
47.68	5.81	6.74	97.64
29.75	6.95	7.92	99.46
48.59	4.76	6.66	97.63
45.84	4.57	6.19	97.99
44.10	3.75	9.68	98.65
47.88	3.30	4.51	96.28
75.76	8.00	-2.22	99.73
58.32	2.81	6.18	95.92
27.05	2.15	17.91	92.99
45.62	1.92	3.18	96.86
65.81	3.03	5.80	98.03
51.69	3.77	5.78	99.81
63.08	3.00	8.21	96.01
71.05	4.97	0.50	98.09
54.69	6.62	6.93	97.76
48.17	3.27	6.84	96.75
51.98	4.33	7.14	97.43
52.53	2.83	7.15	95.46
66.89	1.62	7.97	98.03
60.13	1.99	5.83	97.86
52.45	2.87	4.70	99.06
41.06	2.43	11.74	97.03
43.26	4.56	7.65	98.46
49.69	14.92	11.45	57.67
76.80	2.97	-1.68	98.86
45.38	1.76	9.59	108.45
59.76	0.82	-3.69	98.96

12－11 按行业分国有控股工业企业主要经济效益指标(2011 年)

MAIN INDICATORS ON ECONOMIC BENEFIT OF STATE-OWNED AND STATE-HOLDING INDUSTRIAL ENTERPRISES BY INDUSTRIAL SECTOR(2011)

行　业	Sector	总资产贡献率(％) Ratio of Total Assets to Industrial Output Value(％)
总　计	**Total**	**13.00**
煤炭开采和洗选业	Mining and Washing of Coal	
石油和天然气开采业	Extraction of Petroleum and Natural Gas	
黑色金属矿采选业	Mining of Ferrous Metal Ores	
有色金属矿采选业	Mining of Non-ferrous Metal Ores	
非金属矿采选业	Mining and Processing of Nonmetal Ores	14.24
其他采矿业	Mining of Other Ores	
农副食品加工业	Processing of Food from Agricultural Products	0.96
食品制造业	Manufacture of Foods	
饮料制造业	Manufacture of Beverage	18.49
烟草制品业	Manufacture of Tobacco	
纺织业	Manufacture of Textile	2.45
纺织服装、鞋、帽制造业	Manufacture of Textile Wearing Apparel, Footware, and Caps	2.87
皮革、毛皮、羽毛(绒)及其制品业	Manufacture of Leather, Fur, Feather & Its Products	15.10
木材加工及木、竹、藤、棕、草制品业	Processing of Timbers, Manufacture of Wood, Bamboo, Rattan, Palm, and Straw Products	
家具制造业	Manufacture of Furniture	
造纸及纸制品业	Manufacture of Paper and Paper Products	6.51
印刷业和记录媒介的复制	Printing, Reproduction of Recording Media	8.37
文教体育用品制造业	Manufacture of Articles for Culture, Education and Sport Activity	
石油加工、炼焦及核燃料加工业	Processing of Petroleum, Coking, Processing of Nucleus Fuel	39.54
化学原料及化学制品制造业	Manufacture of Chemical Raw Material and Chemical Products	5.04
医药制造业	Manufacture of Medicines	7.64
化学纤维制造业	Manufacture of Chemical Fiber	
橡胶制品业	Manufacture of Rubber	1.35
塑料制品业	Manufacture of Plastic	5.59
非金属矿物制品业	Manufacture of Non-metallic Mineral Products	10.00
黑色金属冶炼及压延加工业	Smelting and Pressing of Ferrous Metals	8.05
有色金属冶炼及压延加工业	Smelting and Pressing of Non-ferrous Metals	17.68
金属制品业	Manufacture of Metal Products	4.91
通用设备制造业	Manufacture of General Purpose Machinery	6.39
专用设备制造业	Manufacture of Special Purpose Machinery	12.59
交通运输设备制造业	Manufacture of Transport Equipment	9.90
电气机械及器材制造业	Manufacture of Electrical Machinery & Equipment	4.65
通信设备、计算机及其他电子设备制造业	Manufacture of Communication Equipment, Computer and Other Electronic Equipment	20.58
仪器仪表及文化、办公用机械制造业	Manufacture of Measuring Instrument and Machinery for Cultural Activity & Office Work	12.09
工艺品及其他制造业	Manufacture of Artwork, Other Manufacture	5.98
废弃资源和废旧材料回收加工业	Recycling and Disposal of Waste	
电力、热力的生产和供应业	Production and Supply of Electric Power and Heat Power	2.60
燃气生产和供应业	Production and Supply of Gas	0.59
水的生产和供应业	Production and Supply of Water	0.08

资产负债率 (%) Assets-Liability Ratio(%)	流动资产周转次数(次/年) Number of Times of Annual of Turnover Current Assets(time/year)	工业成本费用利润率(%) Ratio of Profits to Industrial Costs(%)	产品销售率 (%) Ratio of Sales to Output(%)
65.25	**2.69**	**2.69**	**101.37**
65.73	3.84	1.46	96.92
8.66	25.85	-0.25	97.17
34.90	3.32	11.06	177.15
105.53	3.99	-1.10	100.00
92.69	1.77	0.89	99.94
56.81	2.23	5.74	103.14
68.49	3.11	0.52	96.00
50.58	0.64	17.61	116.12
76.01	8.12	-2.32	99.72
54.85	2.21	1.81	100.78
39.92	1.49	4.93	99.65
77.78	1.62	-1.20	101.74
41.37	1.43	2.27	86.93
69.87	1.35	6.06	100.96
76.06	5.35	0.33	99.94
43.42	4.07	21.38	99.98
104.82	4.68	0.79	92.18
59.60	1.45	5.04	98.61
83.61	2.61	2.18	83.25
66.16	1.58	7.44	98.55
77.89	3.26	0.25	100.82
53.78	2.51	6.07	99.55
41.83	1.72	2.70	85.65
67.60	1.35	0.37	100.00
76.26	2.68	-2.17	98.68
41.66	0.33	-4.31	100.00
59.56	0.83	-5.49	99.23

12－12 按行业分规模以上外商及港澳台商投资工业企业主要经济效益指标(2011年)

MAIN INDICATORS ON ECONOMIC BENEFIT OF FOREIGN FUNDED ENTERPRISES AND ENTERPRISES WITH FUNDS FROM HONG KONG, MACAO AND TAIWAN ABOVE DESIGNATED SIZE BY INDUSTRIAL SECTOR(2011)

行　业	Sector	总资产贡献率(%) Ratio of Total Assets to Industrial Output Value(%)
总　计	**Total**	**15.64**
煤炭开采和洗选业	Mining and Washing of Coal	
石油和天然气开采业	Extraction of Petroleum and Natural Gas	
黑色金属矿采选业	Mining of Ferrous Metal Ores	124.29
有色金属矿采选业	Mining of Non-ferrous Metal Ores	
非金属矿采选业	Mining and Processing of Nonmetal Ores	35.89
其他采矿业	Mining of Other Ores	
农副食品加工业	Processing of Food from Agricultural Products	13.79
食品制造业	Manufacture of Foods	19.94
饮料制造业	Manufacture of Beverage	17.89
烟草制品业	Manufacture of Tobacco	
纺织业	Manufacture of Textile	18.27
纺织服装、鞋、帽制造业	Manufacture of Textile Wearing Apparel, Footware, and Caps	21.27
皮革、毛皮、羽毛(绒)及其制品业	Manufacture of Leather, Fur, Feather & Its Products	23.67
木材加工及木、竹、藤、棕、草制品业	Processing of Timbers, Manufacture of Wood, Bamboo, Rattan, Palm, and Straw Products	29.54
家具制造业	Manufacture of Furniture	23.71
造纸及纸制品业	Manufacture of Paper and Paper Products	15.60
印刷业和记录媒介的复制	Printing, Reproduction of Recording Media	18.98
文教体育用品制造业	Manufacture of Articles for Culture, Education and Sport Activity	12.83
石油加工、炼焦及核燃料加工业	Processing of Petroleum, Coking, Processing of Nucleus Fuel	21.31
化学原料及化学制品制造业	Manufacture of Chemical Raw Material and Chemical Products	13.42
医药制造业	Manufacture of Medicines	18.11
化学纤维制造业	Manufacture of Chemical Fiber	4.27
橡胶制品业	Manufacture of Rubber	10.20
塑料制品业	Manufacture of Plastic	14.49
非金属矿物制品业	Manufacture of Non-metallic Mineral Products	15.34
黑色金属冶炼及压延加工业	Smelting and Pressing of Ferrous Metals	3.80
有色金属冶炼及压延加工业	Smelting and Pressing of Non-ferrous Metals	11.80
金属制品业	Manufacture of Metal Products	13.99
通用设备制造业	Manufacture of General Purpose Machinery	23.16
专用设备制造业	Manufacture of Special Purpose Machinery	10.96
交通运输设备制造业	Manufacture of Transport Equipment	15.11
电气机械及器材制造业	Manufacture of Electrical Machinery & Equipment	11.86
通信设备、计算机及其他电子设备制造业	Manufacture of Communication Equipment, Computer and Other Electronic Equipment	8.57
仪器仪表及文化、办公用机械制造业	Manufacture of Measuring Instrument and Machinery for Cultural Activity & Office Work	20.35
工艺品及其他制造业	Manufacture of Artwork, Other Manufacture	19.88
废弃资源和废旧材料回收加工业	Recycling and Disposal of Waste	
电力、热力的生产和供应业	Production and Supply of Electric Power and Heat Power	246.06
燃气生产和供应业	Production and Supply of Gas	28.07
水的生产和供应业	Production and Supply of Water	12.85

资产负债率（%）Assets-Liability Ratio（%）	流动资产周转次数（次/年）Number of Times of Annual of Turnover Current Assets（time/year）	工业成本费用利润率（%）Ratio of Profits to Industrial Costs（%）	产品销售率（%）Ratio of Sales to Output（%）
54.04	**2.57**	**6.49**	**100.26**
9.21	91.38	12.28	100.00
16.87	6.37	7.84	97.96
60.05	3.28	3.54	99.12
42.29	1.86	10.74	95.83
33.94	3.44	10.64	185.43
54.58	4.49	4.69	98.71
46.32	3.91	5.44	100.10
55.23	4.99	4.12	97.35
25.37	6.90	4.94	99.18
46.26	3.93	5.50	100.08
48.02	2.86	4.38	99.01
39.49	2.24	9.74	96.06
46.33	2.65	3.54	96.29
56.48	2.83	12.09	101.33
64.95	2.49	6.41	95.63
30.02	3.38	5.26	83.69
50.55	1.51	1.90	95.55
61.84	2.20	5.65	98.87
47.40	3.14	4.37	100.49
40.94	2.77	7.71	96.55
52.00	3.74	0.18	93.36
60.88	3.16	5.00	97.46
58.29	2.87	5.06	98.99
49.14	3.52	8.11	97.19
52.63	2.27	4.35	99.43
65.67	1.06	15.70	99.74
52.33	2.84	3.22	98.65
47.93	3.61	2.47	98.80
37.93	1.68	15.72	98.35
51.82	3.43	5.75	102.85
77.28	111.94	15.06	100.00
48.10	5.22	13.24	119.37
14.74	0.91	15.19	100.00

12－13 按行业分大中型工业企业主要经济效益指标（2011 年）

MAIN INDICATORS ON ECONOMIC BENEFIT OF LARGE AND MEDIUM-SIZED INDUSTRIAL ENTERPRISES BY INDUSTRIAL SECTOR(2011)

行 业	Sector	总资产贡献率(%) Ratio of Total Assets to Industrial Output Value(%)
总 计	**Total**	**12.75**
煤炭开采和洗选业	Mining and Washing of Coal	
石油和天然气开采业	Extraction of Petroleum and Natural Gas	
黑色金属矿采选业	Mining of Ferrous Metal Ores	
有色金属矿采选业	Mining of Non-ferrous Metal Ores	
非金属矿采选业	Mining and Processing of Nonmetal Ores	60.62
其他采矿业	Mining of Other Ores	
农副食品加工业	Processing of Food from Agricultural Products	9.58
食品制造业	Manufacture of Foods	19.31
饮料制造业	Manufacture of Beverage	18.48
烟草制品业	Manufacture of Tobacco	
纺织业	Manufacture of Textile	12.32
纺织服装、鞋、帽制造业	Manufacture of Textile Wearing Apparel, Footware, and Caps	16.63
皮革、毛皮、羽毛(绒)及其制品业	Manufacture of Leather, Fur, Feather & Its Products	24.32
木材加工及木、竹、藤、棕、草制品业	Processing of Timbers, Manufacture of Wood, Bamboo, Rattan, Palm, and Straw Products	33.04
家具制造业	Manufacture of Furniture	21.53
造纸及纸制品业	Manufacture of Paper and Paper Products	10.57
印刷业和记录媒介的复制	Printing, Reproduction of Recording Media	15.55
文教体育用品制造业	Manufacture of Articles for Culture, Education and Sport Activity	7.46
石油加工、炼焦及核燃料加工业	Processing of Petroleum, Coking, Processing of Nucleus Fuel	40.68
化学原料及化学制品制造业	Manufacture of Chemical Raw Material and Chemical Products	9.23
医药制造业	Manufacture of Medicines	21.5
化学纤维制造业	Manufacture of Chemical Fiber	1.57
橡胶制品业	Manufacture of Rubber	8.07
塑料制品业	Manufacture of Plastic	9.31
非金属矿物制品业	Manufacture of Non-metallic Mineral Products	8.8
黑色金属冶炼及压延加工业	Smelting and Pressing of Ferrous Metals	6.94
有色金属冶炼及压延加工业	Smelting and Pressing of Non-ferrous Metals	33.1
金属制品业	Manufacture of Metal Products	11.49
通用设备制造业	Manufacture of General Purpose Machinery	15.81
专用设备制造业	Manufacture of Special Purpose Machinery	12.51
交通运输设备制造业	Manufacture of Transport Equipment	10.17
电气机械及器材制造业	Manufacture of Electrical Machinery & Equipment	10.21
通信设备、计算机及其他电子设备制造业	Manufacture of Communication Equipment, Computer and Other Electronic Equipment	15.81
仪器仪表及文化、办公用机械制造业	Manufacture of Measuring Instrument and Machinery for Cultural Activity & Office Work	32.16
工艺品及其他制造业	Manufacture of Artwork, Other Manufacture	12.98
废弃资源和废旧材料回收加工业	Recycling and Disposal of Waste	
电力、热力的生产和供应业	Production and Supply of Electric Power and Heat Power	3.63
燃气生产和供应业	Production and Supply of Gas	2.41
水的生产和供应业	Production and Supply of Water	0.39

资产负债率 (%) Assets-Liability Ratio(%)	流动资产周转次数(次/年) Number of Times of Annual of Turnover Current Assets(time/year)	工业成本费用利润率(%) Ratio of Profits to Industrial Costs(%)	产品销售率 (%) Ratio of Sales to Output(%)
61.74	**2.37**	**4.52**	**99.61**
38.32	12.1	11.19	98.50
57.74	3.75	2.14	97.73
43.95	1.46	13.61	99.95
35.54	3.44	10.26	165.38
55.76	3.65	3.52	100.7
52.13	2.4	6.66	102.52
54.31	4.89	5.89	95.45
36.78	3.91	5.46	98.83
55.31	4.09	3.23	100.86
60.2	3.26	1.88	95.43
37.67	1.72	10.63	93.64
42.49	1.72	1.15	97.07
78.19	8.2	-2.26	100.21
63.9	2.46	4.97	95.85
24.3	1.23	34.88	97.52
43.42	1.7	-2.16	94.14
70.78	2.19	4.24	98.43
56.1	2.47	2.71	98.96
76.02	1.24	7.97	94.68
71.86	5.17	0.22	99.78
45.4	10.42	9.27	97.75
48.6	2.26	6.53	97.09
59.33	2.74	6.29	98.38
57.96	1.66	5.86	92.32
68.54	1.43	7.99	99.61
62.1	1.74	5.52	98.42
52.38	2.81	4.65	99.12
49.21	2.59	15.66	96.8
47.72	2.35	4.98	97.78
75.42	2.86	-1.44	98.8
44.56	0.84	4.9	100
57.45	1.04	-4.17	98.91

12-14 主要年份主要工业产品产量
MAJOR YEAR'S PRODUCTS OUTPUT OF INDUSTRY ABOVE DESIGNATED SIZE

年份 Year	原盐（万吨）Salt (10000 tons)	发电量（亿千瓦小时）Electricity (100 million kW·h)	饮料酒（万吨）Beverage Liquor (10000 tons)	#啤酒 Beer	卷烟（万箱）Cigarettes (10000 cases)	罐头（吨）Canned Food (ton)	化学纤维（吨）Chemical Fiber (ton)	纱（吨）Yarn (ton)
1949	15.16	1.21	0.18	0.12	2.36			27 447
1952	35.08	2.11	0.37	0.18	12.27			59 674
1957	44.34	2.92	0.96	0.58	23.41			50 699
1962	38.60	3.86	1.58	0.79	16.59		28	17 939
1965	41.34	6.80	2.04	1.34	31.34		205	68 082
1970	29.96	10.57	3.39	2.55	42.16		621	85 591
1975	34.52	10.98	5.30	2.98	36.00		357	79 516
1978	60.68	13.63	6.25	3.75	44.00	4 743	1 413	85 233
1980	41.19	12.50	8.49	4.84	48.79	3 521	2 116	83 389
1985	47.34	26.97	13.76	10.05	51.81	6 400	1 747	91 839
1987	50.64	28.97	23.40	13.85	55.84	16 000	3 442	108 003
1988	53.28	29.35	26.61	15.58	57.01	27 200	3 393	107 720
1989	55.37	29.87	24.57	15.40	58.64	13 200	3 700	118 379
1990	35.70	40.22	29.18	19.61	61.94		2 900	100 381
1991	31.39	54.60	36.75	27.38	56.19	130 510	5 200	96 271
1992	46.24	58.63	44.59	37.01	59.37	3 200	6 000	99 043
1993	48.88	59.39	54.74	45.92	63.46	1 900	27 100	91 351
1994	53.02	59.62	60.00	50.92	69.20	2 300	21 400	86 744
1995	50.84	64.69	60.85	54.16	70.96	4 609	20 973	79 492
1996	41.39	83.02	61.79	54.40	73.04	1 719	22 945	66 832
1997	34.11	95.12	66.64	56.06	88.32	554	26 300	70 402
1998	19.08	79.65	47.33	42.79	77.10		23 858	66 504
1999	30.30	82.00	126.21	120.10	149.00	379	29 967	56 431
2000	41.83	90.84	211.47	206.50	148.10	225	65 362	69 561
2001	31.40	85.73	279.37	274.28	142.95	99	89 989	72 933
2002	42.50	89.70	323.20	320.60	138.10	11 690	91 394	70 888
2003	36.85	87.69	353.90	351.80	148.00		101 752	65 919
2004	34.36	89.01	393.30	390.60	147.10	10 889	115 187	71 931
2005	10.00	98.63	439.70	435.20	150.70	10 097	95 887	72 140
2006	15.30	124.54	101.60(本地)	95.60(本地)	95.16(本地)	1 668	72 381	56 128
2007	19.23	155.30	118.10(本地)	112.50(本地)	100.08(本地)	1 850	68 746	47 850
2008	15.90	164.58	132.07(本地)	124.75(本地)	100.02(本地)	1 510	51 751	43 102
2009	5.90	172.66	137.21(本地)	127.12(本地)	100.08(本地)	4 706	59 852	38 566
2010	11.25	181.93	144.66(本地)	141.65(本地)	102.55(本地)	1 092	68 654	35 278
2011		173.69	164.09	156.50	104.51	78 041	38 640	19 398

注：1998 年以前为乡及乡以上工业。

Note: Before 1998, the data refer to those at and above county level.

12－14 续表 1
continued

年 份 Year	布(万米) Cloth (10000 m)	印染布 (万米) Printed Fabric (10000 m)	机制纸及纸板(万吨) Machine-made Paper and Paperboards (10000 tons)	硫 酸 (万吨) Sulfuric Acid (10000 tons)	烧 碱 (万吨) Caustic Soda (10000 tons)	纯 碱 (万吨) Soda Ash (10000 tons)
1949	10 608	2 947	0.98		0.01	
1952	30 069	13 658	0.44		0.17	
1957	27 806	16 053	1.54		0.74	
1962	7 444	7 375	1.45	0.06	0.89	
1965	29 538	13 670	2.22		1.66	5.32
1970	33 660	21 994	3.14	0.04	2.14	12.01
1975	31 242	22 828	3.10	0.53	2.36	9.15
1978	36 877	25 797	4.55	1.32	3.61	14.04
1980	34 937	22 900	5.25	4.11	4.33	18.18
1985	34 998	17 679	6.20	3.34	5.52	26.03
1987	38 155	21 833	6.52	4.40	6.15	29.53
1988	35 890	21 213	7.42	4.88	6.62	31.12
1989	36 188	19 842	6.20	4.30	6.95	32.25
1990	34 066	21 446	6.02	4.86	6.73	30.48
1991	34 076	19 999	5.99	5.62	5.99	29.50
1992	33 682	21 534	5.95	6.70	5.62	34.60
1993	35 912	16 606	8.84	6.96	6.07	40.43
1994	43 241	16 387	12.36	8.33	6.48	43.36
1995	41 170	17 864	11.06	9.69	7.90	43.20
1996	39 023	16 881	11.31	10.12	7.30	46.91
1997	43 615	15 722	7.78	10.16	8.45	50.55
1998	40 440	9 864	6.91	10.33	9.25	52.80
1999	39 576	4 340	7.77	12.56	8.96	53.70
2000	41 783	3 526	10.96	12.96	10.24	56.20
2001	40 640	3 402	23.05	13.03	11.44	58.47
2002	47 609	5 592	29.92	5.00	13.80	60.70
2003	35 922	10 131	31.76	4.50	13.53	62.50
2004	50 111	7 718	36.38	14.70	14.86	60.80
2005	51 307	16 027	31.95	14.80	16.10	62.50
2006	55 093	20 867	15.50	7.00	15.90	63.95
2007	44 251	18 708	24.04	9.22	14.91	71.02
2008	48 399	58 907	22.41	13.02	12.78	72.03
2009	19 504	28 146	33.44	1.41	12.24	68.21
2010	17 457	29 631	35.43	4.07	13.87	69.35
2011	43 916	29 166	29.59	5.06	13.20	72.07

12－14 续表 2
continued

年 份 Year	合成氨 （万吨） Synthetic Ammonia （10000 tons）	化学肥料 （万吨） Chemical Fertilizer （10000 tons）	化学农药 （吨） Chemical Pesticides （ton）	油 漆 （吨） Paint （ton）	染 料 （吨） Dye （ton）
1949				30	599
1952				480	2 855
1957			1 226	1 247	4 307
1962		0.45	213	910	3 560
1965		1.42	2	4 727	8 667
1970	0.98	5.89	2 313	6 380	9 347
1975	3.46	12.46	4 439	7 016	5 967
1978	7.17	23.66	9 714	8 786	5 877
1980	7.24	7.82	8 333	14 556	2 159
1985	6.31	5.16	2 000	26 055	4 448
1987	8.20	8.32	2 200	28 323	5 316
1988	8.72	9.41	2 400	28 943	5 527
1989	8.47	8.84	2 500	27 713	5 784
1990	7.56	7.55	2 500	29 075	5 119
1991	8.52	8.04	2 800	33 548	5 263
1992	10.45	7.85	3 400	35 058	4 821
1993	10.70	8.02	3 600	33 054	4 550
1994	13.04	12.39	3 600	29 437	5 097
1995	14.98	12.62	4 934	37 772	7 185
1996	18.67	12.62	4 976	26 762	7 668
1997	16.94	12.52	4 600	19 743	11 189
1998	22.36	15.30	6 755	17 594	8 274
1999	26.09	20.19	4 480	3 730	7 866
2000	24.64	20.04	3 758	693	9 306
2001	35.53	28.07	3 915	1 349	9 757
2002	20.30	9.80	4 020	1 701	9 826
2003	21.55	9.70	2 039	2 106	10 734
2004	30.30	19.60	5 061	1 955	3 961
2005	33.80	22.10	6 524	1 687	13 979
2006	33.30	21.30	12 544		26 544
2007	28.22	25.70	16 433	2 957	28 269
2008	17.93	21.51	12 848	12 105	18 263
2009	17.71	15.25	21 037		39 277
2010	16.84	14.10	16 450		41 383
2011	10.78	9.26	17 340		

12－14 续表 3
continued

年　份 Year	化学原料药 （吨） Chemical Medicines(ton)	水　泥 （万吨） Cement (10000 tons)	平板玻璃 （万重量箱） Plate Glass (10000 weight cases)	耐火材料 （万吨） Refractory Material (10000 tons)	钢 （万吨） Crude Steel (10000 tons)	钢　材 （万吨） Rolled-steel (10000 tons)
1949						0.06
1952				0.78	0.36	0.41
1957				3.39	1.77	4.30
1962		2.09		2.41	4.59	2.94
1965		6.59		2.91	11.72	8.43
1970		7.35	16.31	3.23	19.38	14.56
1975	55	20.93	19.44	4.88	21.25	20.01
1978	185	35.40	8.86	5.93	31.06	27.61
1980	123	44.66	70.13	5.38	37.14	32.82
1984	7 228	70.27	91.25	7.98	37.81	32.43
1985	4 222	82.70	77.00	4.35	37.51	32.68
1987	7 457	117.20	87.00	4.90	46.51	38.09
1988	7 655	141.00	108.81	4.56	50.17	38.26
1989	8 348	135.00	96.49	3.68	54.64	39.38
1990	6 913	139.48	83.13	3.91	54.55	38.04
1991	4 754	165.66	96.90	3.71	56.96	39.02
1992	5 743	191.50	120.00	3.86	63.75	50.09
1993	6 566	221.30	148.71	3.55	61.75	44.88
1994	4 238	246.50	145.12	3.06	60.82	46.95
1995	1 993	213.82	426.40	3.88	67.27	49.60
1996	5 505	181.45	423.60	3.54	72.02	50.60
1997	1 693	208.04	570.85	2.45	75.71	51.06
1998	910	131.51	509.38	0.99	84.02	64.93
1999	1 691	149.41	576.50	0.59	108.10	86.58
2000	2 131	137.52	556.58	0.62	101.17	93.35
2001	2 534	148.67	421.51	0.51	124.45	119.77
2002	2 712	140.30	405.40	0.45	145.90	142.20
2003	3 288	154.90	361.40	0.47	204.80	204.30
2004	4 394	181.19	163.30	0.69	225.70	230.97
2005	4 430	210.80	297.50	1.04	309.70	330.30
2006	32 232	232.72	418.74	1.21	325.82	375.52
2007	14 139	425.53	397.79	2.38	327.00	365.55
2008	17 910	363.57	599.87	3.65	300.19	350.14
2009	18 912	358.54	682.69	7.14	307.89	346.38
2010	26 170	442.66	662.04	8.17	300.04	333.46
2011	29 337	530.80	511.52	20.80	318.27	332.19

12-14 续表4
continued

年　份 Year	金属切削机床（台） Metal-cutting Machine Tools(unit)	锻压机械（台） Metal Forming Machinery(unit)	汽　车（辆） Motor Vehicles (set)	交流电动机（万千瓦） AC Motors (10000 kW)
1949				0.02
1952	105			0.50
1957	76			3.61
1962	167	77		3.85
1965	526	111	13	6.48
1970	2 353	531	120	14.53
1975	3 213	788	490	15.56
1978	2 558	379	22	21.72
1980	595	444	1 644	20.11
1985	900	607	4 575	26.08
1987	1 175	887	2 304	27.02
1988	1 336	737	3 722	39.60
1989	1 107	1 010	3 404	38.60
1990	1 049	440	2 317	34.28
1991	869	764	1 514	44.17
1992	1 018	982	3 287	61.08
1993	1 532	919	4 828	64.13
1994	1 505	860	2 793	37.71
1995	972	2 563	5 210	39.18
1996	1 084	584	12 247	22.65
1997	449	416	13 020	20.74
1998	280		15 475	6.43
1999	251		20 038	11.10
2000	384		30 053	38.70
2001	472	2 477	40 658	42.72
2002	588		70 079	68.25
2003	990		65 612	95.63
2004	1 287		62 572	96.13
2005	1 347		31 055	63.50
2006	3 636		50 278	702.02
2007	3 392	1 869	61 016	119.23
2008	8 381	1 230	70 161	96.89
2009	668		458 779	113.53
2010	1 120		566 211	101.10
2011	6 520		488 838	96.37

12－14 续表5
continued

年　份 Year	钢芯铝绞线(吨) Steel-cored Aluminum Stranded Wire(ton)	家用电冰箱(万台) Home Refrigerators (10000 sets)	家用洗衣机(万台) Home Washing Machines (10000 sets)	彩色电视机(万部) Color TV Sets (10000 sets)
1949				
1952				
1957				
1962				
1965	250			
1970	34			
1975	188			
1978	684			
1980	1 232			
1985	2 327	1.66	0.48	6.60
1987	2 849	9.08	22.08	14.20
1988	1 571	15.22	42.38	17.00
1989	2 805	21.65	35.02	18.11
1990	1 880	27.41	45.86	18.50
1991	2 463	31.51	45.70	22.27
1992	2 248	54.84	46.31	28.07
1993	1 144	50.48	56.59	36.08
1994	287	62.50	71.34	60.15
1995	1 659	107.91	64.34	60.53
1996	2 265	193.80	100.94	56.68
1997	2 616	257.10	171.95	124.86
1998	1 725.3	219.23	183.67	96.83
1999	2 805.2	259.60	256.30	285.20
2000	4 201.5	311.10	318.50	379.40
2001	4 498	396.30	367.89	455.40
2002	5 825	518.20	408.60	593.20
2003	4 940	598.30	471.50	671.70
2004	6 608	815.03	575.06	957.90
2005	116 592	908.80	614.90	1 324.30
2006	46 974	1 290.00	649.40	1 205.60
2007	22 564	1 421.40	769.40	1 243.10
2008	29 507	723.19	407.54	836.66
2009		675.71	488.72	1 064.70
2010		801.22	580.87	1 111.19
2011		718.54	604.55	1 154.20

12－15 规模以上工业主要产品产量

OUTPUT OF MAJOR INDUSTRIAL PRODUCTS OF INDUSTRY ABOVE DESIGNATED SIZE

产品名称	Name	计量单位	Unit	2011	2010	2011 年比 2010 年（±%） 2011/2010（±%）
冶金工业产品	**Products of Metallurgical Industry**					
粗钢	Crude Steel	万吨	10000 tons	318.27	300.04	6.07
钢材	Rolled-steel	万吨	10000 tons	332.20	313.11	6.10
耐火材料制品	Refractory Material	万吨	10000 tons	20.80	15.5	34.24
电力工业产品	**Products of Electricity Industry**					
发电量	Electricity	亿千瓦小时	100 million kW·h	173.69	182.27	-4.71
化学工业产品	**Products of Chemical Industry**					
原油加工量	Processing Amount of Crude Oil	万吨	10000 tons	1 273.66	1 362.51	-6.52
汽油	Petrol	万吨	10000 tons	316.42	348.56	-9.22
柴油	Diesel Oil	万吨	10000 tons	517.56	546.68	-5.33
燃料油	Fuel Oil	万吨	10000 tons	16.62	22.31	-25.51
硫酸	Sulfuric Acid	万吨	10000 tons	5.06	4.07	24.32
纯碱	Soda Ash	万吨	10000 tons	72.07	69.35	3.92
烧碱	Caustic Soda	万吨	10000 tons	13.20	13.87	-4.79
农用化肥（100%）	Ag-fertilizer（100%）	万吨	10000 tons	9.26	14.10	-34.34
合成氨	Synthetic Ammonia	万吨	10000 tons	10.78	16.84	-36.01
化学农药	Chemical Pesticides	万吨	10000 tons	1.73	1.31	31.96
染料	Dye	吨	ton		41 383	
油漆	Paint	吨	ton			
塑料制品	Plastic	吨	ton	268 424.67	220 289.35	21.85
化学药品（原料）	Chemical Medicines（Raw Materials）	吨	ton	29 337	19 934	47.17

12－15 续表 1
continued

产品名称	Name	计量单位	Unit	2011	2010	2011 年比 2010 年 (±%) 2011/2010 (±%)
橡胶轮胎外胎	Tires	万条	10000 tires	4 441.59	3 851.91	15.31
机械工业产品	**Products of Machinery Industry**					
工业锅炉	Industrial Boiler	蒸发量吨	ton(evaporation amount)	5 976	1 164.6	413.14
交流电动机	AC Motors	万千瓦	10000 kW	96.37	97.75	-1.41
钢芯铝绞线	Steel-cored Aluminum Stranded Wire	吨	ton			
金属切削机床	Metal-cutting Machine	台	set	6 520	6 124	6.47
汽车	Motor Vehicles	辆	set	488 838	565 114	-13.5
改装汽车	Refitted Motor Vehicles	辆	set	17 548	20 697	-15.21
客车	Passenger Cars	辆	set	508	793	-35.94
民用钢质船舶	Civil Steel Ships	载重吨	syn-ton	1 645 516	1 341 700	22.64
电子产品	**Electronic Products**					
电视机	Television Sets	万部	10000 sets	1 154.2	1 111.19	3.87
#彩电	Color TV Sets	万部	10000 sets	310.18	368.95	-15.93
程控交换机	Program-controlled Switchboards	万线	10000 lines	173 979.45	121 646.8	43.02
电子元件	Electronics	万只	10000 units	1.88	1.94	-3.09
集成电路	Semiconductor Integrated Circuits	万块	10000 pieces			
建材工业产品	**Products of Construction Industry**					
水泥	Cement	万吨	10000 tons	530.8	446.19	18.96
平板玻璃	Plate Glass	万重量箱	10000 weight cases	511.52	660.92	-22.60
砖(折标准砖)	Bricks	万块	10000 pieces	44 975.8	35 911	25.24

12 -15 续表 2
continued

产品名称	Name	计量单位	Unit	2011	2010	2011 年比 2010 年 (±%) 2011/2010 (±%)
纺织工业产品	**Products of Textile Industry**					
纱	Yarn	吨	ton	19 398	16 054	20.83
布	Cloth	万米	10000 m	43 915.69	16 714.51	162.74
印染布	Printed Fabric	万米	10000 m	29 166.45	27 377.97	6.53
帘子布	Cord Fabrics	吨	ton	2 756.73	1 670	65.07
化学纤维	Chemical Fibers	万吨	10000 tons	3.86	3.84	0.5
轻工产品	**Products of Light Industry**					
机制纸及纸板	Machine-made Paper and Paperboards	万吨	10000 tons	29.59	16.48	79.56
家用洗衣机	Home Washing Machines	万台	10000 sets	604.55	580.87	4.08
原盐	Salt	万吨	10000 tons		11.25	
糖果	Sugar	万吨	10000 tons	18 417	5 633	226.95
卷烟	Cigarette	万箱	10000 cases	104.51	102.55	1.92
食用植物油	Vegetable Oil	万吨	10000 tons	36.1	46.16	-21.79
饮料酒	Beverage Liquor	万吨	10000 tons	164.04	156.5	9.98
#白酒	Wine	万吨	10000 tons	1.13	0.81	38.53
#啤酒	Beer	万吨	10000 tons	156.5	143.27	9.24
塑料制品	Plastic Products	吨	ton	268 424.67	220 289.35	21.85
家具	Furniture	万件	10000 units	630.71	559.68	12.69
家用电冰箱	Home Refrigerators	万台	10000 sets	718.54	795.34	-9.66
皮革鞋靴	Leather Shoes	万双	10000 pairs	7 883.58	5 927.34	33.00
服装	Clothing	万件	10000 articles	80 971.05	72 644.15	11.46

12－16 规模以上工业主要产品生产能力
PRODUCTION CAPACITY OF MAJOR PRODUCTS OF INDUSTRY ABOVE DESIGNATED SIZE

产品名称	Name	计算单位	Unit	2011 生产能力 Production Capacity of 2011	2010 生产能力 Production Capacity of 2010
发电设备容量总计/发电量	Total Capacity of Generation Equipment	万千瓦/万千瓦小时	10000 kW/10000 kW·h	349	350
卷烟	Cigarettes	万支	10000 pieces	7 074 000	7 074 000
化学纤维	Chemical Fiber	吨	ton	60 145	52 600
棉纺锭/纺纱量	Knitting Spindle	锭/吨	spindle/ton	135 632	98 104
气流纺锭/纺纱量	Rotor Spindle	头/吨	spindle/ton		400
棉布织机/布	Cotton Cloth Loom	台/万米	set/10000 m	52 100	49 039
焦炭	Coke	吨	ton	1 020 000	1 020 000
农用氮、磷、钾化学肥料总计(折纯)	Chemical Fertilizer	吨	ton	329 520	340 060
水泥	Cement	吨	ton	7 960 000	6 940 000
平板玻璃	Plate Glass	重量箱	weight cases	9 225 000	10 225 000
生铁	Pig Iron	吨	ton	4 000 000	4 000 000
粗钢	Crude Steel	吨	ton	4 000 000	4 000 000
钢材	Rolled-steel	吨	ton	3 945 000	4 281 600
金属切削机床	Metal-cutting Machine	台	set	1 670	1 270
汽车	Motor Vehicles	辆	set	575 000	522 347
家用电冰箱	Home Refrigerators	台	set	8 400 000	9 630 000
房间空气调节器	Air Conditioner	台	set	7 000 000	7 230 000
移动通信手持机(手机)	Cell Phone	台	set	41 800 000	41 600 000
彩色电视机	Color TV Sets	台	set	13 600 000	12 700 000

主要统计指标解释

工业总产值　是以货币表现的工业企业在一定时期内生产的已出售或可供出售工业产品总量，它是反映一定时间内工业生产的总规模和总水平。

工业销售产值　是以货币表现的工业企业在一定时期内销售的本企业生产的工业产品产量。包括已销售的成品、半成品价值，以及对外提供的工业性作业价值和对本单位基本建设部门、生活福利部门等提供的产品和工业性作业及自制设备的价值。

工业增加值　指工业企业在报告期内以货币表现的工业生产活动的最终成果。是企业全部生产活动的总成果扣除了在生产过程中消耗或转移的物质产品和劳务价值后的余额，是企业生产过程中新增加的价值。

资产总计　指企业拥有或控制的能以货币计量的经济资源，包括各种财产、债权和其他权利。资产按其流动性（即资产的变现能力和支付能力）划分为：流动资产、长期投资、固定资产、无形资产、递延资产和其他资产。

负债合计　指企业所承担的能以货币计量，将以资产或劳务偿付的债务，偿还形式包括货币、资产或提供劳务。负债一般按偿还期长短分为流动负债和长期负债。

利润总额　指企业生产经营活动的最终成果，是企业在一定时期内实现的盈亏相抵后的利润总额（亏损以“－”号表示），它等于营业利润加上补贴收入加上投资收益加上营业外净收入再加上以前年度损益调整。

Explanatory Notes on Main Statistical Indicators

Gross Industrial Output Value　is the total volume of final industrial products produced and industrial services provided during a given period. It reflects the total achievements and overall scale of industrial production during a given period.

Sales Output Value of Industry　refers to total sales of products produced by industrial enterprises during a given period, including sales of fished goods, value of semi-products, value of industrial services provided to other units, value of products, industrial services provided for capital construction sector, welfare and self produced equipments within enterprise.

Value-added of Industry　refers to the final results of industrial production of industrial enterprises in money terms during the reference period.

Total Assets　refer to all economic resources, in monetary terms, that is owned or controlled by enterprises, including properties, creditors equity and other economic rights of all forms. Classified by the degree of equitability, total assets include circulating assets, long-term investment, fixed assets, intangible assets and deferred assets, and other assets.

Total Liabilities　refer to payable liabilities of enterprises that have to repay in terms of money, assets or labour services. In terms of payment, it can be divided into liquid liabilities and long-term liabilities.

Total Profits　refer to the final achievements of production and operation of the enterprises, represented by the total profits after deducting losses (loss is expressed by the negative figure). It is the sum of profits from operation, income from subsidies, investment earnings, net income from activities other than operation, and adjustment of profits and losses of previous years.

建筑业 13

CONSTRUCTION

简要说明

一、本篇资料的主要内容

本篇资料主要反映了全市建筑业基本情况，主要包括建筑业总产值、增加值、建筑企业生产指标、财务指标、重点建筑企业名单等方面的内容。

二、本篇资料的来源

本篇资料来源于建筑业统计年报，由市统计局固定资产投资统计处整理提供。

Brief Introduction

I. Main Content

Data in this chapter show the basic conditions of construction of the whole city, mainly including the gross output value of construction, value added, major production and financial indicators and list of key enterprises of construction, etc.

II. Source of Data

Data in this chapter are based on the annual report of construction industry, and complied by the Division of Investment and Construction Statistics of Qingdao Municipal Bureau of Statistics.

13－1 建筑业企业生产情况(2011 年)
PRODUCTION SITUATION OF CONSTRUCTION ENTERPRISES(2011)

项 目	Item	单位	Unit	合计 Total	#中央 of which: Central Enterprises	国有企业 State-owned Enterprises	集体企业 Collective-owned Enterprises	其他所有制企业 Other Ownership Enterprises
施工企业单位数	Number of Construction Enterprises	个	unit	584	7	31	24	529
建筑业总产值	Gross Output Value of Construction	万元	10000 yuan	9 031 344	1 823 986	1 150 432	65 808	7 815 104
#建筑工程	of which: Construction	万元	10000 yuan	7 926 658	1 526 445	826 322	60 372	7 039 964
安装工程	Installation	万元	10000 yuan	884 709	297 541	315 855	5 031	563 823
建筑业增加值	Value Added of Construction	万元	10000 yuan	3 561 600				
全年竣工产值	Output Value of Buildings Completed in the Year	万元	10000 yuan	3 997 034	379 995	459 596	53 374	3 484 064
施工房屋面积	Floor Space of Buildings under Construction	万平方米	10000 sq. m	7 126	695	668	32	6 426
#新开工	of which: Newly Operating	万平方米	10000 sq. m	3 091	270	239	22	2 830
投标承包	Bidding and Contracting	万平方米	10000 sq. m	5 296	695	661	28	4 607
竣工房屋面积	Floor Space of Buildings Completed	万平方米	10000 sq. m	1 717	137	131	17	1 569
#住宅	of which: Residential Buildings	万平方米	10000 sq. m	1 108	96	100	10	998
年末自有施工机械设备台数	Number of Machinery and Equipment Owned (year-end)	台	set	56 078	4 229	4 207	971	50 900
年末自有施工机械设备净值	Net Value of Machinery and Equipment Owned (year-end)	万元	10000 yuan	302 828	81 342	37 945	1 960	262 923
年末自有施工机械设备总功率	Total Power of Machinery and Equipment Owned(year-end)	万千瓦	10000 kw	144	30	28	1	115
计算建筑业劳动生产率平均人数	Average Number of Persons for Calculating the Labor Productivity	人	person	328 375	33 075	32 149	1 954	294 272

13 -2 建筑业企业财务状况(2011 年)
FINANCIAL SITUATION OF CONSTRUCTION ENTERPRISES(2011)

项 目	Item	单位	Unit	合计 Total
流动资产	Circulating Funds	万元	10000 yuan	6 321 428
#存货	of which:Inventory	万元	10000 yuan	1 099 777
年末固定资产原价	Original Value of Fixed Assets(year-end)	万元	10000 yuan	1 263 913
本年固定资产折旧	Depreciation of Fixed Assets in the Year	万元	10000 yuan	82 213
年末固定资产净值	Net Value of Fixed Assets(year-end)	万元	10000 yuan	752 855
年末资产合计	Total Assets(year-end)	万元	10000 yuan	8 215 785
年末负债合计	Total Liabilities(year-end)	万元	10000 yuan	5 596 537
所有者权益合计	Total Owners' Equity	万元	10000 yuan	2 619 247
#实收资本	Paid-in Capitals	万元	10000 yuan	1 613 906
主营业务收入	Revenue from Principal Business	万元	10000 yuan	8 332 623
主营业务成本	Cost of Principal Business	万元	10000 yuan	7 448 777
主营业务税金及附加	Taxes and Extra Charges on Principal Business	万元	10000 yuan	229 903
管理费用	Management Expenses	万元	10000 yuan	276 355
利润总额	Total Profits	万元	10000 yuan	303 823
利税总额	Total Pre-tax Profits	万元	10000 yuan	544 897
年末应收工程款	Account Receivable(year-end)	万元	10000 yuan	1 971 954
#其中:竣工工程	of which:Projects Completed	万元	10000 yuan	760 283

#中央 of which: Central Enterprises	国有企业 State-owned Enterprises	集体企业 Collective-owned Enterprises	其他所有制企业 Other Ownership Enterprises
1 318 056	848 475	60 194	5 412 759
213 111	147 842	10 132	941 803
351 928	265 445	19 343	979 125
34 234	23 393	1 092	57 728
166 791	156 755	12 485	583 615
1 588 048	1 030 338	82 011	7 103 436
1 357 200	819 293	36 674	4 740 570
230 848	211 046	45 338	2 362 863
159 665	142 952	22 516	1 448 438
1 922 107	1 272 043	58 759	7 001 821
1 732 341	1 151 210	52 131	6 245 436
50 573	24 283	1 898	203 722
70 922	48 911	2 859	224 585
43 552	36 244	1 370	266 209
95 390	61 406	3 643	479 848
447 333	244 162	16 506	1 711 286
110 313	87 210	7 199	665 874

13 -3 建筑业企业主要经济效益指标(2011 年)
MAIN INDICATORS ON ECONOMIC BENEFIT OF CONSTRUCTION ENTERPRISES(2011)

项　目	Item	单位	Unit	合计 Total	#中央 of which: Central Enterprises	国有企业 State-owned Enterprises	集体企业 Collective-owned Enterprises	其他所有制企业 Other Ownership Enterprises
建筑业劳动生产率	Labor Productivity of Construction							
按总产值计算	In Terms of Gross Output Value	元/人	yuan/person	275 023	551 469	361 498	339 217	265 260
竣工率	Rate of Buildings Completed							
按产值计算	In Terms of Gross Output Value	%	%	44.3	20.8	39.9	81.1	44.6
产值工资率	Ratio of Wages to Gross Output Value	%	%	6.6	5.5	6.2	11.8	6.6
资金利润率	Ratio of Profit to Funds	%	%	4.3	1.6	2.0	1.0	4.4
产值利润率	Ratio of Profit to Gross Output Value	%	%	3.4	2.4	3.2	2.1	3.4
技术装备率	Value of Machines per Laborer	元/人	yuan/person	9 222	24 593	11 802	10 030	8 934
流动比率	Current Ratio	%	%	124.8	101.5	105.9	168.2	128.0
资产负债率	Assets-Liability Ratio	%	%	68.1	85.5	79.5	44.7	66.7

13 -4 建筑业增加值(2011 年)
VALUE ADDED OF CONSTRUCTION(2011)

单位:亿元(100 million yuan)

市、区名称	Region	增加值 Value Added
总 计	Total	356.16
市南区	Shinan District	28.05
市北区	Shibei District	23.50
四方区	Sifang District	13.98
李沧区	Licang District	11.33
崂山区	Laoshan District	23.14
黄岛区	Huangdao District	49.99
城阳区	Chengyang District	33.52
即墨市	Jimo	38.43
胶州市	Jiaozhou	40.16
胶南市	Jiaonan	37.54
平度市	Pingdu	27.95
莱西市	Laixi	28.57

13 -5 重点建筑企业一览表(2011 年)
LIST OF KEY CONSTRUCTION ENTERPRISES(2011)

序号 Precedence	企业单位名称	Name	所在地区 Location		资质等级 Qualification Criteria
1	中交一航局第二工程有限公司	China Communications 1nd Navigational Bureau 2nd Engineering Co. , Ltd.	市南区	Shinan	A104
2	青建集团股份公司	Qingjian Group Co. ,Ltd.	市北区	Shibei	A001
3	青岛海尔家居集成股份有限公司	Qingdao Haier Home Corp.	崂山区	Laoshan	B103
4	中铁二十局集团第四工程有限公司	China Railway 20th Bureau Group 4th Engineering Co. ,Ltd.	崂山区	Laoshan	A103
5	中启胶建集团有限公司	Zhongqi Jiaozhou Construction Group Co. ,Ltd.	胶州市	Jiaozhou	A001
6	青岛海川建设集团有限公司	Qingdao Haichuan Construction Group Co. ,Ltd.	市北区	Shibei	A101
7	中国石油天然气第七建设公司	China Petroluem 7th Construction Company	胶州市	Jiaozhou	A109
8	青岛一建集团有限公司	Qingdao Yijian Group Co. ,Ltd.	四方区	Sifang	A101
9	中建八局第四建设有限公司	China Construction 8th Devision Corp. Ltd. (Qingdao Branch)	市南区	Shinan	A101
10	山东莱钢建设有限公司	Shandong Laigang Gonstruction Co. ,Ltd.	市南区	Shinan	A108
11	青岛建安建设集团有限公司	Qingdao Jian' an Construction Group Co. ,Ltd.	市南区	Shinan	A101
12	青岛温泉建设集团有限公司	Qingdao Hot Spring Construction Group Co. ,Ltd.	即墨市	Jimo	A101
13	青岛建设集团零零一工程有限公司	Qingdao Construction Group 001 Engineering Co. ,Ltd.	市南区	Shinan	A101
14	莱西市建筑总公司	Laixi Construction Corp.	莱西市	Laixi	A001
15	山东兴华建设集团有限公司	Shandong Xinghua Construction Co. ,Ltd.	黄岛区	Huangdao	A101
16	青岛公路建设集团有限公司	Qingdao Highway Construction Group Co. ,Ltd.	四方区	Sifang	A102
17	青岛福瀛建设集团有限公司	Qingdao Fuying Construction Group Co. ,Ltd.	黄岛区	Huangdao	A101
18	中建筑港集团有限公司	China State Construction Port Engineering Group Co. ,Ltd.	四方区	Sifang	A104
19	通广建工集团有限公司	Qingdao Tongguang Construction Engineering Co. ,Ltd.	即墨市	Jimo	A001
20	青岛城建集团有限公司	Qingdao City Construction Co. ,Ltd.	四方区	Sifang	A110
21	青岛建工集团有限公司	Qingdao Jiangong Group Co. ,Ltd.	崂山区	Laoshan	A102
22	青岛新华友建工集团股份有限公司	Qingdao Xinhuayou Construction Engineering Group Co. ,Ltd.	市北区	Shibei	A101
23	山东省路通工程集团有限公司	Shandong Lutong Engineering Group Co. ,Ltd.	崂山区	Laoshan	A102
24	青岛第一市政工程有限公司	Qingdao No. 1 Municipal Construction Engineering Co. ,Ltd.	四方区	Sifang	A110
25	青岛胶城建设集团有限公司	Qingdao Jiaocheng Construction Co. ,Ltd.	胶州市	Jiaozhou	A101
26	青岛瑞源工程集团有限公司	Qingdao Ruiyuan Engineering Group Co. ,Ltd.	黄岛区	Huangdao	A105
27	青岛土木建工集团有限公司	Qingdao Yinghai Construction Co. ,Ltd.	黄岛区	Huangdao	A101
28	青岛安装建设股份有限公司	Qingdao Installation and Construction Co. ,Ltd.	四方区	Sifang	A112
29	青岛平建建筑安装股份有限公司	Qingdao Pingjian Construction and Installation Co. , Ltd.	平度市	Pingdu	A101
30	青岛东亚建筑装饰有限公司	Qingdao Feiyu Construction and Decoration Co. ,Ltd.	市南区	Shinan	B103
31	青岛德才装饰安装工程有限公司	Qingdao Decai Decoration and Installation Engineering Co. ,Ltd.	市南区	Shinan	B103
32	青岛亿联集团股份有限公司	Qingdao Yilian Group Co. ,Ltd.	胶南市	Jiaonan	A101
33	青岛滨海建设集团有限公司	Qingdao Binhai Construction Group Co. ,Ltd.	黄岛区	Huangdao	A101

13 -5 续表 1
continued

序号 Precedence	企业单位名称	Name	所在地区 Location		资质等级 Qualification Criteria
34	青岛恒生源集团建设有限公司	Qingdao Hengshengyuan Construction Engineering Co. ,Ltd.	即墨市	Jimo	A101
35	青岛建祥建设集团有限公司	Qingdao Jianxiang Construction Group Co. ,Ltd.	胶州市	Jiaozhou	A201
36	青岛三林建筑工程有限公司	Qingdao Sanlin Construction Engineering Co. ,Ltd.	胶南市	Jiaonan	A201
37	青岛营上建设集团有限公司	Qingdao Yingshang Construction Co. ,Ltd.	即墨市	Jimo	A101
38	山东巴龙建设集团有限公司	Shandong Ballon Construction Group Co. ,Ltd.	市南区	Shinan	A201
39	青岛星火建筑工程有限公司	Qingdao Xinghuo Construction Engineering Co. ,Ltd.	胶南市	Jiaonan	A301
40	青岛环海工程贸易发展有限公司	Qingdao Huanhai Enginnering Trade Development Co. ,Ltd.	市北区	Shibei	A201
41	山东兴华建设集团胶南工程有限公司	Shandong Xinghua Construction Group Jiaonan Enginnering Co. ,Ltd.	黄岛区	Huangdao	A301
42	青岛四机建筑安装有限公司	Qingdao Siji Construction and Installation Co. ,Ltd.	四方区	Sifang	B201
43	青岛新城发展建筑工程有限公司	Qingdao New City Development Construction Engineering Co. ,Ltd.	市北区	Shibei	A201
44	青岛港务局港务工程公司	Qingdao Port Engineering Co. ,Ltd.	黄岛区	Huangdao	A204
45	青岛昶德建设集团有限公司	Qingdao Changde Construction Co. ,Ltd.	胶州市	Jiaozhou	A101
46	青岛地矿岩土工程有限公司	Qingdao Mine Engineering Co. ,Ltd.	市南区	Shinan	B101
47	青岛营海建设集团有限公司	Qingdao Civil Engineering Group Co. ,Ltd.	胶州市	Jiaozhou	A101
48	青岛青房建安集团有限公司	Qingdao Qingfang Construction and Installation Co. ,Ltd.	市南区	Shinan	A101
49	青岛恒源送变电工程有限公司	Qingdao Hengyuan Transmission and Distribution Project Co. ,Ltd.	城阳区	Chengyang	A201
50	青岛市一宅建筑集团股份有限公司	Qingdao Yizhai Construction Co. ,Ltd.	市北区	Shibei	A101
51	青岛德泰建设工程有限公司	Qingdao Detai Construction Engineering Co. ,Ltd.	黄岛区	Huangdao	A101
52	青岛豪斯建设工程有限公司	Qingdao Haosi Construction Co. ,Ltd.	崂山区	Laoshan	A101
53	青岛九龙建设集团有限公司	Qingdao Jiulong Construction Co. ,Ltd.	胶州市	Jiaozhou	A201
54	青岛天柱燃气工程公司	Qingdao Tianzhu Gas Enginnering Co. ,Ltd.	平度市	Pingdu	A310
55	青岛望城三宝建设有限公司	Qingdao Wangcheng Sanbao Construction Co. ,Ltd.	莱西市	Laixi	A101
56	青岛市泽惠建设集团有限公司	Qingdao Huize Construction Co. ,Ltd.	城阳区	Chengyang	A101
57	青岛金沙滩建设集团有限公司	Qingdao Jinsha Beach Construction Co. ,Ltd.	黄岛区	Huangdao	A101
58	青岛海德路桥工程股份有限公司	Qingdao Haide Highway & Bridge Engineering Co. ,Ltd.	市南区	Shinan	A210
59	胶州市阳光建筑有限公司	Jiaozhou Sunshine Construction Co. ,Ltd.	胶州市	Jiaozhou	A201
60	胶南市建筑工程公司	Jiaonan Construction Engineering Co. ,Ltd.	胶南市	Jiaonan	A101
61	青岛胶东建设集团有限公司	Qingdao Jiaodong Construction Co. ,Ltd.	胶州市	Jiaozhou	A201
62	青岛建国工程集团有限公司	Qingdao Jianguo Engineering Co. ,Ltd.	黄岛区	Huangdao	A201
63	青岛凯顺建设集团有限公司	Qingdao Kaishun Construction Group Co. ,Ltd.	胶州市	Jiaozhou	A201
64	青岛市热电工程公司	Qingdao Thermal Power Engineering Co. ,Ltd.	市北区	Shibei	A210
65	青岛经济技术开发区建筑安装工程总公司	Qingdao Development Zone Construction and Installation Co. ,Ltd.	黄岛区	Huangdao	A201
66	青岛施运机械施工有限责任公司	Qingdao Shiyun Mechanized Construction Co. ,Ltd.	四方区	Sifang	B101

13 -5 续表 2
continued

序号 Precedence	企业单位名称	Name	所在地区 Location		资质等级 Qualification Criteria
67	青岛康太源建设集团有限公司	Qingdao Kangtaiyuan Construction Group Co. ,Ltd.	李沧区	Licang	A101
68	青岛亿佰建筑工程有限公司	Qingdao Yibai Construction Engineering Co. ,Ltd.	胶南市	Jiaonan	A201
69	青岛铁路工程建筑有限公司	Qingdao Railway Engineering Co. ,Ltd.	市南区	Shinan	A203
70	青岛中奥体育专用地板有限公司	Qingdao Zhongao Sport Wooden Floor Co. ,Ltd.	平度市	Pingdu	B359
71	青岛颐金建筑装饰工程有限公司	Qingdao Yijin Construction and Installation Co. , Ltd.	市南区	Shinan	B103
72	山东省即墨市第二建筑工程公司	Shandong Jimo 2nd Construction Project Co. ,Ltd.	即墨市	Jimo	A201
73	青岛高新建筑安装工程有限公司	Qingdao Gaoxin Construction and Installation Co. , Ltd.	崂山区	Laoshan	A101
74	山东国建建设工程有限公司	Shandong Guojian Construction Project Co. ,Ltd.	崂山区	Laoshan	B201
75	青岛胶州南关建安股份有限公司	Qingdao Jiaonan Nanguan Construction and Installation Co. ,Ltd.	胶州市	Jiaozhou	A201
76	青岛市市政工程集团有限公司	Qingdao Municipal Engineering Co. ,Ltd.	市南区	Shinan	A110
77	青岛鲁赫建筑装饰有限公司	Qingdao Luhe Construction and Decoration Co. ,Ltd.	市南区	Shinan	B203
78	青岛新奥燃气设施开发有限公司	Qingdao ENN Gas Facilities Development Co. ,Ltd.	黄岛区	Huangdao	B225
79	青岛宝利建设有限公司	Qingdao Baoli Construction Co. ,Ltd.	莱西市	Laixi	A201
80	青岛飞宇建设集团有限公司	Qingdao Feiyu Construction Engineering Co. ,Ltd.	胶南市	Jiaonan	A301
81	青岛福海洋建设集团有限公司	Qingdao Fuhaiyuang Construction Co. ,ltd.	胶州市	Jiaozhou	A201
82	青岛隆昌达建筑安装有限公司	Qingdao Longchangda Construction and Installation Co. ,Ltd.	胶州市	Jiaozhou	A201
83	青岛洋河建设集团有限公司	Qingdao Yanghe Construction Group Co. ,Ltd.	胶州市	Jiaozhou	A201
84	青岛铁路红宇建设集团有限公司	Qingdao Railway Hongyu Construction Group Co. , Ltd.	市南区	Shinan	A301
85	青岛田横建筑工程有限公司	Qingdao Tianheng Construction Project Co. ,Ltd.	即墨市	Jimo	A201
86	青岛建设装饰集团有限公司	Qingdao Construction and Decoration Co. ,Ltd.	市南区	Shinan	B103
87	青岛爱华工程有限公司	Qingdao Aihua Engineering Co. ,Ltd.	市北区	Shibei	A201
88	青岛市李沧区东大建筑公司	Qingdao Licang Dongda Construction Co. ,Ltd.	李沧区	Licang	A301
89	青岛政益达实业有限公司	Qingdao Zhengyida Industrial Co. ,Ltd.	市北区	Shibei	A210
90	青岛岳海建设集团有限公司	Qingdao Yuehai Construction Group Co. ,Ltd.	市南区	Shinan	A101
91	平度市金泰建筑有限公司	Pingdu Jintai Construction Co. ,Ltd.	平度市	Pingdu	A201
92	青岛九鼎峰建设集团有限公司	Qingdao Jiudingfeng Construction Co. ,Ltd.	黄岛区	Huangdao	A201
93	青岛一建集团永和工程有限公司	Qingdao 1st Construction Group Yonghe Enginnering Co. ,Ltd.	即墨市	Jimo	A201
94	青岛经济技术开发区市政工程总公司	Qingdao Development Zone Municipal Administration Engineering Co. ,Ltd.	黄岛区	Huangdao	A210
95	青岛通盛达建筑工程有限公司	Qingdao Tongshengda Construction Engineering Co. ,Ltd.	即墨市	Jimo	A201
96	青岛鸿润建设集团有限公司	Qingdao Hongrun Construction Group Co. ,Ltd.	黄岛区	Huangdao	A201
97	青岛润杰建筑工程有限公司	Qingdao Runjie Construction Engineering Co. , Ltd.	莱西市	Laixi	A301
98	青岛鑫隆建设集团有限公司	Qingdao Xinlong Construction Group Co. ,Ltd.	黄岛区	Huangdao	A101
99	青岛金楷装饰工程有限公司	Qingdao Jinkai Decoration Engineering Co. ,Ltd.	市北区	Shibei	B202

13－5 续表 3
continued

序号 Precedence	企业单位名称	Name	所在地区 Location		资质等级 Qualification Criteria
100	青岛市黄岛区园林绿化工程有限公司	Qingdao Huangdao Green Enginnering Co. , Ltd.	黄岛区	Huangdao	B101
101	青岛鑫鸿泰建设工程有限公司	Qingdao Hongxintai Construction Engineering Co. , Ltd.	胶州市	Jiaozhou	A201
102	青岛新世纪路桥工程有限公司	Qingdao New Century Highway & Bridge Engineering Co. , Ltd.	即墨市	Jimo	A202
103	青岛嘉和建造有限公司	Qingdao Jiahe Construcion Co. , Ltd.	即墨市	Jimo	A201
104	山东红建建安集团公司	Shandong Hongjian Construction and Installation Co. , Ltd.	黄岛区	Huangdao	A201
105	青岛胶州水利工程有限公司	Qingdao Jiaozhou Water Engineering Co. , Ltd.	胶州市	Jiaozhou	A205
106	青岛胶州湾建设集团有限公司	Qingdao Jiaozhou Bay Construction Co. , Ltd.	胶州市	Jiaozhou	A101
107	青岛环城建工集团有限公司	Qingdao Huancheng Construction Engineering Group Co. , Ltd.	黄岛区	Huangdao	A201
108	青岛东恒建筑工程有限公司	Qingdao Dongheng Construction Engineering Co. , Ltd.	胶南市	Jiaonan	A201
109	青岛晶城设计装饰工程有限公司	Qingdao Jingcheng Design and Decoration Enginnering Co. , Ltd.	市南区	Shinan	B103
110	青岛盈鑫建设集团有限公司	Qingdao Yingxin Construction Co. , Ltd.	城阳区	Chengyang	A201
111	青岛城阳兴源建筑工程有限公司	Qingdao Chengyang Xingyuan Construction Co. , Ltd.	城阳区	Chengyang	A301
112	青岛莱西九联建筑工程有限公司	Qingdao Laixi Jiulian Construction Project Co. , Ltd.	莱西市	Laixi	A201
113	胶南市公用事业工程公司	Jiaonan Public Service Enginnering Co. , Ltd.	胶南市	Jiaonan	A310
114	青岛多元建设集团有限公司	Qingdao Duoyuan Construction Group Co. , Ltd.	黄岛区	Huangdao	A210
115	平度市永盛建筑有限公司	Pingdu Yongsheng Construction Co. , Ltd.	平度市	Pingdu	A301
116	青岛天一建设集团有限公司	Qingdao Tianyi Construction Group Co. , Ltd.	胶南市	Jiaonan	A201
117	平度市引黄济青建筑安装工程公司	Pingdu Yin Huang Ji Qing Construction and Installation Engineering Corp.	平度市	Pingdu	A205
118	青岛光大集团工程有限公司	Qingdao Guangda Group Co. , Ltd.	胶南市	Jiaonan	A201
119	青岛通力建设集团有限公司	Qingdao Tongli Construction Group Co. , Ltd.	市南区	Shinan	A101
120	青岛城阳恒升建筑安装工程有限公司	Qingdao Chengyang Hengsheng Construction and Installation Co. , Ltd.	城阳区	Chengyang	A201
121	青岛增泉建设集团有限公司	Qingdao Zengquan Construction Group Co. , Ltd.	黄岛区	Huangdao	A201
122	青岛康大诚鑫建筑安装工程有限公司	Qingdao Kangda Chengxin Construction and Installation Co. , Ltd.	胶南市	Jiaonan	A301
123	青岛鲁城建设有限公司	Qingdao Lucheng Construction Co. , Ltd.	市南区	Shinan	A201
124	青岛市城阳区夏庄建筑工程有限公司	Qingdao Chengyang Xiazhuang Construction Engineering Co. , Ltd.	城阳区	Chengyang	A301
125	青岛市崂山区古建建筑工程有限公司	Qingdao Laoshan Gujian Construction Engineering Co. , Ltd.	崂山区	Laoshan	A201
126	青岛泓鑫源建筑安装工程有限公司	Qingdao Hongxinyuan Construction and Installion Project Co. , Ltd.	胶州市	Jiaozhou	A201
127	即墨市水利建筑安装工程公司	Jimo Water Construction and Installation Engineering Corp.	即墨市	Jimo	A205
128	青岛泰能工程股份有限公司	Qingdao Taineng Engineering Co. , Ltd.	四方区	Sifang	A210
129	青岛昊海建筑工程有限公司	Qingdao Haohai Construction Engineering Co. , Ltd.	莱西市	Laixi	A301
130	青岛市自来水物资工程公司	Qingdao Tap Water Project Co. , Ltd.	四方区	Sifang	A310
131	青岛伟信建设工程有限公司	Qingdao Weixin Construction Engineering Co. , Ltd.	平度市	Pingdu	A201
132	青岛金东建筑安装有限公司	Qingdao Jindong Construction and Installation Co. , Ltd.	莱西市	Laixi	A301

13 -5 续表4
continued

序号 Precedence	企业单位名称	Name	所在地区	Location	资质等级 Qualification Criteria
133	青岛市神州建筑工程有限公司	Qingdao Shenzhou Construction Engineering Co. ,Ltd.	胶州市	Jiaozhou	A201
134	平度市东苑建筑工程有限公司	Pingdu Dongyuan Construction Engineering Co. ,Ltd.	平度市	Pingdu	A201
135	青岛高科技工业园市政有限公司	Qingdao High-tech Industrial Park Municipal Co. , Ltd.	崂山区	Laoshan	A210
136	青岛经济技术开发区天龙建筑安装工程有限公司	Qingdao Development Zone Tianlong Construction and Installion Co. ,Ltd.	黄岛区	Huangdao	A201
137	青岛宇鑫锋建设工程有限公司	Qingdao Xinyufeng Construction Engineering Co. ,Ltd.	黄岛区	Huangdao	A210
138	青岛宏远建筑工程有限公司	Qingdao Hongyuan Construction Engineering Co. , Ltd.	莱西市	Laixi	A201
139	青岛环海建设集团有限公司	Qingdao Huanhai Construction Group Co. ,Ltd.	黄岛区	Huangdao	A201
140	青岛滨泰建筑工程有限公司	Qingdao Bintai Construction Co. ,Ltd.	莱西市	Laixi	A301
141	青岛新凯达市政工程有限公司	Qingdao Xinkaida Municipal Enginnering Co. , Ltd.	市北区	Shibei	A210
142	青岛东方铁塔安装工程有限公司	Qingdao Orient Iron Tower Project Co. ,Ltd.	胶州市	Jiaozhou	B108
143	青岛软控安装工程有限公司	Qingdao Mesnac Installation Engineering Co. ,Ltd.	四方区	Sifang	B253
144	青岛市益水工程股份有限公司	Qingdao Yishui Engineering Co. ,Ltd.	市南区	Shinan	A210
145	青岛市丰水市政工程有限公司	Qingdao Shunyuan Construction Engineering Co. ,Ltd.	即墨市	Jimo	A210
146	青岛泰华集团有限公司	Qingdao Taihua Group Co. ,Ltd.	胶南市	Jiaonan	A201
147	青岛天润工程有限公司	Qingdao Tianrun Enginnering Co. ,Ltd.	莱西市	Laixi	A305
148	山东省引黄济青青岛建筑安装有限公司	Shandong Yellow River Diversion Project Qingdao Construction and Installation Co. ,Ltd.	胶州市	Jiaozhou	B201
149	青岛润佳建筑工程有限公司	Qingdao Runjia Construction Project Co. ,Ltd.	即墨市	Jimo	A201
150	青岛即建建设集团有限公司	Qingdao Jijian Construction Group Co. ,Ltd.	即墨市	Jimo	A101
151	青岛市李沧区东李建筑工程有限公司	Qingdao Licang Dongli Construction Project Co. , Ltd.	李沧区	Licang	A201
152	青岛中天伟业建设工程有限公司	Qingdao Zhongtian Weiye Construction Engineering Co. ,Ltd.	黄岛区	Huangdao	A201
153	青岛润达建设工程有限公司	Qingdao Runda Construction Engineering Co. ,Ltd.	黄岛区	Huangdao	A210
154	即墨市七级建筑工程有限公司	Jimo 7-class Construction Engineering Co. ,Ltd.	即墨市	Jimo	A201
155	青岛凌云建设集团有限公司	Qingdao Lingyun Construction Co. ,Ltd.	胶州市	Jiaozhou	A201
156	青岛琅琊建筑有限公司	Qingdao Langyatai Construction Engineering Co. ,Ltd.	胶南市	Jiaonan	A201
157	青岛市市南区市政工程养护建设有限公司	Qingdao Shinan Municipal Engineering Construction Co. ,Ltd.	市南区	Shinan	A310
158	山东森泰源建设工程有限公司	Shandong Sentaiyuan Construction Engineering Co. ,Ltd.	黄岛区	Huangdao	A210
159	青岛新隆安建筑安装有限公司	Qingdao Xinlongan Construction and Installion Co. ,Ltd.	四方区	Sifang	A201
160	青岛暖万家市政工程有限公司	Qingdao Nuanwanjia Municipal Engineering Co. ,Ltd.	黄岛区	Huangdao	A210
161	青岛建泰建筑工程有限公司	Qingdao Jiantai Construction Co. ,Ltd.	黄岛区	Huangdao	A201
162	青岛市沙子口第二建筑工程有限公司	Qingdao Shazikou 2nd Construction Engineering Co. ,Ltd.	崂山区	Laoshan	A301
163	青岛市房产工程公司	Qingdao Real Estate Enginnering Co. ,Ltd.	市南区	Shinan	B103
164	青岛凯盛源建筑安装工程有限公司	Construction and Installation Co. ,Ltd.	平度市	Pingdu	A201
165	青岛市城阳区上马建筑工程有限公司	Qingdao Chengyang Shangma Construction Co. ,Ltd.	城阳区	Chengyang	A201

13 –5 续表 5
continued

序号 Precedence	企业单位名称	Name	所在地区 Location		资质等级 Qualification Criteria
166	青岛金原建筑工程有限公司	Qingdao Jinyuan Construction Co. ,Ltd.	胶南市	Jiaonan	A201
167	青岛恒瑞工程建设有限公司	Qingdao Hengrui Engineering Construction Co. ,Ltd.	黄岛区	Huangdao	A210
168	青岛静力工程有限公司	Qingdao Static Project Co. ,Ltd.	市南区	Shinan	B301
169	青岛易简电力工程有限公司	Qingdao Yijian Power Enginnering Co. ,Ltd.	莱西市	Laixi	B349
170	青岛经典建设工程有限公司	Qingdao Classical Construction Project Co. ,Ltd.	胶州市	Jiaozhou	A201
171	青岛恒辉建设工程有限公司	Qingdao Henghui Construction Enginnering Co. , Ltd.	黄岛区	Huangdao	A201
172	青岛易通建安有限公司	Qingdao Yitong Construction and Installation Co. ,Ltd.	黄岛区	Huangdao	A201
173	青岛平度市粮食局建筑公司	Qingdao Pingdu Grain Bureau Construction Co. , Ltd.	平度市	Pingdu	A301
174	青岛城阳太阳城建筑有限公司	Qingdao Chengyang Suncity Construction Co. ,Ltd.	城阳区	Chengyang	A301
175	青岛市城阳区建设工程有限公司	Qingdao Chengyang Construction Engineering Co. ,Ltd.	城阳区	Chengyang	A301
176	即墨市地质基础工程公司	Jimo Geological Engineering Co. ,Ltd.	即墨市	Jimo	A205
177	青岛平度江北建筑工程有限公司	Qingdao Pingdu Jiangbei Construction Engineering Co. ,Ltd.	平度市	Pingdu	A201
178	青岛国龙市政建设工程有限公司	Qingdao Guolong Municipal Construction Engineering Co. ,Ltd.	城阳区	Chengyang	A310
179	青岛金星科技工程有限公司	Qingdao Jinxing Science and Technology Enginnering Co. ,Ltd.	市南区	Shinan	B111
180	青岛柳源鑫瑞市政园林建设集团有限公司	Qingdao Liuyuan Xinrui Municipal Green Construction Co. ,Ltd.	黄岛区	Huangdao	A210
181	青岛正东建设集团有限公司	Qingdao Zhengdong Construction Co. ,Ltd.	黄岛区	Huangdao	A204
182	青岛德惠建筑工程有限公司	Qingdao Dehui Construction Engineering Co. ,Ltd.	即墨市	Jimo	A201
183	青岛东部电气工程有限 u 公司	Qingdao Eastern Electrical Engineering Co. ,Ltd.	崂山区	Laoshan	B349
184	青岛胶南万德建筑工程有限公司	Qingdao Jiaonan Wande Construction Engineering Co. ,Ltd.	胶南市	Jiaonan	A301
185	胶南市市政工程公司	Jiaonan Municipal Engineering Corp.	胶南市	Jiaonan	A301
186	青岛御景建设工程有限公司	Qingdao Yujing Construction Engineering Co. , Ltd.	胶州市	Jiaozhou	A301
187	青岛汉河电气工程有限公司	Qingdao Hanhe Electrical Engineering Co. ,Ltd.	崂山区	Laoshan	B349
188	青岛庆顺建设工程有限公司	Qingdao Qingshun Construction Engineering Co. , Ltd.	莱西市	Laixi	A301
189	青岛腾达建筑工程有限公司	Qingdao Tengda Construction Engineering Co. ,Ltd.	即墨市	Jimo	A201
190	平度市光华建筑工程有限公司	Pingdu guanghua Construction Engineering Co. , Ltd.	平度市	Pingdu	A301
191	青岛平运路桥工程有限公司	Qingdao Pingyun Road & Bridge Project Co. ,Ltd.	平度市	Pingdu	A202
192	青岛金美建防腐保温有限公司	Qingdao Jinmei Anticorrosive Insulation Co. ,Ltd.	崂山区	Laoshan	B213
193	青岛金坤建筑有限公司	Qingdao Jinkun Construction Co. ,Ltd.	平度市	Pingdu	A201
194	青岛奔腾路桥建设工程有限公司	Qingdao Benteng Road and Bridge Construction Engineering Co. ,Ltd.	黄岛区	Huangdao	A210
195	青岛永鑫建筑工程有限公司	Qingdao Yongxin Construction Co. ,Ltd.	平度市	Pingdu	A301
196	青岛德瑞建筑装饰有限公司	Qingdao Derui Construction and Decoration Co. , Ltd.	崂山区	Laoshan	B103
197	青岛岩土基础工程公司	Qingdao Geotechnical Engineering Co. ,Ltd.	市南区	Shinan	B201
198	青岛旭阳建设工程有限公司	Qingdao Xuyang Construction Engineering Co. , Ltd.	城阳区	Chengyang	A301
199	青岛华烨建设工程有限公司	Qingdao Huaye Construction Engineering Co. , Ltd.	黄岛区	Huangdao	A301
200	青岛金浩源建筑工程有限公司	Qingdao Jinhaoyuan Construction Engineering Co. ,Ltd.	城阳区	Chengyang	A301

主要统计指标解释

建筑业统计单位 指从事房屋、构筑物建造和设备安装活动的法人企业。建筑业法人企业应具有建筑业资质并能够独立核算,同时其应具备以下条件:①依法成立,有自己的名称、组织机构和场所,能够承担民事责任;②独立拥有和使用资产,承担负债,有权与其他单位签订合同;③独立核算盈亏,能够编制资产负债表。

建筑业总产值 是以货币形式表现的建筑业企业在一定时期内生产的建筑业产品和提供的服务的总和。建筑业总产值包括:

(1)建筑工程产值:指列入建筑工程预算内的各种工程价值。

(2)安装工程产值:指设备安装工程价值,不包括被安装设备本身的价值。

(3)其他产值:建筑业总产值中除建筑工程、安装工程以外的产值。包括房屋构筑物修理产值、非标准设备制造产值、总包企业向分包企业收取的管理费以及不能明确划分的施工活动所完成的产值。

建筑业增加值 指建筑业企业在报告期内以货币形式表现的建筑业生产经营活动的最终成果。建筑业增加值 = 劳动者报酬 + 生产税净额 + 本年折旧 + 营业盈余

Explanatory Notes on Main Statistical Indicators

Statistical Unit in Construction refers to corporate enterprise engaged in the construction of buildings and structures and in the installation of equipment. A corporate construction enterprise should have qualification certificates with independent accounting system, and should meet the following 3 requirements: a) being set up in line with relevant legal basis, having its full name, organization and location, and capable of taking civil liabilities; b) independently possessing and using its assets and assuming its liabilities, and entitled to sign contracts with other institutions; and c) making independent accounts of its profits and losses, and capable of compiling its own balance sheet.

Gross Output Value of Construction refers to total of construction products and services, expressed in money terms, produced or rendered by construction and installation enterprises during a given period of time. It includes:

(1) Output value of construction projects, that is the value of projects covered by the project budgets;

(2) Output value of installation projects, that is the value of the installation of equipment, (excluding the value of the equipment to be installed);

(3) Output value of others, that is the output value of construction industry excluding that of construction projects and installation projects. It includes: output value of repair of buildings and structures; output value of non-standard equipment manufacturing; overhead expenses received by contracted enterprises to the sub-contracted enterprises and the completed output value of construction activities that have no clear definition.

Value-added of Construction refers to the final result of the activities of production and management of construction industry in monetary terms in the reference period.

Value-added of Construction = Compensation of Employees + Net Taxes on Production + Depreciation of Fixed Assets + Operating Surplus.

运输、邮电 14

TRANSPORT, POSTAL AND TELECOMMUNICATION SERVICES

简要说明

一、本篇资料的主要内容

本篇资料主要反映了全市交通运输业和邮电业通讯业发展的基本情况，主要包括客货运输及港口吞吐量、民用汽车拥有量、独立核算运输邮电单位主要财务指标、邮电通讯基本情况等方面的内容。

二、本篇资料的来源

1、本篇资料中交通运输资料来源于全市交通运输业统计年报。

2、邮电通讯业资料来源于邮电通讯基本情况统计年报。

3、民用汽车拥有量资料来源于青岛市公安局交警支队车辆管理所。

本篇资料由市统计局工业（能源）统计处整理提供。

Brief Introduction

I. Main Content

Data in this chapter show the basic conditions of the development of transport, post and telecommunications in Shandong Province, mainly including the freight traffic and passenger traffic, cargo handled at port, possession of civil motor vehicles， major financial indices and basic conditions of transport， postal and telecommunication services.

II. Source of Data

（1）Data on transport are based on the annual report of transport.

（2）Data on postal and telecommunication are based on the annual report of postal and telecommunication.

（3）Data on possession of civil motor vehicles are provided by Traffic Police Office of Vehicle Management of Qingdao Municipal Bureau of Public Security.

Data in this chapter are prepared and provide by the Division of Industry（Energy） Statistics of Qingdao Municipal Bureau of Statistics.

14 –1 主要年份客货运输及港口吞吐量

MAJOR YEAR'S PASSENGER & FREIGHT TRAFFIC AND HANDLING CAPACITY OF THE PORTS

年份 Year	客运量(万人) Passenger Traffic(10000 persons)				货运量(万吨) Freight Traffic(10000 tons)				港口吞吐量(万吨)Cargo Handled at Ports (10000 tons)	集装箱吞吐量(万标箱) Containers (10000 TEU)
	铁路 Railways	公路 Highways	海运 Waterways	航空 Civil Aviation	铁路 Railways	公路 Highways	海运 Waterways	航空 Civil Aviation		
1949	327	14	9		386	162	22		73	
1952	571	49	13		447	399	44		181	
1957	1 054	149	13		747	548	118		269	
1962	3 100	141	39		909	524	97		391	
1965	1 424	230	19		1 257	690	158		524	
1970	1 329	373	20		1 856	736	232		695	
1975	1 803	159	30		2 325	817	282		1 542	
1978	1 986	274	49		2 917	1 561	528		2 081	
1980	1 896	713	73		2 596	1 642	941		1 779	
1985	2 063	1 894	86	1.0	3 009	2 303	919	0.03	2 610	
1987	2 019	2 133	159	7.0	3 288	4 948	1 085	0.04	3 070	
1988	2 083	3 300	234	8.8	3 418	6 486	1 160	0.04	3 153	
1989	1 802	3 441	308	11.3	3 717	8 926	1 450	0.10	3 145	
1990	1 488	3 639	316	14.1	3 741	6 433	1 556	0.20	3 068	
1991	1 453	4 144	366	19.0	3 774	6 896	1 789	0.31	3 194	
1992	1 488	4 965	437	27.0	3 899	6 822	1 981	0.45	3 240	
1993	1 499	6 436	499	35.3	4 044	7 685	1 910	0.64	3 650	
1994	1 564	6 787		47.0	4 112	8 336	1 804		4 331	
1995	1 480	9 785		66.6	4 205	11 788	2 185		5 165	
1996	1 230	10 738		79.9	4 415	10 749	474		6 056	81.1
1997	1 308	11 855			4 466	11 232	544		6 944	103.3
1998	1 549	11 754			4 028	14 311	1 792	1.44	7 044	121.3
1999	1 674	12 103			3 919	14 550	1 926	1.96	7 282	154.3
2000	1 780	12 145		124.1	4 256	17 234	2 998	2.30	8 661	212.0
2001	1 678	13 686		143.0	4 778	20 906	3 432	2.40	10 423	264.0
2002	1 530	14 516	777	163.7	5 079	24 480	2 530	3.00	12 252	341.0
2003	1 366	13 132	786	174.7	4 929	27 241	2 773	3.60	14 135	424.0
2004	1 496	16 420	862	241.9	5 119	29 937	3 503	5.30	16 303	514.0
2005	552	17 212	972	280.9	2 299	31 009	4 471	4.60	18 727	630.7
2006	810	17 752	999	320.2	2 790	32 047	4 768	5.10	22 438	770.0
2007	1 101	18 800	1 080	366.9	2 781	33 336	4 019	5.90	2 6507	946.6
2008	1 278	19 909	1 055	377.9	3 225	34 172	5 080	7.20	30 029	1 037.7
2009	1 425	19 612	1 145	440.9	3 772	16 297	4 332	7.19	31 668	1 027.6
2010	1 537	20 460	1 302	505.5	5 031	17 525	4 407	8.44	35 012	1 201.0
2011	1 693	21 560	791	537.4	5 697	19 208	4 220	8.93	37 971	1 302.0

14 -2 民用车辆拥有量(2011 年底)

POSSESSION OF CIVIL MOTOR VEHICLES(END OF 2011)

单位:辆(unit)

项　目	Item	合计 Total 辆数 Number	#个人 of which:Private Vehicles 辆数 Number
一、汽车	**Automobile**	**1 163 211**	**895 124**
1.载客汽车	Passenger Vehicles	961 326	795 116
其中:轿车	of which:Sedan	586 434	501 381
2.载货汽车	Trucks	156 316	61 414
3.其他汽车	Other Automobile	45 569	38 594
二、电车	**Tram**	**73**	
三、摩托车	**Motorcycle**	**603 244**	**599 520**
四、农用运输车	**Agricultural Camion**		
五、挂车	**Trailer Trucks**	**17 121**	**1 038**
六、其他类型车	**Other Vehicles**	**243**	**16**

补充资料:机动车驾驶员(人)Motor drivers(person) 1996420

其中:汽车驾驶员(人)of which:Automobile drivers(person) 1846188

14 –3 客货运输及港口吞吐量(2011 年)
PASSENGER & FREIGHT TRAFFIC AND HANDLING CAPACITY OF THE PORTS(2011)

项 目	Item	货运量（万吨）Freight Traffic (10000 tons)	货物周转量（亿吨公里）Freight Ton-kilometers(100 million tons · km)	客运量（万人）Passenger Traffic (10000 persons)	旅客周转量（亿人公里）Passenger-Kilometers(100 million person-km)	旅客吞吐量（万人）Volume of Passenger Handled (10000 persons)	货物吞吐量（万吨）Volume of Freight Handled (10000 tons)	集装箱（万标箱）Containers (10000 TEU)
总 计	**Total**	**29 125.26**	**3 819.45**	**24 044.55**	**184.57**	**1 188.22**	**37 987.43**	**1 302.00**
铁路	Railways	5 697.10	173.19	1 693.40	51.65			
公路	Highways	19 208.00	408.86	21 560.00	131.82			
水运	Waterways	4 220.16	3 237.40	791.15	1.10			
民航	Civil Aviation					1 171.64	16.65	
港口	Ports					16.58	37 970.78	1 302.00

14 –4 独立核算运输邮电单位主要财务指标(2011 年)
MAIN FINANCIAL INDICATORS OF INDEPENDENT ACCOUNTING UNITS OF TRANSPORT, POSTAL AND TELECOMMUNICATION SERVICES(2011)

单位:万元(10 000 yuan)

项目	Item	主营业务收入 Revenue from principal Business	主营业务成本 Cost of principal Business	营业利润 Operating Profits	营业税金及附加 Operating Taxes and Extra Charges	利润总额 Total Profits
总 计	**Total**					
铁路	Railways					
公路	Highways	464 094.5	390 584.7	15 650.1	7 575.9	15 722.5
水运	Waterways	590 088.9	649 832.8	-88 663.0	5 300.0	-105 770.8
民航	Civil Aviation	69 858.4	45 628.1	10 487.6	2 716.8	10 874.3
港口	Ports	1 763 693.6	1 338 270.3	280 932.0	33 960.6	287 387.3
邮政	Postal Services	63 037.1	54 784.9	1 432.6	552.0	2 579.9
电信	Telecommunication Services	901 451.5	370 763.1	306 449.8	28 949.0	296 457.3

14 -5 邮电通讯基本情况(2011 年)

BASIC CONDITIONS OF POSTAL AND TELECOMMUNICATION SERVICES(2011)

市、区名称	Region	邮电局(处) Post Office (unit)	#提供邮政全功能服务的 of which:Providing Omni-directional Services	邮路总长度(公里) Length of Postal Routes(km)	邮运汽车(辆) Vehicles for Postal Services(unit)	信筒、信箱(个) Post Boxes (unit)
总 计	**Total**	**739**	**215**	**7 131**	**294**	**743**
市 区	Urban Area	164	32	4 583	127	274
#崂山区	Huangdao District	38	8	127	27	56
黄岛区	Laoshan District	41	9	205	25	29
即墨市	Jimo	103	34	522	28	75
胶州市	Jiaozhou	77	29	295	27	63
胶南市	Jiaonan	91	28	463	12	63
平度市	Pingdu	142	50	636	29	127
莱西市	Laixi	83	25	300	25	56

14 -5 续表 1

continued

市、区名称	Region	固定电话市话交换机容量(门) Capacity of Urban Fixed Telephone Exchanges(line)	固定电话市话用户数(户) Urban Fixed Telephone Subscribers (subscriber)	固定电话农村交换机容量(门) Capacity of Rural Fixed Telephone Exchanges(line)	固定电话农村用户数(户) Rural Fixed Telephone Subscribers (subscriber)	移动电话交换机容量(户) Capacity of Mobile Telephone Exchanges (subscriber)	年末移动电话用户(户) Mobile Telephone Subscribersat Year-end (subscriber)
总 计	**Total**	**3 493 702**	**1 575 211**	**1 126 136**	**888 288**	**20 390 000**	**10 948 844**
市 区	Urban Area	2 719 093	909 603	167 621	188 329	10 135 992	4 573 142
#崂山区	Huangdao District	83 903	116 118	65 270	37 866	801 509	537 978
黄岛区	Laoshan District	125 334	118 424	28 912	34 072	1 603 297	835 158
即墨市	Jimo	106 454	105 318	218 023	190 264	2 226 403	1 415 193
胶州市	Jiaozhou	117 065	105 116	106 016	96 148	1 553 221	918 621
胶南市	Jiaonan	91 388	78 995	103 828	92 594	1 394 716	841 161
平度市	Pingdu	46 754	68 404	173 920	177 001	1 666 722	1 136 496
莱西市	Laixi	57 983	51 942	133 138	72 014	908 141	581 383

14 -5 续表2
continued

市、区名称	Region	函件(出口)(万件) Number of Letters (10000 pcs)	邮政储蓄期末余额(万元) Balance of Postal Savings at Term-end (10 000 yuan)	特快专递(万件) Express Mail Services (10000 pcs)	邮电业务总量(万元2010年价)Busine Volume of Postal and Telecommunication Services(10000 yuan at 2010 price)	报纸期发份数(万份) Issue of Newspapers (10000 copies)	杂志期发份数(万份) Issue of Magazines (10000 copies)
总　计	**Total**	**9 280.28**	**1 700 808.38**	**87.89**	**1 978 289.24**	**61.18**	**26.67**
市　区	Urban Area	5 087.89	230 217.77	27.75	1 178 765.75	21.32	11.37
#崂山区	Huangdao District	583.78	67 952.53	14.26	131 951.89	5.53	3.35
黄岛区	Laoshan District	401.83	98 729.16	11.07	101 684.07	3.90	1.99
即墨市	Jimo	536.20	298 755.90	7.88	157 669.65	5.88	1.83
胶州市	Jiaozhou	815.15	287 518.09	8.49	122 258.27	5.60	2.90
胶南市	Jiaonan	613.78	185 445.81	6.10	105 244.99	4.19	2.21
平度市	Pingdu	743.03	381 516.73	7.96	113 454.89	11.05	1.53
莱西市	Laixi	498.62	150 672.39	4.39	67 261.83	3.71	1.49

主要统计指标解释

货(客)运量 指在一定时期内,各运输部门实际运送的货物(旅客)数量。是反映运输业为国民经济和人民生活服务的数量指标,也是制定和检查运输生产计划,研究运输发展规模和速度的重要指标。货运按吨计算,客运按人计算。货物不论运输距离长短,货物类别,均按实际重量统计;旅客不论行程远近或票价多少,均按一人一次作为客运量统计。半价票、小孩票也按一人统计。

货物(旅客)周转量 指在一定时期内,由各种运输工具运送的货物(旅客)数量与其相应运输距离的乘积之总和,是反映运输业生产总成果的重要指标,也是编制和检查运输生产计划,计算运输效益、劳动生产率以及核算运输单位成本的主要基础资料。通常以吨公里和人公里为计算单位。计算货物周转量通常按发出站与到达站之间的最短距离,也就是计费距离计算。

港口货物吞吐量 指经水运进出沿海主要港区范围,并经过装卸的货物数量,包括邮件及办理托运手续的行李、包裹以及补给运输船舶的燃、物料和淡水。货物吞吐量按货物流向分为进口、出口吞吐量,按货物交流性质分为外贸货物吞吐量和国内贸易货物吞吐量。货物吞吐量的货类构成及其流向,是衡量港口生产能力大小的重要指标。

邮电业务总量 指以货币表现的邮电部门用于传递信息和提供其他邮电服务的总数量。它综合反映了一定时期邮电工作的总成果,是研究邮电业务量构成和发展趋势的重要指标。根据邮电管理体制不同,分为中央国营业务总量和地方国营业务总量。它用各种邮电分类业务量,如函件件数、电报份数、长话张数、市内电话和农村电话的年均户数、订销报刊累计份数等,分别乘以相应的平均单位(不变价),加总后再加上出租电路和设备的收入、代用户维护电话交换机和线路等设备的收入、其他业务收入求得。

Explanatory Notes on Main Statistical Indicators

Freight (Passenger) Traffic refers to the volume of freight (passenger) transported with various means. Freight transport is calculated in tons and passenger traffic is calculated in the number of persons. Despite the type of freight and traveling distance, the freight transport is calculated in the actual weight of the goods: and despite the traveling distance and ticket price, the passenger traffic is calculated by the principle that one person can be counted only once in one travel. The passengers who travel with a half price ticket or a child ticket is also calculated as one person. The freight (passenger) traffic provides a quantitative measure to show how the transport industry serves the national economy and people, and is also an important indicator for planning the transport industry and for studying the development scale and speed of the transport industry.

Freight Ton-kilometers (Passenger-kilometers) refer to the sum of the products of the volume of transported cargo (passengers) multiplying by the transport distance. It is an important indicator to reflect the achievement of transportation industry. Normally, the shortest distance between the departure station and the destination station (i. e. , the payable distance) is the basis to calculate the freight ton-kilometers. This is an important indicator to show the total results of the transport industry, to prepare and examine the transport plan and to measure the efficiency, the labour productivity and the unit cost of transport.

Volume of Freight Handled in Ports refers to the volume of cargo passing in and out the harbor area of the major coastal ports and having been loaded and unloaded. The volume includes that of the postal matters, registered luggage and fuels, materials and fresh water as supplies of the ships. The volume of freight handled may be classified by direction of flow as freight for import and freight for export, or by nature of cargo as freight for domestic trade and freight for foreign trade. As an important indicator, the volume of freight handled by type of cargo and by main flow direction reflects the production capacity of ports.

Businesss Volume of Postal and Telecommunication Services refers to the total amount of the information delivered and other post and telecommunication services provided by the post and telecommunication departments for the customers. It is arrived by first multiplying the business volume of different types, such as number of letters, telegrams, long distance calls, city and rural telephone (fixed price) and then adding these products together, plus the income from maintenance of telephone switchboards and lines, and the income from other business operations. The service revenue of posts and telecommunications reflects the total achievements by the post and telecommunication departments during a given period of time in a comprehensive way, and is an important indicator to study the composition and development of the post and telecommunication business.

批发和零售业 15

WHOLESALE AND RETAIL TRADES

简要说明

一、本篇资料的主要内容

本篇资料主要反映了全市批发和零售业经营情况和效益情况，主要包括批发和零售业商品流转及财务情况、批发和零售业网点及从业人员、亿元以上商品交易市场、社会消费品零售总额等内容。

二、本篇资料的来源

本篇资料来源于批发和零售业统计年报和定期报表统计资料；网点资料依据市工商局提供的个体私营经济注册登记资料测算。由市统计局外经贸易统计处整理提供。

Brief Introduction

I. Main Content

Data in this chapter show the development of wholesale and retail trade of the whole city, mainly including the circulation and financial indices of commodities in the wholesale and retail trade, outlets and employment of wholesale and retail trade, commodity exchange markets over 100 million yuan, Total retail sales of consumer goods, etc.

II. Source of Data

Data in this chapter are based on annual report and regular reports of wholesale and retail trade. Data on outlets are based on registration information of individual and private economy provided by Qingdao Municipal Bureau of Industry and Commerce.

Data in this chapter are prepared and compiled by the Division of Trade and External Economic Relations Statistics of Qingdao Municipal Bureau of Statistics.

15－1 社会消费品零售总额(1985－2011 年)

TOTAL RETAIL SALES OF CONSUMER GOODS(1985-2011)

单位:万元(10 000 yuan)

年份 Year	消费品零售总额 Total Retail Sales of Consumer Goods	批发零售业 Wholesale and Retail Trades	住宿餐饮业 Hotels and Catering Services	其他行业 Others
1985	307 222	231 477	16 996	18 753
1986	364 091	269 418	21 384	27 118
1987	432 569	310 658	23 319	32 617
1988	590 538	434 572	32 304	45 449
1989	619 941	450 812	34 083	56 303
1990	658 264	484 770	35 568	67 863
1991	760 562	566 767	43 320	56 812
1992	888 411	666 911	53 045	67 392
1993	1 384 533	1 031 794	80 077	96 759
1994	1 880 654	1 352 073	127 313	202 937
1995	2 376 776	1 637 349	186 028	305 947
1996	2 708 527	1 873 008	220 322	321 325
1997	3 008 981	2 105 728	241 928	361 248
1998	3 368 736	2 322 209	277 696	411 210
1999	3 762 754	2 715 635	315 307	391 388
2000	4 282 871	3 116 990	387 944	403 854
2001	4 911 735	3 561 731	507 012	433 851
2002	5 574 364	4 162 676	638 358	402 654
2003	6 455 113	5 283 584	849 032	322 497
2004	7 475 022	6 266 750	1 017 193	191 079
2005	8 701 057	7 304 660	1 176 539	219 858
2006	10 163 457	8 458 226	1 443 120	262 111
2007	12 162 246	9 995 772	1 837 754	328 720
2008	14 922 153	12 995 842	1 554 086	372 225
2009	17 302 231	14 232 954	2 549 203	520 074
2010	19 611 331	17 151 504	2 459 827	
2011	23 023 703	20 153 079	2 870 624	

注:1. 自 2003 年开始消费品零售总额不再包括制造业零售额和农民对非农居民的销售额分组。
2. 自 2005 年起,住宿业从其它行业调整到住宿餐饮业中。
3. 根据第二次经济普查结果,对 2005 年以来的历史数据进行了调整。

Note:1. Since 2003, retail sales of manufacturing and retail sales of rural residents to urban residents are excluded in total retail sales of consumer goods.
2. Since 2005, hotels is adjusted to hotels and catering services from the others.
3. Historical data since 2005 have been adjusted according to results of the Second China Economic Census.

15－2 分市、区社会消费品零售总额(2011 年)

TOTAL RETAIL SALES OF CONSUMER GOODS BY REGION(2011)

单位:万元(10 000 yuan)

市、区名称	Region	消费品零售总额 Total Retail Sales of Consumer Goods	按行业分 Grouped By Sector	
			批发零售业 Wholesale and Retail Trades	住宿餐饮业 Hotels and Catering Services
总计	**Total**	**23 023 703**	**20 153 079**	**2 870 624**
市区	Urban Area	13 184 540	11 385 475	1 799 065
市南区	Shinan District	3 266 698	2 652 530	614 168
市北区	Shibei District	2 750 427	2 406 602	343 825
四方区	Sifang District	1 546 557	1 471 358	75 199
李沧区	Licang District	2 003 950	1 803 844	200 106
崂山区	Laoshan District	1 083 786	965 145	118 641
黄岛区	Huangdao District	1 265 995	1 030 680	235 315
城阳区	Chengyang District	1 267 127	1 055 316	211 811
即墨市	Jimo	2 346 797	2 146 884	199 913
胶州市	Jiaozhou	1 976 759	1 713 327	263 432
胶南市	Jiaonan	1 730 151	1 548 702	181 449
平度市	Pingdu	2 151 185	1 928 481	222 704
莱西市	Laixi	1 634 271	1 430 210	204 061

15－3 限额以上批发和零售业商品购销存总额(2011 年)

TOTAL PURCHASES,SALES AND STOCK OF ENTERPRISES ABOVE DESIGNATED SIZE OF WHOLESALE AND RETAIL TRADES(2011)

单位:万元(10 000 yuan)

项　目	Item	商品销售总额 Total Sales Value	批发总额 Wholesale Value	零售总额 Retail Value	库存总额 Stock
总计	**Total**	**41 742 747.8**	**32 868 859.5**	**8 873 888.3**	**2 736 286.0**
国有企业	State-owned Enterprises	5 361 163.4	5 192 146.5	169 016.9	305 000.5
集体企业	Collective-owned Enterprises	1 779 990.1	1 768 040.1	11 950.0	74 656.4
其它企业	Other Enterprises	34 601 594.3	25 908 672.9	8 692 921.4	2 356 629.1
农畜产品批发业	Wholesale of Farm Produce and Livestock Products	994 079.1	994 049.2	29.9	88 130.0
食品饮料及烟草制品批发业	Wholesale of Food, Beverages and Tobaccos	1 909 135.3	1 882 675.8	26 459.5	719 512.4
纺织服装及日用品批发业	Wholesale of Textiles, Garments and Daily Consumer Articles	3 663 923.8	3 365 148.8	298 775.0	355 515.5
文化体育用品及器材批发业	Wholesale of Culture, Sports Appliances and Equipments	219 984.4	214 149.0	5 835.4	23 728.9
医药及医疗器械批发业	Wholesale of Medicines and Medical Appliances	646 664.7	625 627.4	21 037.3	33 599.7
矿产品建材及化工产品批发业	Wholesale of Mineral Products, Building Materials and Chemical Products	18 100 622.7	16 985 554.5	1 115 068.2	558 218.9
机械设备五金交电及电子产品批发业	Wholesale of Machinery, Hardware and Electronic Equipment	7 568 055.3	7 514 581.8	53 473.5	230 911.6
贸易经济与代理	Trade Broker and Agency	39 910.9	38 910.9	1 000.0	1 739.9
其它批发业	Other Wholesale not Classified Elsewhere	617 397.8	617 397.8		22 778.8
综合零售业	Integrated Retail Trade	3 032 311.9	154 831.0	2 877 480.9	238 608.1
食品饮料及烟草制品专门零售业	Retail of Food, Beverages and Tobaccos	43 518.2	6 127.3	37 390.9	8 091.2
纺织服装及日用品专门零售业	Retail of Textiles, Garments and Daily Consumer Articles	67 851.0	18 249.4	49 601.6	21 051.5
文化体育用品及器材专门零售业	Retail of Culture, Sports Appliances and Equipments	129 914.5	35 448.6	94 465.9	32 686.9
医药及医疗器械专门零售业	Retail of Medicines and Medical Appliances	106 338.2	14 461.9	91 876.3	34 490.1
汽车摩托车燃料及零配件专门零售业	Retail of Motor Vehicles, Motorcycles, Fuel and Parts	3 768 439.9	189 694.4	3 578 745.5	295 954.5
机动车燃料零售业	Retail of Fuel of Motor Vehicles	814 839.1	90 063.2	724 775.9	16 493.3
家用电器及电子产品专门零售业	Retail of Household Electric Appliances and Electronic Products	622 497.5	132 088.1	490 409.4	44 754.5
五金家具及室内装潢材料专门零售业	Retail of Hardware, Furniture and Decoration Materials	67 481.5	28 109.7	39 371.8	8 837.4
无店铺及其他零售业	Non-shop and Other Retails	144 621.1	51 753.9	92 867.2	17 676.1

15－4 限额以上批发和零售业商品分类销售额(2011 年)

SALES VALUE OF ENTERPRISES ABOVE DESIGNATED SIZE OF WHOLESALE AND RETAIL TRADES BY CATEGORY OF COMMODITIES(2011)

单位:万元(10 000 yuan)

项　　目	Item	销售总额 Total Sales Value	批发总额 Wholesale Value	零售总额 Retail Value
销售总额	**Total Sales Value**	**38 280 549.5**	**29 576 363.3**	**8 704 186.2**
一、粮油、食品、饮料、烟酒类	Grain & Oil, Food, Beverages, Tobacco and Liquor	2 868 069.6	1 825 590.3	1 042 479.3
#粮油、食品类	Grain & Oil and Food	1 560 409.9	798 966.3	761 443.6
粮油类	Grain and Oil	388 609.1	263 660.9	124 948.2
肉禽蛋类	Meat, Poultry and Eggs	190 016.0	34 963.9	155 052.1
水产品类	Aquatic Products	127 212.8	97 312.0	29 900.8
蔬果类	Vegetable and Fruit	29 523.1	17 214.2	12 308.9
干鲜果品类	Dried and Fresh Fruit	51 234.1	19 052.4	32 181.7
饮料类	Beverages	152 712.4	54 431.4	98 281.0
烟酒类	Tobacco and Liquor	1 154 947.3	972 192.6	182 754.7
二、服装鞋帽、针、纺织品类	Clothing, Shoes, Hats and Textiles	2 772 953.0	1 627 317.9	1 145 635.1
#服装类	Clothing	1 660 723.9	829 902.1	830 821.8
鞋帽类	Shoes and Hats	437 968.3	189 332.5	248 635.8
针、纺织品类	Knitwear and Textiles	674 260.8	608 083.3	66 177.5
三、化妆品类	Cosmetics	213 018.5	50 454.9	162 563.6
四、金银珠宝类	Gold, Silver and Jewellery	257 298.0	40 919.7	216 378.3
五、日用品类	Articles for Daily Use	474 061.9	217 323.2	256 738.7
#洗涤用品类	Washing Articles	102 307.0	52 098.3	50 208.7
儿童玩具类	Children Toys	20 160.0	9 189.2	10 970.8
六、五金、电料类	Hardware and Electrical Materials	358 396.3	298 761.9	59 634.4
七、体育、娱乐用品类	Sports and Recreation Articles	102 285.8	29 803.4	72 482.4
八、书报杂志类	Newspapers and Magazines	103 778.2	29 992.0	73 786.2
九、电子出版物及音像制品类	E-journals and Video Products	9 212.7	2 391.4	6 821.3
十、家用电器和音像器材类	Household Appliances and Video Appliances	3 277 485.0	2 537 198.0	740 287.0
十一、中西药品类	Traditional Chinese and Western Medicines	689 347.8	576 583.8	112 764.0
#西药	Western Medicines	620 540.9	525 595.4	94 945.5
中草药及中成药	Traditional Chinese Medicines	68 806.7	52 988.4	15 818.3
十二、文化办公用品类	Cultural and Offices Appliances	349 404.0	147 022.9	202 381.1
十三、家具类	Furniture	123 610.8	14 579.6	109 031.2
十四、通讯器材类	Communication Appliances	197 765.4	32 257.9	165 507.5
十五、煤炭及制品类	Coal and Related Products	684 666.5	678 285.0	6 381.5
十六、木材及制品类	Wood and Wooden Products	86 941.2	86 941.2	
十七、石油及制品类	Petroleum and Related Products	3 899 214.7	2 869 916.8	1 029 297.9
十八、化工材料及制品类	Chemical Materials and Related Products	3 052 636.1	3 052 636.1	
#化肥类	Fertilizers	136 893.6	136 893.6	
十九、金属材料类	Metal Materials	9 862 414.0	9 862 414.0	
二十、建筑及装潢材料类	Building and Decoration Materials	636 277.6	469 146.2	167 131.4
二十一、机电产品及设备类	Mechanical and Electrical Products	1 706 006.0	1 696 394.9	9 611.1
#农机类	Agricultural Machineries	24 702.8	24 702.8	
二十二、汽车类	Automobiles	3 587 245.8	551 688.6	3 035 557.2
二十三、种子饲料类	Seeds and Feedstuff	538 170.5	538 170.5	
二十四、棉麻类	Cotton, Hemp	235 508.8	235 508.8	
二十五、其他类	Others	2 194 781.3	2 105 064.3	89 717.0

15－5 限额以上批发业财务状况(2011 年)

FINANCIAL POSITION OF ENTERPRISES ABOVE DESIGNATED SIZE OF WHOLESALE TRADE(2011)

单位:万元(10 000 yuan)

指标	Indicator	合计 Total	国有经济 State-owned Enterprises	集体经济 Collective-owned Enterprises	外商及港澳台经济 Foreign Funded Enterprises and Enterprises with Funds from Hong Kong, Macao and Taiwan	其它 Other Enterprises
单位数	**Number of Enterprises**	**799**	**32**	**8**	**52**	**707**
年末资产负债	**Year-end Assets-Liability**					
资产合计	Total Assets	13 946 570	2 664 351	994 731	467 438	9 820 049
流动资产小计	Sub-total of Current Assets	11 952 346	2 410 314	926 100	423 563	8 192 368
负债合计	Total Liabilities	11 894 293	2 235 315	968 035	297 831	8 393 111
所有者权益合计	Total Owners' Equities	2 052 277	429 036	26 696	169 607	1 426 938
损益及分配	**Loss, Profits and Distribution**					
主营业务收入	Revenue from Principal Business	29 811 891	4 818 193	1 628 158	1 972 060	21 393 480
主营业务成本	Cost of Principal Business	28 351 686	4 509 532	1 610 193	1 841 235	20 390 726
主营业务税金及附加	Taxes and Extra Charges on Principal Business	70 237	44 917	913	1 503	22 905
主营业务利润	Profits from Principal Business	1 389 968	263 744	17 052	129 323	979 849
其他业务利润	Profits from other Business	74 488	4 438	9 827	6 163	54 060
营业费用	Operating Costs	654 540	72 140	12 228	69 279	500 893
管理费用	Management Expenses	338 508	60 763	21 140	25 215	231 390
财务费用	Financial Expenses	93 342	4 615	－4 021	2 929	89 819
利润总额	Total Profits	456 490	134 931	4 099	36 440	281 020
经济效益	**Economic Benefit**					
商品经营费用率%	Ratio of Operating Costs to Revenue from Principal Business	2.20	1.50	0.75	3.51	2.34
商品销售利润率%	Ratio of Profit to Sales Revenue	4.66	5.47	1.05	6.56	4.58

15－6 限额以上零售业财务状况(2011 年)

FINANCIAL POSITION OF ENTERPRISES ABOVE DESIGNATED SIZE OF RETAIL TRADE(2011)

单位:万元(10 000 yuan)

指标	Indicator	合计 Total	国有经济 State-owned Enterprises	集体经济 Collective-owned Enterprises	外商及港澳台经济 Foreign Funded Enterprises and Enterprises with Funds from Hong Kong, Macao and Taiwan	其它 Other Enterprises
单位数	**Number of Enterprises**	**511**	**15**	**6**	**26**	**464**
年末资产负债	**Year-end Assets-Liability**					
资产合计	Total Assets	3 929 415	52 059	3 992	614 744	3 258 620
流动资产小计	Sub-total of Current Assets	2 533 344	34 446	2 247	383 604	2 113 047
负债合计	Total Liabilities	2 983 703	37 338	3 525	445 810	2 497 030
所有者权益合计	Total Owners' Equities	945 712	14 721	467	168 934	761 590
损益及分配	**Loss, Profits and Distribution**					
主营业务收入	Revenue from Principal Business	6 726 086	92 823	8 470	869 688	5 755 105
主营业务成本	Cost of Principal Business	6 082 491	82 150	7 460	742 561	5 250 321
主营业务税金及附加	Taxes and Extra Charges on Principal Business	20 348	136	130	3 017	17 065
主营业务利润	Profits from Principal Business	623 246	10 537	880	124 110	487 719
其他业务利润	Profits from other Business	103 266	572	1	34 473	68 221
营业费用	Operating Costs	318 059	5 049	179	74 578	238 253
管理费用	Management Expenses	279 879	4 620	527	73 634	201 097
财务费用	Financial Expenses	55 570	110	49	689	54 722
利润总额	Total Profits	62 666	3 266	77	8 159	51 164
经济效益	**Economic Benefit**					
商品经营费用率%	Ratio of Operating Costs to Revenue from Principal Business	4.73	5.44	2.11	8.58	4.14
商品销售利润率%	Ratio of Profit to Sales Revenue	9.27	11.35	10.39	14.27	8.47

15－7 分市、区城乡亿元商品交易市场分布情况(2011 年)
BASIC STATISTICS ON COMMODITY EXCHANGE MARKETS OF TRANSACTION VALUE OVER 100 MILLION YUAN BY REGION(2011)

市、区名称	Region	亿元商品交易市场数量(个) Number of Commodity Exchange Markets of Transaction Value over 100 Million Yuan(unit)			亿元商品交易市场成交额(亿元) Turnover of Commodity Exchange Markets of Transaction Value over 100 Million Yuan (100 million yuan)		
		合计 Total	#综合市场 Integrated Markets	专业市场 Special Markets	合计 Total	#综合市场 Integrated Markets	专业市场 Special Markets
总计	**Total**	**68**	**9**	**59**	**1 109.2**	**171.2**	**937.9**
市区	Urban Area	30	2	28	452.4	44.1	408.3
#崂山区	Laoshan District	2		2	2.7		2.7
黄岛区	Huangdao District	3		3	10.2		10.2
城阳区	Chengyang District	4		4	194.9		194.9
即墨市	Jimo	12	1	11	371.5	64.9	306.6
胶州市	Jiaozhou	8	2	6	136.6	40.4	96.2
胶南市	Jiaonan	4	1	3	30.7	5.6	25.1
平度市	Pingdu	13	3	10	104.0	16.2	87.8
莱西市	Laixi	1		1	13.9		13.9

15－8 按经济类型分批发业企业网点数(2011 年底)
OUTLETS OF WHOLESALE TRADES BY ECONOMIC TYPE(END OF 2011)

单位:个(unit)

市、区名称	Region	合计 Total	分经济类型 Grouped By Economic Type 国有及控股 State-owned and State-holding	私营 Private	其他 Others	外商投资 Foreign Funded
全市总计	**Total**	**22 850**	**236**	**20 834**	**1 380**	**400**
市　区	Urban Area	17 975	172	16 406	1 024	373
市南区	Shinan District	5 474	61	4 696	550	167
市北区	Shibei District	3 059	23	3 010	20	6
四方区	Sifang District	2 455	30	2 405	10	10
李沧区	Licang District	1 447	26	1 390	11	20
崂山区	Laoshan District	1 383	9	1 196	135	43
黄岛区	Huangdao District	2 615	22	2 363	182	48
城阳区	Chengyang District	1 542	1	1 346	116	79
即墨市	Jimo	1 398	6	1 329	55	8
胶州市	Jiaozhou	1 232	6	1 153	71	2
胶南市	Jiaonan	659	23	445	187	4
平度市	Pingdu	758	23	698	32	5
莱西市	Laixi	828	6	803	11	8

15－9 按经济类型分批发业企业从业人员(2011 年底)
EMPLOYMENT OF WHOLESALE TRADES BY ECONOMIC TYPE(END OF 2011)

单位:人(person)

市、区名称	Region	合计 Total Trades	分经济类型 Grouped By Economic Type 国有及控股 State-owned and State-holding	私营 Private	其他 Others	外商投资 Foreign Funded
全市总计	**Total**	**212 541**	**9 418**	**171 800**	**26 227**	**5 096**
市　区	Urban Area	156 122	7 615	121 950	21 842	4 715
市南区	Shinan District	52 315	1 975	37 584	10 976	1 780
市北区	Shibei District	26 502	2 180	24 118	146	58
四方区	Sifang District	16 221	774	12 282	3 105	60
李沧区	Licang District	10 982	453	10 196	43	290
崂山区	Laoshan District	17 878	1 905	9 383	5 398	1 192
黄岛区	Huangdao District	17 727	318	14 961	1 733	715
城阳区	Chengyang District	14 497	10	13 426	441	620
即墨市	Jimo	10 904	162	9 978	703	61
胶州市	Jiaozhou	14 446	230	13 203	993	20
胶南市	Jiaonan	7 083	317	4 537	2 165	64
平度市	Pingdu	9 071	876	7 865	256	74
莱西市	Laixi	14 915	218	14 267	268	162

15－10 按经济类型分零售业企业网点数(2011 年底)

OUTLETS OF RETAIL TRADES BY ECONOMIC TYPE(END OF 2011)

单位:个(unit)

市、区名称	Region	合 计 Total	分经济类型 Grouped By Economic Type 国有及控股 State-owned and State-holding	私营 Private	其他 Others	外商投资 Foreign Funded
全市总计	**Total**	**11 175**	**225**	**9 502**	**1 295**	**153**
市 区	Urban Area	6 754	125	5 902	581	146
市南区	Shinan District	1 232	23	992	185	32
市北区	Shibei District	2 224	18	2 140	56	10
四方区	Sifang District	401	23	255	123	
李沧区	Licang District	675	22	626	13	14
崂山区	Laoshan District	461	7	409	39	6
黄岛区	Huangdao District	824	5	721	90	8
城阳区	Chengyang District	937	27	759	75	76
即墨市	Jimo	836	16	744	73	3
胶州市	Jiaozhou	840	11	793	35	1
胶南市	Jiaonan	1 212	39	904	268	1
平度市	Pingdu	824	19	585	219	1
莱西市	Laixi	709	15	574	119	1

15－11 按经济类型分零售业企业从业人员(2011 年底)

EMPLOYMENT OF RETAIL TRADES BY ECONOMIC TYPE(END OF 2011)

单位:人(person)

市、区名称	Region	合 计 Total	分经济类型 Grouped By Economic Type 国有及控股 State-owned and State-holding	私营 Private	其他 Others	外商投资 Foreign Funded
全市总计	**Total**	**116 497**	**2 916**	**85 686**	**17 181**	**10 714**
市 区	Urban Area	72 159	1 723	52 187	8 538	9 711
市南区	Shinan District	17 035	781	7 109	3 253	5 892
市北区	Shibei District	19 073	133	18 098	489	353
四方区	Sifang District	6 021	158	2 925	2 938	
李沧区	Licang District	7 860	137	7 336	251	136
崂山区	Laoshan District	5 006	92	3 820	18	1 076
黄岛区	Huangdao District	6 122	16	4 787	1 286	33
城阳区	Chengyang District	11 042	406	8 112	303	2 221
即墨市	Jimo	7 514	148	5 251	1 399	716
胶州市	Jiaozhou	8 091	245	7 560	259	27
胶南市	Jiaonan	11 076	282	8 328	2 457	9
平度市	Pingdu	9 081	312	5 672	2 965	132
莱西市	Laixi	8 576	206	6 688	1 563	119

15－12 按行业分批发业企业网点(2011 年底)

OUTLETS OF WHOLESALE TRADE BY SECTOR(END OF 2011)

单位:个(unit)

市、区名称	Region	合 计 Total	农畜产品 Wholesale of Farm Produce and Livestock Products	食品饮料烟草制品 Wholesale of Food, Beverages and Tobaccos	纺织服装及日用品 Wholesale of Textiles, Garmentsand Daily Consumer Articles
全市总计	**Total**	**22 850**	**715**	**2 160**	**3 351**
市　区	Urban Area	17 975	256	1 523	2 685
市南区	Shinan District	5 474	92	562	1 158
市北区	Shibei District	3 059	20	304	590
四方区	Sifang District	2 455	12	139	208
李沧区	Licang District	1 447	16	80	172
崂山区	Laoshan District	1 383	46	95	178
黄岛区	Huangdao District	2 615	44	158	277
城阳区	Chengyang District	1 542	26	185	102
即墨市	Jimo	1 398	52	146	329
胶州市	Jiaozhou	1 232	99	153	107
胶南市	Jiaonan	659	48	47	25
平度市	Pingdu	758	158	133	126
莱西市	Laixi	828	102	158	79

15－12 续表

continued

单位:个(unit)

市、区名称	Region	文化体育用品及器材 Wholesale of Culture, Sports Appliances and Equipments	医药及医疗器械 Wholesale of Medicines and Medical Appliances	矿产品建材及化工产品 Wholesale of Mineral Products, Building Materials and Chemical Products	机械设备五金交电及电子产品 Wholesale of Machinery, Hardware and Electronic Equipment	其他批发 Other Wholesale not Classified Elsewhere
全市总计	**Total**	**1 132**	**563**	**6 028**	**6 496**	**2 405**
市　区	Urban Area	1 063	495	4 236	5 728	1 989
市南区	Shinan District	467	186	966	1 205	838
市北区	Shibei District	209	88	527	1 071	250
四方区	Sifang District	102	42	466	1 321	165
李沧区	Licang District	65	27	486	521	80
崂山区	Laoshan District	76	69	443	394	82
黄岛区	Huangdao District	98	26	1 029	928	55
城阳区	Chengyang District	46	57	319	288	519
即墨市	Jimo	26	15	578	204	48
胶州市	Jiaozhou	20	9	408	287	149
胶南市	Jiaonan	6	14	283	128	108
平度市	Pingdu	12	22	148	104	55
莱西市	Laixi	5	8	375	45	56

15－13 按行业分批发业企业从业人员(2011 年底)

EMPLOYMENT OF WHOLESALE TRADE BY SECTOR(END OF 2011)

单位:人(person)

市、区名称	Region	合　计 Total	农畜产品 Wholesale of Farm Produce and Livestock Products	食品饮料烟草制品 Wholesale of Food, Beverages and Tobaccos	纺织服装及日用品 Wholesale of Textiles, Garmentsand Daily Consumer Articles
全市总计	**Total**	**212 541**	**8 358**	**27 215**	**36 555**
市　　区	Urban Area	156 122	2 222	16 592	30 092
市南区	Shinan District	52 315	605	5 275	17 294
市北区	Shibei District	26 502	186	3 330	4 798
四方区	Sifang District	16 221	191	2 211	2 458
李沧区	Licang District	10 982	136	796	901
崂山区	Laoshan District	17 878	374	2 061	1 602
黄岛区	Huangdao District	17 727	280	1 463	1 993
城阳区	Chengyang District	14 497	450	1 456	1 046
即墨市	Jimo	10 904	508	1 295	3 198
胶州市	Jiaozhou	14 446	1 671	2 237	797
胶南市	Jiaonan	7 083	422	1 263	228
平度市	Pingdu	9 071	1 205	1 436	1 545
莱西市	Laixi	14 915	2 330	4 392	695

15－13 续表

continued

单位:人(person)

市、区名称	Region	文化体育用品及器材 Wholesale of Culture, Sports Appliances and Equipments	医药及医疗器械 Wholesale of Medicines and Medical Appliances	矿产品建材及化工产品 Wholesale of Mineral Products, Building Materials and Chemical Products	机械设备五金交电及电子产品 Wholesale of Machinery, Hardware and Electronic Equipment	其他批发 Other Wholesale not Classified Elsewhere
全市总计	**Total**	**9 257**	**6 322**	**51 111**	**52 653**	**21 070**
市　　区	Urban Area	8 430	5 287	33 499	43 142	16 858
市南区	Shinan District	2 839	1 971	9 196	8 772	6 363
市北区	Shibei District	1 575	1 438	4 346	8 883	1 946
四方区	Sifang District	402	535	2 355	5 598	2 471
李沧区	Licang District	297	596	3 876	4 308	72
崂山区	Laoshan District	2 281	343	3 751	6 577	889
黄岛区	Huangdao District	520	185	6 330	6 557	399
城阳区	Chengyang District	516	219	3 645	2 447	4 718
即墨市	Jimo	134	68	3 589	2 094	18
胶州市	Jiaozhou	195	148	4 350	3 022	2 026
胶南市	Jiaonan	129	289	2 445	1 218	1 089
平度市	Pingdu	238	405	1 690	2 242	310
莱西市	Laixi	131	125	5 538	935	769

15－14 按行业分零售业企业网点数(2011 年底)

OUTLETS OF RETAIL TRADE BY SECTOR(END OF 2011)

单位：个(unit)

市、区名称	Region	合 计 Total	综合零售 Integrated Retail Trade	食品饮料烟草制品 Retail of Food, Beverages and Tobaccos	纺织服装及日用品 Retail of Textiles, Garments and Daily Consumer Articles	文化体育用品及器材 Retail of Culture, Sports Appliances and Equipments
全市总计	**Total**	**11 175**	**1 081**	**1 090**	**1 145**	**736**
市　区	Urban Area	6 754	500	587	745	511
市南区	Shinan District	1 232	102	136	249	142
市北区	Shibei District	2 224	134	181	256	196
四方区	Sifang District	401	39	39	35	27
李沧区	Licang District	675	49	53	41	32
崂山区	Laoshan District	461	30	56	39	26
黄岛区	Huangdao District	824	58	72	86	66
城阳区	Chengyang District	937	88	50	39	22
即墨市	Jimo	836	67	40	99	49
胶州市	Jiaozhou	840	148	91	54	30
胶南市	Jiaonan	1 212	128	228	114	57
平度市	Pingdu	824	129	95	65	41
莱西市	Laixi	709	109	49	68	48

15－14 续表

continued

单位：个(unit)

市、区名称	Region	医药及医疗器械 Retail of Medicines and Medical Appliances	汽车摩托车燃料及零配件 Retail of Motor Vehicles, Motorcycles, Fuel and Parts	家用电器及电子产品 Retail of Household Electric Appliances and Electronic Products	五金家具及室内装潢材料 Retail of Hardware, Furniture and Decoration Materials	无店铺及其他零售 Non-shop and Other Retails
全市总计	**Total**	**1 656**	**1 597**	**1 511**	**1 490**	**869**
市　区	Urban Area	981	793	1 080	1 016	541
市南区	Shinan District	170	70	113	177	73
市北区	Shibei District	233	101	593	378	152
四方区	Sifang District	64	125	32	36	4
李沧区	Licang District	80	156	83	155	26
崂山区	Laoshan District	35	78	67	76	54
黄岛区	Huangdao District	156	86	148	136	16
城阳区	Chengyang District	243	177	44	58	216
即墨市	Jimo	184	179	69	88	61
胶州市	Jiaozhou	151	155	79	83	49
胶南市	Jiaonan	112	166	101	178	128
平度市	Pingdu	138	151	98	61	46
莱西市	Laixi	90	153	84	64	44

15－15 按行业分零售业企业从业人员(2011 年底)
EMPLOYMENT OF RETAIL TRADE BY SECTOR(END OF 2011)

单位:人(person)

市、区名称	Region	合计 Total	综合零售 Integrated Retail Trade	食品饮料烟草制品 Retail of Food, Beverages and Tobaccos	纺织服装及日用品 Retail of Textiles, Garments and Daily Consumer Articles	文化体育用品及器材 Retail of Culture, Sports Appliances and Equipments
全市总计	**Total**	**116 497**	**32 020**	**8 062**	**9 658**	**5 060**
市　区	Urban Area	72 159	20 599	4 788	5 538	3 359
市南区	Shinan District	17 035	7 749	1 279	1 818	1 009
市北区	Shibei District	19 073	3 260	1 402	1 626	1 320
四方区	Sifang District	6 021	1 187	295	352	152
李沧区	Licang District	7 860	3 196	305	274	143
崂山区	Laoshan District	5 006	508	456	283	183
黄岛区	Huangdao District	6 122	1 780	384	560	356
城阳区	Chengyang District	11 042	2 919	667	625	196
即墨市	Jimo	7 514	1 841	352	1 084	331
胶州市	Jiaozhou	8 091	2 296	424	659	336
胶南市	Jiaonan	11 076	2 516	1 280	708	325
平度市	Pingdu	9 081	2 587	860	808	338
莱西市	Laixi	8 576	2 181	358	861	371

15－15 续表
continued

单位:人(person)

市、区名称	Region	医药及医疗器械 Retail of Medicines and Medical Appliances	汽车摩托车燃料及零配件 Retail of Motor Vehicles, Motorcycles, Fuel and Parts	家用电器及电子产品 Retail of Household Electric Appliances and Electronic Products	五金家具及室内装潢材料 Retail of Hardware, Furniture and Decoration Materials	无店铺及其他零售 Non-shop and Other Retails
全市总计	**Total**	**10 878**	**19 146**	**14 617**	**10 696**	**6 360**
市　区	Urban Area	6 522	11 398	9 656	6 214	4 085
市南区	Shinan District	832	1 048	1 140	1 128	1 032
市北区	Shibei District	1 645	1 241	4 824	2 648	1 107
四方区	Sifang District	485	2 854	466	121	109
李沧区	Licang District	424	1 695	751	862	210
崂山区	Laoshan District	343	2 035	526	461	211
黄岛区	Huangdao District	493	613	1 284	582	70
城阳区	Chengyang District	2 300	1 912	665	412	1 346
即墨市	Jimo	693	1 515	755	598	345
胶州市	Jiaozhou	904	1 298	865	769	540
胶南市	Jiaonan	853	1 853	1 073	1 772	696
平度市	Pingdu	1 170	1 349	1 049	612	308
莱西市	Laixi	736	1 733	1 219	731	386

15－16 按行业分零售业企业营业面积(2011年底)

OPERATING AREA OF RETAIL TRADE BY SECTOR(END OF 2011)

单位:平方米(sq. m)

市、区名称	Region	零售业 Retail Trade	综合零售 Integrated Retail Trade	食品饮料烟草制品 Retail of Food, Beverages and Tobaccos	纺织服装及日用品 Retail of Textiles, Garments and Daily Consumer Articles	文化体育用品及器材 Retail of Culture, Sports Appliances and Equipments
全市总计	**Total**	**6 713 103**	**2 094 444**	**496 836**	**204 180**	**149 947**
市　区	Urban Area	3 784 322	1 357 501	162 412	92 736	72 057
市南区	Shinan District	712 922	532 875	8 421	19 240	21 860
市北区	Shibei District	467 704	121 596	22 129	24 488	22 797
四方区	Sifang District	265 307	78 541	3 968	3 958	1 750
李沧区	Licang District	436 026	251 072	4 837	15 674	3 970
崂山区	Laoshan District	148 507	20 352	6 969	2 323	2 743
黄岛区	Huangdao District	413 627	184 941	11 276	18 446	13 199
城阳区	Chengyang District	1 340 229	168 124	104 812	8 607	5 738
即墨市	Jimo	412 699	115 458	8 267	17 414	14 012
胶州市	Jiaozhou	606 403	131 820	11 496	18 242	16 133
胶南市	Jiaonan	826 738	131 818	302 818	26 087	15 168
平度市	Pingdu	648 431	212 393	6 205	26 145	14 908
莱西市	Laixi	434 510	145 454	5 638	23 556	17 669

15－16 续表

continued

单位:平方米(sq. m)

市、区名称	Region	医药及医疗器械 Retail of Medicines and Medical Appliances	汽车摩托车燃料及零配件 Retail of Motor Vehicles, Motorcycles, Fuel and Parts	家用电器及电子产品 Retail of Household Electric Appliances and Electronic Products	五金家具及室内装潢材料 Retail of Hardware, Furniture and Decoration Materials	无店铺及其他零售 Non-shop and Other Retails
全市总计	**Total**	**251 211**	**2 306 193**	**637 384**	**285 804**	**287 104**
市　区	Urban Area	134 808	1 220 907	492 713	152 036	99 152
市南区	Shinan District	13 586	31 318	61 675	21 687	2 260
市北区	Shibei District	33 549	62 119	104 467	66 034	10 525
四方区	Sifang District	6 841	154 474	9 211	3 210	3 354
李沧区	Licang District	8 305	65 743	59 840	19 580	7 005
崂山区	Laoshan District	3 333	98 576	4 040	6 121	4 050
黄岛区	Huangdao District	18 787	88 374	52 679	24 567	1 358
城阳区	Chengyang District	50 407	720 303	200 801	10 837	70 600
即墨市	Jimo	22 871	151 024	24 123	28 443	31 087
胶州市	Jiaozhou	23 142	283 176	55 532	19 453	47 409
胶南市	Jiaonan	14 491	239 727	19 693	33 518	43 418
平度市	Pingdu	43 763	254 658	22 075	31 286	36 998
莱西市	Laixi	12 136	156 701	23 248	21 068	29 040

15 -17 批发和零售业个体网点数(2011 年底)
INDIVIDUAL OUTLETS OF WHOLESALE AND RETAIL TRADES(END OF 2011)

单位:个(unit)

市、区名称	Region	合 计 Total	批发业 Wholesale Trade	零售业 Retail Trade
合计	**Total**	**357 010**	**68 186**	**288 824**
市　区	Urban Area	121 194	11 034	110 160
市南区	Shinan District	11 756	196	11 560
市北区	Shibei District	20 476	1 271	19 205
四方区	Sifang District	10 528	1 387	9 141
李沧区	Licang District	18 020	1 907	16 113
崂山区	Laoshan District	6 190	311	5 879
黄岛区	Huangdao District	31 436	1 450	29 986
城阳区	Chengyang District	22 788	4 512	18 276
即墨市	Jimo	55 929	14 156	41 773
胶州市	Jiaozhou	46 219	12 278	33 941
胶南市	Jiaonan	41 110	6 878	34 232
平度市	Pingdu	61 210	14 358	46 852
莱西市	Laixi	31 348	9 482	21 866

15 -18 批发和零售业个体从业人员(2011 年底)
INDIVIDUAL EMPLOYMENT OF WHOLESALE AND RETAIL TRADES(END OF 2011)

单位:人(person)

市、区名称	Region	合 计 Total	批发业 Wholesale Trade	零售业 Retail Trade
合计	**Total**	**825 649**	**183 945**	**641 704**
市　区	Urban Area	287 107	23 736	263 371
市南区	Shinan District	32 151	611	31 540
市北区	Shibei District	66 318	4 502	61 816
四方区	Sifang District	17 428	2 554	14 874
李沧区	Licang District	35 979	1 012	34 967
崂山区	Laoshan District	12 839	713	12 126
黄岛区	Huangdao District	73 877	3 882	69 995
城阳区	Chengyang District	48 515	10 462	38 053
即墨市	Jimo	134 414	50 365	84 049
胶州市	Jiaozhou	108 679	30 656	78 023
胶南市	Jiaonan	107 841	18 799	89 042
平度市	Pingdu	117 119	36 085	81 034
莱西市	Laixi	70 489	24 304	46 185

主要统计指标解释

社会消费品零售总额 指各种经济类型的批发和零售业、住宿和餐饮业以及其他行业对城乡居民和社会集团的消费品零售额总和。该指标从2003年开始不再包括制造业零售额和农民对非农居民的零售额。

商品购进总额 指从本企业(单位)以外的单位和个人购进(包括从国外直接进口)作为转卖或加工后转卖的商品。这个指标反映批发零售贸易业从国内、国外市场上购进商品的总量。商品购进总额包括:(1)从工农业生产者购进的商品;(2)从出版社、报社的出版发行部门购进的图书、杂志和报纸;(3)从各种类型的批发零售贸易企业(单位)购进的商品;(4)从其他单位购进的商品,如从机关、团体、企业、单位购进的剩余物资,从餐饮业、服务业购进的商品,从海关、市场管理部门购进的缉私和没收的商品,向居民收购的废旧商品等;(5)从国(境)外直接进口的商品,但不包括企业(单位)为自身经营用和未通过买卖行为而收入的商品以及销售退回、商品损益等。

商品销售总额 指对本企业(单位)以外的单位和个人出售(包括对国(境)外直接出口)的商品。这个指标反映批发零售贸易业在国内市场上销售商品以及出口商品的总量。商品销售总额包括:(1)售给城乡居民和社会集团消费用的商品;(2)售给工业、农业、建筑业、运输邮电业、批发零售贸易业、餐饮业、服务业等作为生产、经营使用的商品;(3)售给批发零售贸易业作为转卖或加工后转卖的商品;(4)对国(境)外直接出口的商品。不包括:出售本企业(单位)自用的废旧包装用品,未通过买卖行为付出的商品,经本单位介绍,由买卖双方直接结算,本单位只收取手续费的业务,购货退出的商品以及商品损耗和损失等。

Explanatory Notes on Main Statistical Indicators

Total Retail Sales of Consumer Goods refers to the sum of retail sales of consumer goods sold by all sectors of the national economy to urban and rural residents and social groups. Sectors of the national economy include wholesale and retail trade, accommodation and catering trade and others. Since 2003, retail sales of manufacture and retail sales of rural residents to urban residents are excluded in total retail sales.

Total Purchases of Commodities refer to the total value of purchases of commodities by the enterprises (establishments) from other establishments or individuals (including direct import from abroad) for the purpose of re-selling, either with or without further processing of the commodities purchased. This indicator is used to show the total value of purchases of commodities by wholesale and retail establishments from domestic and overseas markets. The total purchases include: (1) agricultural and industrial products purchased from producers; (2) books, magazines and newspapers purchased from distribution departments of the publishers; (3) commodities purchased from wholesale and retail establishments of different status of registration; (4) commodities purchased from other units, such as surplus materials purchased from government agencies, enterprises or institutions, commodities purchased from catering and service establishments, confiscated goods purchased from customs authorities or market management agencies, second-hand goods and wastes purchased from residents; and (5) commodities directly imported from abroad. Excluded are commodities purchased by enterprises (establishments) for use in their own business operation, commodities obtained without buying or selling procedures, rejected commodities, etc.

Total Sales of Commodities refer to value of commodities sold by the establishments to other establishments and individuals (including direct export). This indicator is used to show the total value of sales of commodities at domestic markets and export. The total sales include: (1) commodities sold to urban and rural residents and social groups for their consumption; (2) commodities sold to establishments in industry, agriculture, construction, transportation, post and telecommunications, wholesale and retail trades, hotels and catering services, and public utility for their production and operation; (3) commodities sold to wholesale and retail establishments for re-selling, with or without further processing; and (4) commodities for direct export to other countries. Excluded are selling of waste packaging materials used by the establishments (units) themselves, commodities transferred without buying or selling procedures, commission income from brokerage in transactions for which settlement is directly handled by buyers and sellers, rejected commodities in the purchase, loss in commodities, etc.

住宿、餐饮业和旅游 16

HOTELS, CATERING SERVICES AND TOURISM

简要说明

一、本篇资料的主要内容

本篇资料主要反映了全市住宿和餐饮业的经营情况和效益情况以及旅游的基本情况，主要包括住宿和餐饮业经营情况和财务情况、网点及从业人员、涉外以及国内旅游基本情况等方面的内容。

二、本篇资料的来源

1、本篇资料中住宿和餐饮业经营情况和财务情况资料来源于住宿和餐饮业统计年报和定期报表统计资料；网点资料依据市工商局提供的个体私营经济注册登记资料测算；涉外旅游资料来源于市旅游局。由市统计局外经贸易统计处整理提供。

2、国内旅游资料来源于国内旅游抽样调查，由国家统计局青岛调查队专项调查处整理提供。

Brief Introduction

I. Main Content

Data in this chapter show the development of wholesale and retail trade and tourism of the whole city, mainly including the circulation and financial indices of hotels and catering services, outlets and employment, international and domestic tourism, etc.

II. Source of Data

(1) Data on hotels and catering services are based on annual report and regular reports of hotels and catering services. Data on outlets are based on registration information of individual and private economy, and provided by Qingdao Municipal Bureau of Industry and Commerce. Data on international tourism are provided by Qingdao Municipal Tourism Bureau. The above data are prepared and compiled by the Division of Trade and External Economic Relations Statistics of Qingdao Municipal Bureau of Statistics.

(2) Data on domestic tourism are based on sample survey of domestic tourism and provided by the Division of Special Survey of Survey Office of the National Bureau of Statistics in Qingdao.

16－1 限额以上住宿和餐饮业法人企业经营情况(2011 年)
BUSINESS CONDITIONS OF ENTERPRISES OF HOTELS AND CATERING SERVICES ABOVE DESIGNATED SIZE(2011)

单位:万元(10 000 yuan)

项目	Item	营业额 Turnover	客房收入 Income from Guest Rooms	餐费收入 Catering Income	商品销售收入 Income from Commodity Sales	其他收入 Other Income
总　计	**Total**	**928 587.8**	**218 218.1**	**634 070.6**	**28 743.0**	**47 556.1**
一、住宿业	**Hotels**	**418 351.8**	**203 277.5**	**159 748.2**	**13 304.1**	**42 022.0**
国有企业	State-owned Enterprises	131 942.0	51 828.5	48 043.4	6 774.1	25 296.0
集体企业	Collective-owned Enterprises	3 663.5	1 204.1	2 117.8	122.4	219.2
其他企业	Other Enterprises	282 746.3	150 244.9	109 587.0	6 407.6	16 506.8
独立门店	Freestanding Stores	353 413.1	170 064.2	138 867.8	10 265.1	34 216.0
连锁总店	General Chain Stores	12 974.3	11 155.8	1 434.6	292.6	91.3
连锁门店	Chain Stores	15 460.6	8 026.8	5 476.1	836.4	1 121.3
其他门店	Other Stores	36 503.8	14 030.7	13 969.7	1 910.0	6 593.4
五星	Five Star Class	127 898.4	62 426.9	48 319.7	2 056.4	15 095.4
四星	Four Star Class	132 008.2	52 704.6	61 517.3	5 725.1	12 061.2
三星	Three Star Class	63 542.3	31 612.5	24 000.0	2 999.7	4 930.1
二星	Two Star Class	16 814.6	11 802.4	4 403.0	416.7	192.5
一星	One Star Class	980.3	658.3	237.6	68.3	16.1
其他	Others	77 108.0	44 072.8	21 270.6	2 037.9	9 726.7
二、餐饮业	**Catering Services**	**510 236.0**	**14 940.6**	**474 322.4**	**15 438.9**	**5 534.1**
国有企业	State-owned Enterprises	3 414.1	1 117.5	2 109.3	127.3	60.0
集体企业	Collective-owned Enterprises	110.0		67.0	39.0	4.0
其他企业	Other Enterprises	506 711.9	13 823.1	472 146.1	15 272.6	5 470.1
独立门店	Freestanding Stores	238 094.3	13 848.9	205 953.7	13 348.6	4 943.1
连锁总店	General Chain Stores	248 588.0		247 285.6	1 284.5	17.9
连锁门店	Chain Stores	8 289.4	691.1	7 164.9	241.5	191.9
其他门店	Other Stores	15 264.3	400.6	13 918.2	564.3	381.2

16-2 限额以上住宿业财务状况(2011年)
FINANCIAL SITUATION OF HOTELS ABOVE DESIGNATED SIZE(2011)

单位:万元(10 000 yuan)

指标	Indicator	合 计 Total	国有经济 State-owned Enterprises	集体经济 Collective-owned Enterprises	外商及港澳台经济 Foreign Funded Enterprises and Enterprises with Funds from Hong Kong, Macao and Taiwan	其它 Other Enterprises
单位数	**Number of Enterprises**	**152**	**35**	**5**	**12**	**100**
年末资产负债	**Year-end Assets-Liability**					
资产合计	Total Assets	832 413	247 260	7 051	241 686	336 417
流动资产小计	Sub-total of Current Assets	293 468	86 560	2 911	47 455	156 541
负债合计	Total Liabilities	558 389	107 914	6 438	186 005	258 033
所有者权益合计	Total Owners' Equities	274 024	139 346	613	55 681	78 384
损益及分配	**Loss Profits and Distribution**					
主营业务收入	Revenue from Principal Business	398 213	127 979	3 635	91 863	174 736
主营业务成本	Cost of Principal Business	124 034	46 860	2 311	15 893	58 969
主营业务税金及附加	Taxes and Extra Charges on Principal Business	21 149	6 026	200	5 116	9 806
主营业务利润	Profits from Principal Business	253 031	75 093	1 123	70 854	105 961
其他业务利润	Profits from other Business	7 651	2 062	1	4 800	788
营业费用	Operating Costs	114 668	39 898	669	22 027	52 074
管理费用	Management Expenses	126 049	34 669	521	41 905	48 955
财务费用	Financial Expenses	15 017	1 678	16	5 494	7 829
利润总额	Total Profits	3 565	301	-94	5 690	-2 332
其他	**Others**					
本年应付工资总额	Total Wages Payable in This Year	128 805	26 680	638	10 788	28 638
主营业务利润率	Profitability of Principal Business	63.54	58.68	30.90	77.13	60.64

16－3 限额以上餐饮业财务状况(2011 年)

FINANCIAL SITUATION OF CATERING SERVICES ABOVE DESIGNATED SIZE(2011)

单位:万元(10 000 yuan)

指标	Indicator	合　计 Total	国有经济 State-owned Enterprises	集体经济 Collective-owned Enterprises	外商及港澳台经济 Foreign Funded Enterprises and Enterprises with Funds from Hong Kong, Macao and Taiwan	其它 Other Enterprises
单位数	**Number of Enterprises**	**191**	**4**	**1**	**21**	**165**
年末资产负债	**Year-end Assets-Liability**					
资产合计	Total Assets	458 522	7 107	81	158 153	293 182
流动资产小计	Sub-total of Current Assets	199 827	1 472	38	52 997	145 321
负债合计	Total Liabilities	309 518	2 123	42	106 121	201 232
所有者权益合计	Total Owners' Equities	149 005	4 984	39	52 032	91 950
损益及分配	**Loss Profits and Distribution**					
主营业务收入	Revenue from Principal Business	478 610	3 414	110	239 306	235 779
主营业务成本	Cost of Principal Business	240 874	2 151	90	116 013	122 621
主营业务税金及附加	Taxes and Extra Charges on Principal Business	26 114	177	1	13 347	12 589
主营业务利润	Profits from Principal Business	211 622	1 087	19	109 947	100 570
其他业务利润	Profits from other Business	708	22		1	686
营业费用	Operating Costs	125 632	608		65 681	59 343
管理费用	Management Expenses	45 950	642		20 499	24 809
财务费用	Financial Expenses	9 070	50		1 921	7 099
利润总额	Total Profits	33 709	－197	19	24 635	9 252
其他	**Others**					
本年应付工资总额	Total Wages Payable in This Year	62 061	741	48	29 243	32 028
主营业务利润率	Profitability of Principal Business	44.22	31.83	17.27	45.94	42.65

16－4 按经济类型分餐饮业企业网点数(2011 年底)

OUTLETS OF CATERING SERVICES BY ECONOMIC TYPE(END OF 2011)

单位:个(unit)

市、区名称	Region	餐饮业 Catering Services	分经济类型 Grouped by Economic Types			
			国有及控股 State-owned and State-holding	私营 Private	其他 Others	外商投资 Foreign Funded
全市总计	**Total**	**1 815**	**20**	**1 473**	**152**	**170**
市　区	Urban Area	1 032	15	781	81	155
市南区	Shinan District	305	7	202	44	52
市北区	Shibei District	175	1	157		17
四方区	Sifang District	60		50		10
李沧区	Licang District	92	2	69	3	18
崂山区	Laoshan District	93	3	67		23
黄岛区	Huangdao District	174	2	152	6	14
城阳区	Chengyang District	133		84	28	21
即墨市	Jimo	192		183	7	2
胶州市	Jiaozhou	129	2	112	10	5
胶南市	Jiaonan	123	1	107	13	2
平度市	Pingdu	183	1	141	40	1
莱西市	Laixi	156	1	149	1	5

16－5 按经济类型分餐饮业企业从业人员(2011 年底)

EMPLOYMENT OF CATERING SERVICES BY ECONOMIC TYPE(END OF 2011)

单位:人(person)

市、区名称	Region	合　计 Total	分经济类型 Grouped by Economic Types			
			国有及控股 State-owned and State-holding	私营 Private	其他 Others	外商投资 Foreign Funded
全市总计	**Total**	**44 271**	**1 697**	**32 546**	**4 177**	**5 851**
市　区	Urban Area	27 989	845	19 333	2 756	5 055
市南区	Shinan District	9 670	664	5 214	2 201	1 591
市北区	Shibei District	5 044	15	3 948		1 081
四方区	Sifang District	1 222		1 078		144
李沧区	Licang District	2 510	30	1 986	63	431
崂山区	Laoshan District	2 747	111	1 929		707
黄岛区	Huangdao District	3 102	25	2 735	86	256
城阳区	Chengyang District	3 694		2 443	406	845
即墨市	Jimo	4 146		3 794	239	113
胶州市	Jiaozhou	3 074	521	2 105	316	132
胶南市	Jiaonan	2 313	13	1 893	305	102
平度市	Pingdu	3 019	126	2 286	490	117
莱西市	Laixi	3 730	192	3 135	71	332

16－6 按经济类型分住宿业企业网点数(2011 年底)
OUTLETS OF HOTELS BY ECONOMIC TYPE(END OF 2011)

单位:个(unit)

市、区名称	Region	合 计 Total	分经济类型 Grouped by Economic Types			
			国有及控股 State-owned and State-holding	私营 Private	其他 Others	外商投资 Foreign Funded
合 计	**Total**	**758**	**78**	**570**	**94**	**16**
市 区	Urban Area	647	70	470	92	15
市南区	Shinan District	216	35	121	52	8
市北区	Shibei District	151	10	137	1	3
四方区	Sifang District	60	[illegible]	47		
李沧区	Licang District	58	2	56		
崂山区	Laoshan District	48	7	30	9	2
黄岛区	Huangdao District	87	3	66	18	
城阳区	Chengyang District	27		13	12	2
即墨市	Jimo	26	3	22		1
胶州市	Jiaozhou	28	1	27		
胶南市	Jiaonan	29	3	26		
平度市	Pingdu	20	1	19		
莱西市	Laixi	8		6	2	

16－7 按经济类型分住宿业企业从业人员(2011 年底)
EMPLOYMENT OF HOTELS BY ECONOMIC TYPE(END OF 2011)

单位:人(person)

市、区名称	Region	住宿业 Hotels	分经济类型 Grouped by Economic Types			
			国有及控股 State-owned and State-holding	私营 Private	其他 Others	外商投资 Foreign Funded
合 计	**Total**	**30 592**	**7 058**	**13 448**	**8 046**	**2 040**
市 区	Urban Area	26 172	5 939	10 525	7 908	1 800
市南区	Shinan District	14 773	4 787	2 996	5 310	1 680
市北区	Shibei District	2 180	585	1 553	6	36
四方区	Sifang District	758	130	628		
李沧区	Licang District	1 325	90	1 235		
崂山区	Laoshan District	2 301	175	1 404	722	
黄岛区	Huangdao District	2 500	172	1 560	768	
城阳区	Chengyang District	2 335		1 149	102	84
即墨市	Jimo	1 232	474	518		240
胶州市	Jiaozhou	921	236	685		
胶南市	Jiaonan	683	285	398		
平度市	Pingdu	883	124	759		
莱西市	Laixi	701		563	138	

16-8 住宿和餐饮业个体网点数(2011 年底)

INDIVIDUAL OUTLETS OF HOTELS AND CATERING SERVICES(END OF 2011)

单位:个(unit)

市、区名称	Region	合计 Total	住宿业 Hotels	餐饮业 Catering Services
合计	**Total**	**49 613**	**9 333**	**40 280**
市区	Urban Area	26 028	5 393	20 635
市南区	Shinan District	3 122	1 195	1 927
市北区	Shibei District	2 934	691	2 243
四方区	Sifang District	2 052	701	1 351
李沧区	Licang District	3 128	621	2 507
崂山区	Laoshan District	1 745	326	1 419
黄岛区	Huangdao District	6 623	624	5 999
城阳区	Chengyang District	6 424	1 235	5 189
即墨市	Jimo	4 193	509	3 684
胶州市	Jiaozhou	6 988	1 159	5 829
胶南市	Jiaonan	4 096	918	3 178
平度市	Pingdu	5 504	1 135	4 369
莱西市	Laixi	2 804	219	2 585

16-9 住宿和餐饮业个体从业人员(2011 年底)

INDIVIDUAL EMPLOYMENT OF HOTELS AND CATERING SERVICES(END OF 2011)

单位：人(person)

市、区名称	Region	合计 Total	住宿业 Hotels	餐饮业 Catering Services
合计	**Total**	**192 850**	**39 750**	**153 100**
市区	Urban Area	112 116	25 207	86 909
市南区	Shinan District	17 361	4 502	12 859
市北区	Shibei District	16 285	3 002	13 283
四方区	Sifang District	13 499	9 924	3 575
李沧区	Licang District	9 973	1 403	8 570
崂山区	Laoshan District	6 575	818	5 757
黄岛区	Huangdao District	26 903	2 442	24 461
城阳区	Chengyang District	21 520	3 116	18 404
即墨市	Jimo	14 007	1 226	12 781
胶州市	Jiaozhou	22 463	3 810	18 653
胶南市	Jiaonan	15 976	3 028	12 948
平度市	Pingdu	15 670	4 416	11 254
莱西市	Laixi	12 618	2 063	10 555

16 -10 入境旅游人数(1990 -2011 年)
NUMBER OF OVERSEA VISITOR ARRIVALS (1990 - 2011)

单位:人次(person-time)

项目	Item	1990	1995	2000	2005	2006	2007	2008	2009	2010	2011
总　计	**Total**	**72 019**	**177 797**	**260 592**	**684 407**	**854 462**	**1 081 476**	**800 455**	**1 000 670**	**1 080 511**	**1 156 391**
一、外国人	**Foreigner**	**22 329**	**79 469**	**177 098**	**596 177**	**751 403**	**925 384**	**697 391**	**801 424**	**826 628**	**809 043**
#韩国	Korea		20 330	69 878	295 111	373 712	509 369	340 648	363 181	382 225	298 096
日本	Japan	9 426	34 296	67 215	177 121	221 542	242 500	210 090	261 553	242 082	216 755
美国	United States	2 454	5 607	10 384	23 284	32 256	37 509	28 998	28 745	35 539	45 842
俄罗斯	Russia	163	449	4 820	12 062	17 457	10 949	3 774	9 525	15 793	15 750
德国	Germany	1 494	2 660	3 820	10 646	14 440	14 560	11 261	14 735	21 626	26 178
新加坡	Singapore	626	2 998	6 321	6 060	8 332	10 918	10 683	17 453	13 444	16 626
英国	United Kingdom	712	1 545	2 798	5 744	10 047	12 175	10 657	9 103	17 639	23 955
加拿大	Canada	556	930	1 865	4 397	5 727	7 095	5 467	7 741	9 279	12 007
法国	France	461	825	2 491	5 166	7 377	8 452	6 067	7 030	11 766	12 019
意大利	Italy	437	746	1 555	3 963	4 022	6 062	3 871	3 747	3 867	7 028
澳大利亚	Australia	351	1 009	1 817	4 257	7 106	8 505	7 940	6 641	8 223	15 465
菲律宾	Philippines	270	558	7 947	3 459	1 812	2 461	2 075	7 800	14 140	14 259
泰国	Thailand	406	299	780	3 261	2 464	2 682	2 236	3 685	2 572	3 271
印尼	Indonesia	237	670	1 241	2 349	2 301	3 127	1 589	4 221	7 863	8 128
新西兰	New Zealand	68	192	442	710	980	1 106	1 161	2 029	1 597	6 265
二、港澳和台湾同胞	**Chinese Compatriots from Hong Kong, Macao and Taiwan**	**29 276**	**39 223**	**60 367**	**88 230**	**103 059**	**156 092**	**103 064**	**199 246**	**253 883**	**347 348**

16 -11 入境旅游收入(1990 -2011 年)
EARNINGS FROM INTERNATIONAL TOURISM (1990 - 2011)

单位:万元(10 000 yuan)

项　目	Item	1990	1995	2000	2005	2006	2007	2008	2009	2010	2011
总　计	**Total**	**13 534**	**48 320**	**118 164**	**340 899**	**434 100**	**502 926**	**347 645**	**377 000**	**399 688**	**441 171**
旅游购物	Shopping	4 409	5 933	20 742	67 047	78 882	95 705	66 053	70 763	74 104	80 823
住宿费	Accommodation	3 267	18 509	17 443	37 277	44 011	53 662	37 198	41 093	43 933	59 823
餐饮费	Dining	1 160	5 361	11 223	33 557	39 611	48 182	33 374	36 569	38 747	40 191
交通费	Transportation	3 619	11 404	35 252	128 112	140 831	183 425	9 039	9 877	145 551	134 425
邮电费	Postal and Telecommunication Services	585	3 246	5 502	18 394	21 654	26 111	17 382	18 812	19 081	16 720
文化娱乐费	Culture and Entertainment	89	1 302	6 894	20 240	23 900	29 180	20 163	22 394	24 032	36 132
游览	Sightseeing						26 502	18 773	21 037	22 978	51 705
其他	Other Services				36 272	85 210	40 158	145 663	29 745	31 262	21 353

16－12 国内旅游人数(2011 年)

NUMBER OF DOMESTIC TOURISTS(2011)

指　标	Indicator	单位	Unit
国内旅游人数	**Number of Domestic Tourists**	**万人次**	**10000 person－times**
1. 过夜旅游者人数	Number of Overnight Tourists	万人次	10000 person－times
(1)旅游住宿设施国内旅游人数	Domestic Tourists Staying Overnight at Hotels	万人次	10000 person－times
(2)住亲友家去景点的国内旅游人数	Domestic Tourists Staying Overnight at Relatives and Friends' s Home	万人次	10000 person－times
2. 不过夜旅游者(一日游人数)	Number of Same-day(One-day Sightseeing) Tourists	万人次	10000 person－times
旅游景点接待一日游人数	One-day Sightseeing Tourists Received by Tour Scenes	万人次	10000 person－times
(1)本地一日游人数	Number of Local One-day Sightseeing Tourists	万人次	10000 person－times
(2)外地一日游人数	Number of One-day Sightseeing Tourists from Outside Areas	万人次	10000 person－times
国内旅游人均花费	**Per Capita Expenditure of Domestic Tourist**	**元**	**yuan**
其中:旅游住宿设施国内旅游者人均花费	of which: Staying Overnight at Hotels	元	yuan
住亲友家去景点的国内旅游者人均花费	Staying Overnight at Relatives and Friends' s Home	元	yuan
一日游旅游者人均花费	Per Capita Expenditure of One-day Sightseeing Tourist	元	yuan
国内旅游收入	**Earings from Domestic Tourism**	**万元**	**10000 yuan**
1. 接待过夜旅游者收入	Earings from Overnight Tourists	万元	10000 yuan
(1) 旅游住宿设施接待国内旅游者收入	of which: Staying Overnight at Hotels	万元	10000 yuan
(2)住亲友家去景点的国内旅游者旅游花费	Staying Overnight at Relatives and Friends' s Home	万元	10000 yuan
2. 接待不过夜旅游者（一日游）收入	Earings from Same-day(One-day Sightseeing) Tourists	万元	10000 yuan

一季度 1st Quarter	二季度 2nd Quarter	三季度 3rd Quarter	四季度 4th Quarter	全年 Annual Total
729.56	**1 398.82**	**1 853.68**	**974.05**	**4 956.11**
528.28	837.91	1 309.38	683.97	3 359.54
448.81	728.17	911.04	504.69	2 592.71
79.47	109.74	398.34	179.28	766.83
201.28	560.91	544.30	290.08	1 596.57
201.28	560.91	544.30	290.08	1 596.57
91.89	334.97	299.36	185.32	911.54
109.39	225.94	244.94	104.76	685.03
1 279.94	**1 145.41**	**1 296.23**	**1 472.77**	**1 285.96**
1 748.35	1 714.87	1 956.58	2 004.50	1 861.98
1 003.21	1 200.99	1 036.16	1 559.68	1 178.73
344.74	395.26	381.28	493.94	402.05
933 792.70	**1 602 219.56**	**2 402 798.65**	**1 434 554.41**	**6 373 365.32**
864 404.10	1 380 514.52	2 195 268.57	1 291 271.58	5 731 458.77
784 678.70	1 248 717.55	1 782 525.59	1 011 652.30	4 827 574.14
79 725.40	131 796.97	412 742.98	279 619.28	903 884.63
69 388.60	221 705.04	207 530.08	143 282.83	641 906.55

主要统计指标解释

住宿餐饮业营业额 指住宿和餐饮业法人企业、产业活动单位在经营活动中因提供服务或销售商品等取得的收入，包括客房收入、餐费收入、商品销售收入和其他收入。客房收入指住宿和餐饮业法人企业、产业活动单位在经营活动中因提供住宿服务取得的客房收入。餐费收入指住宿和餐饮业法人企业、产业活动单位因为顾客提供就餐服务取得的收入，包括经烹饪、调制加工后出售的各种食品，如主食、炒菜、凉拌菜等的收入。商品销售收入指住宿和餐饮业法人企业、产业活动单位伴随服务而出售商品所取得的收入。其他收入指营业收入中除客房收入、餐费收入、商品销售收入以外的其他收入，包括娱乐、健身和商务服务等。

国内旅游者 是指不以谋求职业、获取报酬为目的，离开惯常居住环境，到国内其它地方从事参观、游览、度假等旅游活动（包括外出探亲、疗养、考察、参加会议和从事商务、科技、文化、教育、宗教活动过程中的旅游活动），出行距离超过10公里，出游时间超过6小时，但不超过12个月的我国大陆居民。

入境旅游者 指来我国参观、访问、旅行、探亲、访友、休养、考察、参加会议和从事经济、科技、文化、教育、体育、宗教等活动的外国人、华侨、港澳和台湾同胞的人数。不包括外国在我国的常驻机构，如领事馆、通讯社、企业办事处的工作人员；来我国常住的外国专家、留学生以及在岸逗留不过夜人员。

Explanatory Notes on Main Statistical Indicators

Business Revenue of Hotels and Catering Services refer to revenue received from providing services or selling commodities by corporate enterprises and establishments engaged in hotel and catering services, including income from hotel rooms, from catering services, from selling of commodities and from other services. Income from hotel rooms refers to income of corporate enterprises and establishments by providing lodging services. Income from catering services refers to income of corporate enterprises and establishments by providing catering services, including selling of cooked or prepared foods such as stable food, cooked dishes or cold dishes. Income from selling of commodities refers to income of corporate enterprises and establishments by selling commodities that accompany the services they provide. Income from other activities refers to income received other than income from hotel rooms, catering services or selling of commodities, such as income from providing recreation, fitness or business services.

Domestic Tourists refers to residents in mainland China who are not for the purpose of seeking employment, remuneration, and leaving the usual living environment, elsewhere to engage in domestic visitors, sightseeing, vacation travel (including to go out to visit relatives, infirmary, observing, participate in the meeting and engage in business, science and technology, culture, education, religious activities in the course of tourism activities), trip distance of more than 10 km, trips longer than six hours, but not more than 12 months.

Entrance Tourists refers to foreigners, overseas Chinese, Chinese compatriots from Hong Kong, Macao and Taiwan coming to China for sight-seeing, visits, tours, family reunions, vacations, study tours, conferences and other activities of a business, scientific and technological, cultural, educational and religious nature. It does not include representatives and employees of resident institutions of foreign countries in China such as embassies, consulates, news agencies and offices of foreign companies and organizations, nor does it include long-term foreign experts or students residing in China, or persons in transition without spending a night in China.

教育、科技和文化 17

EDUCATION, SCIENCE & TECHNOLOY AND CULTURE

简要说明

一、本篇资料的主要内容

本篇资料主要反映了全市教育、科技和文化事业基本情况。教育部分主要包括高等教育、中等教育、初等教育、成人教育、职业教育、幼儿园等方面的基本情况。科技部分主要包括科研机构、科学技术奖励、大中型工业企业技术开发情况。文化部分主要包括文化、文物、广播、电视、报纸杂志出版、图书出版等方面的发展状况。

二、本篇资料的来源

1、教育部分，技工学校的资料来源于市人力资源和社会保障局，其他资料来源于市教育局。

2、科技部分，科研机构及科技奖励资料来源于市科技局，大中型工业企业科技活动资料来源于市统计局统计调查年报。

3、文化部分，图书、杂志、报纸出版有关资料来源于青岛出版集团、海大出版社其他资料来源于市文化广电新闻出版局。

本篇资料由市统计局人口和社会科技统计处整理提供。

Brief Introduction

I. Main Content

Data in this chapter show the basic conditions of education, science & technology and culture. Data on education show the development of higher education, secondary education, primary education, adult education, vocational education and kindergartens. Data on science & technology show the basic conditions of science research institutions, scientific and technological achievements and prizes, scientific & technological activities of large and medium-size industrial enterprises. Data on culture show the basic conditions of arts, cultural relics, broadcasting, television and publication of newspapers, magazines and books.

II. Source of Data

（1）In education component, data on the basic conditions of technical schools are provided by Qingdao Municipal Bureau of Human Resources and Social Security, and the other data on education are provided by Qingdao Municipal Bureau of Education.

（2）In science & technology component, data on science research institutions and scientific & technological achievements and prizes are provided by Qingdao Municipal Bureau of Science and Technology. Data on scientific and technological activities are from the annual report of scientific and technological activities, which is provided by Qingdao Municipal Bureau of Statistics.

（3）In culture component, data on publication of books, magazines and newspapers are provided by Qingdao Publishing Group and Ocean University Press. The other data are provided by Qingdao Municipal Bureau of Cluture, Broadcasting, Television, Press and Publication.

Data in this chapter are provided and compiled by the Division of Population and Science & Technology of Qingdao Municipal Bureau of Statistics.

17－1 各级各类学校基本情况(2011 年)
BASIC STATISTICS ON SCHOOLS BY LEVEL AND TYPE OF SCHOOL(2011)

项　目	Item	学校数(所) Schools (unit)	毕业生数(人) Graduates (person)	招生数(人) New Students Enrollment(person)	在校学生数(人) Students Enrollment(person)	教职工数(人) Teachers and Staff(person)	#专任教师 of which: Full-time Teachers
研究生	Postgraduates		6 806	9 340	26 072		5 756
普通高等学校	Regular Institutions of Higher Education	22	79 466	84 434	291 453	28 151	17 120
#普通本专科	Regular College Course & Specialized Subject		78 837	84 434	291 024		
自考助学班	Guidance Class for Students Learning Themselves and Examination		629		429		
中等专业学校	Specialized Secondary Schools	7	6 491	9 364	25 905	1 016	662
技工学校	Technical Schools	24	10 586	10 276	31 028	2 172	1 544
职业学校	Vocational Schools	53	39 060	21 940	74 892	7 724	5 642
普通中学	Regular Secondary Schools	290	122 332	119 255	373 226	36 738	31 402
初中	Junior Secondary Schools	232	90 194	75 733	253 446		22 008
高中	Senior Secondary Schools	58	32 138	43 522	119 780		9 394
小学	Primary Schools	889	76 249	92 860	479 513	33 704	31 554
特殊教育学校	Special Education Schools	13	286	311	1 481	585	444
幼儿园	Kindergartens	2 476	72 093	72 966	218 725	20 783	14 063
成人高等学校	Adult Institutions of Higher Education	2	29 880	35 674	81 008	638	226
成人中等学校	Adult Secondary Education Schools	8	3 457	6 020	15 897	327	219
成人初等学校	Adult Primary Education Schools						

注:1. 研究生栏中专任教师指的是指导教师。
2. 成人中等学校仅包括成人中学和成人中专。

Note:1. Full-time teachers of postgraduates refer to instructors.
2. Adult secondary education schools refer to adult secondary schools and adult specialized secondary schools.

17－2 主要年份各级各类学校在校学生数

MAJOR YEAR'S STUDENTS ENROLLMENT OF SCHOOLS BY LEVEL AND TYPE OF SCHOOL

单位：人(person)

年份 Year	普通高等学校 Regular Institutions of Higher Education	中等学校 Secondary Schools	中等专业学校 Specialized Secondary Schools	普通中学 Regular Secondary Schools	职业中学 Vocational Schools	技工学校 Technical Schools	小学 Primary Schools
1949	1 007	13 804	1 600	12 204			213 470
1952	2 761	27 951	3 770	24 181			413 286
1957	3 133	56 689	4 985	51 604	100		482 397
1962	4 381	62 646	2 791	58 639	243	973	522 921
1965	2 987	99 605	9 405	88 187	1 490	523	788 485
1970	320	222 521	105	220 262	2 154		728 433
1975	1 151	350 309	3 144	346 403		762	928 153
1978	3 465	464 584	4 269	457 460	2 000	865	634 905
1980	6 783	325 935	5 195	318 193	1 344	1 203	816 970
1985	10 631	327 446	11 475	279 915	33 945	2 111	691 341
1988	14 408	352 576	11 819	306 943	28 933	4 881	629 212
1989	15 183	348 367	14 401	296 318	32 283	5 365	634 794
1990	15 433	351 365	15 118	296 163	34 568	5 516	632 314
1991	15 491	353 410	14 618	298 568	34 421	5 803	612 772
1992	16 470	367 480	14 763	307 903	38 242	6 572	585 381
1993	23 858	383 043	16 877	318 179	40 743	7 244	583 585
1994	25 018	420 077	20 582	347 667	43 734	8 094	593 419
1995	24 908	450 212	23 744	372 335	46 044	8 089	595 891
1996	26 076	468 561	26 951	382 760	50 131	8 719	607 284
1997	27 434	463 619	28 543	362 305	61 640	11 131	626 749
1998	29 507	442 525	28 757	336 918	65 989	10 861	625 308
1999	33 681	459 520	26 955	352 238	70 236	10 091	583 594
2000	46 131	497 391	25 192	398 458	63 894	9 847	534 922
2001	60 728	542 400	25 358	443 693	62 003	11 346	499 147
2002	82 539	575 599	27 421	467 628	67 085	13 465	478 634
2003	168 439	586 704	28 948	461 435	75 221	21 100	467 560
2004	201 739	598 804	30 881	436 117	101 553	30 253	476 897
2005	239 761	569 230	33 522	391 148	106 400	38 160	479 781
2006	260 339	554 308	32 051	365 192	116 487	40 578	483 892
2007	264 917	558 527	28 011	360 410	130 156	39 950	484 775
2008	269 314	582 932	25 330	373 884	143 126	40 592	477 230
2009	275 157	564 476	22 739	377 427	127 792	36 518	465 031
2010	284 788	535 079	24 014	380 025	98 560	32 480	462 722
2011	291 453	505 051	25 905	373 226	74 892	31 028	479 513

17 -3 主要年份普通高等学校基本情况

MAJOR YEAR'S BASIC STATISTICS ON REGULAR INSTITUTIONS OF HIGHER EDUCATION

单位:人(person)

年份 Year	学校数(所) Schools (unit)	毕业生数 Graduates	招生数 New Students Enrollment	在校学生数 Students Enrollment	教职工数 Teachers and Staff	#专任教师 of which: Full-time Teachers
1949	1		250	1 007	779	226
1952	2	262	565	2 761	12 530	308
1957	2	356	755	3 133	1 308	622
1962	5	647	653	4 381	1 866	749
1965	3	741	529	2 987	1 539	623
1970	2	684		320	1 178	486
1975	2	460	473	1 151	1 353	582
1978	4	739	1 782	3 465	2 829	1 176
1980	6	431	1 717	6 783	4 182	1 606
1985	7	1 828	3 823	10 631	5 561	2 181
1988	7	3 496	4 687	14 408	6 875	2 499
1989	7	3 891	4 567	15 183	7 174	2 554
1990	7	4 495	4 745	15 433	7 305	2 624
1991	7	4 880	4 954	15 491	7 282	2 489
1992	7	4 458	5 428	16 470	7 344	2 523
1993	7	3 140	9 449	23 858	7 366	2 520
1994	4	7 059	8 042	25 018	7 466	2 650
1995	4	7 828	7 978	24 908	7 545	2 682
1996	4	6 691	7 956	26 076	7 606	2 745
1997	4	7 091	8 503	27 434	7 790	2 813
1998	4	6 912	8 849	29 507	7 662	2 907
1999	4	7 202	11 584	33 681	7 662	2 928
2000	6	7 128	18 427	46 131	8 030	3 278
2001	6	8 991	22 787	60 728	8 706	4 058
2002	7	13 053	29 731	82 539	9 517	4 723
2003	25	25 747	61 975	168 439	18 911	10 293
2004	25	34 860	70 022	201 739	21 437	12 347
2005	25	46 114	79 725	239 761	23 078	13 894
2006	25	55 931	79 094	260 339	24 881	15 195
2007	25	68 354	78 728	264 917	25 956	16 005
2008	25	75 198	86 878	269 314	26 654	16 805
2009	25	69 475	81 025	275 157	26 983	16 870
2010	25	70 450	82 220	284 788	28 145	16 996
2011	22	79 466	84 434	291 453	28 151	17 120

17－4 各类成人教育基本情况(2011 年)
BASIC STATISTICS ON ADULT EDUCATION(2011)

单位:人(person)

各类学校	Schools by Type of School	学校数(所) Schools (unit)	毕业生数 Graduates	招生数 New Students Enrollment	在校学生数 Students Enrollment	教职工数 Teachers and Staff	#专任教师 of which: Full-time Teachers
总 计	**Total**	**10**	**33 337**	**41 694**	**96 905**	**965**	**445**
成人高等教育	Adult Higher Education	2	29 880	35 674	81 008	638	226
广播电视大学	Broadcasting and TV Universities	1	59	252	630	104	57
职工、农民大学	Universities of Vocational and Agricultural Education						
函授、夜大学	Correspondence and Evening College Education		29 265	35 422	80 134		
管理干部学校	Cadre Management Schools	1	556		244	534	169
成人中等教育	Adult Secondary Education	8	3 457	6 020	15 897	327	219
成人中等专业学校	Adult Specialized Secondary Schools	8	3 457	6 020	15 897	327	219

注:本年度成人高等自学考试毕业 3880 人;参加成人高等单科班、进修班、短训班、专业证书班学习毕业(结业)38785 人。

Note:3880 persons have been graduated from adult higher tech-oneself tests in the year, 38785 persons have been graduated from adult higher single subject courses, training courses, short-term training course and specialized diploma courses.

17 -5 分市、区普通中学情况(2011 年)
BASIC STATISTICS ON REGULAR SECONDARY SCHOOLS BY REGION(2011)

单位:人(person)

市、区名称	Region	普通高中 Regular Senior Secondary Schools				普通初中 Regular Junior Secondary Schools			
		学校数(所) Schools (unit)	毕业生数 Graduates	招生数 New Students Enrollment	在校生数 Students Enrollment	学校数(所) Schools (unit)	毕业生数 Graduates	招生数 New Students Enrollment	在校生数 Students Enrollment
总　计	**Total**	**58**	**32 138**	**43 522**	**119 780**	**232**	**90 194**	**75 733**	**253 446**
市　区	Urban Area	32	12 633	14 308	42 232	75	26 428	26 849	81 938
#崂山区	Laoshan District	7	1 412	1 807	5 025	8	2 648	2 108	6 801
黄岛区	Huangdao District	3	1 547	1 943	6 039	9	3 770	3 964	12 301
城阳区	Chengyang District	3	2 008	2 804	7 756	15	6 055	5 556	17 562
即墨市	Jimo	7	4 683	6 234	18 059	29	14 864	11 135	37 317
胶州市	Jiaozhou	5	3 147	4 931	12 795	23	9 995	8 610	30 056
胶南市	Jiaonan	7	3 309	5 434	13 713	25	10 981	8 219	28 055
平度市	Pingdu	5	5 124	8 236	21 251	46	18 070	14 454	46 919
莱西市	Laixi	2	3 242	4 379	11 730	34	9 856	6 466	29 161

17 -6 分市、区职业中学、小学情况(2011 年)
BASIC STATISTICS ON VOCATIONAL SECONDARY SCHOOLS AND PRIMARY SCHOOLS BY REGION(2011)

单位:人(person)

市、区名称	Region	职业中学 Vocational Secondary Schools				小学 Primary Schools			
		学校数(所) Schools (unit)	毕业生数 Graduates	招生数 New Students Enrollment	在校生数 Students Enrollment	学校数(所) Schools (unit)	毕业生数 Graduates	招生数 New Students Enrollment	在校生数 Students Enrollment
总　计	**Total**	**53**	**39 060**	**21 940**	**74 892**	**889**	**76 249**	**92 860**	**479 513**
市　区	Urban Area	30	20 044	8 102	28 897	247	26 852	33 592	176 307
#崂山区	Laoshan District	1	552	1 413	2 929	24	2 270	2 855	14 799
黄岛区	Huangdao District	8	10 889	1 711	10 252	32	4 047	5 726	28 317
城阳区	Chengyang District	4	3 135	717	2 266	61	5 561	7 886	39 115
即墨市	Jimo	5	1 530	1 875	6 523	174	11 212	14 637	74 911
胶州市	Jiaozhou	1	2 013	2 838	7 132	96	8 966	11 347	58 354
胶南市	Jiaonan	11	12 153	4 653	19 994	76	8 179	10 171	53 141
平度市	Pingdu	2	2 494	2 993	7 806	190	14 610	14 886	80 769
莱西市	Laixi	4	826	1 479	4 540	106	6 430	8 227	36 031

17 -7 分市、区中小学教职工情况(2011 年)
BASIC STATISTICS ON TEACHERS AND STAFF IN SECONDARY AND PRIMARY SCHOOLS BY REGION(2011)

单位:人(person)

市、区名称	Region	普通中学 Regular Secondary Schools		职业中学 Vocational Secondary Schools		小学 Primary Schools	
		教职工数 Teachers and Staff	#专任教师 of which: Full-time Teachers	教职工数 Teachers and Staff	#专任教师 of which: Full-time Teachers	教职工数 Teachers and Staff	#专任教师 of which: Full-time Teachers
总 计	**Total**	**36 738**	**31 402**	**7 724**	**5 642**	**33 704**	**31 554**
市 区	Urban Area	12 287	9 871	4 174	2 840	11 830	10 852
#崂山区	Laoshan District	1 488	1 077	245	148	1 163	1 061
黄岛区	Huangdao District	1 416	1 325	854	687	1 447	1 405
城阳区	Chengyang District	2 491	2 266	894	575	2 221	2 092
即墨市	Jimo	5 442	4 709	708	575	5 176	4 867
胶州市	Jiaozhou	3 974	3 331	648	459	4 025	3 864
胶南市	Jiaonan	4 475	4 087	829	687	4 052	3 917
平度市	Pingdu	6 480	5 747	738	625	5 668	5 327
莱西市	Laixi	4 080	3 657	627	456	2 953	2 727

17 -8 分市、区幼儿园基本情况(2011 年)
BASIC STATISTICS ON KINDERGARTENS BY REGION(2011)

单位:人(person)

市、区名称	Region	幼儿园(所) Kindergartens(unit)	幼儿数 Children	教职工数 Teachers and Staff	#专任教师 of which: Full-time teachers
总 计	**Total**	**2 476**	**218 725**	**20 783**	**14 063**
市 区	Urban Area	582	86 393	10 950	6 635
#崂山区	Laoshan District	98	7 845	1 267	793
黄岛区	Huangdao District	88	14 648	1 853	1 131
城阳区	Chengyang District	132	18 443	2 009	1 508
即墨市	Jimo	431	38 767	2 397	1 700
胶州市	Jiaozhou	474	25 792	2 154	1 547
胶南市	Jiaonan	235	21 563	2 180	1 770
平度市	Pingdu	548	30 049	1 969	1 539
莱西市	Laixi	206	16 161	1 133	872

17 -9 科研机构基本情况(1978 -2011 年)
BASIC STATISTICS ON SCIENTIFIC RESEARCH INSTITUTIONS(1978 -2011)

年份 Year	独立自然科研机构(个) Independent Institutions of Natural Scientific Research(unit)	独立自然科研机构中科技人员(人) Personnel of Independent Institutions of Natural Scientific Research(person)	完成科研项目(项) Number of Scientific Research Projects Completed(item)	取得科技成果(项) Number of Achievements in S&T(item)
1978	31	2 701	306	306
1980			481	297
1982	41	2 345	451	451
1983	48	3 182	530	530
1984	53	3 312	507	507
1985	52	3 673	552	552
1986	63	3 998	577	577
1987	76	4 629	579	579
1988	101	5 199	544	510
1989	111	5 885	544	688
1990	141	6 046	414	931
1991	72	5 665	753	753
1992	71	5 726	659	659
1993	69	5 545	546	546
1994	69	5 540	467	467
1995	59	5 286	441	441
1996	58	4 738	613	613
1997	54	4 577	418	418
1998	52	4 142	517	517
1999	58	3 771	606	606
2000	54	3 637	621	621
2001	50	3 191	457	457
2002	52	3 248	406	406
2003	53	3 246	589	589
2004	50	3 226	506	506
2005	50	3 234	438	438
2006	50	3 291	548	548
2007	50	3 432	506	506
2008	42	3 709	416	416
2009	43	3 727	572	572
2010	44	4 088	472	472
2011	47	4 548	345	345

注:1991 年以后不包括民办科研机构。

Note:Since 1991,private institutions of scientific research are not included.

17－10 独立科学研究机构情况(2011 年)

BASIC STATISTICS ON INDEPENDENT INSTITUTIONS OF SCIENTIFIC RESEARCH(2011)

项　目	Item	计量单位	Unit	总　计 Total	中央属 Central	省属 Provincial	地市属 Local	县级市属 County
机构数	Number of Institutions	个	unit	47	10	11	24	2
职工人数	Staff and Workers	人	person	5 699	2 771	1 272	1 643	13
科技人员	Personnel Engaged in S&T	人	person	4 548	2 497	816	1 222	13
经费收入	Funding for S&T	万元	10000 yuan	240 384.6	154 324.6	42 255.3	43 727.7	77.0
经费支出	Expenditures for S&T	万元	10000 yuan	231 433.3	149 546.2	38 264.5	43 545.6	77.0

17－11 科学技术奖励情况(2011 年)

AWARD STATISTICS ON SCIENCE AND TECHNOLOGY(2011)

项　目	Item	单位	Unit	自然科学奖 Natural Science Prizes Awarded	技术发明奖 Invention Prizes Awarded	科技进步奖 Scientific And Technological Progress Prizes Awarded	科学技术功勋奖 Scientific And Technological Credit Prizes Awarded	国际科技合作奖 International S&T Cooperation Prizes Award	最高奖 Highest Prizes Award
国家级	**National Level**	**项**	**item**		**2**	**12**			
#一等	First Prize	项	item						
二等	Second Prize	项	item		2	12			
省级	**Provincial Level**	**项**	**item**	**4**	**4**	**88**		**1**	
#一等	First Prize	项	item	1	2	10			
二等	Second Prize	项	item	3	1	25			
三等	Third Prize	项	item		1	53			
市级	**Municipal Level**	**项**	**item**	**20**	**10**	**120**			
#一等	First Prize	项	item	2	1	15			
二等	Second Prize	项	item	10	4	43			
三等	Third Prize	项	item	8	5	62			

注:国际科技合作奖、最高奖不分等级。

Note:There is no grade in international scientific and technological cooperation prizes award and highest prizes award.

17-12 大中型工业企业技术开发主要相对指标(1990-2011年)

MAJOR INDICATORS OF TECHNOLOGY DEVELOPMENT OF LARGE AND MEDIUM-SIZE INDUSTRIAL ENTERPRISES (1990-2011)

项目	Item	单位	Unit	1990	1995	2000	2005	2006	2007	2008	2009	2010	2011
企业技术开发人员占全部职工比重	Percentage of Technology Development Personnel to Staff and Workers	%	%	2.3	2.6	5.7	4.4	4.9	5.9	5.6	5.8	6.7	7.7
科学家工程师占技术开发人员比重	Percentage of Scientists and Engineers to Technology Development Personnel	%	%	32.4	39.0	62.3	66.1	63.1	62.4	63.0			
设有开发机构的企业占企业总数比重	Percentage of Enterprises Having Development Institutions to Total Number of Enterprises	%	%	59.5	59.3	29.7	20.8	21.8	26.1	24.6	24.0	26.2	28.1
科学家工程师占开发机构人员比重	Percentage of Scientists and Engineers to Personnel of Development Institutions	%	%	37.1	48.1	77.6							
平均每个企业技术开发经费筹集额	Average Funding for Technology Development of Each Enterprise	万元	10 000 yuan	144.0	118.2	873.0	1 535.8	1 577.0	1 805.0	1 815.6			
平均每个企业技术开发经费支出额	Average Expenditures for Technology Development of Each Enterprise	万元	10 000 yuan	125.0	114.5	812.0	1 626.0	1 716.0	1 931.0	1 894.9			
开发新产品用款占经费支出比重	Percentage of Expenditures on New Product Development to Total Expenditures	%	%	81.9	50.8	52.6	55.9	58.4	63.3	66.2			
技术开发经费支出占产品销售收入比重	Percentage of Expenditures on Technology Development to Revenue from Product Sales	%	%	2.1	1.0	3.1	2.7	2.7	2.6	2.3			
新产品产值比重	Percentage of Output Value of New Products	%	%	8.2		35.5	31.3	32.7	28.4	26.8	27.4	28.4	28.8
新产品销售额比重	Percentage of Sales Volume of New Products	%	%	8.0	12.2	32.7	32.5	32.4	30.5	28.7	28.8	28.9	29.3
新产品利税额比重	Percentage of Profits and Taxes of New Products	%	%	7.4	18.7	30.6							

17－13 主要年份文化机构数
MAJOR YEAR'S INSTITUTIONS OF CULTURE

单位:个(unit)

年　份 Year	合计 Total	#影剧院 Cinemas	文化馆 Cultural Centers	艺术表演团体 Art Performance Troupes
1949	24	9	3	3
1952	50	11	15	8
1957	99	16	11	15
1962	103	17	12	13
1965	117	18	13	13
1970	121	20	12	13
1975	249	21	12	16
1978	402	24	13	15
1980	661	24	12	17
1985	1 290	81	12	11
1988	1 473	84	12	11
1989	1 308	106	12	11
1990	1 323	106	12	11
1991	1 185	108	12	11
1992	1 167	108	12	11
1993	1 079	103	12	11
1994	964	78	12	11
1995	767	61	13	11
1996	761	61	13	11
1997	634	61	12	11
1998	491	51	12	11
1999	638	43	12	11
2000	637	45	12	11
2001	614	44	12	11
2002	590	44	11	11
2003	492	50	11	11
2004	476	29	12	11
2005	478	39	12	12
2006	446	40	12	12
2007	451	40	12	12
2008	456	40	12	12
2009	459	40	12	12
2010	465	40	12	12
2011	470	40	12	10

17－14 文化、文物事业机构、人员数(2011 年)

NUMBER OF INSTITUTIONS AND PERSONNEL IN CULTURE AND CULTURAL RELICS(2011)

项 目	Item	文化机构数(个) Number of Cultural Institutions(unit)		文化人员数(人) Number of Cultural Personnel(person)	
		2011	2010	2011	2010
总 计	**Total**	**259**	**257**	**2 406**	**2 056**
文化事业合计	**Culture**	**242**	**240**	**2 169**	**1 831**
一、艺术事业	Art	21	23	856	850
1. 艺术表演团体	Art Performance Troupes	10	12	732	719
2. 艺术表演场所	Art Centers	9	9	106	114
3. 艺术创作机构	Art Creation Institutions				
4. 艺术研究机构	Art Research Institutions	2	2	18	17
5. 艺术展览机构	Art Exhibition Institutions				
6. 其他	Others				
二、图书馆事业	Libraries	13	13	267	268
公共图书馆	Public Libraries	13	13	267	268
#县(区)级图书馆	County Libraries	12	12	158	159
三、群众文化事业	Mass Culture	186	184	688	671
1. 群众艺术馆	Mass Art Centers	1	1	55	53
2. 文化馆	Cultural Palaces	12	12	182	186
3. 文化站	Cultural Centers	173	171	451	432
4. 其他	Others				
四、其他文化事业	Other Cultural Units	22	20	358	42
文物事业合计	**Cultural Relics**	**17**	**17**	**237**	**223**
一、文物机构	Cultural Relics Institutions	5	5	16	16
二、博物馆纪念馆	Museums and Memorial Halls	10	10	202	187
三、文物商店	Cultural Relics Shops	1	1	8	11
四、文物科研机构	Scientific and Research Institutions of Cultural Relics	1	1	11	11

17－15 分市、区艺术表演、电影发行及放映机构数(2011 年)

NUMBER OF INSTITUTIONS OF ART PERFORMANCE,FILMS DISTRIBUTION AND PROJECTION BY REGION(2011)

单位:个(unit)

市、区名称	Region	合计 Total	影剧院 Cinemas	电影发行机构 Institutions of Films Distribution	流动放映单位 Travelling Projection Units
总　计	**Total**	**276**	**40**	**9**	**227**
市　区	Urban Area	47	20	4	23
#崂山区	Laoshan District	5	2		3
黄岛区	Huangdao District	10	3	1	6
城阳区	Chengyang District	9			9
即墨市	Jimo	45	7	1	37
胶州市	Jiaozhou	33	1	1	31
胶南市	Jiaonan	44	1	1	42
平度市	Pingdu	64	3	1	60
莱西市	Laixi	43	8	1	34

17－16 艺术表演、电影放映情况(2011 年)

STATISTICS ON ART PERFORMANCE AND FILMS PROJECTION(2011)

项　目	Item	机构数(个) Number of Institutions (unit)	座位数(个) Number of Seats (unit)	演出场次(场) Number of Performances (show)	观众人数(万人次) Number of Spectators (10 000 person-times)	票款收入(万元) Income from Ticket Sales (10 000 yuan)
艺术表演总计	Art Performance	9	4 680	115	11	148
电影放映总计	Films Projection	267	25 373	277 239	1 831	11 989
#影剧院	Cinemas	40	25 373	204 951	369	11 989
流动放映单位	Travelling Projection Units	227		72 288	1 462	

17－17 文化部门艺术剧团情况(2011 年)
STATISTICS ON ART TROUPES OF CULTURAL DEPARTMENT(2011)

项目	Item	剧团数（个）Number of Troupes (unit)	职工人数（人）Staff and Workers (person)	演出场次（场）Number of Performances (show)	观众人数(万人次) Number of Spectators (10 000 person-times)	演出收入（万元）Income from Performance (10 000 yuan)	拨款经费（万元）Appropriation Funds (10 000 yuan)
总计	**Total**	**10**	**732**	**1 689**	**213.8**	**1 161.7**	**5 707.3**
一、按隶属关系分	**Grouped by Administrative Relationship**						
国营剧团	State-run Troupes	10	732	1 689	213.8	1 161.7	5 707.3
集体经营剧团	Collective-owned Troupes						
二、按剧种分	**Grouped by Type of Drama**						
1. 话剧团	Drama Troupes	1	99	236	13.2	217.9	737.9
2. 歌舞团	Song and Dance Troupes	1	214	250	13.7	577.3	1 601.1
3. 戏曲剧团	Local Opera Troupes	5	230	896	151.3	189.8	1 580.5
#京剧	of which:Beijing Opera	1	82	150	6.4	88.2	622.7
4. 曲艺团	Recitation and Ballad Troupes						
5. 文工团(艺术团)	Cultural and Performance Troupes	3	189	307	35.6	176.7	1 787.8

17－18 图书馆、博物馆、文化馆情况
STATISTICS ON LIBRARIES,MUSEUMS AND CULTURAL CENTERS

项目	Item	单位	Unit	2011		2010	
				全市合计 Total	#市区 Urban Area	全市合计 Total	#市区 Urban Area
公共图书馆	**Public Libraries**	个	**unit**	**13**	**8**	**13**	**8**
工作人员	Staff and Workers	人	person	267	196	268	198
藏书册数	Collection Books	千册	1000 copies	4 709	3 506	4 442	3 318
阅览席位	Seating Capacity of Reading Rooms	张	seat	5 507	3 884	5 735	4 112
读者人数	Readers	万人次	10 000 person-times	326.7	233.7	300.9	238.5
博物馆、纪念馆	**Museums and Memorial Halls**	个	**unit**	**10**	**5**	**10**	**4**
工作人员	Staff and Workers	人	person	202	153	187	139
藏品数量	Collections	万件	10 000 copies	15.7	10.9	15.7	10.9
参观人数	Visitors	万人次	10 000 person-times	161.5	96.5	139.3	110.6
文化馆	**Cultural Centers**	个	**unit**	**12**	**7**	**12**	**7**

17－19 图书、杂志、报纸出版情况(1990－2011年)

PUBLICATION OF BOOKS, MAGAZINES AND NEWSPAPERS(1990－2011)

项　目	Item	单位	Unit	1990	1995
图书出版	**Publication of Books**				
种数	Number of Publication	种	kind	292	530
总印数	Total Printed Copies	万册	10 000 copies	1 626	2 109
总印张数	Total Printed Sheets	千印张	1 000 sheets	40 358	75 242
杂志出版	**Publication of Magazines**				
种数	Number of Publication	种	kind	32	34
每期平均印数	Average Printed Copies per Issue	万册(份)	10 000 copies	41.71	37.42
总印数	Total Printed Copies	万册	10 000 copies	452	409
总印张数	Total Printed Sheets	千印张	1 000 sheets	6 422	5 630
报纸出版	**Publication of Newspapers**				
种数	Number of Publication	种	kind	4	8
每期平均印数	Average Printed Copies per Issue	万份	10 000 copies	64.25	81.51
总印数	Total Printed Copies	万份	10 000 copies	7 127	16 318
总印张数	Total Printed Sheets	千印张	1 000 sheets	56 670	231 642

注:自2008年图书出版种数改按种次统计,总印数,总印张数均按此口径进行统计。

Note: Number of book publication in 2008 are according to the type and times of statistical. The total printed copies and total printed sheets are the same calibre.

2000	2005	2006	2007	2008	2009	2010	2011
572	896	926	788	3 609	3 642	2 562	4 102
1 542	2 873	1 697	1 376	6 055	6 124	6 443	6 713
71 826	191 671	194 584	112 337	376 404	396 753	413 917	412 686
35	44	44	44	45	49	50	47
75.41	76.95	85.41	72.26	106.5	99.97	100.93	96.3
1 249	1 755	1 779	1 936	2 587	2 616	2 650	2 766
31 946	69 635	56 913	63 235	83 748	86 064	98 136	80 345
14	12	12	12	13	14	15	15
84.74	174.16	183.26	202.82	231.20	257.89	291.54	297.48
21 309	53 947	57 135	63 800	74 143	78 239	93 255	107 615
555 503	4 188 151	3 944 883	4 773 915	5 624 658	5 877 377	7 130 931	12 346 098

17 -20 广播电视业基本情况(1990 -2011 年)

BASIC STATISTICS ON RADIO AND TELEVISION STATIONS(1990 -2011)

项　目	Item	单位	Unit	1990	1995
一、广播基本情况	**Basic Statistics on Radio**				
电台个数	Number of Radio Stations	座	set	6	8
发射台个数	Number of Transmission Stations	座	set	7	9
节目套数	Number of Programs	套	set	7	10
平均日播音时间	Broadcasting Hours per Day	时:分	hour: minute	53:35	126:35
#自办节目	of which: Self-programs	时:分	hour: minute	41:15	117:05
#本年自制广播节目时间	Hours of Programs Making in the Year	小时	hour		
广播人口覆盖率	Radio Coverage of Population	%	%	94	94
二、电视基本情况	**Basic Statistics on Television**				
电视台个数	Number of Television Stations	座	set	4	8
发射台个数	Number of Transmission Stations	座	set	42	48
节目套数	Number of Programs	套	set	4	9
平均每周播出时间	Broadcasting Hour per Week	时:分	hour: minute	129:10	382:18
#自办节目	of which: Self-programs	时:分	hour: minute	38:25	327:35
#本年自制广播节目时间	Hours of Programs Making in the Year	小时	hour		
电视人口覆盖率	TV Coverage of Population	%	%	90.87	92.00
三、有线电视基本情况	**Basic Statistics on CATV**				
总用户数	Number of Users of CATV	万户	10 000 households		
有线电视入户率	CATV Coverage of Household	%	%		
网络总长	Length of the Network	公里	km		
广播电视卫星收转系统	Satellite Relaying Systems of Radio and Television	座	set		

2000	2005	2006	2007	2008	2009	2010	2011
1	1	1	1	1	1	1	1
9	11	10	10	10	10	10	10
10	12	12	12	12	12	12	12
119: 15	174:01	190:43	195:23	221:09	220:39	237:23	237:12
107: 50	111:12	139:25	137:48	163:49	174:44	183:40	182:48
	36 964	48 604	50 853	60 892	61 642	64 146	66 075
96.0	97.9	98.0	98.1	98.2	98.3	98.4	98.5
1	1	1	1	1	1	1	1
29	11	10	10	10	10	10	10
9	15	15	15	15	15	15	15
489: 20	1 522:38	1 653:25	1 659:37	1 618:56	1 640:32	1 771:36	1712:36
410: 54	597:55	827:06	717:47	652:41	660:52	760:18	727:01
	11 977	12 774	13 089	11 874	9 713	15 406	12 974
95.04	97.70	97.80	97.90	98.00	98.10	98.20	98.30
	176.60	201.60	218.48	218.57	241.55	253.83	268.2
	75.05	84.96	91.29	90.48	93.79	103.72	
	44 827	46 479	49 303	50 871	51 297	52 617	
	1 062	168	178	162	121	113	

主要统计指标解释

普通高等学校 指按照国家规定的设置标准和审批程序批准举办,通过国家统一招生考试,招收高中毕业生为主要培养对象,实施高等教育的全日制大学、独立设置的学院和高等专科学校、短期职业大学。

成人高等学校 指按照国家有关规定审批,招收通过全国成人高教统一招生考试的具有高中毕业或同等学历的在职从业人员,利用脱产、半脱产、业余或函授等多种形式对其实施高等学历教育,培养高等教育专科或本科毕业水平的专门人才,修业年限、课程设置和总学时数均按高等学历教育要求付诸实施的学校。包括广播电视大学、职工高等学校、农民高等学校、管理干部学院;教育学院、独立设置的函授学院等。

科技活动人员 指直接从事科技活动、以及专门从事科技活动管理和为科技活动提供直接服务,累计的实际工作时间占全年制度工作时间10%及以上的人员。

文化事业机构 指从事专业文化工作和为专业文化工作服务的独立建制的单独核算的单位。不包括这些单位另外举办独立核算的其他机构和各部门的业余文化组织。

Explanatory Notes on Main Statistical Indicators

Regular Institutions of Higher Education refer to educational establishments set up according to the government evaluation and approval procedures, enrolling graduates from senior secondary schools and providing higher education courses and training for senior professionals. They include full-time universities, colleges, high professional schools, high professional vocational schools and others.

Adult Institutions of Higher Education refer to educational establishments, set up in line with relevant rules approved by the government, enrolling staff and workers with senior secondary school or equivalent education, and providing higher education courses in many forms of correspondence, spare time, or full time for adults. Professionals thus trained receive a qualification equivalent to graduates studying regular courses at regular universities, colleges and professional colleges. Institutions of higher learning for adults include schools of high education for staff and workers, schools of high education for peasants, colleges for management cadres, pedagogical colleges, independent correspondence colleges, Radio and TV universities and other educational establishments.

Personnel Engaged in S&T Activities refer to personnel directly engaged in S&T activities, in the management of S&T activities, and in providing direct service to S&T activities, who spend over 10% of the total working hours in a year in S&T activities.

Cultural Institutions refer to units, which have their own organizational system and independent accounting system and specialize in or serve cultural development. They exclude other establishments run by these cultural institutions and amateur cultural groups established by various departments.

体育、卫生和民政、司法 18

SPORTS, PUBLIC HEALTH AND CIVIL AFFAIRS, JUDICIAL AFFAIRS

简要说明

一、本篇资料的主要内容

本篇资料反映了全市体育、卫生、民政、司法等社会事业的基本情况。体育部分主要包括主要年份运动员、教练员、裁判员发展人数、体育运动破纪录、获奖情况。卫生部分主要包括各类卫生机构及其人员、床位数。民政部分主要包括婚姻登记、社会救济、社会福利事业基本情况、殡葬服务情况。司法部分主要包括律师、公证、调解、社会治安基本情况。

二、本篇资料的来源

1、体育部分来源于市体育局。

2、卫生部分来源于市卫生局。

3、民政部分来源于市民政局。

4、司法部分，社会治安资料来源于市公安局，其他资料来源于市司法局。

本篇资料由市统计局人口和社会科技统计处整理提供。

Brief Introduction

I. Main Content

Data in this chapter show the basic conditions of sports, public health, civil affairs and judicial affairs. Data on sports are mainly including the number of athletes, coaches and referees, conditions of record and awards. Data on public health are mainly including the number of health institutions, personnel and beds. Data on civil affairs are mainly including the conditions of marriage registration, social relief, social welfare and funeral services. Data on judicial affairs are mainly including the conditions of lawyers, notarization, mediation and social order.

II. Source of Data

（1）Data on sports are provided by Qingdao Municipal Bureau of Physical.

（2）Data on public health are provided by Qingdao Municipal Bureau of Health.

（3）Data on civil affairs are provided by Qingdao Municipal Bureau of Civil Affairs.

（4）In judicial affairs component, data on social order are provided by Qingdao Municipal Bureau of Public Security and the other data are provided by Qingdao Municipal Bureau of Justice.

Data in this chapter are provided and compiled by the Division of Population and Science & Technology of Qingdao Municipal Bureau of Statistics.

18－1 体育事业情况(1985－2011年)

STATISTICS ON SPORTS(1985－2011)

单位:人(person)

项目	Item	1985	1990	1995	2000	2005	2006	2007	2008	2009	2010	2011
体育部门职工人数	**Staff and Workers in Sports Commissions**	**464**	**714**	**902**	**849**	**834**	**848**	**772**	**1210**	**910**	**1 015**	
#运动员	Athletes	31	88	121	90	87	81	55	452	512	287	
教练员	Coaches	129	166	175	174	235	221	211	173	106	170	136
重点体校	Key Sports Schools	6	70	141	126	117	166	249	109	97	115	129
业余体校	Sparetime Sports Schools	83	174	117	142	223	220	145		160		
体育专业队	Professional Sports Teams	31	120	158	135	132	154	121		144	192	87
优秀运动员	Excellent Athletes	31	82	121	90	87	81	55	71	72	146	57
优秀运动队专职教练员	Full-time Coaches of Excellent Sports Teams	3	14	15	18	23	48	47	106	92	97	54
等级裁判员发展人数	**Certified Referees**	**977**	**827**	**223**	**1 114**	**275**	**1 068**	**781**	**205**	**292**	**212**	**510**
#二级	Second Grades	381	402	50	451	275	1 068	781	181	252	169	510
三级	Third Grades	596	425	136	616							
等级运动员发展人数	**Certified Athletes**	**1 115**	**868**	**249**	**343**	**260**	**267**	**108**	**310**	**512**	**229**	**436**
#二级	Second Grades		7	135	209	260	267	108	281	448	229	436
三级	Third Grades	682	454	114	46							
少年级	Juvenile	433	395		88							

18 -1 续表
continued

项目	Item	单位	Unit	1985	1990	1995	2000	2005	2006	2007	2008	2009	2010	2011
全年获得奖牌数	**Number of Medals Won in the Year**	**枚**	**unit**	**184**	**281**	**278**	**347.5**	**669**	**829**	**481**	**494**	**602**	**754**	**829**
#国家级金牌	Golden Medals at National Level	枚	unit	28	20	34	45	62	71	61	26	30	14	105
国家级银牌	Silver Medal at National Level	枚	unit	36	23	18	28	48	54	38	21	23	7	49
省级金牌	Golden Medals at Provincial Level	枚	unit		83	94	116.5	187	363	116	168	207	459	225
省级银牌	Silver Medals at Provincial Level	枚	unit		79	47	62	174	144	93	122	149	116	155
体育运动破全国记录	**Records Broken the National Records**													
项目	Number of Events	项	item		5	2		2		1		1	1	2
人数	Number of Persons	人	person		8	2		2		1		1	1	2
次数	Number of Times	人次	person-time		7	2		4		1		1	1	2
体育运动破全省记录	**Records Broken the Provincial Records**													
项目	Number of Events	项	item		3	4	7	3	5		2		1	
人数	Number of Persons	人	person		3	5	7	1	3		2		1	
次数	Number of Times	人次	person-time		2	5	7	3	5		2		1	

18 -2 主要年份卫生事业基本情况
MAJOR YEAR'S BASIC STATISTICS ON PUBLIC HEALTH

年份 Year	卫生机构数(个) Health Institutions (unit)	#医院 of which: Hospitals	医疗床位数(张) Beds in Health Institutions (bed)	#医院 of which: Hospitals	卫生技术人员(人) Medical and Technical Personnel(person)	#医生 of which: Doctors	每千人口拥有医生数(人) Number of Doctors per 1000 Population(person)	每千人口拥有床位数(张) Number of Hospital Beds per 1000 Population(bed)
1949	80	26	1 079	970	2 637	1 292	0.32	0.27
1952	260	34	2 943	1 691	3 748	1 559	0.37	0.70
1957	624	45	5 163	2 656	6 941	2 578	0.53	1.07
1962	849	149	7 167	4 526	8 279	2 972	0.64	1.55
1965	912	162	8 428	5 003	9 051	3 586	0.73	1.72
1970	712	170	8 613	6 603	9 591	3 761	0.70	1.60
1975	959	181	10 902	9 078	13 558	4 566	0.80	1.90
1978	1 192	212	13 084	10 709	16 921	5 893	1.01	2.24
1980	1 253	212	14 170	11 345	19 265	6 781	1.14	2.38
1985	1 517	219	18 469	13 214	23 413	9 694	1.55	2.95
1987	1 553	228	21 667	15 463	26 669	11 738	1.81	3.34
1989	1 566	232	22 668	15 670	27 195	13 555	2.06	3.46
1990	1 563	235	23 541	16 586	27 932	13 761	2.08	3.56
1991	1 579	235	23 727	16 796	27 772	13 227	1.98	3.54
1992	1 562	236	24 765	17 269	28 305	13 157	1.95	3.67
1993	1 540	237	24 885	17 469	28 705	13 312	1.97	3.68
1994	1 335	242	24 732	17 882	28 938	13 535	1.99	3.64
1995	1 347	228	25 282	18 126	29 816	13 840	2.02	3.69
1996	2 216	228	24 334	18 344	30 048	13 790	2.00	3.53
1997	2 193	239	25 201	19 046	31 121	14 400	2.07	3.62
1998	2 190	237	24 887	19 083	31 623	14 327	2.05	3.56
1999	2 185	235	25 481	19 798	31 965	14 453	2.06	3.62
2000	2 911	231	24 392	20 057	32 160	14 860	2.10	3.45
2001	3 199	217	24 755	20 313	32 765	15 772	2.22	3.48
2002	3 050	213	21 370	20 662	31 469	13 371	1.87	2.99
2003	3 111	213	23 980	21 605	32 337	13 452	1.87	3.33
2004	2 923	219	25 432	23 465	32 937	13 953	1.91	3.48
2005	2 609	235	30 627	28 564	33 942	15 008	2.03	4.13
2006	2 834	232	28 724	26 653	34 360	15 451	2.06	3.83
2007	2 116	251	30 062	28 107	33 807	15 018	1.98	3.97
2008	1 985	249	32 350	29 874	36 574	16 260	2.14	4.25
2009	2 017	252	32 803	30 527	40 217	16 734	2.19	4.30
2010	2 147	254	36 066	33 383	43 285	17 696	2.32	4.72
2011	2 549	280	39 980	35 600	47 347	18 310	2.39	5.22

18－3 各类卫生机构、床位、人员数(2011 年底)

NUMBER OF HEALTH INSTITUTIONS, BEDS AND EMPLOYED PERSONS(END OF 2011)

项　　目	Item	机构数(个) Health Institutions (unit)	床位数(张) Beds in Health Institutions (bed)	人员数(人) Personnel (person)
总　计		**2 549**	**39 980**	**56 343**
一、医院合计	**Sub-total of Hospitals**	**280**	**35 600**	**43 415**
1. 医院	Hospitals	170	28 862	37 276
综合医院	General Hospitals	96	19 801	27 009
中医医院	Hospitals Specialized in Traditional Chinese Medicine	16	2 591	3 272
中西医结合医院	Hospitals of Combination of Chinese and Western Medicine	3	475	487
专科医院	Specialized Hospitals	53	5 935	6 482
口腔医院	Stomatological Hospitals	2		122
眼科医院	Ophthalmology Hospitals	3	171	193
肿瘤医院	Tumor Hospitals	2	565	571
心血管病医院	Cardiovascular Diseases Hospitals	5	646	921
精神病医院	Mental Hospitals	6	1 320	756
传染病医院	Infectious Disease Hospitals	2	640	469
妇产科医院	Obstetrics and Gynecology Hospitals	7	513	757
骨科医院	Orthopaedics Hospitals	5	711	654
其它专科医院	Other Specialized Hospitals	21	1 369	2 039
护理院	Nursing Homes	2	60	26
2. 卫生院	Sanitation Stations	110	6 738	6 139
二、社区卫生服务中心	**Neighborhood Service Centers**	**55**	**536**	**1 630**
三、社区卫生服务站	**Neighborhood Service Stations**	**241**	**515**	**1 993**
四、门诊部	**Outpatient Service Stations**	**41**	**34**	**698**
五、诊所、卫生所、医务室	**Clinics Medical Houses**	**1 818**		**4 547**
六、急救中心	**First Aid Centers**	**2**		**148**
七、采供血机构	**Institutions of Blood Collection and Supply**	**1**		**226**
八、妇幼保健院(所、站)	**Maternity and Child Care Centers**	**13**	**382**	**930**
九、专科疾病防治院(所、站)	**Specialized Disease Prevention & Treatment Institutions**	**10**	**338**	**361**
十、疾病预防控制中心(防疫站)	**Centers for Disease Control and Prevention (Epidemic Prevention Stations)**	**28**		**998**
十一、卫生监督所(中心)	**Sanitation Control Stations**	**13**		**364**
十二、卫生监督检验所(站)	**Sanitation Control and Test Stations**			
十三、医学科学研究机构	**Institutions of Medical Science**			
十四、医学在职培训机构	**Institutions of Medical Training for Working Personnel**			
十五、临床检验中心(所、站)		**1**		**3**
十六、健康教育所(站、中心)	**Health Education Stations**	**1**		**4**
十七、其它卫生机构	**Other Health Institutions**	**33**		**289**
十八、疗养院	**Sanatoriums**	**12**	**2 575**	**737**

#卫生技术人员 Medical and Technical Personnel	#医生 Doctors	注册护士 Registered Nurses	药剂人员 Pharmacists	检验人员 Laboratory Technicians
47 347	**18 310**	**19 574**	**2 865**	**1 669**
36 463	**12 635**	**16 338**	**2 361**	**1 282**
30 957	10 401	14 671	1 815	1 028
22 774	7 470	11 011	1 332	706
2 764	1 019	1 163	190	92
404	149	211	24	13
4 997	1 754	2 278	268	217
108	88	10	3	1
133	56	70	5	1
434	132	224	21	13
719	192	310	31	24
589	174	350	23	14
352	113	172	25	28
562	187	240	27	29
532	250	190	34	21
1 568	562	712	99	86
18	9	8	1	
5 506	2 234	1 667	546	254
1 376	**541**	**450**	**137**	**62**
1 672	**803**	**598**	**121**	**66**
533	**224**	**198**	**32**	**28**
4 467	**2 928**	**1 343**	**114**	**22**
77	**30**	**40**	**2**	**1**
155	**49**	**48**	**1**	**53**
734	**351**	**232**	**26**	**49**
279	**110**	**89**	**32**	**20**
781	**372**	**56**	**16**	**73**
223				
3	**1**	**1**	**1**	
3	**2**		**1**	
241	**156**	**47**	**8**	**5**
340	**108**	**134**	**13**	**8**

18 -4 分市、区各类卫生机构、床位、人员数(2011 年底)

NUMBER OF HEALTH INSTITUTIONS, BEDS AND EMPLOYED PERSONS BY REGION (END OF 2011)

市、区名称	Region	机构数（个）Institutions (unit)	医院小计 Sub-total of Hospitals	#医院 Hospitals	卫生院 Sanitation Stations	社区卫生服务中心 Neighborhood Service Centers
总　计	**Total**	**2 549**	**280**	**170**	**110**	**55**
市　区	Urban Area	1 732	129	116	13	52
#崂山区	Laoshan District	186	15	11	4	1
黄岛区	Huangdao District	184	14	10	4	2
城阳区	Chengyang District	165	19	14	5	3
即墨市	Jimo	185	36	14	22	
胶州市	Jiaozhou	143	25	11	14	
胶南市	Jiaonan	225	20	4	16	1
平度市	Pingdu	172	39	10	29	
莱西市	Laixi	80	31	15	16	2

18 -4 续表 1

continued

市、区名称	Region	采供血机构 Institutions of Blood Collection and Supply	妇幼保健院(所、站) Maternity and Child Care Centers	专科疾病防治院(所、站) Specialized Disease Prevention & Treatment Institutions
总　计	**Total**	**1**	**13**	**10**
市　区	Urban Area	1	8	2
#崂山区	Laoshan District		1	
黄岛区	Huangdao District		1	
城阳区	Chengyang District		1	
即墨市	Jimo		1	1
胶州市	Jiaozhou		1	
胶南市	Jiaonan		1	2
平度市	Pingdu		1	3
莱西市	Laixi		1	2

社区卫生服务站 Neighborhood Service Stations	门诊部 Outpatient Service Stations	诊所、卫生所、医务室 Clinics Medical Houses	急救中心 First Aid Centers
241	**41**	**1 818**	**2**
187	37	1 284	1
17	9	141	
38	16	105	
		132	
36		84	
4		107	1
4	4	189	
		125	
10		29	

疾病预防控制中心(防疫站) Centers for Disease Control and Prevention (Epidemic Prevention Stations)	卫生监督所 Sanitation Control Stations	卫生监督检疫所(站) Sanitation Control and Test stations	医学科学研究机构 Institutions of Medical Science	医学在职培训机构 Institutions of Medical Training for Working Personnel
28	**13**			
22	8			
1	1			
7	1			
9	1			
1	1			
1	1			
1	1			
1	1			
2	1			

18－4 续表2
continued

市、区名称	Region	健康教育所（站、中心） Health Education Station	临床检验中心（所、站）	其他卫生机构 Other Health Institutions	疗养院 Sanatoriums	床位数(张) Beds in Health Institutions(bed)
总　计	**Total**	**1**	**1**	**33**	**12**	**39 980**
市　区	Urban Area		1		11	23 025
#崂山区	Laoshan District				1	784
黄岛区	Huangdao District					2 324
城阳区	Chengyang District					2 550
即墨市	Jimo	1		24	1	4 494
胶州市	Jiaozhou			3		3 063
胶南市	Jiaonan			2		2 488
平度市	Pingdu			2		3 446
莱西市	Laixi			2		3 464

18－4 续表3
continued

市、区名称	Region	专科疾病防治院(所、站) Specialized Disease Centers	人员数(人) Personnel (person)	卫生技术人员 Medical and Technical Personnel
总　计	**Total**	**338**	**56 343**	**47 347**
市　区	Urban Area	25	36 714	30 230
#崂山区	Laoshan District		1 554	1 276
黄岛区	Huangdao District		4 140	3 556
城阳区	Chengyang District		3 591	3 041
即墨市	Jimo		4 740	4 178
胶州市	Jiaozhou		3 834	3 319
胶南市	Jiaonan	75	3 485	3 170
平度市	Pingdu	193	3 923	3 403
莱西市	Laixi	45	3 647	3 047

医院小计 Sub-total of Hospitals	#医院 Hospitals	卫生院 Sanitation Stations	门诊部 Outpatient Service Stations	妇幼保健院(所、站) Maternity and Child Care Centers
35 600	**28 862**	**6 738**	**34**	**382**
19 780	19 164	616	24	
725	640	85	3	
2 259	2 078	181	21	
2 501	2 151	350		
4 044	2 647	1 397		100
3 008	2 071	937		55
2 268	1 153	1 115	10	110
3 181	1 579	1 602		72
3 319	2 248	1 071		45

执业医师 Certified Doctors	执业助理医师 Assistant Doctors	注册护士 Registered Nurses	药剂人员 Pharmacists	检验人员 Laboratory Technicians	其他人员 Other Personnel
16 917	**1 393**	**19 574**	**2 865**	**1 669**	**3 047**
11 049	660	12 774	1 733	1 086	2 213
521	65	499	65	45	49
1 227	87	1 615	167	124	340
1 083	105	1 238	163	104	254
1 463	121	1 609	285	133	195
1 062	167	1 516	178	96	120
1 120	119	1 232	192	114	119
1 289	177	1 245	241	110	214
934	149	1 198	236	130	186

18－5 收养性社会福利单位情况(2011 年)

BASIC STATICTICS ON SOCIAL WELFARE INSTITUTIONS(2011)

市、区名称	Region	单位数(个) Number of Institutions (unit)	年末职工人数(人) Number of Staff and Workers at Year-end (person)	年末床位数(张) Number of Beds at Year-end (bed)
总　计	**Total**	**263**	**3 177**	**27 383**
市　区	Urban Area	131	2 210	14 300
#崂山区	Laoshan District	10	64	388
黄岛区	Huangdao District	2	22	220
城阳区	Chengyang District	8	43	884
即墨市	Jimo	32	223	3 851
胶州市	Jiaozhou	17	150	2 038
胶南市	Jiaonan	28	275	2 630
平度市	Pingdu	33	121	2 217
莱西市	Laixi	22	198	2 347

18－6 社会救济情况(2011 年)

BASIC STATISTICS ON SOCIAL RELIEF(2011)

市、区名称	Region	城镇居民最低生活保障人数(人) Number of Persons Receiving Minimum Living Allowance in Urban Area(person)	城镇居民最低生活保障家庭数(户) Number of Households Receiving Minimum Living Allowance in Urban Area(household)	城镇低保资金计划支出(万元) Planned Expense of Funds for Minimum Living Allowance in Urban Area (10 000 yuan)	城镇临时救济人数(人次) Number of Persons Receiving Temporary Relief in Urban Area(person-time)
总　计	**Total**	**41 191**	**20 069**	**20 928.2**	**9 409**
市　区	Urban Area	34 954	16 843	19247.3	6 453
#崂山区	Laoshan District	545	253	175.8	384
黄岛区	Huangdao District	573	342	151.0	
城阳区	Chengyang District	643	338	207.3	121
即墨市	Jimo	1 493	849	399.7	281
胶州市	Jiaozhou	1 013	564	303.7	933
胶南市	Jiaonan	1 354	669	366.3	
平度市	Pingdu	975	513	262.2	
莱西市	Laixi	1 402	631	349.0	1 742

注：农村低保含农村五保供养。

Note: Minimum living allowance in rural area contains rural households with livelihood guaranteed in five aspects.

年末在院人数(人) Residences at Year-end (person)	优抚对象 Disabled Military Servicemen and Family Members of War Heroes and Military Servicemen	"三无"对象 Senior Citizen, Disabled Persons, Minors Non-ability to Work, Non-source of income and Non-supports the human or the provider	自费人员 Self-supporting Persons
18 930	**489**	**7 700**	**10 741**
11 388	106	1 780	9 502
388	1	365	22
92		82	10
689	15	271	403
1 433	67	656	710
1 495	15	1 406	74
1 367	220	1 039	108
1 173	26	1 147	
2 074	55	1 672	347

农村居民最低生活保障人数(人) Number of Persons Receiving Minimum Living Allowance in Rural Area (person)	农村居民最低生活保障家庭数(户) Number of Households Receiving Minimum Living Allowance in Rural Area (household)	农村低保资金计划支出(万元) Planned Expense of Funds for Minimum Living Allowance in Rural Area (10 000 yuan)	农村临时救济人数(人次) Number of Persons Receiving Temporary Relief in Rural Area (person-time)
90 449	**54 979**	**14 037.7**	**2003**
12 244	6 099	2 190.2	1212
3 468	1 630	574.1	467
2 769	1 365	646.5	
6 007	3 104	969.6	745
19 646	12 102	3 024.6	791
13 759	8 331	2 371.3	
14 119	8 934	1 483.7	
16 306	10 324	2 179.7	
14 375	9 189	2 788.2	

18－7 分市、区婚姻登记情况(2011 年)
BASIC STATISTICS ON MARRIAGE REGISTRATION BY REGION(2011)

市、区名称	Region	准予登记结婚 Registered Marriages					准予登记离婚(对) Registered Divorces (couple)	涉外婚姻登记(对) Registered Marriages with Foreigner(couple)
		合计(对) Total(couple)	初婚(人) First Marriages (person)	恢复结婚(对) Resumed Marriages (couple)	再婚(人) Remarriages(person) 男 Male	女 Female		
总　计	**Total**	**78 903**	**138 600**	**1 146**	**9 652**	**9 554**	**14 466**	**341**
市　区	Urban Area	35 071	65 502	462	2 556	2 084	6 645	341
#崂山区	Laoshan District	3 302	5 878		395	331	359	
黄岛区	Huangdao District	4 620	9 240				899	
城阳区	Chengyang District	4 779	8 292	95	693	573	585	
即墨市	Jimo	9 416	15 504	28	1 667	1 661	1 888	
胶州市	Jiaozhou	7 348	12 265	171	1 211	1 220	1 381	
胶南市	Jiaonan	7 612	12 816		1 124	1 284	1 462	
平度市	Pingdu	12 650	21 019	200	1 970	2 311	2 061	
莱西市	Laixi	6 806	11 494	285	1 124	994	1 029	

18-8 律师、公证、调解、社会治安基本情况(1985-2011年)

BASIC STATISTICS ON LAWYERS,NOTARIZATION,MEDIATION AND SOCIAL ORDER (1985-2011)

项目	Item	单位	Unit	1985	1990	1995	2000	2005
一、律师工作	**Lawyers**							
律师事务所	Law Offices	个	unit	13	16	61	76	116
律师工作者	Lawyers	人	person	152	278	783	1 439	1 941
专职	Full-time Lawyers	人	person	68	111	458	971	1 542
兼职(含特邀)	Part-time Lawyers	人	person	84	167	325	150	73
聘请常年法律顾问单位	Units with Permanent Legal Advisors	个	unit	162	731	2 028	2 508	3 564
全年办理民事代理	Agent of Civil Cases	件	case	309	1 512	1 650	5 571	11 104
刑事辩护	Defender of Criminal Cases	件	case	275	1 172	1 009	1 755	3 003
非诉讼事件	Agent of Non-litigious Legal Affairs	件	case	128	252	3 885	5 251	6 501
解答法律询问	Agent of Legal Advisory Services	件	case	8 305	15 489	23 758	58 385	27 880
代写法律事务文书	Agent of Legal Documents Written on Behalf of Clients	件	case	1 460	2 237	4 635	9 335	8 595
二、公证工作	**Notarization**							
公证处	Notary Offices	个	unit	13	13	15	15	15
公证人员	Notarial Personnel	人	person	71	103	111	152	196
公证员	Notaries	人	person	46	56	89	106	112
办理公证文书	Notarized Documents	件	case	22 627	68 954	106 205	120 849	105 787
三、人民调解	**People's Mediation**							
人民调解委员会	People's Mediation Committees	个	unit	8 009	8 718	9 631	9 750	11 480
调解人员	Mediators	人	person	38 721	41 061	64 806	34 714	46 735
调解民间纠纷	Civil Disputes Mediated	件	case	22 409	21 175	17 552	18 501	13 658
四、社会治安	**Social Order**							
交通事故发生次数	Traffic Accidents	次	time	360	1 047	917	15 601	7 051
死亡人数	Deaths	人	person	90	345	600	1 371	776
受伤人数	Injuries	人	person	282	409	329	8 620	6 639
经济损失	Losses	万元	10 000 yuan	32.70	125.30	381.55	4 815.70	2 208.20
火灾发生次数	Fire Accidents	次	time	206	422	221	3 088	1 948
死亡人数	Deaths	人	person	18	12	18	10	3
受伤人数	Injuries	人	person	15	18	33	43	3
经济损失	Losses	万元	10 000 yuan	77.96	401.62	3 542.29	1 531.06	550.40

注:火灾发生次数自1997年统计方法及口径范围发生变化,与往年不可比。交通事故发生次数自1998年统计方法及口径范围发生变化,与往年不可比。

Note:The statistical method and coverage have been adopted in fire accidents since 1997 and in traffic accidents since 1998. The data are not comparable with those in preceding year.

18 -8 续表
continued

项　目	Item	单位	Unit	2006	2007	2008	2009	2010	2011
一、律师工作	**Lawyers**								
律师事务所	Law Offices	个	unit	122	140	159	203	222	247
律师工作者	Lawyers	人	person	2 218	2 594	2 915	3 144	2 487	2 801
专职	Full-time Lawyers	人	person	1 616	1 738	1 855	1 934	2 377	2 643
兼职(含特邀)	Part-time Lawyers	人	person	75	79	90	86	94	105
聘请常年法律顾问单位	Units with Permanent Legal Advisors	个	unit	4 032	4 075	4 086	4 457	4 779	5 180
全年办理民事代理	Agent of Civil Cases	件	case	10 556	19 460	20 547	29 025	26 935	27 702
刑事辩护	Defender of Criminal Cases	件	case	2 917	3 311	3 655	3 758	3 964	4 535
非诉讼事件	Agent of Non-litigious Legal Affairs	件	case	10 049	7 710	5 467	5 897	4 274	3 576
解答法律询问	Agent of Legal Advisory Services	件	case	26 518	27 393	31 571	30 123	21 102	42 428
代写法律事务文书	Agent of Legal Documents Written on Behalf of Clients	件	case	8 171	8 012	9 077	6 015	6 210	6 762
二、公证工作	**Notarization**								
公证处	Notary Offices	个	unit	15	13	13	13	13	13
公证人员	Notarial Personnel	人	person	209	208	214	214	214	221
公证员	Notaries	人	person	117	116	117	118	117	119
办理公证文书	Notarized Documents	件	case	100 513	95 704	101 766	97 019	94 077	88 506
三、人民调解	**People's Mediation**								
人民调解委员会	People's Mediation Committees	个	unit	10 897	11 216	11 223	9 643	8 014	8 486
调解人员	Mediators	人	person	34 487	35 553	33 875	32 675	27 820	28 094
调解民间纠纷	Civil Disputes Mediated	件	case	14 094	16 586	12 803	14 660	20 550	22 882
四、社会治安	**Social Order**								
交通事故发生次数	Traffic Accidents	次	time	5 559	4 465	3 025	2 570	2 313	2 164
死亡人数	Deaths	人	person	689	556	489	402	393	374
受伤人数	Injuries	人	person	5 685	4 603	3 273	2 943	2 504	2 240
经济损失	Losses	万元	10 000 yuan	1 514.00	1 291.40	991.50	854.80	811.27	861.05
火灾发生次数	Fire Accidents	次	time	1 400	962	840	773	683	369
死亡人数	Deaths	人	person	8	9	16	5	9	1
受伤人数	Injuries	人	person	5		13		4	2
经济损失	Losses	万元	10 000 yuan	544.00	929.60	979.70	865.50	5 566.11	598.20

18－9 分区、市殡葬服务情况(2011 年)
BASIC STATISTICS ON FUNERAL SERVICES(2011)

市、区名称	Region	单位数(个) Number of Institutions (unit)	年末职工人数(人) Number of Staff and Workers at Year-end (person)	火化炉数(台) Number of Cremators (unit)	处理遗体数(具) Number of Remains Cremated (body)
总计	**Total**	**11**	**211**	**46**	**56 962**
市本级	Municipal Level	1	60	10	10 965
市南区	Shinan District				
市北区	Shibei District				
四方区	Sifang District				
李沧区	Licang District				
崂山区	Laoshan District				
黄岛区	Huangdao District	1	3		
城阳区	Chengyang District	1	19	5	5 727
即墨市	Jimo	1	18	6	8 474
胶州市	Jiaozhou	1	10	4	6 481
胶南市	Jiaonan	1	23	7	8 158
平度市	Pingdu	3	32	8	11 509
莱西市	Laixi	2	46	6	5 648

18－9 续表
continued

市、区名称	Region	穴位数(个) Number of Graves (unit)	本年销售穴位数 Number of Graves Saled in the Year	安葬数(具) Number of Remains Buried(body)	本年安葬数 Number of Remains Buried in the Year
总计	**Total**	**22 088**	**571**	**20 318**	**1 663**
市本级	Municipal Level	18 796	432	18 006	1 499
市南区	Shinan District				
市北区	Shibei District				
四方区	Sifang District				
李沧区	Licang District				
崂山区	Laoshan District				
黄岛区	Huangdao District				
城阳区	Chengyang District				
即墨市	Jimo				
胶州市	Jiaozhou				
胶南市	Jiaonan				
平度市	Pingdu	1 197	62	1 133	81
莱西市	Laixi	2 095	77	1 179	83

主要统计指标解释

卫生机构　包括医疗机构、疾病预防控制中心(防疫站)、采供血机构、卫生监督及监测(检验)机构、医学科研和在职培训机构、健康教育所等。

医疗机构　包括医院、社区卫生服务中心(站)、疗养院、卫生院、门诊部、诊所(卫生所、医务室)、妇幼保健院(所、站)、专科疾病防治院(所、站)、急救中心(站)和临床检验中心。医疗机构分为非赢利性医疗机构和赢利性医疗机构。

医院　包括综合医院、中医医院、中西医结合医院、民族医院、各类专科医院和护理院。

医生　指在医疗、预防保健机构工作且取得《执业医师证书》的执业医师和执业助理医师。

卫生技术人员　指卫生事业机构中现任职务为卫生技术工作的人员。包括中医师、西医师、中西医结合高级医师、护师、中药师、西药师、检验师、其他技师、中医士、西医士、护士、助产士、中药剂士、西药剂士、检验士、其他技士、其他中医、护理员、中药剂员、西药剂员、检验员、其他初级卫生技术人员。

社会福利事业单位　指集中收养社会孤老、残、幼的机构,包括由民政部门管理的社会福利院、儿童福利院、精神病人福利院和城镇集体举办的福利院及农村集体举办的敬老院以及优抚医院和具有收养能力的社区服务中心等。

Explanatory Notes on Main Statistical Indicators

Health Care Institutions include: medical institutions, disease prevention and control centers (epidemic prevention stations), blood gathering and supplying institutions, health supervision and inspection (check up) institutions, medicinal scientific research and on-job training institutions, health education and so on.

Medical Organizations include: hospitals, health service centers (stations) of communities, nursing homes, health centers, clinics, clinics (health stations and infirmaries), maternity and child care agencies (centers and stations), special disease prevention and curing agencies (centers and stations), first aid centers (stations) and clinical inspection centers. Medical organizations are grouped by two types: profit-making and non-profit-making medical organizations.

Hospitals include: polyclinics, traditional Chinese medical hospitals, hospitals integrated with traditional Chinese therapeutics and western therapeutics, ethical hospitals, various specialties hospitals and nursing hospitals.

Doctors refer to certified physicians and certified assistant physicians with certifications working in medical and health care and prevention agencies.

Medical Technical Personnel refers to those medical workers employed institutions, including doctors of Chinese and Western medicine, senior doctors of integrated Chinese-Western medicine, head nurses, pharmacists of Chinese and Western medicine, laboratory specialists, other specialists, junior doctors of Chinese and Western medicine, nurses, midwives, druggists of Chinese and Western medicine, laboratory technicians, other technicians, other practitioners of Chinese medicine, nursing attendants, pharmacological workers of Chinese and Western medicine, laboratory workers, and other primary medical personnel.

Social Welfare Institutions refer to institutions taking care of old people without children, handicapped people and orphans. They include social welfare institutions run by civil affairs departments, children welfare institutions, social welfare institutions for mental patients, collective-owned old people's homes in rural areas, convalescent homes and community service centers with the capacity of receiving those people.

企业调查 19

ENTEPRISES SURVEY

简要说明

一、本篇资料的主要内容

本篇资料主要反映了全市企业景气方面的内容。

二、本篇资料的来源

本篇资料来源于企业景气调查报表，由国家统计局青岛调查队统计监测处整理提供。

Brief Introduction

I. Main Content

Data in this chapter show the conditions of business climate.

II. Source of Data

Data in this chapter are based on reports of business climate survey and enterprise corporations, and provided by the Division of Statistics Monitoring of Survey Office of the National Bureau of Statistics in Qingdao.

19－1 企业家信心指数(2011 年)
ENTREPRENEURS' CONFIDENCE INDEX(2011)

单位：点(point)

项　　目	Item	1 季度 First Quarter	2 季度 Second Quarter	3 季度 Third Quarter	4 季度 Fourth Quarter
总体状况	**General Condition**	**136.76**	**132.33**	**127.82**	**114.27**
一、按行业门类分	**Grouped by Sectors**				
(一)工业	Industry	134.54	124.07	123.66	112.55
1.采掘业	Mining	200.00	180.00	160.00	160.00
2.制造业	Manufacturing	133.30	122.26	120.88	108.66
3.电力、煤气及水的生产和供应业	Production and Supply of Electricty, Gas and Water	122.61	145.85	161.80	162.97
(二)建筑业	Construction	164.65	155.88	157.32	148.98
(三)交通运输、仓储和邮政业	Transport, Storage and Post	123.70	136.79	120.37	100.12
(四)批发和零售业	Wholesale and Retail Trade	142.41	138.48	140.27	130.98
(五)房地产业	Real Estate	109.21	115.79	84.93	33.83
(六)社会服务业	Social Services	144.81	162.50	143.75	126.06
(七)信息传输、计算机服务和软件	Information Transmission, Computer Services and Software	175.00	165.37	148.71	148.71
(八)住宿和餐饮业	Hotels and Catering Services	130.77	134.62	134.62	126.92
二、按企业登记注册类型分	**Grouped by Status of Registration**				
#国有企业	State-owned Enterprises	154.39	144.76	136.45	125.71
集体企业	Collective-owned Enterprises	140.06	130.06	130.00	116.77
股份合作企业	Share Holding Enterprises	103.70	103.70	100.00	70.37
有限责任公司	Companies with Limited Liabilities	136.48	128.73	128.66	111.61
股份有限公司	Stock-holding Companies with Limited Liabilities	127.88	125.10	116.07	114.65
私营企业	Private Enterprises	130.00	130.00	135.00	120.00
港、澳、台投资企业	Hong Kong, Macao and Taiwan Funded Companies	130.00	120.00	130.00	100.00
外商投资企业	Foreign Funded Companies	136.40	141.28	142.01	121.23
三、按企业规模分	**Grouped by Size of Enterprises**				
大中型	Large and Medium-sized	141.65	135.62	136.06	122.33
#大型	Large Sized	144.17	130.20	136.50	119.44
中型	Medium Sized	140.12	138.89	135.80	124.07
中小型	Medium and Small-sized	132.20	129.10	124.15	109.91
#小型	Small Sized	124.22	119.25	112.42	95.65

19-2 企业景气指数(2011年)

BUSINESS CLIMATE INDEX(2011)

单位:点(point)

项　目	Item	1季度 First Quarter	2季度 Second Quarter	3季度 Third Quarter	4季度 Fourth Quarter
总体状况	**General Condition**	**141.72**	**138.47**	**136.16**	**127.74**
一、按行业门类分	**Grouped by Sectors**				
(一)工业	Industry	142.92	138.46	136.49	130.54
1.采掘业	Excavation	140.00	160.00	180.00	140.00
2.制造业	Manufacturing	142.88	138.36	134.46	128.16
3.电力、煤气及水的生产和供应业	Power, Gas and Tap Water Production and Supply	144.91	134.74	144.91	154.43
(二)建筑业	Construction	158.24	160.19	154.87	146.14
(三)交通运输、仓储和邮政业	Transportation, Storage, Postal and Telecommunication Services	130.37	137.03	133.70	116.79
(四)批发和零售业	Wholesale and Retail Trade	140.24	130.00	133.64	137.35
(五)房地产业	Real Estate	122.13	133.12	111.02	76.55
(六)社会服务业	Social Services	150.00	130.19	131.25	117.69
(七)信息传输、计算机服务和软件	Information Transmission, Computer Service and Software	166.67	158.33	158.33	150.00
(八)住宿和餐饮业	Hotels and Catering Services	119.23	142.31	142.31	115.38
二、按企业登记注册类型分	**Grouped by Status of Registration**				
#国有企业	State-owned Enterprises	139.00	132.42	143.44	131.06
集体企业	Collective-owned Enterprises	125.06	140.00	135.00	115.00
股份合作企业	Share Holding Enterprises	107.41	107.41	92.59	85.19
有限责任公司	Companies with Limited Liabilities	142.64	142.29	140.07	127.15
股份有限公司	Stock-holding Companies with Limited Liabilities	155.01	152.41	142.54	144.38
私营企业	Private Enterprises	135.00	130.00	135.00	125.00
港、澳、台投资企业	Hong Kong, Macao and Taiwan Funded Companies	150.00	140.00	150.00	130.00
外商投资企业	Foreign Funded Companies	139.80	133.42	133.96	128.55
三、按企业规模分	**Grouped by Size of Enterprises**				
大中型	Large and Medium-sized	153.53	152.45	149.88	141.17
#大型	Large Sized	173.64	174.87	178.26	169.44
中型	Medium Sized	141.36	138.89	132.72	124.07
中小型	Medium and Small-sized	131.58	127.86	125.39	115.48
#小型	Small Sized	121.74	116.77	118.01	106.83

19-3 企业盈利(亏损)变化景气指数(2011年)
PROFIT AND LOSS OF ENTERPRISES INDEX(2011)

单位:点(point)

项目	Item	1季度 First Quarter	2季度 Second Quarter	3季度 Third Quarter	4季度 Fourth Quarter
总体状况	**General Condition**	**107.12**	**122.71**	**118.36**	**111.82**
一、按行业门类分	**Grouped by Sectors**				
(一)工业	Industry	108.05	116.90	118.25	117.87
1.采掘业	Excavation	140.00	140.00	180.00	120.00
2.制造业	Manufacturing	107.73	116.22	117.31	118.08
3.电力、煤气及水的生产和供应业	Power, Gas and Tap Water Production and Supply	80.18	127.23	105.85	103.27
(二)建筑业	Construction	107.70	141.08	121.85	133.31
(三)交通运输、仓储和邮政业	Transportation, Storage, Postal and Telecommunication Services	109.60	136.52	133.19	99.60
(四)批发和零售业	Wholesale and Retail Trade	114.87	127.09	127.04	134.61
(五)房地产业	Real Estate	77.42	90.32	60.97	35.17
(六)社会服务业	Social Services	107.31	144.81	131.25	81.25
(七)信息传输、计算机服务和软件	Information Transmission, Computer Service and Software	116.67	132.04	83.33	109.63
(八)住宿和餐饮业	Hotels and Catering Services	88.46	134.62	134.62	84.62
二、按企业登记注册类型分	**Grouped by Status of Registration**				
#国有企业	State-owned Enterprises	81.32	117.94	112.89	92.52
集体企业	Collective-owned Enterprises	93.53	101.65	128.23	125.00
股份合作企业	Share Holding Enterprises	92.59	107.41	85.19	70.37
有限责任公司	Companies with Limited Liabilities	107.76	122.00	118.71	114.42
股份有限公司	Stock-holding Companies with Limited Liabilities	136.69	139.03	138.63	126.55
私营企业	Private Enterprises	90.00	115.00	100.00	115.00
港、澳、台投资企业	Hong Kong, Macao and Taiwan Funded Companies	80.00	120.00	80.00	110.00
外商投资企业	Foreign Funded Companies	106.77	118.13	120.53	111.37
三、按企业规模分	**Grouped by Size of Enterprises**				
大中型	Large and Medium-sized	114.95	128.21	130.20	126.40
#大型	Large Sized	128.44	146.27	145.42	147.58
中型	Medium Sized	106.79	117.28	120.99	113.58
中小型	Medium and Small-sized	100.00	114.86	109.91	100.31
#小型	Small Sized	93.17	112.42	98.76	86.96

19-4 企业货款拖欠景气指数(2011年)

LOANS OF ENTERPRISES IN APPEARS INDEX(2011)

单位:点(point)

项目	Item	1季度 First Quarter	2季度 Second Quarter	3季度 Third Quarter	4季度 Fourth Quarter
总体状况	**General Condition**	**114.97**	**106.39**	**104.99**	**103.70**
一、按行业门类分	**Grouped by Sectors**				
(一)工业	Industry	112.63	108.19	106.92	107.55
1.采掘业	Excavation	100.00	120.00	80.00	60.00
2.制造业	Manufacturing	113.50	107.53	107.48	108.41
3.电力、煤气及水的生产和供应业	Power, Gas and Tap Water Production and Supply	116.81	119.08	88.72	83.88
(二)建筑业	Construction	111.92	105.18	65.17	66.04
(三)交通运输、仓储和邮政业	Transportation, Storage, Postal and Telecommunication Services	127.05	93.33	93.33	93.33
(四)批发和零售业	Wholesale and Retail Trade	117.04	115.85	125.49	115.56
(五)房地产业	Real Estate	133.94	112.24	116.13	108.15
(六)社会服务业	Social Services	119.81	106.25	113.56	106.25
(七)信息传输、计算机服务和软件	Information Transmission, Computer Service and Software	84.63	82.04	83.33	75.00
(八)住宿和餐饮业	Hotels and Catering Services	103.85	84.62	80.77	103.85
二、按企业登记注册类型分	**Grouped by Status of Registration**				
#国有企业	State-owned Enterprises	100.90	110.35	91.47	107.15
集体企业	Collective-owned Enterprises	106.53	81.53	91.47	78.18
股份合作企业	Share Holding Enterprises	125.93	103.70	100.00	100.00
有限责任公司	Companies with Limited Liabilities	105.54	101.26	100.18	90.90
股份有限公司	Stock-holding Companies with Limited Liabilities	134.03	131.87	119.84	136.87
私营企业	Private Enterprises	125.00	110.00	100.00	95.00
港、澳、台投资企业	Hong Kong, Macao and Taiwan Funded Companies	90.00	100.00	120.00	100.00
外商投资企业	Foreign Funded Companies	118.78	92.91	102.44	103.91
三、按企业规模分	**Grouped by Size of Enterprises**				
大中型	Large and Medium-sized	117.67	111.85	102.09	106.68
#大型	Large Sized	130.55	140.61	112.69	124.86
中型	Medium Sized	109.88	94.44	95.68	95.68
中小型	Medium and Small-sized	108.98	96.90	101.55	97.83
#小型	Small Sized	108.07	99.38	107.45	100.00

19-5 企业流动资金景气指数(2011 年)

CIRCULATING CAPITAL OF ENTERPRISES INDEX(2011)

单位:点(point)

项　　目	Item	1 季度 First Quarter	2 季度 Second Quarter	3 季度 Third Quarter	4 季度 Fourth Quarter
总体状况	**General Condition**	**107.70**	**104.71**	**105.32**	**91.92**
一、按行业门类分	**Grouped by Sectors**				
(一)工业	Industry	108.69	104.43	102.93	91.45
1.采掘业	Excavation	120.00	100.00	80.00	40.00
2.制造业	Manufacturing	107.48	104.61	102.90	91.94
3.电力、煤气及水的生产和供应业	Power, Gas and Tap Water Production and Supply	122.37	106.38	101.61	98.48
(二)建筑业	Construction	108.85	103.40	112.75	92.94
(三)交通运输、仓储和邮政业	Transportation, Storage, Postal and Telecommunication Services	96.52	86.52	93.19	81.03
(四)批发和零售业	Wholesale and Retail Trade	111.20	113.51	116.51	104.49
(五)房地产业	Real Estate	117.64	105.66	83.58	56.09
(六)社会服务业	Social Services	98.94	105.19	112.50	86.44
(七)信息传输、计算机服务和软件	Information Transmission, Computer Service and Software	117.96	117.96	126.29	142.96
(八)住宿和餐饮业	Hotels and Catering Services	96.15	115.38	126.92	103.85
二、按企业登记注册类型分	**Grouped by Status of Registration**				
#国有企业	State-owned Enterprises	99.48	103.00	101.91	92.36
集体企业	Collective-owned Enterprises	103.23	73.29	93.23	48.29
股份合作企业	Share Holding Enterprises	96.30	92.59	85.19	70.37
有限责任公司	Companies with Limited Liabilities	99.79	97.97	99.34	82.44
股份有限公司	Stock-holding Companies with Limited Liabilities	132.88	124.29	118.25	116.13
私营企业	Private Enterprises	95.00	110.00	100.00	90.00
港、澳、台投资企业	Hong Kong, Macao and Taiwan Funded Companies	150.00	130.00	140.00	130.00
外商投资企业	Foreign Funded Companies	116.47	125.32	126.22	115.35
三、按企业规模分	**Grouped by Size of Enterprises**				
大中型	Large and Medium-sized	116.07	111.59	110.19	98.39
#大型	Large Sized	149.77	142.98	132.14	118.18
中型	Medium Sized	95.68	92.59	96.91	86.42
中小型	Medium and Small-sized	95.67	95.05	97.83	84.52
#小型	Small Sized	95.65	97.52	98.76	82.61

19-6 企业劳动力需求景气指数(2011年)
REQUIREMENT FOR ENTERPRISES LABOR INDEX(2011)

单位:点(point)

项　目	Item	1季度 First Quarter	2季度 Second Quarter	3季度 Third Quarter	4季度 Fourth Quarter
总体状况	**General Condition**	**132.43**	**129.17**	**123.46**	**115.23**
一、按行业门类分	**Grouped by Sectors**				
(一)工业	Industry	143.28	125.14	121.79	123.30
1. 采掘业	Excavation	80.00	120.00	140.00	120.00
2. 制造业	Manufacturing	145.74	127.97	121.07	122.14
3. 电力、煤气及水的生产和供应业	Power, Gas and Tap Water Production and Supply	132.79	86.56	137.40	140.63
(二)建筑业	Construction	104.32	151.72	156.35	137.24
(三)交通运输、仓储和邮政业	Transportation, Storage, Postal and Telecommunication Services	116.67	113.85	100.90	93.85
(四)批发和零售业	Wholesale and Retail Trade	115.73	128.50	120.55	108.48
(五)房地产业	Real Estate	123.33	117.01	115.71	90.59
(六)社会服务业	Social Services	143.75	156.25	125.00	87.50
(七)信息传输、计算机服务和软件	Information Transmission, Computer Service and Software	117.96	159.63	166.67	126.29
(八)住宿和餐饮业	Hotels and Catering Services	115.38	146.15	138.46	100.00
二、按企业登记注册类型分	**Grouped by Status of Registration**				
#国有企业	State-owned Enterprises	114.72	119.81	126.31	101.03
集体企业	Collective-owned Enterprises	120.00	111.71	121.71	125.00
股份合作企业	Share Holding Enterprises	125.93	111.11	103.70	92.59
有限责任公司	Companies with Limited Liabilities	132.49	134.78	128.90	120.07
股份有限公司	Stock-holding Companies with Limited Liabilities	156.52	125.41	114.54	134.88
私营企业	Private Enterprises	120.00	125.00	110.00	75.00
港、澳、台投资企业	Hong Kong, Macao and Taiwan Funded Companies	140.00	150.00	150.00	140.00
外商投资企业	Foreign Funded Companies	148.46	142.17	135.27	125.83
三、按企业规模分	**Grouped by Size of Enterprises**				
大中型	Large and Medium-sized	141.58	130.83	128.08	128.02
#大型	Large Sized	157.26	130.77	122.46	148.83
中型	Medium Sized	132.10	130.86	131.48	115.43
中小型	Medium and Small-sized	127.24	127.55	123.53	107.43
#小型	Small Sized	122.36	124.22	115.53	99.38

19－7 企业固定资产投资景气指数(2011 年)
INVESTMENT OF ENTERPRISES IN FIXED ASSETS INDEX(2011)

单位:点(point)

项　　目	Item	1 季度 First Quarter	2 季度 Second Quarter	3 季度 Third Quarter	4 季度 Fourth Quarter
总体状况	**General Condition**	**109.04**	**116.17**	**112.65**	**112.68**
一、按行业门类分	**Grouped by Sectors**				
(一)工业	Industry	115.75	118.03	115.76	114.27
1.采掘业	Excavation	120.00	140.00	100.00	120.00
2.制造业	Manufacturing	114.84	115.75	114.71	112.73
3.电力、煤气及水的生产和供应业	Power, Gas and Tap Water Production and Supply	94.09	148.28	140.19	135.56
(二)建筑业	Construction	87.70	130.86	117.62	123.28
(三)交通运输、仓储和邮政业	Transportation, Storage, Postal and Telecommunication Services	124.09	121.67	122.18	122.79
(四)批发和零售业	Wholesale and Retail Trade	89.64	98.88	108.60	112.01
(五)房地产业	Real Estate	107.20	114.32	89.66	74.39
(六)社会服务业	Social Services	93.75	118.75	93.75	119.81
(七)信息传输、计算机服务和软件	Information Transmission, Computer Service and Software	110.92	123.71	107.04	98.71
(八)住宿和餐饮业	Hotels and Catering Services	100.00	100.00	115.38	96.15
二、按企业登记注册类型分	**Grouped by Status of Registration**				
#国有企业	State-owned Enterprises	98.84	136.19	128.57	129.18
集体企业	Collective-owned Enterprises	98.35	128.23	106.47	96.65
股份合作企业	Share Holding Enterprises	85.19	92.59	81.48	92.59
有限责任公司	Companies with Limited Liabilities	107.14	107.88	105.50	105.53
股份有限公司	Stock-holding Companies with Limited Liabilities	125.33	132.74	139.04	130.05
私营企业	Private Enterprises	95.00	100.00	100.00	105.00
港、澳、台投资企业	Hong Kong, Macao and Taiwan Funded Companies	110.00	140.00	120.00	130.00
外商投资企业	Foreign Funded Companies	114.64	117.96	116.48	107.20
三、按企业规模分	**Grouped by Size of Enterprises**				
大中型	Large and Medium-sized	115.08	124.89	125.01	119.80
#大型	Large Sized	123.68	144.59	149.01	146.41
中型	Medium Sized	109.88	112.96	110.49	103.70
中小型	Medium and Small-sized	104.33	108.67	103.10	102.17
#小型	Small Sized	98.76	104.35	95.65	100.62

主要统计指标解释

景气指数 又称景气度。它是对景气调查中定性经济指标的量化描述，以直观地反映经济所处状态。景气指数的数值介于0－200之间，当景气指数为100时，说明经济处于景气的边缘；大于100时，则表示经济状况处于景气状态，越接近200，状态越好；小于100时，表示经济处于不景气状态，越接近于0，状态越差。

企业景气指数 亦称企业综合生产经营景气指数，是根据企业家对本企业综合生产经营情况的判断与预期（通常为对“良好”、“一般”、“不佳”的选择）而编制的指数，用以综合反映企业的生产经营状况。

企业家信心指数 亦称宏观经济景气指数，是根据企业家对企业对外部市场经济环境与宏观政策的认识、看法、判断与预期（通常为对“乐观”、“一般”、“不乐观”的选择）而编制的指数，用以综合反映企业家对宏观经济环境的感受与信心。

Explanatory Notes on Main Statistical Indicators

Climate Index is also called climate scores. It is an indicator which comprehensively reflects the situation or the trend of development of a certain group surveyed or a certain socio-economic phenomenon. The numerical values of the business climate index lie between 0 and 200. 100 is the critical value of the business climate index. When the business climate index is greater than 100, it indicates that the ecomomic indicators are picking up and the economic situation is improving and it is in a state of prosperity. The closer the value is to 200, the better the economic situation is. When the business climate index is smaller than 100, it indicates that the economic indicators are declining and the economic situation is worse than before and it is in a state of depression. The closer the value is to 0, the worse the economic situation is.

Business Climate Index refers the index reflecting soundness of general operation, derived from management's judgment and estimation on performance of the company, (variables being sound, common and bad), which is used to reflect the general operation status of the enterprises.

Entrepreneurs' Confidence Index also refers to macro economic climate index, derived from entrepreneurs' understanding, opinions, judgment and estimation of macro market situations as well as macro economic polices, (variables being optimistic, common and not optimistic) so as to reflect comprehensively entrepreneurs' perception and confidence regarding the macro economic environment.

附　录

APPENDIX

2011 年省内各市主要经济指标对比情况
MAJOR ECONOMIC INDICATORS ON CITIES OF THE PROVINCE(2011)

主要指标 Indicator	单位 Unit	青岛市 Qingdao	济南市 Jinan	淄博市 Zibo	枣庄市 Zaozhuang	东营市 Dongying	烟台市 Yantai	潍坊市 Weifang
全市生产总值 GDP	亿元 (100 million yuan)	6 615.60	4 406.29	3 280.23	1 561.68	2 676.35	4 906.83	3 541.85
比上年增长 YOY Growth	%	11.7	10.6	12.0	10.9	12.7	12.1	11.0
规模以上工业增加值比上年增长 YOY Growth of Industrial Added Value above Designated Size	%	13.46	13.08	14.22	13.01	13.94	14.38	15.52
固定资产投资 Investmentin Fixed Assets	亿元 (100 million yuan)	3 502.5	1 934.3	1 499.2	823.8	1 574.4	2 883.8	2 603.2
比上年增长 YOY Growth	%	23.4	18.1	23.7	24.1	24.5	22.4	22.9
进出口(含中央省公司) Imports and Exports (including central and provincial companies)	亿美元 (100 million USD)	721.5	104.0	90.4	10.7	102.2	453.5	140.9
比上年增长 YOY Growth	%	26.5	39.8	34.7	17.2	26.1	3.6	20.0
其中:出口 of which:Exports	亿美元 (100 million USD)	406.1	60.5	53.2	8.4	43.6	266.9	103.6
比上年增长 YOY Growth	%	19.7	49.4	32.1	13.2	58.1	4.8	19.2
社会消费品零售总额 Total Retail Sales of Consumer Goods	亿元 (100 million yuan)	2 232.9	2 023.1	1 186.25	480.6	448.85	1 616.49	1 349.82
比上年增长 YOY Growth	%	17.4	17.3	18.0	17.3	17.4	17.3	17.3
地方财政一般预算收入 General Budgetary Revenue of Local Government Finance	亿元 (100 million yuan)	566.0	325.4	203.6	100.1	135.3	303.2	253.9
比上年增长 YOY Growth	%	25.1	22.3	25.4	30.5	29.0	27.5	25.4
城市居民人均可支配收入 Per Capita Disposable Income of Urban Households	元 (yuan)	28 567	28 892	24 955	20 193	27 343	26 542	22 508
比上年增长 YOY Growth	%	14.3	14.1	14.6	14.5	14.9	14.0	14.4
农民人均纯收入 Per Capital Net Income of Rural Households	元 (yuan)	12 370	10 412	10 878	8 397	10 025	11 716	10 409
比上年增长 YOY Growth	%	17.25	16.9	18.3	18.2	19.0	18.2	17.3

注:各市数据为快报数。

Note:The data are preliminary statistics.

济宁市 Jining	泰安市 Taian	威海市 Weihai	日照市 Rizhao	莱芜市 Laiwu	临沂市 Linyi	德州市 Dezhou	聊城市 Liaocheng	滨州市 Binzhou	菏泽市 Heze
2 896.69	2 304.3	2 110.95	1 214.1	611.88	2 770.5	1 950.71	1 905.19	1 817.58	1 475.68
10.8	11.5	10.7	12.1	10.6	12.0	11.7	12.3	12.0	14.0
13.84	13.98	13.62	16.08	13.53	16.38	15.80	16.21	15.92	22.55
1 391.7	1 473.7	1 341.6	880.7	350.1	1 608.6	1 153.7	1 041.1	1 010.7	552.3
20.0	22.9	22.7	23.7	20.0	23.9	23.8	23.4	23.8	24.8
57.5	18.2	169.2	208.4	35.9	68.3	26.8	56.5	66.9	27.4
28.8	14.6	21.7	55.7	31.5	43.2	37.7	52.7	31.7	49.0
30.7	11.9	107.4	39.1	11.4	36.2	17.5	18.8	28.4	14.4
33.5	28.0	20.5	76.7	10.6	28.2	30.7	45.4	11.6	18.9
1 130.10	806.7	802.79	365.4	198.4	1 366.1	757.50	629.95	505.75	775.20
17.3	17.4	17.4	17.3	16.0	18.1	17.3	17.4	17.3	18.1
207.1	138.1	136.4	68.5	39.2	141.3	95.1	96.6	130.8	111.6
22.4	18.1	15.4	23.2	11.1	22.3	30.4	37.0	25.8	31.8
22 406	22 687	25 290	20 098	23 509	24 232	19 771	20 649	22 540	16 658
13.0	13.7	13.7	14.5	12.0	15.2	13.6	15.4	14.5	15.5
8 712	8 974	12 334	8 756	9 626	8 018	8 350	7 735	8 744	7 119
16.9	18.2	17.3	16.7	15.8	18.6	18.8	21.3	21.5	22.5

2011 年十五个副省级城市主要经济指标对比资料

MAJOR ECONOMIC INDICATORS ON CITIES UNDER PROVINCIAL LEVELS(2011)

指标名称 Indicator	单位 Unit	青岛 Qingdao	沈阳 Shenyang	大连 Dalian	长春 Changchun	哈尔滨 Harbin	南京 Nanjing
全市生产总值 GDP	亿元 (100 million yuan)	6 615.6	5 914.9	6 150.1	4 003.1	4 243.4	6 145.52
比上年增长 YOY Growth	%	11.7	12.3	13.5	13.3	12.3	12
第一产业 Primary Industry	亿元 (100 million yuan)	306.38	279.1	395.7	290.1	447.2	163.61
比上年增长 YOY Growth	%	5.0	6.5	6.5	4.7	7	4.1
第二产业 Secondary Industry	亿元 (100 million yuan)	3 150.72	3 027.6	3 204.2	2 092.7	1 647.2	2 760.99
比上年增长 YOY Growth	%	11.6	14	16.3	14.9	14.4	12.3
第三产业 Tertiary Industry	亿元 (100 million yuan)	3 158.50	2 608.2	2 550.2	1 620.2	2 149	3 220.91
比上年增长 YOY Growth	%	12.4	11	11.3	13	12	12.3
规模以上工业增加值比上年增长 YOY Growth of Industrial Added Value above Designated Size	%	13.46	16	16.3	13.3	14	13
固定资产投资额 Investment in Fixed Assets	亿元 (100 million yuan)	3 502.5	4 560.6	4 553.6	2 433.4	3 012	3 757.25
比上年增长 YOY Growth	%	23.4	29.2	30	30.3	32.1	21.5
社会消费品零售总额 Total Retail Sales of Consumer Goods	亿元 (100 million yuan)	2 232.88	2 426.9	1 924.8	1 512.2	2 070.4	2 670.3
比上年增长 YOY Growth	%	17.4	17.5	17.4	17.5	17.4	17.8
进出口(含中央省公司) Imports and Exports(including central and provincial companies)	亿美元 (100 million USD)	721.52	106.2	600.09	173.4	51.2	573.44
比上年增长 YOY Growth	%	26.5	35.2	15.1	31.2	16.6	25.8
其中:出口总额 of which:Exports	亿美元 (100 million USD)	406.13	48.3	311.93	22.7	22.6	308.65
比上年增长 YOY Growth	%	19.7	18.4	13.9	13.3	13.1	24
实际使用外资金额 Foreign Investment Actually Utilized	亿美元 (100 million USD)	36.34	55	110.1	7.7	7.9	35.66
比上年增长 YOY Growth	%	27.8	8.9	10	10.7	13.4	33.3
地方财政一般预算收入 General Budgetary Revenue of Local Government Finance	亿元 (100 million yuan)	566	620.1	651	288.6	300.3	635
比上年增长 YOY Growth	%	25.1	33.3	30	59.6	27	22.4
城市居民人均可支配收入 Per Capita Disposable Income of Urban Households	元 (yuan)	28 567	23 320	24 276	20 487	20 031	32 200
比上年增长 YOY Growth	%	14.3	13.5	14	14.3	14.1	13.7
农民人均纯收入 Per Capita Net Income of Rural Households	元 (yuan)	12 370	11 575	14 213	7 400	9 608	13 108
比上年增长 YOY Growth	%	17.3	15.5	15.4	12	19.8	17.8
居民消费价格指数 Consumer Price Index	%	105.0	105.4	105.4	105.5	105.6	105.4

注:各市数据为快报数。

Note:The data are preliminary statistics.

杭州 Hangzhou	宁波 Ningbo	厦门 Xiamen	济南 Jinan	武汉 Wuhan	广州 Guangzhou	深圳 Shenzhen	成都 Chengdu	西安 Xi'an
7 011.8	6 010.48	2 535.8	4 406.29	6 536.81	12 303.12	11 502.06	6 854.58	3 864.21
10.1	10	15.1	10.6	12.1	11	10	15.2	13.8
236.07	255.76	24.68	237.86	192	203.06	5.7	327.3	173.14
2.5	4	-4	4.4	4	3.1	-22.3	3.7	6.7
3 322.15	3 335.37	1 304.1	1 828.97	3 119.66	4 532.52	5 343.33	3 143.86	1 697.16
9.8	10	17.4	11.7	15.5	11.5	11.8	19.8	16.4
3 453.58	2 419.35	1 207.02	2 339.46	3 225.15	7 567.54	6 153.03	3 383.42	1 993.91
11	10.7	13.1	10.3	9.6	11	8.5	12.4	12.1
12.7	12.2	19.5	13.1	16	12	12.6	22.3	17.2
3 105.16	2 392.9	1 126.28	1 934.3	4 255.16	3 413.58	2 136.39	5 006.02	3 352.12
17.1	17.6	30.2	18.1	22.1	10	10.1	19.2	30.2
2 548.36	2 018.9	810.69	2 023.1	2 959.04	5 243.02	3 520.87	2 861.28	1 935.18
18.7	18.4	16.4	17.3	18	17.1	17.8	18.4	20.1
639.7	981.9	701.67	104.02	227.9	1 161.72	4141	379.06	125.78
22.2	18.4	23	40.4	25.9	12	19.4	53.9	21
415.2	608.3	426.47	60.48	117.33	564.73	2455.25	229.56	58.04
17.5	17.1	20.7	49.1	34	16.7	20.2	65.5	9.2
47.22	28.09	17.26	11	37.6	42.7	45.99	65.5	20.05
8.4	20.9	1.7	5.8	14.2	7.3	7	34.9	28
785.15	657.55	370.68	325.4	673.26	979.47	1 339.59	680.71	318.55
17	23.8	32.6	22.3	40	20.5	21	30.1	31.7
34 065	34 058	33 565	28 892	23 738	34 438	36 505	23 932	25 981
13.4	12.9	14.7	14.1	14.1	12.3	12.7	14.9	16.8
15 245	16 518	11 928	10 412	9 814	14 818	-	9 895	9 788
15.6	15.8	18.9	16.9	18.3	16.9	-	20.6	26.3
104.8	105.3	105.2	105.4	105.2	105.5	105.4	105.4	105.6